Benjamin Disraeli, Isaac Disraeli

The calamities and quarrels of authors; with some inquiries

respecting their moral and literary characters, and memoirs for our

literary history

Benjamin Disraeli, Isaac Disraeli

The calamities and quarrels of authors; with some inquiries respecting their moral and literary characters, and memoirs for our literary history

ISBN/EAN: 9783337305512

Printed in Europe, USA, Canada, Australia, Japan

Cover: Foto ©Thomas Meinert / pixelio.de

More available books at **www.hansebooks.com**

THE

CALAMITIES AND QUARRELS

OF

AUTHORS:

WITH

SOME INQUIRIES RESPECTING THEIR MORAL AND
LITERARY CHARACTERS,

And Memoirs for our Literary History.

By ISAAC DISRAELI.

EDITED BY HIS SON,

THE RIGHT HON. B. DISRAELI.

IN TWO VOLUMES.

VOL. II.

NEW YORK:

W. J. WIDDLETON, PUBLISHER.

1875.

Cambridge:
Presswork by John Wilson and Son.

QUARRELS OF AUTHORS;

OR,

SOME MEMOIRS FOR OUR LITERARY HISTORY.

"The use and end of this Work I do not so much design for curiosity, or satisfaction of those that are the lovers of learning, but chiefly for a more grave and serious purpose: which is, that it will make *learned men wise in the use and administration of learning.*"—LORD BACON, "Of Learning."

CONTENTS.

QUARRELS OF AUTHORS.

PREFACE.

The Quarrels of Authors may be considered as a continuation of the Calamities of Authors; and both, as some Memoirs for Literary History.

These Quarrels of Authors are not designed to wound the Literary Character, but to expose the secret arts of calumny, the malignity of witty ridicule, and the evil prepossessions of unjust hatreds.

The present, like the preceding work, includes other subjects than the one indicated by the title, and indeed they are both subservient to a higher purpose—that of our Literary History.

There is a French work, entitled "Querelles Littéraires," quoted in "Curiosities of Literature," many years ago. Whether I derive the idea of the present from the French source I cannot tell. I could point out a passage in the great Lord Bacon which might have afforded the hint. But I am inclined to think that what induced me to select this topic was the interest which Johnson has given to the literary quarrels between *Dryden* and *Settle*, *Dennis* and *Addison*, &c.; and which Sir Walter Scott, who, amid the fresh creations of fancy, could delve for the buried truths of research, has thrown into his narrative of the quarrel of *Dryden* and *Luke Milbourne*.

From the French work I could derive no aid; and my plan is my own. I have fixed on each literary controversy to illustrate some principle, to portray some character, and to investigate some topic. Almost every controversy which occurred opened new views. With the subject, the character

of the author connected itself; and with the character were
associated those events of his life which reciprocally act on
each other. I have always considered an author as a human
being, who possesses at once two sorts of lives, the intellectual and the vulgar: in his books we trace the history of his
mind, and in his actions those of human nature. It is this
combination which interests the philosopher and the man of
feeling; which provides the richest materials for reflection;
and all those original details which spring from the constituent
principles of man. Johnson's passion for literary history,
and his great knowledge of the human heart, inspired at
once the first and the finest model in this class of composition.

The Philosophy of Literary History was indeed the creation of Bayle. He was the first who, by attempting a *critical dictionary*, taught us to think, and to be curious and vast
in our researches. He ennobled a collection of facts by his
reasonings, and exhibited them with the most miscellaneous
illustrations; and thus conducting an apparently humble
pursuit with a higher spirit, he gave a new turn to our
studies. It was felt through Europe; and many celebrated
authors studied and repeated Bayle. This father of a numerous race has an English as well as a French progeny.

Johnson wrote under many disadvantages; but, with
scanty means, he has taught us a great end. Dr. Birch was
the contemporary of Johnson. He excelled his predecessors;
and yet he forms a striking contrast as a literary historian.
Birch was no philosopher, and I adduce him as an instance
how a writer, possessing the most ample knowledge, and the
most vigilant curiosity—one practised in all the secret arts
of literary research in public repositories and in private collections, and eminently skilled in the whole science of bibli-
ography—may yet fail with the public. The diligence of
Birch has perpetuated his memory by a monument of MSS.,
but his touch was mortal to genius! He palsied the character

which could never die; heroes sunk pusillanimously under
his hand; and in his torpid silence, even Milton seemed
suddenly deprived of his genius.

I have freely enlarged in the *notes* to this work; a practice
which is objectionable to many, but indispensable perhaps in
this species of literary history.

The late Mr. Cumberland, in a conversation I once held
with him on this subject, triumphantly exclaimed, " You will
not find a single note through the whole volume of my ' Life.'
I never wrote a note. The ancients never wrote notes; but
they introduced into their text all which was proper for the
reader to know."

I agreed with that elegant writer, that a fine piece of essay-
writing, such as his own "Life," required notes no more than
his novels and his comedies, among which it may be classed.
I observed that the ancients had no literary history; this
was the result of the discovery of printing, the institution of
national libraries, the general literary intercourse of Europe,
and some other causes which are the growth almost of our
own times. The ancients have written history without producing authorities.

Mr. Cumberland was then occupied on a review of Fox's
History; and of Clarendon, which lay open before him,—
he had been complaining, with all the irritable feelings of a
dramatist, of the frequent suspensions, and the tedious
minuteness of his story.

I observed that *notes* had not then been discovered. Had
Lord Clarendon known their use, he had preserved the unity
of design in his text. His Lordship has unskilfully filled it
with all that historical furniture his diligence had collected,
and with those minute discussions which his anxiety for truth,
and his lawyer-like mode of scrutinising into facts and sub-
stantiating evidence, amassed. Had these been cast into
notes, and were it now possible to pass them over in the
present text, how would the story of the noble historian clear

up! The greatness of his genius will appear when disencumbered of its unwieldy and misplaced accompaniments.

If this observation be just, it will apply with greater force to literary history itself, which, being often the mere history of the human mind, has to record opinions as well as events—to discuss as well as to narrate—to show how accepted truths become suspicious—or to confirm what has hitherto rested in obscure uncertainty, and to balance contending opinions and opposite facts with critical nicety. The multiplied means of our knowledge now opened to us, have only rendered our curiosity more urgent in its claims, and raised up the most diversified objects. These, though accessories to the leading one of our inquiries, can never melt together in the continuity of a text. It is to prevent all this disorder, and to enjoy all the usefulness and the pleasure of this various knowledge, which has produced the invention of *notes* in literary history. All this forms a sort of knowledge peculiar to the present more enlarged state of literature. Writers who delight in curious and rare extracts, and in the discovery of new facts and new views of things, warmed by a fervour of research which brings everything nearer to our eye and close to our touch, study to throw contemporary feelings in their page. Such rare extracts and such new facts Bayle eagerly sought, and they delighted Johnson; but all this luxury of literature can only be produced to the public eye in the variegated forms of *notes*.

WARBURTON, AND HIS QUARRELS;

INCLUDING AN ILLUSTRATION OF

HIS LITERARY CHARACTER.

The name of Warburton more familiar to us than his Works—declared to be "a Colossus" by a Warburtonian, who afterwards shrinks the image into "a human size "—Lowth's caustic retort on his Attorney-ship—motives for the change to Divinity—his first literary mis-chances—Warburton and his Welsh Prophet—his Dedications—his mean flatteries—his taste more struck by the monstrous than the beautiful—the effects of his opposite studies—the SECRET PRINCIPLE which conducted Warburton through all his Works —the *curious* ar-gument of his Alliance between Church and State—the *bold* paradox of his Divine Legation—the demonstration ends in a conjecture—Warburton lost in the labyrinth he had ingeniously constructed—confesses the harassed state of his mind—attacked by Infidels and Christians—his SECRET PRINCIPLE turns the poetical narrative of Æneas into the Eleusinian Mysteries—Hurd attacks Jortin; his Attic irony translated into plain English—Warburton's paradox on Eloquence; his levity of ideas renders his sincerity suspected—Le-land refutes the whimsical paradox—Hurd attacks Leland—Leland's noble triumph—Warburton's SECRET PRINCIPLE operating in Modern Literature: on Pope's Essay on Man—Lord Bolingbroke the author of the Essay—Pope received Warburton as his tutelary genius—Warburton's systematic treatment of his friends and rival editors—his literary artifices and little intrigues—his Shakspeare—the whimsical labours of Warburton on Shakspeare annihilated by Ed-wards's " Canons of Criticism "—Warburton and Johnson—Edwards and Warburton's mutual attacks—the concealed motive of his edi-tion of Shakspeare avowed in his justification—his SECRET PRINCIPLE further displayed in Pope's Works—attacks Akenside; Dyson's generous defence—correct Ridicule is a test of Truth, illustrated by

a well-known case—Warburton a literary revolutionist; aimed to
be a perpetual dictator—the ambiguous tendency of his speculations
—the Warburtonian School supported by the most licentious principles—specimens of its peculiar style—the use to which Warburton
applied the Dunciad—his party: attentive to raise recruits—the
the active and subtle Hurd—his extreme sycophancy—Warburton,
to maintain his usurped authority, adopted his system of literary
quarrels.

THE name of Warburton is more familiar to us than
his works: thus was it early,* thus it continues, and
thus it will be with posterity! The cause may be
worth our inquiry. Nor is there, in the whole compass
of our literary history, a character more instructive for
its greatness and its failures; none more adapted to
excite our curiosity, and which can more completely
gratify it.

Of great characters, whose actions are well known,
and of those who, whatever claim they may have to distinction, are not so, Aristotle has delivered a precept
with his accustomed sagacity. If *Achilles*, says the
Stagirite, be the subject of our inquiries, since all know
what he has done, we are simply to indicate his actions,
without stopping to detail; but this would not serve for
Critias; for whatever relates to him must be fully told,
since he is known to few;†—a critical precept, which
ought to be frequently applied in the composition of this
work.

The history of Warburton is now well known, the facts

---

* One of his lively adversaries, the author of the "Canons of Criticism," observed the difficulty of writing against an author whose reputation so much exceeded the knowledge of his works. "It is my
misfortune," says Edwards, " in this controversy, to be engaged with a
person who is better known by his *name* than his *works;* or, to speak
more properly, whose *works* are *more known than read.*"--*Preface to
the Canons of Criticism.*

† Aristotle's Rhetoric, B. III. c. 16.

lie dispersed in the chronological biographer;* but the
secret connexion which exists between them, if there
shall be found to be any, has not yet been brought out;
and it is my business to press these together; hence to
demonstrate principles, or to deduce inferences.

The literary fame of Warburton was a portentous
meteor: it seemed unconnected with the whole planetary
system through which it rolled, and it was imagined to
be darting amid new creations, as the tail of each hy-
pothesis blazed with idle fancies.† Such extraordinary
natures cannot be looked on with calm admiration, nor
common hostility; all is the tumult of wonder about
such a man; and his adversaries, as well as his friends,
though differently affected, are often overcome by the
same astonishment.

To a Warburtonian, the object of his worship looks
indeed of colossal magnitude, in the glare thrown about
that hallowed spot; nor is the divinity of common
stature; but the light which makes him appear so great,
must not be suffered to conceal from us the real standard
by which only his greatness can be determined:‡ even

* The materials for a " Life of Warburton " have been arranged by
Mr. Nichols with his accustomed fidelity.—*See his Literary Anecdotes.*

† It is probable I may have drawn my meteor from our volcanic
author himself, who had his lucid moments, even in the deliriums of
his imagination. Warburton has rightly observed, in his "Divine
Legation," p. 203, that "*Systems, Schemes*, and *Hypotheses*, all bred of
heat, in the warm regions of *Controversy*, like meteors in a troubled
sky, have each its turn to *blaze* and *fly* away."

‡ It seems, even by the confession of a Warburtonian, that his
master was of "a human size;" for when Bishop Lowth rallies the
Warburtonians for their subserviency and credulity to their master,
he aimed a gentle stroke at Dr. Brown, who, in his "Essays on the
Characteristics," had poured forth the most vehement panegyric. In
his "Estimate of Manners of the Times," too, after a long *tirade* of
their badness in regard to taste and learning, he thus again eulogizes
his mighty master:—"Himself is abused, and his friends insulted for

literary enthusiasm, delightful to all generous tempers,
may be too prodigal of its splendours, wasting itself while
it shines; but truth remains behind! Truth, which, like
the asbestos, is still unconsumed and unaltered amidst
these glowing fires.

The genius of Warburton has called forth two re-

his sake, by those who never read his writings; or. if they did, could
neither taste nor comprehend them: while every little aspiring or de-
spairing scribbler eyes him as Cassius did Cæsar: and whispers to his
fellow—

> 'Why, man, he doth bestride the narrow world
> Like a Colossus; and we petty men
> Walk under his huge legs, and peep about
> To find ourselves dishonourable graves.'

No wonder, then. if the malice of the Lilliputian tribe be bent against
this dreaded Gulliver; if they attack him with poisoned arrows, whom
they cannot subdue by strength."

On this Lowth observes. that "this Lord Paramount in his pretensions *doth bestride the narrow world* of literature. and has cast out his
shoe over all the regions of science." This leads to a ludicrous comparison of Warburton, with King Pichrochole and his three ministers,
who, in Urquhart's admirable version of the French wit. are Count
Merdaille. the Duke of Smalltrash. and the Earl Swashbuckler, who
set up for universal monarchy, and made an imaginary expedition
through all the quarters of the world, as Rabelais records, and the
bishop facetiously quotes. Dr. Brown afterwards seemed to repent
his panegyric, and contrives to make his gigantic hero shrink into a
moderate size. "I believe still. every little aspiring fellow continues
thus to eye him. For myself, I have ever considered him as *a man*,
yet considerable among his species, as the following part of the paragraph clearly demonstrates. I speak of him here as *a Gulliver* indeed;
yet still of *no more than human size*, and only apprehended to be of
colossal magnitude by certain of his Lilliputian enemies." Thus subtilely would poor Dr. Brown save appearances! It must be confessed
that. in a dilemma, never was a giant got rid of so easily!—The plain
truth, however. was, that Brown was then on the point of quarrelling
with Warburton; for he laments, in a letter to a friend. that "he had
not avoided all personal panegyric. I had thus saved myself the
trouble of setting right a character which I far over-painted." A part
of this letter is quoted in the "Biographia Britannica."

markable anonymous criticisms—in one, all that the most
splendid eloquence can bring to bear against this chief
and his adherents;* and in the other, all that taste
warmed by a spark of Warburtonian fire, can discrimi-

* " Tracts by Warburton and a Warburtonian, not admitted into the
collections of their respective works," itself a collection which our
shelves could ill spare, though maliciously republished by Dr. Parr.
The dedication by Parr stands unparalleled for comparative criticism.
It is the eruption of a volcano; it sparkles, it blazes, and scatters light
and destruction. How deeply ought we to regret that this Nazarite
suffered his strength to be shorn by the Delilahs of spurious fame.
Never did this man, with his gifted strength, grasp the pillars of a
temple, to shake its atoms over Philistines; but pleased the child-like
simplicity of his mind by pulling down houses over the heads of their
unlucky inhabitants. He consumed, in local and personal literary
quarrels, a genius which might have made the next age his own.
With all the stores of erudition, and all the eloquence of genius, he
mortified a country parson for his politics, and a London accoucheur
for certain obstetrical labours performed on Horace; and now his collected writings lie before us, volumes unsaleable and unread. His
insatiate vanity was so little delicate, as often to snatch its sweet-
meat from a foul plate; it now appears, by the secret revelations in
Griffith's own copy of his " Monthly Review," that the writer of a very
elaborate article on the works of Dr. Parr, was no less a personage
than the Doctor himself. His egotism was so declamatory, that it
unnaturalized a great mind, by the distortions of Johnsonian mimicry;
his fierceness, which was pushed on to brutality on the unresisting, retreated with a child's terrors when resisted; and the pomp of petty
pride in table triumphs and evening circles, ill compensated for the
lost century he might have made his own !

> Lord o'er the greatest, to the least a slave,
> Half-weak, half-strong, half-timid, and half-brave;
> To take a compliment of too much pride,
> And yet most hurt when praises are denied.
> Thou art so deep discerning, yet so blind,
> So learn'd, so ignorant, cruel, yet so kind;
> So good, so bad, so foolish, and so wise;—
> By turns I love thee, and by turns despise.
>   MS. ANON. (said to be by the late Dr. Homer.)

nate in an impartial decision.* Mine is a colder and less
grateful task. I am but a historian! I have to creep
along in the darkness of human events, to lay my hand
cautiously on truths so difficult to touch, and which
either the panegyrist or the writer of an invective cover
over, and throw aside into corners.

Much of the moral, and something too of the physical
dispositions of the man enter into the literary character;
and, moreover, there are localities—the place where he
resides, the circumstances which arise, and the habits he
contracts; to all these the excellences and the defects
of some of our great literary characters may often be
traced. With this clue we may thread our way
through the labyrinth of Genius.

Warburton long resided in an obscure provincial
town, the articled clerk of a country attorney,† and

* The "Quarterly Review," vol. vii. p. 383.—So masterly a piece
of criticism has rarely surprised the public in the leaves of a periodical publication. It comes, indeed, with the feelings of another age,
and the reminiscences of the old and vigorous school. I cannot im-
plicitly adopt all the sentiments of the critic, but it exhibits a highly-
finished portrait, enamelled by the love of the artist.—This article was
written by the late Dr. Whitaker, the historian of Craven, &c.

† When Warburton, sore at having been refused academical honours at Oxford, which were offered to Pope, then his fellow-traveller,
and who, in consequence of this refusal, did himself not accept them—
in his controversy with Lowth (then the Oxford Professor), gave way
to his angry spirit, and struck at the University itself, for its political
jesuitism, being a place where men "were taught to distinguish
between *de facto* and *de jure*." caustic was the retort. Lowth, by singular felicity of application, touched on Warburton's original designa-
tion, in a character he hit on in Clarendon. After remonstrating with
spirit and dignity on this petulant attack, which was not merely personal, Lowth continues:—"Had I not your lordship's example to justify me, I should think it a piece of extreme impertinence to inquire
where you were bred: though one might justly plead, in excuse for
it, a natural curiosity to know *where* and *how* such a phenomenon was
produced. It is commonly said that your lordship's education was of

then an unsuccessful practising one. He seems, too, once to have figured as "a wine-merchant in the Borough," and rose into notice as "the orator of a disputing club;" but, in all his shapes, still keen in literary pur-

that particular kind, concerning which it is a remark of that great judge of men and manners, Lord Clarendon (on whom you have, therefore, with a wonderful happiness of allusion, justness of application, and elegance of express'on, conferred 'the unrivalled title of the Chancellor of Human Nature'), that it peculiarly disposes men to be proud, insolent, and pragmatical." Lowth, in a note, inserts Clarendon's character of Colonel Harrison: "He had been bred up in the place of a clerk, under a lawyer of good account in those parts; which kind of education introduces men into the language and practice of business; and if it be not resisted by the great ingenuity of the person. inclines young men to more pride than any other kind of breeding, and disposes them to be pragmatical and insolent." "Now, my lord (Lowth continues), as you have in your whole behaviour, and in all your writings, remarkably distinguished yourself by your humility, lenity, meekness, forbearance, candour, humanity, civility, decency, good manners, good temper, moderation with regard to the opinions of others, and a modest diffidence of your own, this unpromising circumstance of your education is so far from being a disgrace to you, that it highly redounds to your praise."—*Lowth's Letter to the Author of the D. L.* p. 63.

Was ever weapon more polished and keen? This Attic style of controversy finely contrasts with the tasteless and fierce invective of the Warburtonians, although one of them is well known to have managed too adroitly the cutting instrument of irony; but the frigid malignancy of Hurd diminishes the pleasure we might find in his skill. Warburton ill concealed his vexation in the contempt he vented in a letter to Hurd on this occasion. "All you say about Lowth's pamphlet breathes the purest spirit of friendship. His *wit* and his *r a ou-ing.* God knows, and I also, (as a certain critic said once in a matter of the like great importance), are much below the qualities that deserve those names."—He writes too of "this man's boldness in publishing his letters."—"If he expects an answer, he will certainly find himself disappointed; though I believe I could make *as good sport with this devil of a vice,* for the public diversion, as ever was made with him in the old Moralities."—But Warburton did reply! Had he ever possessed one feeling of taste, never would he have figured the elegant

suits, without literary connexions; struggling with all
the defects of a desultory and self-taught education, but
of a bold aspiring character, he rejected, either in pride
or in despair, his little trades, and took Deacon's orders
—to exchange a profession, unfavourable to continuity of
study, for another more propitious to its indulgence.*

Lowth as this grotesque personage. He was, however, at that moment sharply stung!

This circumstance of *Attorneyship* was not passed over in Mallet's
"Familiar Epistle to the Most Impudent Man Living." Comparing,
in the spirit of "familiarity," Arnall, an impudent scribbling attorney and political scribe, with Warburton, he says, " You have been
an attorney as well as he, but a little more impudent than he was; for
Arnall never presumed to conceal his turpitude under the gown and
the scarf." But this is mere invective!

* I have given a tempered opinion of his motive for this sudden
conversion from Attorneyship to Divinity; for it must not be concealed. in our inquiry into Warburton's character, that he has frequently been accused of a more worldly one. He was so fierce an
advocate for some important causes he undertook, that his sincerity
has been liable to suspicion: the pleader. in some points, certainly acting
the part of a sophist. Were we to decide by the early appearances
of his conduct, by the rapid change of his profession, by his obsequi-
ous servility to his country squire, and by what have been termed the
hazardous "fooleries in criticism, and outrages in controversy," which
he systematically pursued, he looks like one not in earnest, and more
zealous to maintain the character of his own genius, than the cause he
had espoused. Leland once exclaimed, "What are we to think of
the writer and his intentions? Is he really sincere in his reasonings?"
Certain it is, his paradoxes often alarmed his friends, to repeat the
words of a great critic. by "the absurdity of his criticism, the hetero-
doxy of his tenets, and the brutality of his invectives." Our Juvenal,
who, whatever might be the vehemence of his declamation, reflected
always those opinions which floated about him, has drawn a full-
length figure. He accounts for Warburton's early motive in taking
the cassock, as being

" ——— ——————— thereto drawn
By some faint omens of the Lawn,
And on the truly Christian plan,
To make himself a gentleman;

In a word, he set off as a literary adventurer, who was to win his way by earning it from patronage.
His first mischances were not of a nature to call forth

> A title, in which Form arrayed him,
> Tho' Fate ne'er thought of when she made him.
> To make himself a man of note,
> He in defence of Scripture wrote:
> So long he wrote, and long about it,
> That e'en believers 'gan to doubt it.
> He wrote too of the Holy Ghost;
> Of whom, no more than doth a post,
> He knew; nor, should an angel show him,
> Would he or know, or choose to know him."
>
> Churchill's "Duellist."

I would not insinuate that Warburton is to be ranked among the class he so loudly denounced, that of "Free-thinkers;" his mind, warm with imagination, seemed often tinged with credulity. But from his want of sober-mindedness, we cannot always prove his earnestness in the cause he advocated. He often sports with his fancies; he breaks out into the most familiar levity; and maintains, too broadly, subtile and refined principles, which evince more of the political than the primitive Christian. It is certain his infidelity was greatly suspected; and Hurd, to pass over the stigma of Warburton's sudden conversion to the Church, insinuates that "*an early seriousness of mind* determined him to the ecclesiastical profession."—" It may be so," says the critic in the "Quarterly Review," no languid admirer of this great man; "but the symptoms of that *seriousness were very equivocal afterwards;* and the *certainty of an early provision, from a generous patron in the country,* may perhaps be considered by those who are disposed to assign human conduct to ordinary motives, as quite adequate to the effect."

Dr. Parr is indignant at such surmises; but the feeling is more honourable than the decision! In an admirable character of Warburton in the "Westminster Magazine" for 1779, it is acknowledged, "at his outset in life he was suspected of being inclined to infidelity; and it was not till many years had elapsed, that the orthodoxy of his opinions was generally assented to." On this Dr. Parr observes, "Why Dr. Warburton was *ever* suspected of secret infidelity I know not. What he was *inclined to think* on subjects of religion, before, perhaps, he had leisure or ability to examine them, depends only upon obscure surmise, or vague report." The words *inclined to think* seems a

that intrepidity which afterwards hardened into the
leading feature of his character. Few great authors
have begun their race with less auspicious omens,
though an extraordinary event in the life of an author
happened to Warburton—he had secured a patron before he was an author.

The first publication of his which we know, was his
"Translations in Prose and Verse from Roman Poets,
Orators, and Historians." 1724. He was then about
twenty-five years of age. The fine forms of classic
beauty could never be cast in so rough a mould as his
prose; and his turgid unmusical verses betrayed qualities of mind incompatible with the delicacy of poetry.
Four years afterwards he repeated another bolder attempt, in his "Critical and Philosophical Inquiry into
the Causes of Prodigies and Miracles." After this publication, I wonder Warburton was ever suspected of
infidelity or even scepticism.* So radically deficient in

periphrase for *secret infidelity*. Our critic attributes these reports to
"an English dunce, whose blunders and calumnies are now happily
forgotten, and repeated by a French buffoon, whose morality is not
commensurate with his wit."—*Tracts* by Warburton, &c., p. 136.

"The English Dunce" I do not recollect: of this sort there are so
many! Voltaire is "the French buffoon;" who, indeed, compares
Warburton in his bishopric, to Peachum in the Beggar's Opera—who,
as Keeper of Newgate, was for hanging all his old accomplices!

* Warburton was far more extravagant in a later attempt which he
made to expound the odd visions of a crack-brained Welshman, a
prophesying knave; a knave by his own confession, and a prophet by
Warburton's. This commentary, inserted in Jortin's "Remarks on
Ecclesiastical History," considerably injured the reputation of Jortin.
The story of Warburton and his Welsh Prophet would of itself be sufficient to detect the shiftings and artifices of his genius. Rice or Arise
Evans! was one of the many prophets who rose up in Oliver's fanatical days; and Warburton had the hardihood to insert, in Jortin's
learned work, a strange commentary to prove that Arise Evans, in
Cromwell's time, in his "Echo from Heaven," had manifestly *prophe-
sied the Hanoverian Succession!* The Welshman was a knave by his

Warburton was that fine internal feeling which we call taste, that through his early writings he acquired not one solitary charm of diction,* and scarcely betrayed,

own account in subscribing with his *right* hand the confession he calls his prophecy, before a justice, and with his *left*, that which was his recantation, signed before the recorder, adding, "I know the bench and the people thought I recanted; but, alas! they were deceived;" and this Warburton calls "an uncommon fetch of wit," to save the truth of the prophecy, though not the honour of the prophet. If Evans meant anything, he meant what was then floating in all men's minds, the probable restoration of the Stuarts. By this prelude of that inventive genius which afterwards commented, in the same spirit, on the Æneid of Virgil, and the "Divine Legation, itself," and made the same sort of discoveries, he fixed himself in this dilemma: either Warburton was a greater impostor than Arise Evans, or he was more credulous than even any follower of the Welsh prophet, if he really had any. But the truth is, that Warburton was always writing for a present purpose, and believed, and did not believe, as it happened. "Ordinary men believe *one* side of a contradiction at a time, whereas his lordship" (says his admirable antagonist) "frequently believes, or at least defends *both*. So that it would have been no great wonder if he should maintain that Evans was both a real prophet and an impostor." Yet this is not the only awkward attitude into which Warburton has here thrown himself. To strain the vision of the raving Welshman to events of which he could have no notion, Warburton has plunged into the most ludicrous difficulties, all which ended, as all his discoveries have done, in making the fortune of an adversary who, like the Momus of Homer, has raised through the skies "inextinguishable laughter," in the amusing tract of "Confusion worse Confounded, Rout on Rout, or the Bishop of G——'s Commentary on Arise Evans; by Indignatio." 1772. The writer was the learned Henry Taylor, the author of Ben Mordecai's Apology.

* The correct taste of Lowth with some humour describes the last sentence of the "Enquiry on Prodigies" as "the Musa Pedestris got on horseback in a high prancing style." He printed it in measured lines, without, however, changing the place of a single word, and it produced blank verse. Thus it reads—

"Methinks I see her like the mighty Eagle
renewing her immortal youth, and purging
her opening sight at the unobstructed beams
of our benign meridian Sun," &c.

amid his impurity of taste, that nerve and spirit which afterwards crushed all rival force. His translations *in imitation of Milton's style* betray his utter want of ear and imagination. He attempted to suppress both these works during his lifetime.

When these unlucky productions were republished by Dr. Parr, the *Dedications* were not forgotten; they were both addressed to the same opulent baronet, not omitting "the virtues" of his lady the Countess of Sunderland, whose marriage he calls "so divine a union." Warburton had shown no want of judgment in the choice of his patrons; for they had more than one living in their gift —and perhaps, knowing his patrons, none in the dedications themselves. They had, however, this absurdity, that in freely exposing the servile practices of dedicators, the writer was himself indulging in that luxurious sin, which he so forcibly terms "Public Prostitution." This early management betrays no equivocal symptoms of that traffic in *Dedications*, of which he has been so severely accused,* and of that paradoxical turn and

Such a glowing metaphor, in the uncouth prose of Warburton, startled Lowth's classical ear. It was indeed "the Musa Pedestris who had got on horseback in a high prancing style;" for as it has since been pointed out. it is a well-known passage towards the close of the Areopagitica of Milton, whose prose is so often purely poetical. See Birch's Edition of Milton's Prose Works, I. 158. Warburton was familiarly conversant with our great vernacular writers at a time when their names generally were better known than their works, and when it was considered safe to pillage their most glorious passages. Warburton has been convicted of snatching their purple patches, and sewing them into his coarser web, without any acknowledgment; he did this in the present remarkable instance. and at a later day, in the preface to his "Julian," he laid violent hands on one of Raleigh's splendid metaphors.

* When Warburton was considered as a Colossus of literature, Ralph, the political writer, pointed a severe allusion to the awkward figure he makes in these Dedications. "The Colossus himself creeps

hardy effrontery which distinguished his after-life. These dedications led to preferment, and thus hardily was laid the foundation-stone of his aspiring fortunes.

between the legs of the late Sir Robert Sutton ; in what posture, or for what purpose, need not be explained."

Churchill has not passed by unnoticed Warburton's humility, even to weakness, combined with pride which could rise to haughtiness.

> " He was so proud, that should he meet
> The twelve apostles in the street,
> He'd turn his nose up at them all,
> And shove his Saviour from the wall."

Yet this man

> ——" Fawned through all his life
> For patrons first, then for a wife;
> Wrote *Dedications*, which must make
> The heart of every Christian quake."
>
> *The Duellist.*

It is certain that the proud and supercilious Warburton long crouched and fawned. Mallet, at least, well knew all that passed between Warburton and Pope. In the "Familiar Epistle" he asserts that Warburton was introduced to Pope by his "nauseous flattery." A remarkable instance, besides the dedications we have noticed, occurred in his correspondence with Sir Thomas Hanmer. He did not venture to attack " The Oxford Editor." as he sarcastically distinguishes him, without first demanding back his letters, which were immediately returned, from Sir Thomas's high sense of honour. Warburton might otherwise have been shown strangely to contradict himself, for in these letters he had been most lavish of his flatteries and encomiums on the man whom he covered with ridicule in the preface to his Shakspeare. See " An Answer to certain Passages in Mr. W.'s Preface to Shakspeare," 1748.

His dedication to the plain unlettered Ralph Allen of Bath, his greatest of patrons, of his "Commentary on Pope's Essay on Man," is written in the same spirit as those to Sir Robert Sutton ; but the former unlucky gentleman was more publicly exposed by it. The subject of this dedication turns on " the growth and progress of *Fate*, divided into four principal branches!" There is an episode about *Free-will* and *Nature* and *Grace*, and "a *contrivance* of Leibnitz about *Fatalism* " Ralph Allen was a good Quaker-like man, but he must have lost his temper if he ever read the dedication ! Let us not, however, imagine

Till his thirtieth year, Warburton evinced a depraved taste, but a craving appetite for knowledge. His mind was constituted to be more struck by the Monstrous than the Beautiful, much like that Sicilian prince who furnished his villa with the most hideous figures imaginable:* the

that Warburton was at all insensible to this violation of literary decorum; he only sacrificed *propriety* to what he considered a more urgent principle—his own personal interest. No one had a juster conception of the true nature of *dedications;* for he says in the famous one "to the Free-thinkers:"—"I could never approve the custom of dedicating books to men whose professions made them strangers to the subject. A Discourse on the Ten Predicaments to a Leader of Armies, or a System of Casuistry to a Minister of State, always appeared to me a high absurdity."

All human characters are mixed—true! yet still we feel indignant to discover some of the greatest often combining the most opposite qualities; and then they are not so much mixed as the parts are naturally joined together. Could one imagine that so lofty a character as Warburton could have been liable to have incurred even the random stroke of the satirist? whether true or false, the events of his life, better known at this day than in his own, will show. Churchill says that

> " He could cringe and creep, be civil,
> And hold a stirrup to the devil,
> If, *in a journey to his mind,*
> He'd let him mount, and ride behind."

The author of the "Canons of Criticism," with all his sprightly sarcasm, gives a history of Warburton's later Dedications. "The first edition of 'The Alliance' came out without a dedication. but was presented to the bishops; and when nothing came of that, the second was addressed to both the Universities; and when nothing came of that, the third was dedicated to a noble Earl. and nothing has yet come of that." Appendix to "Canons of Criticism," seventh edit. 261.

* The palace here alluded to is fully described in a volume of "Travels through Sicily and Malta," by P. Brydone, F. R. S., in 1770. He describes it as belonging to "the Prince of Palermo, a man of immense fortune, who has devoted his whole life to the study of monsters and chimeras, greater and more ridiculous than ever entered into the imagination of the wildest writers of romance and knight-

delight resulting from harmonious and delicate forms
raised emotions of too weak a nature to move his obliquity of taste ; roused, however, by the surprise excited
by colossal ugliness. The discovery of his intellectual
tastes, at this obscure period of his life, besides in those
works we have noticed, is confirmed by one of the most
untoward accidents which ever happened to a literary
man ; it was the chance-discovery of a letter he had written to one of the heroes of the Dunciad, forty years
before. At the time that letter was written, his literary
connexions were formed with second-rate authors ; he
was in strict intimacy with Concanen and Theobald, and
other "ingenious gentlemen who made up our last night's
conversation," as he expresses himself. * This letter is

errantry." He tells us this palace was surrounded by an army of
statues, "not one made to represent any object in nature. He has
put the heads of men to the bodies of every sort of animal, and the
heads of every other animal to the bodies of men. Sometimes he
makes a compound of five or six animals that have no sort of resemblance in nature. He puts the head of a lion on the neck of a goose,
the body of a lizard, the legs of a goat, the tail of a fox ; on the back
of this monster he puts another, if possible still more hideous, with
five or six heads, and a bush of horns. There is no kind of horn in
the world he has not collected, and his pleasure is to see them all
flourishing upon the same head." The interior of the house was deco-
rated in the same monstrous style, and the description, unique of its
kind, occupies several pages of Mr. Brydone's book.—ED.

* This letter was written in 1726, and first found by Dr. Knight in
1750, in fitting up a house where Concanen had probably lodged. It
was suppressed, till Akenside, in 1766, printed it in a sixpenny pamphlet, entitled "An Ode to Mr. Edwards." He preserved the curiosity, with "all its peculiarities of grammar, spelling, and punctuation."
The insulted poet took a deep revenge for the contemptuous treatment
he had received from the modern Stagirite. The "peculiarities" betray most evident marks of the self-taught lawyer ; the orthography
and the double letters were minted in the office. [Thus he speaks of
Addison as this " exact Mr. of propriety," and of his own studies of
the English poets " to trace them to their sources ; and observe what

full of the heresies of taste: one of the most anomalous
is the comment on that well-known passage in Shakspeare
on "the genius and the mortal instruments;" Warburton's is a miraculous specimen of fantastical sagacity and
critical delirium, or the art of discovering meanings never
meant, and of illustrations the author could never have
known. Warburton declares to "the ingenious gentlemen," (whom afterwards with a Pharaoh's heart he
hanged by dozens to posterity in the "Dunciad,") that
"Pope borrowed for want of genius;" that poet, who,
when the day arrived, he was to comment on as the first
of poets! His insulting criticisms on the popular writings of Addison,—his contempt for what Young calls
"sweet elegant Virgilian prose,"—show how utterly insensible he was to that classical taste in which Addison
had constructed his materials. But he who could not taste
the delicacy of Addison, it may be imagined might be in
raptures with the rant of Lee. There is an unerring
principle in the false sublime: it seems to be governed
by laws, though they are not ours; and we know what
it will like, that is, we know what it will mistake for
what ought not to be liked, as surely as we can anticipate what will delight correct taste. Warburton has

oar, as well as what slime and gravel they brought down with them."]
When I looked for the letter in *Akenside's Works*, I discovered that it
had been silently dropped. Some interest, doubtless, had been made
to suppress it, for Warburton was humbled when reminded of it.
Malone, fortunately, has preserved it in his Shakspeare, where it may
be found, in a place not likely to be looked into for it, at the close of
Julius Cæsar: this literary curiosity had otherwise been lost for posterity; its whole history is a series of wonderful escapes.

By this document we became acquainted with the astonishing fact,
that Warburton, early in life, was himself one of those very dunces
whom he has so unmercifully registered in their Doomsday-book; one
who admired the genius of his brothers, and spoke of Pope with the
utmost contempt! [Thus he says, "Dryden, I observe, borrows for
want of leisure, and Pope for want of genius!"]

pronounced one of the raving passages of poor Nat "to
contain not only the most sublime, but the most judicious
imagery that poetry could conceive or paint." Joseph
Warton, who indignantly rejects it from his edition of
Pope, asserts that "we have not in our language a more
striking example of true turgid expression, and genuine
fustian and bombast."* Yet such was the man whom
ill-fortune (for the public at least) had chosen to become
the commentator of our greater poets! Again Churchill
throws light on our character:—

> He, with an all-sufficient air
> Places him-elf in the critic's chair,
> And wrote, to advance his Maker's praise,
> Comments on rhymes, and notes on plays—
> A judge of genius, though, confest,
> With not one spark of genius blest:
> Among the first of critics placed,
> Though free from every taint of taste.

Not encouraged by the reception his first literary
efforts received, but having obtained some preferment
from his patron, we now come to a critical point in his
life. He retreated from the world, and, during a seclusion of near twenty years, persevered in uninter-

* Lee introduces Alexander the Great, saying,

> "When Glory, like the dazzling eagle, stood
> Perch'd on my beaver in the Granic flood.
> When Fortune's self my standard trembling bore,
> And the pale Fates stood frighted on the shore;
> When the Immortals on the billows rode,
> And I myself appear'd the leading god!"

In the province of taste Warburton was always at sea without chart
or compass, and was as unlucky in his panegyric on Milton as on Lee.
He calls the "Paradise Regained" "a charming poem, *nothing inferior*
in the *poetry* and the *sentiments* to the Paradise Lost." Such extravagance could only have proceeded from a critic too little sensible to the
essential requisites of poetry itself.

rupted studies. The force of his character placed him
in the first order of thinking beings. This resolution
no more to court the world for literary favours, but to
command it by hardy preparation for mighty labours,
displays a noble retention of the appetite for fame;
Warburton scorned to be a scribbler!

Had this great man journalised his readings, as Gibbon has done, we should perhaps be more astonished
at his miscellaneous pursuits. He read everything,
and, I suspect, with little distinction, and equal delight.*

* Such opposite studies shot themselves into the most fantastical
forms in his rocket-writings, whether they streamed in "The Divine
Legation," or sparkled in "The Origin of Romances," or played about
in giving double senses to Virgil, Pope, and Shakspeare. Churchill,
with a good deal of ill-nature and some truth, describes them :—

> "A curate first, he read and read,
> And laid in, while he should have fed
> The souls of his neglected flock,
> Of reading, such a mighty stock,
> That he o'ercharged the weary brain
> With more than she could well contain;
> More than she was with spirit fraught
> To turn and methodise to thought;
> And which, *like ill-digested food,*
> *To humours turn'd, and not to blood.*"

The opinion of Bentley, when he saw "The Divine Legation," was a
sensible one. "This man," said he, "has a monstrous appetite, with a
very bad digestion."

The Warburtonians seemed to consider his great work, as the Bible
by which all literary men were to be sworn. Lowth ridicules their
credulity. "'The Divine Legation,' it seems, contains in it all knowledge, divine and human, ancient and modern: it is a perfect Ency-
clopædia, including all history, criticism, divinity, law, politics, from the
law of Moses down to the Jew bill, and from Egyptian hieroglyphics
to modern Rebus-writing, &c."

"In the 2014 pages of the unfinished 'Divine Legation,'" observes
the sarcastic Gibbon, "four hundred authors are quoted, from St.
Austin down to Scarron and Rabelais!"

Curiosity, even to its delirium, was his first passion; which produced those new systems of hypothetical reasoning by which he startled the world; and his efforts to save his most ingenious theories from absurdity resembled, to use his own emphatic words applied to the philosophy of Leibnitz, "a contrivance against Fatalism," for though his genius has given a value to the wildest paradoxes, paradoxes they remain.

But if Warburton read so much, it was not to enforce opinions already furnished to his hands, or with cold scepticism to reject them, leaving the reader in despair. He read that he might write what no one else had written, and which at least required to be refuted before it was condemned. He hit upon a SECRET PRINCIPLE, which prevails through all his works, and this was INVENTION; a talent, indeed, somewhat dangerous to introduce in researches where Truth, and not Fancy, was to be addressed. But even with all this originality he was not free from imitation, and has even been accused of borrowing largely without hinting at his obligations. He had certainly one favourite model before him : Warburton has delineated the portrait of a certain author with inimitable minuteness, while he caught its general effect; we feel that the artist, in tracing the resemblance of another, is inspired by all

' Yet, after all that satire and wit have denounced, listen to an enlightened votary of Warburton. He asserts that "The 'Divine Legation' has taken its place at the head, not to say of English theology, but almost of English literature. To the composition of this prodigious performance. Hooker and Stillingfleet could have contributed the erudition, Chillingworth and Locke the acuteness, Taylor an imagination even more wild and copious, Swift, and perhaps, Eachard, the sarcastic vein of wit; but what power of understanding, except Warburton's, could first have amassed all these materials, and then compacted them into a bulky and elaborate work, so consistent and harmonious."—*Quarterly Review*, vol. vii.

the flattery of a self-painter—he perceived the kindred
features, and he loved them!

This author was Bayle! And I am unfolding the character of Warburton, in copying the very original portrait:
" Mr. Bayle is of a quite different character from these
Italian sophists: a writer, whose strength and clearness
of *reasoning* can be equalled only by the gaiety, easiness,
and delicacy of his *wit; who, pervading human nature
with a glance*, STRUCK INTO THE PROVINCE OF PARADOX,
as an exercise for the restless vigour of his mind: who,
with a soul superior to the sharpest attacks of fortune, and
a heart practised to the best philosophy, had *not yet enough
of real greatness to overcome that last foible of superior
geniuses*, the temptation of honour, which the ACADEMIC
EXERCISE OF WIT is conceived to bring to its professors." *

Here, then, we discover the SECRET PRINCIPLE which
conducted Warburton through all his works, although
of the most opposite natures. I do not give this as an
opinion to be discussed, but as a fact to be demonstrated.

The faculties so eminent in Bayle were equally so in
Warburton. In his early studies he had particularly
applied himself to logic; and was not only a vigorous
reasoner, but one practised in all the *finesse* of dialectics.
He had wit, fertile indeed, rather than delicate; and a
vast body of erudition, collected in the uninterrupted
studies of twenty years. But it was the SECRET PRIN-
CIPLE, or, as he calls it, " *the Academic exercise of Wit*,"
on an enlarged system, which carried him so far in the
new world of INVENTION he was creating.

* "The Divine Legation of Moses Demonstrated," vol. i. sec. iv.
Observe the remarkable expression, "that last foible of superior
genius." He had evidently running in his mind Milton's line on Fame—

"That last infirmity of noble minds."

In such an exalted state was Warburton's mind when he was
writing this, his own character.

This was a new characteristic of investigation; it led him on to pursue his profounder inquiries beyond the clouds of antiquity; for what he could not *discover*, he CONJECTURED and ASSERTED. Objects, which in the hands of other men were merely matters resting on authentic researches, now received the stamp and lustre of original invention. Nothing was to be seen in the state in which others had viewed it; the hardiest paradoxes served his purpose best, and this licentious principle produced unlooked-for discoveries. He humoured his taste, always wild and unchastised, in search of the monstrous and the extravagant; and, being a wit, he delighted in finding resemblances in objects which to more regulated minds had no similarity whatever. *Wit* may exercise its ingenuity as much in combining *things* unconnected with each other, as in its odd assemblage of *ideas;* and Warburton, as a literary antiquary, proved to be as witty in his combinations as Butler and Congreve in their comic images. As this principle took full possession of the mind of this man of genius, the practice became so familiar, that it is possible he might at times have been credulous enough to have confided in his own reveries. As he forcibly expressed himself on one of his adversaries, Dr. Stebbing, "Thus it is to have to do with a head whose *sense is all run to system.*" "His Academic Wit" now sported amid whimsical theories, pursued bold but inconclusive arguments, marked out subtile distinctions, and discovered incongruous resemblances; but they were maintained by an imposing air of conviction, furnished with the most prodigal erudition, and they struck out many ingenious combinations. The importance or the curiosity of the topics awed or delighted his readers; the principle, however licentious, by the surprise it raised, seduced the lovers of novelties. Father Hardouin had studied as hard as

Warburton, rose as early, and retired to rest as late, and
the obliquity of his intellect resembled that of Warburton—but he was a far inferior genius; he only discovered
that the classical works of antiquity, the finest compositions of the human mind, in ages of its utmost refinement, had been composed by the droning monks of the
middle ages; a discovery which only surprised by its
tasteless absurdity—but the absurdities of Warburton
had more dignity, were more delightful, and more
dangerous: they existed, as it were, in a state of illusion, but illusion which required as much genius and
learning as his own to dissipate. His spells were to be
disturbed only by a magician, great as himself. Conducted by this solitary principle, Warburton undertook,
as it were, a magical voyage into antiquity. He passed
over the ocean of time, sailing amid rocks, and half lost
on quicksands; but he never failed to raise up some
terra incognita; or point at some scene of the *Fata
Morgana,* some earthly spot, painted in the heaven one
knows not how.

In this secret principle of resolving to *invent* what no
other had before conceived, by means of *conjecture* and
assertion, and of maintaining his theories with all the
pride of a sophist, and all the fierceness of an inquisitor,
we have the key to all the contests by which this great
mind so long supported his literary usurpations.

The first step the giant took showed the mightiness of
his stride. His first great work was the famous "Alliance between Church and State." It surprised the
world, who saw the most important subject depending
on a mere *curious* argument, which, like all political
theories, was liable to be overthrown by writers of
opposite principles.* The term "Alliance" seemed to

* The author of "The Canons of Criticism" addressed a severe son-
nct to Warburton; and alludes to the "Alliance":—

the dissenters to infer that the *Church* was an independent power, forming a contract with the *State*, and not acknowledging that it is only an integral part, like that of the *army* or the *navy*.* Warburton had not probably decided, at that time, on the principle of ecclesiastical power: whether it was paramount by its divine origin, as one party asserted; or whether, as the new philosophers, Hobbes, Selden, and others, insisted, the spiritual was secondary to the civil power.†

The intrepidity of this vast genius appears in the plan of his greater work. The omission of a future state of reward and punishment, in the Mosaic writings, was perpetually urged as a proof that the mission was not of divine origin: the ablest defenders strained at obscure

> " Reign he sole king in paradoxal land,
> And for Utopia plan his idle schemes
> Of *visionary leagues, alliance vain*
> '*Twixt* Will *and* Warburton—"

On which he adds this note, humorously stating the grand position of the work:—"The whole argument by which the *alliance between Church and State* is established, Mr. Warburton founds upon this supposition—'That people, considering themselves in a religious capacity, may contract with themselves, considered in a civil capacity.' The conceit is ingenious, but is not his own. *Scrub*, in the *Beaux Stratagem*, had found it out long ago: he considers himself as acting the different parts of all the servants in the family; and so *Scrub*, the coachman, ploughman, or justice's clerk, might contract with *Scrub*, the butler, for such a quantity of ale as the other assumed character demanded."—Appendix, p. 261.

* " Monthly Review," vol. xvi. p. 324, the organ of the dissenters.

† See article Hobbes, for his system. The great Selden was an *Erastian;* a distinction extremely obscure. *Erastus* was a Swiss physician of little note, who was for restraining the ecclesiastical power from all temporal jurisdiction. Selden did him the honour of adopting his principles. Selden wrote against the *divine right* of tithes, but allowed the *legal* right, which gave at first great offence to the clergy, who afterwards perceived the propriety of his argument, as Wotton has fully acknowledged

or figurative passages, to force unsatisfactory inferences; but they were looking after what could not be found. Warburton at once boldly acknowledged it was not there; at once adopted all the objections of the infidels: and roused the curiosity of both parties by the hardy assertion, that this very *omission* was a *demonstration* of its divine origin.*

* It does not always enter into the design of these volumes to examine those great works which produced *literary quarrels*. But some may be glad to find here a word on this original project.

The grand position of the *Divine Legation* is, that the knowledge of the immortality of the soul, or a future state of reward and punishment, is absolutely necessary in the moral government of the universe. The author shows how it has been inculcated by all good legislators, so that no religion could ever exist without it; but the Jewish could, from its peculiar government, which was theocracy—a government where the presence of God himself was perpetually manifested by miracles and new ordinances; and hence temporal rewards and punishments were sufficient for that people, to whom the unity and power of the Godhead were never doubtful. As he proceeded, he would have opened a new argument, viz., that the Jewish religion was only the *pa't* of a revelation, showing the necessity of a further one *for* its *completion*, which produced Christianity.

When Warburton was in good spirits with his great work (for he was not always so), he wrote thus to a friend:—" You judge right, that the *next* volume of the D. L. will not be the *last*. I thought I had told you that I had divided the work into three parts: the first gives you a view of Paganism; the second, of Judaism; and the third, of Christianity. *You will wonder* how this last inquiry can come into *so simple an argument* as that which I undertake to enforce. I have not room to tell you more than this—that after I have proved a future state not to be, *in fact*, in the Mosaic dispensation. I next show that, if Christianity be true, *it could not possibly be there;* and this necessitates me to explain the nature of Christianity, with which the whole ends. But this *inter nos*. If it be known, I should possibly have somebody writing against *this part too* before it appears."—Nichols's "Literary Anecdotes," vol. v. p. 551.

Thus he exults in the true tone, and with all the levity of a sophist. It is well that a true feeling of religion does not depend on the quirks and quibbles of human reasonings, or, what are as fallible, on masses of fanciful erudition.

The first idea of this new project was bold and delightful, and the plan magnificent. Paganism, Judaism, and
Christianity, the three great religions of mankind, were
to be marshalled in all their pomp, and their awe, and
their mystery.. But the procession changed to a battle!
To maintain one great paradox, he was branching out
into innumerable ones. This great work was never concluded: the author wearied himself, without, however,
wearying his readers; and, as his volumes appeared, he
was still referring to his argument, "as far as it is yet
advanced." The *demonstration* appeared in great danger of ending in a *conjecture;* and this work, always
beginning and never ending, proved to be the glory and
misery of his life.* In perpetual conflict with those
numerous adversaries it roused, Warburton often shifted

* Warburton lost himself in the labyrinth he had so ingeniously
constructed. This work harassed his days and exhausted his intellect.
Observe the tortures of a mind, even of so great a mind as that of
Warburton's, when it sacrifices all to the perishable vanity of sudden
celebrity. Often he flew from his task in utter exhaustion and despair. He had quitted the smooth and even line of truth, to wind
about and split himself on all the crookedness of paradoxes. He
paints his feelings in a letter to Birch. He says—"I was so disgusted
with an old subject, that I had deferred it from month to month and
year to year." He had recourse to "an expedient;" which was, "to
set the press on work, and so oblige himself to supply copy." Such is
the confession of the author of the "Divine Legation!" this "ency-
clopædia" of all ancient and modern lore—all to proceed from "a simple argument!" But when he describes his sufferings, hard is the
heart of that literary man who cannot sympathise with such a giant
caught in the toils! I give his words:—" Distractions of various
kinds, inseparable from human life. joined with a naturally melancholy habit, contribute greatly to increase my indolence. This makes
my reading wild and desultory; and I seek refuge from *the uneasiness
of thought,* from any book, let it be what it will. *By my manner of
writing upon subjects, you would naturally imagine they afford me pleasure, and attach me thoroughly. I will assure you, No!*"—Nichols's
" Literary Anecdotes," vol. v. p. 562.

his ground, and broke into so many divisions, that when
he cried out, Victory! his scattered forces seemed rather
to be in flight than in pursuit.*

The same SECRET PRINCIPLE led him to turn the poetical narrative of Æneas in the infernal regions, an episode evidently imitated by Virgil from his Grecian master,

Warburton had not the cares of a family—they were merely literary
ones. The secret cause of his "melancholy," and his "indolence,"
and that "want of attachment and pleasure to his subjects," which his
friends "naturally imagined" afforded him so much, was the controversies he had kindled, and the polemical battles he had raised about
him. However boldly he attacked in return, his heart often sickened in
privacy: for how often must he have beheld his noble and his whimsical
edifices built on sands, which the waters were perpetually eating into!
At the last interview of Warburton with Pope, the dying poet ex-
horted him to proceed with "The Divine Legation." "Your reputation," said he, "as well as your duty, is concerned in it. People say
you can get no farther in your proof. Nay, Lord Bolingbroke himself bids me expect no such thing." This anecdote is rather extraordinary: for it appears in "Owen Ruffhead's Life of Pope," p. 497,
a work written under the eye of Warburton himself: and in which I
think I could point out some strong touches from his own hand on
certain important occasions, when he would not trust to the creeping
dulness of Ruffhead.

* His temerity had raised against him not only infidels, but Christians. If any pious clergyman now wrote in favour of the opinion
that God's people believed in the immortality of the soul—which can
we doubt they did? and which Manasseh Ben Israel has written his
treatise, "De Resurrectione Mortuorum," to prove—it was a strange
sight to behold a bishop seeming to deny so rational and religious a
creed! Even Dr. Balguy confessed to Warburton, that "there was
one thing in the argument of the 'Divine Legation' that stuck more
with candid men than all the rest—how a religion without a future
state could be worthy of God!" This Warburton promised to satisfy,
by a fresh appendix. His volatile genius, however, was condemned
to "the pelting of a merciless storm." Lowth told him—"You give
yourself out as *demonstrator* of the *divine legation* of Moses; it has
been often demonstrated before; a young student in theology might
undertake to give a better—that is, a more satisfactory and irrefragable demonstration of it in five pages than you have done in five
volumes."—Lowth's "Letter to Warburton," p. 12.

into a minute description of the initiation into the Eleusinian Mysteries. A notion so perfectly new was at least
worth a commonplace truth. Was it not delightful to
have so many particulars detailed of a secret transaction,
which even its contemporaries of two thousand years ago
did not presume to know anything about? Father
Hardouin seems to have opened the way for Warburton,
since he had discovered that the whole Æneid was an
allegorical voyage of St. Peter to Rome! When Jortin,
in one of his "Six Dissertations," modestly illustrated
Virgil by an interpretation inconsistent with Warburton's
strange discovery, it produced a memorable quarrel.
Then Hurd, the future shield, scarcely the sword, of
Warburton, made his first sally; a dapper, subtle, and
cold-blooded champion, who could dexterously turn
about the polished weapon of irony.* So much our

* Hurd was the son of a Staffordshire farmer, and was placed by
him at Rugely, from whence he was removed to Emmanuel College,
Cambridge. At the age of twenty-six he published a pamphlet entitled "Remarks on a late Book entitled ' An Inquiry into the Rejection of the Christian Miracles by the Heathens, by William Weston,' "
which met with considerable attention. In 1749, on the occasion of
publishing a commentary on Horace's " Ars Poetica," he complimented
Warburton so strongly as to ensure his favour. Warburton returned
it by a puff for Hurd in his edition of Pope, and the two became fast
friends. It was a profitable connexion to Hurd, for by the intercession of Warburton he was appointed one of the Whitehall preachers,
a preacher at Lincoln's Inn, and Archdeacon of Gloucester. He re-
paid Warburton by constant praises in print, and so far succeeded
with that vain man, that when he read the dedication he made to him
of his "Commentary on the Epistle to Augustus," he wrote to him
with mock humility—"I will confess to you how much satisfaction the
groundless part of it, that which relates to myself, gave me." When
Dr. Jortin very properly spoke of Warburton with less of subserviency
than the overbearing bishop desired, Hurd at once came forward to
fight for Warburton in print, in a satirical treatise on "The Delicacy
of Friendship," which highly delighted his patron, who at once wrote
to Dr. Lowth, stating him to be "a man of very superior talents, of

Railleur admired the volume of Jortin, that he favoured
him with "A Seventh Dissertation, addressed to the
Author of the Sixth, on the Delicacy of Friendship,"
one of the most malicious, but the keenest pieces of
irony. It served as the foundation of a new School of
Criticism, in which the arrogance of the master was to
be supported by the pupil's contempt of men often his
superiors. To interpret Virgil differently from the
modern Stagirite, was, by the aggravating art of the
ridiculer, to be considered as the violation of a moral
feeling.* Jortin bore the slow torture and the teasing
of Hurd's dissecting-knife in dignified silence.

At length a rising genius demonstrated how Virgil
could not have described the Eleusinian Mysteries in the

genius, learning, and virtue; indeed, a principal ornament of the age
he lives in." Hurd was made Bishop of Lichfield in 1775, and of
Winchester in 1779. He died in the year 1808.—ED.

* The Attic irony was translated into plain English, in " Remarks
on Dr. Warburton's Account of the Sentiments of the Early Jews,"
1757; and the following rules for all who dissented from Warburton
are deduced:—" You must not write on the same subject that he
does. You must not glance at his arguments, even without naming
him or so much as referring to him. If you find his reasonings ever
so faulty, you must not presume to furnish him with better of your
own, even though you prove, and are desirous to support his conclusions. When you design him a compliment, you must express it in
full form, and with all the circumstance of panegyrical approbation,
without impertinently qualifying your civilities by assigning a reason
why you think he deserves them, as this might possibly be taken for
a hint that you know something of the matter he is writing about as
well as himself. You must never call any of his *discoveries* by the
name of *conjectures*, though you allow them their full proportion of
elegance, learning, &c.; for you ought to know that this capital genius
never proposed anything to the judgment of the public (though ever
so new and uncommon) with diffidence in his life. Thus stands the
decree prescribing our demeanour towards this sovereign in the Republic of Letters, as we find it promulged, and bearing date at the
palace of Lincoln's Inn, Nov. 25, 1755."—From whence Hurd's " Sev
enth Dissertation" was dated.

sixth book of the Æneid. One blow from the arm of Gibbon shivered the allegorical fairy palace into glittering fragments.*

When the sceptical Middleton, in his "Essay on the Gift of Tongues," pretended to think that "an inspired language would be perfect in its kind, with all the purity of Plato and the eloquence of Cicero," and then asserted that "the style of the New Testament was utterly rude and barbarous, and abounding with every fault that can possibly deform a language," Warburton, as was his custom, instantly acquiesced; but hardily maintained that "*this very barbarism was one certain mark of a divine original.*"†—The curious may follow his subtile argument in his "Doctrine of Grace;" but, in delivering this paradox, he struck at the fundamental principles of eloquence : he dilated on all the abuses of that human

* Gibbon's "Critical Observations on the Design of the Sixth Book of the Æneid." Dr. Parr considers this clear, elegant, and decisive work of criticism, as a complete refutation of Warburton's discovery.

† It is curious enough to observe that Warburton himself, acknowledging this to be a paradox, exultingly exclaims. "Which, *like so many others* I have had the ODD FORTUNE to advance, will be seen to be only another name for Truth." This has all the levity of a sophist's language! Hence we must infer that some of the most important subjects could not be understood and defended, but by Warburton's "*odd fortune!*" It was this levity of ideas that raised a suspicion that he was not always sincere. He writes, in a letter, of "living in mere spite, to rub another volume of the 'Divine Legation' in the noses of bigots and zealots." He employs the most ludicrous images, and the coarsest phrases, on the most solemn subjects. In one of his most unlucky paradoxes with Lowth, on the age and style of the writings of Job, he accuses that elegant scholar of deficient discernment; and, in respect to style, as not "distinguishing partridge from horseflesh;" and in quoting some of the poetical passages, of "paying with an old song," and "giving rhyme for reason." Alluding to some one of his adversaries, whom he calls "the weakest, as well as the wickedest of all mankind," he employs a striking image—"I shall hang him and his fellows, as they do vermin in a warren, and leave them to posterity, to stink and blacken in the wind."

art. It was precisely his utter want of taste which
afforded him so copious an argument; for he asserted
that the principles of eloquence were arbitrary and
chimerical, and its various modes "mostly fantastical;"
and that, consequently, there was no such thing as a
good taste,* except what the *consent of the learned* had
made; an expression borrowed from Quintilian. A
plausible and a consolatory argument for the greater
part of mankind! It, however, roused the indignation
of Leland, the eloquent translator of Demosthenes, and
the rhetorical professor at Trinity College, in Dublin,
who has nobly defended the cause of classical taste and
feeling by profounder principles. His classic anger produced his "Dissertation on the Principles of Human
Eloquence;" a volume so much esteemed that it is still
reprinted. Leland refuted the whimsical paradox, yet
complimented Warburton, who, "with the spirit and
energy of an ancient orator, was writing against eloquence," while he showed that the style of the New
Testament was defensible on surer grounds. Hurd, who
had fleshed his polished weapon on poor Jortin, and had
been received into the arms of the hero under whom he
now fought, adventured to cast his javelin at Leland: it

* Warburton, in this work (the "Doctrine of Grace,") has a
curious passage, too long to quote, where he observes, that "The
Indian and Asiatic eloquence was esteemed hyperbolic and puerile by
the more phlegmatic inhabitants of Rome and Athens: and the
Western eloquence, in its turn, frigid or insipid, to the hardy and inflamed imaginations of the East. The same expression, which in one
place had the utmost simplicity, had in another the utmost sublime."
The jackal, too, echoes the roar of the lion; for the polished Hurd,
whose taste was far more decided than Warburton's, was bold enough
to add, in his Letter to Leland, "That which is thought supremely
elegant in one country, passes in another for *finical;* while what in this
country is accepted under the idea of *sublimity,* is derided in that other
as no better than *bombast.*" So unsettled were the *no-taste* of Warburton, and the *prim-taste* of Hurd!

was dipped in the cold poison of contempt and petulance.
It struck, but did not canker, leaves that were immortal.*
Leland, with the native warmth of his soil, could not
resist the gratification of a reply; but the nobler part
of the triumph was, the assistance he lent to the circulation of Hurd's letter, by reprinting it with his own
reply, to accompany a new edition of his "Dissertation
on Eloquence."†

We now pursue the SECRET PRINCIPLE, operating on
lighter topics; when, turning commentator, with the
same originality as when an author, his character as a
literary adventurer is still more prominent, extorting
double senses, discovering the most fantastical allusions,
and making men of genius but of confined reading,
learned, with all the lumber of his own unwieldy
erudition.

When the German professor Crousaz published a rigid
examen of the doctrines in Pope's "Essay on Man,"
Warburton volunteered a defence of Pope. Some years
before, it appears that Warburton himself, in a literary
club at Newark, had produced a dissertation against
those very doctrines! where he asserted that "the Essay
was collected from the worst passages of the worst
authors." This probably occurred at the time he declared that Pope had no genius! Bolingbroke really

* The Letter to Leland is characterised in the "Critical Review"
for April, 1765, as the work of "a preferment-hunting toad-eater, who,
while his patron happened to go out of his depth, tells him that he is
treading good ground; but at the same time offers him the use of a
cork-jacket to keep him above water."

† Dr. Thomas Leland was born in Dublin in 1722, and was educated
in Trinity College, in that city. Having obtained a Fellowship
there, he depended on that alone, and devoted a long life to study,
and the production of various historical and theological works: as
well as a "History of Ireland," published in 1773. He died in
1785.—ED.

WROTE the "Essay on Man," which Pope *versified.*
His principles may be often objectionable; but those
who only read this fine philosophical poem for its condensed verse, its imagery, and its generous sentiments,
will run no danger from a metaphysical system they will
not care to comprehend.

But this serves not as an apology for Warburton, who

* In a rough attack on Warburton, respecting Pope's privately
printing 1500 copies of the "Patriot King" of Bolingbroke, which I
conceive to have been written by Mallet. I find a particular account
of the manner in which the "Essay on Man" was written, over which
Johnson seems to throw great doubts.

The writer of this angry epistle, in addressing Warburton, says:
"If you were as intimate with Mr. Pope as you pretend, you must
know the truth of a fact which several others, as well as I, who never
had the honour of a personal acquaintance with Lord Bolingbroke or
Mr. Pope, have heard. The fact was related to me by a certain
Senior Fellow of one of our Universities, who was very intimate with
Mr. Pope. He started some objections, one day, at Mr. Pope's house,
to the doctrine contained in the Ethic Epistles; upon which Mr. Pope
told him that he would soon convince him of the truth of it, by laying
the argument at large before him; for which purpose he gave him
a large prose manuscript to peruse, telling him, at the same time, the
author's name. From this perusal, whatever other conviction the
doctor might receive, he collected at least this: that Mr. Pope had
from his friend not only the *doctrine*, but even the *finest and strongest
ornaments of his Ethics.* Now, if this fact be true (as I question not
but you know it to be so), I believe no man of candour will attribute
such merit to Mr. Pope as you would insinuate, for acknowledging the
wisdom and the friendship of the man who was his instructor in philosophy; nor consequently that this acknowledgment, and the *dedication of his own system, put into a poetical dress by Mr. Pope,* laid his
lordship under the necessity of never resenting any injury done to him
by the poet afterwards. Mr. Pope told no more than literal truth, in
calling Lord Bolingbroke his *guide, philosopher, and friend.*" The
existence of this very manuscript volume was authenticated by Lord
Bathurst, in a conversation with Dr. Blair and others, where he said,
"he had read the MS. in Lord Bolingbroke's handwriting, and was at
a loss whether most to admire the elegance of Lord Bolingbroke s
prose, or the beauty of Mr. Pope's verse."—See the letter of Dr. Blair
in "Boswell's Life of Johnson."

now undertook an elaborate defence of what he had himself condemned, and for which purpose he has most unjustly depressed Crousaz—an able logician, and a writer ardent in the cause of religion. This commentary on the "Essay on Man," then, looks much like the work of a sophist and an adventurer! Pope, who was now alarmed at the tendency of some of those principles he had so innocently versified, received Warburton as his tutelary genius. A mere poet was soon dazzled by the sorcery of erudition; and he himself, having nothing of that kind of learning, believed Warburton to be the Scaliger of the age, for his gratitude far exceeded his knowledge.* The poet died in this delusion: he consigned his immortal works to the mercy of a ridiculous commentary and a tasteless commentator, whose labours have cost so much pains to subsequent editors to remove. Yet from this moment we date the worldly fortunes of Warburton.—Pope presented him with the entire property of his works; introduced him to a blind and obedient patron, who bestowed on him a rich wife, by whom he secured a fine mansion; till at length, the

---

* Of many instances, the following one is the most curious. When Jarvis published his "Don Quixote," Warburton, who was prompt on whatever subject was started, presented him with "A Dissertation on the Origin of the Books of Chivalry." When it appeared, it threw Pope, their common friend, into raptures. He writes, " I knew you as certainly as the ancients did the gods, by the first pace and the very gait." True enough! Warburton's strong genius stamped itself on all his works. But neither the translating painter, nor the simple poet, could imagine the heap of absurdities they were admiring! Whatever Warburton here asserted was false, and whatever he conjectured was erroneous; but his blunders were quite original.—The good sense and knowledge of Tyrwhitt have demolished the whole edifice, without leaving a single brick standing. The absurd rhapsody has been worth preserving, for the sake of the masterly confutation: no uncommon result of Warburton's literary labours!

It forms the concluding note in Shakspeare's *Love's Labour Lost.*

mitre crowned his last ambition. Such was the large
chapter of accidents in Warburton's life!

There appears in Warburton's conduct respecting the
editions of the great poets which he afterwards published, something systematic; he treated the several
editors of those very poets, Theobald, Hanmer, and
Grey, who were his friends, with the same odd sort of
kindness: when he was unknown to the world, he cheerfully contributed to all their labours, and afterwards
abused them with the liveliest severity.* It is probable

* Of Theobald he was once the companion, and to Sir Thomas Hanmer he offered his notes for his edition. [Hanmer's Shakspeare was
given in 1742 to the University of Oxford, for its benefit, and was
printed at the University Press, under the management of Dr. Smith
and Dr. Shippon. Sir Thomas paid the expenses of the engravings
by Gravelot prefixed to each play. The edition was published in 4to.
in 1744, it was printed on the "finest royal paper," and does not
warrant the severity of Pope, whose editing was equally faulty.] Sir
Thomas says he found Warburton's notes " sometimes just, but mostly
wild and out of the way." Warburton paid a visit to Sir Thomas for
a week, which he conceived was to assist him in perfecting his darling
text; but hints were now dropped by Warburton, that he might publish the work corrected, by which a greater sum of money might be
got than could be by that plaything of Sir Thomas, which shines in all
its splendour in the Dunciad; but this project did not suit Hanmer,
whose life seemed greatly to depend on the magnificent Oxford edition, which " was not to go into the hands of booksellers." On this,
Warburton, we are told by Hanmer, " flew into a great rage, and
there is an end of the story." With what haughtiness he treats these
two friends, for once they were such! Had the Dey of Algiers been
the editor of Shakspeare, he could not have issued his orders more
peremptorily for the decapitation of his rivals. Of Theobald and Hanmer he says, "the one was recommended to me as a poor man, the
other as a poor critic: and to each of them at different times I communicated a great number of observations, which they managed, as
they saw fit, to the relief of their several distresses. Mr. Theobald
was naturally turned to industry and labour. What he read he could
transcribe; but as to what he thought, if ever he did think, he could
but ill express, so he read on: and by that means got a character of
learning, without risking to every observer the imputation of wanting

that he had himself projected these editions as a source
of profit, but had contributed to the more advanced
labours of his rival editors, merely as specimens of his
talent, that the public might hereafter be thus prepared
for his own more perfect commentaries.

Warburton employed no little art* to excite the pub-

a better talent."—See what it is to enjoy too close an intimacy with a
:..n of wit! " As for the Oxford Editor, he wanted nothing (alluding
to Theobald's want of money) but what he might very well be without, the reputation of a critic," &c., &c.— *Warburton's Preface to Shakspeare.*

His conduct to Dr. Grey, the editor of Hudibras, cannot be accounted
for by any known fact. I have already noticed their quarrels in the
"Calamities of Authors." Warburton cheerfully supplied Grey with
various notes on Hudibras, though he said he had thought of an edition himself, and they were gratefully acknowledged in Grey's Preface;
but behold! shortly afterwards they are saluted by Warburton as "an
execrable heap of nonsense;" further, he insulted Dr. Grey for the
number of his publications! Poor Dr. Grey and his " Coadjutors," as
Warburton sneeringly called others of his friends, resented this by
" A Free and Familiar Letter to that Great Preserver of Pope and
Shakspeare, the Rev. Mr. William Warburton." The doctor insisted
that Warburton had had sufficient share in those very notes to be considered as one of the " Coadjutors." "I may venture to say, that
whoever was the *fool of the company* before he entered (or the *fool of
the piece*, in his own diction) he was certainly so after he engaged in
that work: for, as Ben Jonson observes, 'he that *thinks* himself the
Master-Wit is commonly the *Master-Fool*.' "

* Warburton certainly used little intrigues: he trafficked with the
obscure Reviews of the times. He was a correspondent in "The
Works of the Learned," where the account of his first volume of the
Divine Legation, he says, is "a nonsensical piece of stuff;" and when
Dr. Doddridge offered to draw up an article for his second, the favour
was accepted, and it was sent to the miserable journal, though acknowledged " to be too good for it." In the same journal were published all his specimens of Shakspeare, some years after they had
appeared in the " General Dictionary," with a high character of these
wonderful discoveries.—"The Alliance," when first published, was
announced in " The Present State of the Republic of Letters," to be
the work of a gentleman whose capacity, judgment, and learning

.ic curiosity respecting his future Shakspeare : he liberally presented Dr. Birch with his MS. notes for that
great work the " General Dictionary," no doubt as the
prelude of his after-celebrated edition. Birch was here
only a dupe : he escaped, unlike Theobald, Hanmer, and
Grey, from being overwhelmed with ridicule and contempt. When these extraordinary specimens of emen-
datory and illustrative criticism appeared in the "General Dictionary," with general readers they excited all
the astonishment of perfect novelty. It must have oc-

deserve some eminent dignity in the Church of England, of which
he is "now an inferior minister."—One may presume to guess at
" the gentleman," a little impatient for promotion, who so much cared
whether Warburton was only " now an inferior minister."
    These are little arts. Another was, that Warburton sometimes
acted Falstaff's part, and ran his sword through the dead ! In more
instances than one this occurred. Sir Thomas Hanmer was dead when
Warburton, then a bishop, ventured to assert that Sir Thomas's letter
concerning their intercourse about Shakspeare was " one continued
falsehood from beginning to end." The honour and veracity of Hanmer
must prevail over the " liveliness " of Warburton, for Hurd lauds his
'*lively* preface to his Shakspeare." But the " Biographia Britannica "
bears marks of Warburton's violence, in a cancelled sheet. See the
Index, art. Hanmer; [where we are told "the sheet being castrated at
the instance of Mr., now Dr. Warburton, Bishop of Gloucester, it has
been reprinted as an appendix to the work." it consisted in the suppression of one of Hanmer's letters.] He did not choose to attack Dr.
Middleton in form, during his lifetime, but reserved his blow when his
antagonist was no more. I find in Cole's MSS. this curious passage :
—"It was thought, at Cambridge, that Dr. Middleton and Dr. Warburton did not cordially esteem one another; yet both being keen and
thorough sportsmen, they were mutually afraid to engage to each
other, for fear of a fall. If that was the case, the bishop judged
prudently, however fairly it may be looked upon, to stay till it was
out of the power of his adversary to make any reply, before he gave
his answer." Warburton only replied to Middleton's " Letter from
Rome," in his fourth edition of the " Divine Legation," 1765.—When
Dyson firmly defended his friend Akenside from the rude attacks of
Warburton, it is observed, that he bore them with " prudent patience:"
he never replied !

curred to them, that no one as yet had understood
Shakspeare; and, indeed, that it required no less erudition than that of the new luminary now rising in the
critical horizon to display the amazing erudition of this
most recondite poet. Conjectural criticism not only
changed the words but the thoughts of the author; per-
verse interpretations of plain matters. Many a striking
passage was wrested into a new meaning: plain words
were subtilised to remove conceits; here one line was
rejected, and there an interpolation, inspired alone by
critical sagacity, pretended to restore a lost one; and
finally, a source of knowledge was opened in the notes,
on subjects which no other critic suspected could, by
any ingenuity, stand connected with Shakspeare's text.

At length the memorable edition appeared: all the
world knows its chimeras.* One of its most remarkable

* These critical *extravaganzas* are scarcely to be paralleled by
"Bentley's Notes on Milton." How Warburton turned "an allegorical mermaid" into "the Queen of Scots;"—showed how Shakspeare,
in one word, and with one epithet "the majestic world," described the
Orbis Romanus, alluded to the Olympic Games, &c.; yet, after all this
discovery, seems rather to allude to a story about Alexander, which
Warburton happened to recollect at that moment;—and how he illustrated Octavia's idea of the fatal consequences of a civil war between
Cæsar and Antony, who said it would "cleave the world," by the
story of Curtius leaping into the chasm;—how he rejected "*allowed*,
with absolute power," as not English, and read "*hallowed*," on the
authority of the Roman Tribuneship being called *Sacro-sancta Potestas;*
how his emendations often rose from puns; as for instance, when, in
Romeo and Juliet, it is said of the Friar, that "the city is much
obliged to *him*," our new critic consents to the sound of the word, but
not to the spelling, and reads *hymn;* that is, to laud, to praise! These,
and more extraordinary instances of perverting ingenuity and abused
erudition, would form an uncommon specimen of criticism, which may
be justly ridiculed, but which none, except an exuberant genius, could
have produced. The most amusing work possible would be a real
Warburton's Shakspeare, which would contain not a single thought,
and scarcely an expression, of Shakspeare's!

results was the production of that work, which annihilated the whimsical labours of Warburton, Edwards's
" Canons of Criticism," one of those successful facetious
criticisms which enliven our literary history. Johnson,
awed by the learning of Warburton, and warmed by a
personal feeling for a great genius who had condescended to encourage his first critical labour, grudg-
ingly bestows a moderated praise on this exquisite
satire, which he characterises for " its airy petulance,
suitable enough to the levity of the controversy." He
compared this attack "to a fly, which may sting and
tease a horse, but yet the horse is the nobler animal."*
Among the prejudices of criticism, is one which hinders
us from relishing a masterly performance, when it ridi-

---

* Had Johnson known as much as we do of Warburton's opinion of
his critical powers, it would have gone far to have cured his amiable
prejudice in favour of Warburton, who really was a critic without
taste, and who considered literature as some do politics, merely as a
party business. I shall give a remarkable instance. When Johnson
published his first critical attempt on *Macbeth*, he commended the critical talents of Warburton; and Warburton returned the compliment in
the preface to his Shakspeare, and distinguishes Johnson as ''a man
of parts and genius." But, unluckily, Johnson afterwards published
his own edition; and, in his editorial capacity, his public duty prevailed over his personal feelings: all this went against Warburton:
and the opinions he now formed of Johnson were suddenly those of
insolent contempt. In a letter to Hurd, he writes: "Of *this Johnson*,
you and I, I believe, think alike!" And to another friend: "The
remarks he makes, in every page, on *my Commentaries*, are full of
insolence and malignant reflections, which, had they not in them *as much
folly as malignity*, I should have reason to be offended with." He
consoles himself, however, that Johnson's notes, accompanying his
own, will enable even ''the trifling part of the public'' not to mistake
in the comparison.—Nichols's " Literary Anecdotes," vol. v. p. 595.
   And what became of Johnson's noble Preface to Shakspeare? Not
a word on that!—Warburton, who himself had written so many
spirited ones, perhaps did not like to read one finer than his own,—so
he passed it by! He travelled through Egypt, but held his hands
before his eyes at a pyramid!

cules a favourite author; but to us, mere historians,
truth will always prevail over literary favouritism.
The work of Edwards effected its purpose, that of
" laughing down Warburton to his proper rank and
character."*

Warburton designates himself as "a critic by profession;" and tells us, he gave this edition " to deter the
unlearned writer from wantonly trifling with an art he is
a stranger to, at the expense of the integrity of the text
of established authors." Edwards has placed a N. B.
on this declaration:—" A writer may properly be called
unlearned who, notwithstanding all his other knowledge,
does not understand the subject which he writes upon."
But the most dogmatical absurdity was Warburton's
declaration, that it was once his design to have given
" a body of canons for criticism, drawn out in form, with
a glossary;" and further he informs the reader, that
though this has not been done by him, if the reader will
take the trouble, he may supply himself, as these canons
of criticism lie scattered in the course of the notes.
This idea was seized on with infinite humour by Edwards, who, from these very notes, has framed a set of
" Canons of Criticism," as ridiculous as possible, but
every one illustrated by authentic examples, drawn from
the labours of our new Stagirite.†

* Thomas Edwards chiefly led the life of a literary student, though
he studied for the Bar at Lincoln's-Inn, and was fully admitted a
member thereof. He died unmarried at the age of 58. He descended
from a family of lawyers; possessed a sufficient private property to
ensure independence, and died on his own estate of Turrick, in Buck-
inghamshire. Dr. Warton observes, "This attack on Mr. Edwards is
not of weight sufficient to weaken the effects of his excellent 'Canons
of Criticism,' all impartial critics allow these remarks to have been
decisive and judicious, and his book remains unrefuted and unanswer-
able."—ED.

† Some grave dull men, who did not relish the jests, doubtless the
booksellers, who, to buy the *name of Warburton*, had paid down 500l.

52 QUARRELS OF AUTHORS.

At length, when the public had decided on the fact
of Warburton's edition, it was confessed that the editor's
design had never been to explain Shakspeare! and that
he was even conscious he had frequently imputed to the

for the edition, loudly complained that Edwards had injured both him
and them, by stopping the sale! On this Edwards expresses his surprise, how "a little twelvepenny pamphlet could stop the progress of
eight large octavo volumes;" and apologises, by applying a humorous
story to Warburton, for "puffing himself off in the world for what he
is not, and now being discovered."—"I am just in the case of a friend
of mine, who, going to visit an acquaintance, upon entering his room,
met a person going out of it:—'Prythee, Jack,' says he, 'what do you
do with that fellow?' 'Why, 'tis Don Pedro di Mondongo, my Spanish
master.'—'Spanish master!' replies my friend; 'why, he's an errant
Teague; I know the fellow well enough; 'tis Rory Gehagan. He may
possibly have been in Spain: but, depend on't, he will sell you the
Tipperary brogue for pure Castilian.' Now honest Rory has just the
same reason of complaint against this gentleman as Mr. Warburton
has against me, and I suppose abused him as heartily for it; but
nevertheless the gentleman did both parties justice."

Some secret history is attached to this publication, so fatal to Warburton's critical character in English literature. This satire, like too
many which have sprung out of literary quarrels, arose from *pers nal
motives!* When Edwards, in early life, after quitting college, entered
the army, he was on a visit at Mr. Allen's, at Bath, whose niece Warburton afterwards married. Literary subjects formed the usual conversation. Warburton, not suspecting the red coat of covering any
Greek, showed his accustomed dogmatical superiority. Once, when
the controversy was running high, Edwards taking down a Greek
author, explained a passage in a manner quite contrary to Warburton.
He did unluckily something more—he showed that Warburton's mistake had arisen from having used a French translation!—and all this
before Ralph Allen and his niece! The doughty critic was at once
silenced, in sullen indignation and mortal hatred. To this circumstance is attributed Edwards's "Canons of Criticism," which were
followed up by Warburton with incessant attacks: in every new
edition of Pope, in the "Essay on Criticism," and the Dunciad.
Warburton asserts that Edwards is a very dull writer (witness the
pleasantry that carries one through a volume of no small size), that he
is a libeller (because he ruined the critical character of Warburton)—
and "a libellor (says Warburton, with poignancy), is nothing but a

poet meanings which he never thought! Our critic's great object was to display his own learning! Warburton wrote for Warburton, and not for Shakspeare! and the literary imposture almost rivals the confessions of Lauder or Psalmanazar!

The same SECRET PRINCIPLE was pursued in his absurd edition of Pope. He formed an unbroken Commentary on the "Essay on Criticism," to show that that admirable collection of precepts had been constructed by a systematical method, which it is well known the poet never designed; and the same instruments of torture were here used as in the "Essay on Man," to reconcile a system of fatalism to the doctrines of Revelation.*

Grub-street critic run to seed."—He compares Edwards's wit and learning to his ancestor Tom Thimble's, in the *Rehearsal* (because Edwards read Greek authors in their original), and his air of good-nature and politeness, to Caliban's in the *Tempest* (because he had so keenly written the "Canons of Criticism").—I once saw a great literary curiosity: some *proof-sheets* of the Dunciad of Warburton's edition. I observed that some of the bitterest notes were *after-thoughts*, written on those proof-sheets after he had prepared the book for the press—one of these additions was his note on Edwards. Thus Pope's book afforded renewed opportunities for all the personal hostilities of this singular genius!

* In the "Richardsoniana," p. 264, the younger Richardson, who was admitted to the intimacy of Pope, and collated the press for him gives some curious information about Warburton's Commentary, both upon the "Essay on Man," and the "Essay on Criticism." "Warburton's discovery of the 'regularity' of Pope's 'Essay on Criticism,' and 'the whole scheme' of his 'Essay on Man,' I happen to *know* to be mere absurd refinement in creating conformities; and this from Pope himself, though he thought fit to adopt them afterwards." The genius of Warburton might not have found an invincible difficulty in proving that the "Essay on Criticism" was in fact an Essay on Man, and the reverse. Pope, before he knew Warburton, always spoke of his "Essay on Criticism" as "an irregular collection of thoughts thrown together as Horace's 'Art of Poetry' was." "As for the 'Essay on Man,'" says Richardson, "I *know* that he never dreamed of the scheme he afterwards adopted; but he had taken terror about

Warton had to remove the incumbrance of his Commentaries on Pope, while a most laborious confederacy zealously performed the same task to relieve Shakspeare. Thus Warburton pursued ONE SECRET PRINCIPLE in all his labours; thus he raised edifices which could not be securely inhabited, and were only impediments in the roadway; and these works are now known by the labours of those who have exerted their skill in laying them in ruins.

Warburton was probably aware that the SECRET PRINCIPLE which regulated his public opinions might lay him open, at numerous points, to the strokes of ridicule. It is a weapon which every one is willing to use, but which seems to terrify every one when it is pointed against themselves. There is no party or sect which have not employed it in their most serious controversies: the grave part of mankind protest against it, often at the moment they have been directing it for their own purpose. And the inquiry, whether ridicule be a test of truth, is one of the large controversies in our own literature. It was opened by Lord Shaftesbury, and zealously maintained by his school. Akenside, in a note to his celebrated poem, asserts the efficacy of ridicule as a test of truth: Lord Kaimes had just done the same. Warburton levelled his piece at the lord in the bush-fighting of a note; but came down in the open field with a full discharge of his artillery on the luckless bard.*

the clergy, and Warburton himself, at the general alarm of his fatalism and deistical tendency, of which my father and I talked with him frequently at Twickenham, without his appearing to understand it, or ever thinking to alter those passages which we suggested."—This extract is to be valued, for the information is authentic; and it assists us in throwing some light on the subtilty of Warburton's critical impositions.

* The postscript to Warburton's "Dedication to the Freethinkers," is entirely devoted to Akenside; with this bitter opening, "The Poet was too full of the subject and of himself."

Warburton designates Akenside under the sneering appellative of "The Poet," and alluding to his "sublime account" of the use of ridicule, insultingly reminds him of "his Master," Shaftesbury, and of that school which made morality an object of taste, shrewdly hinting that Akenside was "a man of taste;" a new term, as we are to infer from Warburton, for "a Deist;" or, as Akenside had alluded to Spinoza, he might be something worse. The great critic loudly protested against the practice of ridicule; but, in attacking its advocate, he is himself an evidence of its efficacy, by keenly ridiculing "the Poet" and his opinions. Dyson, the patron of Akenside, nobly stepped forwards to rescue his Eagle, panting in the tremendous grip of the critical Lion. His defence of Akenside is an argumentative piece of criticism on the nature of ridicule, curious, but wanting the graces of the genius who inspired it.*

I shall stop one moment, since it falls into our subject, to record this great literary battle on the use of ridicule, which has been fought till both parties, after having shed their ink, divide the field without victory or defeat, and now stand looking on each other.

The advocates for the use of RIDICULE maintain that it is a natural sense or feeling, bestowed on us for wise purposes by the Supreme Being, as are the other feelings of beauty and of sublimity;—the sense of beauty to

* "An Epistle to the Rev. Mr. Warburton, occasioned by his Treatment of the Author of 'The Pleasures of the Imagination,'" 1744. While Dyson repels Warburton's accusations against "the Poet," he retorts some against the critic himself. Warburton often perplexed a controversy by a subtile change of a word; or by breaking up a sentence; or by contriving some absurdity in the shape of an inference, to get rid of it in a mock triumph. These little weapons against the laws of war are insidiously practised in the war of words. Warburton never replied

detect the deformity, as the sense of ridicule the absurdity of an object: and they further maintain, that no real
virtues, such as wisdom, honesty, bravery, or generosity,
can be ridiculed.

The great Adversary of Ridicule replied that they did
not dare to ridicule the virtues openly; but, by over-
charging and distorting them they could laugh at leisure.
"Give them other names," he says, "call them but
Temerity, Prodigality, Simplicity, &c., and your business
is done. Make them ridiculous, and you may go on, in
the freedom of wit and humour (as Shaftesbury distinguishes ridicule), till there be never a virtue left to laugh
out of countenance."

The ridiculers acknowledge that their favourite art
may do mischief, when *dishonest men obtrude circumstances foreign to the object.* But, they justly urge, that
the use of reason itself is full as liable to the same objection: grant Spinoza his false premises, and his conclusions
will be considered as true. Dyson threw out an ingenious
illustration. "It is so equally in the mathematics;
where, in reasoning about a circle, if we join along with
its real properties others that do not belong to it, our
conclusions will certainly be erroneous. Yet who would
infer from hence that *the manner of proof* is defective
or fallacious?"

Warburton urged the strongest *case* against the use
of ridicule, in that of Socrates and Aristophanes. In his
strong and coarse illustration he shows, that "by clap-
ping a fool's coat on the most immaculate virtue, it stuck
on Socrates like a San Benito, and at last brought him
to his execution: it made the owner resemble his direct
opposite; that character he was most unlike. The consequences are well known."

Warburton here adopted the popular notion, that the
witty buffoon Aristophanes was the occasion of the death

of the philosopher Socrates. The defence is skilful on the part of Dyson; and we may easily conceive that on so important a point Akenside had been consulted. I shall give it in his own words:—

"The Socrates of Aristophanes is as truly ridiculous a character as ever was drawn; but it is not the character of Socrates himself. The object was perverted, and the mischief which ensued was owing to the dishonesty of him who persuaded the people that that was the real character of Socrates, not from any error in the faculty of ridicule itself."—Dyson then states the fact as it concerned Socrates. "The real intention of the contrivers of this ridicule was not so much to mislead the people, by giving them a bad opinion of Socrates, as to sound what was at the time the general opinion of him, that from thence they might judge whether it would be safe to bring a direct accusation against him. The most effectual way of making this trial was by ridiculing him; for they knew, if the people saw his character in its true light, they would be displeased with the misrepresentation, and not endure the ridicule. On trial this appeared: the play met with its deserved fate; and, notwithstanding the exquisiteness of the wit, was absolutely *rejected*. A second attempt succeeded no better; and the abettors of the poet were so discouraged from pursuing their design against Socrates, that it was not till ABOVE TWENTY YEARS after *the publication of the play* that they brought their accusation against him! It was not, therefore, ridicule that did, or could destroy Socrates: he was rather sacrificed for the right use of it himself, against the Sophists, who could not bear the test."

Thus, then, stands the argument.—Warburton, reasoning on the abuses of ridicule, has opened to us all its dangers. Its advocate concedes that Ridicule, to be a

test of Truth, must not impose on us circumstances which
are foreign to the object. No object can be ridiculed
that is not ridiculous. Should this happen, then the
ridicule is false; and, as such, can be proved as much as
any piece of false reasoning. We may therefore conclude, that ridicule is a taste of congruity and propriety
not possessed by every one; a test which separates truth
from imposture; a talent against the exercise of which
most men are interested to protest; but which, being
founded on the constituent principles of the human mind,
is often indulged at the very moment it is decried and
complained of.

But we must not leave this great man without some
notice of that peculiar style of controversy which he
adopted, and which may be distinguished among our
LITERARY QUARRELS. He has left his name to a school—
a school which the more liberal spirit of the day we live
in would not any longer endure. Who has not heard of
THE WARBURTONIANS?

That SECRET PRINCIPLE which directed Warburton in
all his works, and which we have attempted to pursue,
could not of itself have been sufficient to have filled the
world with the name of Warburton. Other scholars
have published reveries, and they have passed away,
after showing themselves for a time, leaving no impression; like those coloured and shifting shadows on a wall,
with which children are amused; but Warburton was a
literary Revolutionist, who, to maintain a new order of
things, exercised all the despotism of a perpetual dictator. The bold unblushing energy which could lay down
the most extravagant positions, was maintained by a
fierce dogmatic spirit, and by a peculiar style of morda-
cious contempt and intolerant insolence, beating down
his opponents from all quarters with an animating shout
of triumph, to encourage those more serious minds, who,

overcome by his genius, were yet often alarmed by the
ambiguous tendency of his speculations.*

The Warburtonian School was to be supported by the
most licentious principles; by dictatorial arrogance,† by
gross invective, and by airy sarcasm;‡ the bitter con-

* The paradoxical title of his great work was evidently designed to
attract the unwary. "The Divine Legation of Moses demonstrated—
from the omission of a future state!" It was long uncertain whether
it was "a covert attack on Christianity, instead of a defence of it." I
have here no concern with Warburton's character as a polemical the-
ologist; this has been the business of that polished and elegant scholar,
Bishop Lowth, who has shown what it is to be in Hebrew literature
"a Quack in Commentatorship, and a Mountebank in Criticism." He
has fully entered into all the absurdity of Warburton's "ill-starred
Dissertation on Job." It is curious to observe that Warburton in the
wild chase of originality, often too boldly took the bull by the horns,
for he often adopted the very reasonings and objections of infidels!—
for instance, in arguing on the truth of the Hebrew text, because the
words had no points when a living language, he absolutely prefers the
Koran for correctness! On this Lowth observes: "You have been
urging the same argument that *Spinoza* employed, in order to destroy
the authority of the Hebrew Scriptures, and to introduce infidelity and
atheism." Lowth shows further, that "this was also done by 'a society of gentlemen,' in their 'Sacerdotism Displayed,' said to be written
by 'a select committee of the Deists and Freethinkers of Great Britain,'
whose author Warburton himself had represented to be 'the forward-
est devil of the whole legion.'" Lowth, however, concludes that all
the mischief has arisen only from "your lordship's undertaking to
treat of a subject with which you appear to be very much unacquainted."—Lowth's *Letter*, p. 91.

† Lowth remonstrated with Warburton on his "supreme authority:"—"I did not care to protest against the authoritative manner in
which you proceeded, or to question *your investiture in the high office of
Inquisitor General and Supreme Judge of the Opinions of the Learned,*
which you had long before assumed, and had *exercised with a ferocity
and a despotism without example in the Republic of Letters, and hardly
to be paralleled among the disciples of Dominic;* exacting their opinions
to the standard of your infallibility, and prosecuting with implacable
hatred every one that presumed to differ from you."—Lowth's *Letter
to W.*, p. 9.

‡ Warburton had the most cutting way of designating his adver-

tempt which, with its many little artifices, lowers an adversary in the public opinion, was more peculiarly the talent of one of the aptest scholars, the cool, the keen, the sophistical Hurd. The lowest arts of confederacy

saries, either by the most vehement abuse or the light petulance that expressed his ineffable contempt. He says to one. "Though your teeth are short, what you want in teeth you have in venom, and know, as all other creatures do, where your strength lies." He thus announces in one of the prefaces to the " Divine Legation " the name of the author of a work on " A Future State of Rewards and Punishments." in which were some objections to Warburton's theory :—" I sha'L therefore, but do what indeed would be justly reckoned the cruellest of all things, *te'l my reader the name of this miserable;* which we find to be J. Tillard." "Mr. Tillard was first condemned (says the author of ' Confusion Worse Confounded,') as a ruffian that stabs a man in the dark. because he did *not* put his name to his book against the ' Divine Legation :' and afterwards condemned as lost to shame. both as a man and a writer, because he *did* put his name to it." Would not one imagine this person to be one of the lowest of miscreants? He was a man of fortune and literature. Of this person Warburton says in a letter. "This is a man of fortune, and it is well he is so, for I have spoiled his trade as a writer; and as he was very abusive. free-thinking. and anonymous, I have not spared to expose his ignorance and ill faith." But afterwards, having discovered that he was a particular friend to Dr. Oliver. he makes awkward apologies, and declares he would not have *gone so far* had he known this ! He was often so vehement in his abuse that I find he confessed it himself, for in preparing a new edition of the " Divine Legation," he tells Dr. Birch that he has made "several omissions of passages which were thought *vain, insolent. and ill-natured.*"

It is amusing enough to observe how he designates men as great as himself. When he mentions the learned Hyde, he places him " at the head of a rabble of lying orientalists." When he alludes to Peters. a very learned and ingenious clergyman, he passes by him as " The Cornish Critic." A friend of Peters observed that "he had given Warburton 'a Cornish hug,' of which he might be sore as long as he lived." Dr. Taylor, the learned editor of Demosthenes, he selects from "his fellows." that is. other dunces: a delicacy of expression which offended scholars. He threatens Dr. Stebbing. who had preserved an anonymous character, "to catch this Eel of Controversy, since he hides his head, by the tail, the only part that sticks out of the

were connived at by all the disciples, prodigal of praise to themselves, and retentive of it to all others; the world was to be divided into two parts, the *Warburtonians* and the *Anti*.

mud, more dirty indeed than slippery, and still more weak than dirty, as passing through a trap where he was forced at every step to leave part of his skin—that is, his system." Warburton has often true wit. With what provoking contempt he calls Sir Thomas Hanmer always "The Oxford Editor!" and in his attack on Akenside, never fails to nickname him, in derision, "The Poet!" I refer the reader to a postscript of his "Dedication to the Freethinkers," for a curious specimen of supercilious causticity in his description of Lord Kaimes as a critic, and Akenside as "The Poet!" Of this pair he tells us, in bitter derision, "they are both men of taste." Hurd imitated his master successfully, by using some qualifying epithet, or giving an adversary some odd nickname, or discreetly dispensing a little mortifying praise. The antagonists he encounters were men sometimes his superiors, and these he calls "sizeable men" Some are styled "insect blasphemers!" The learned Lardner is reduced to "the laborious Dr. Lardner;" and "Hume's History" is treated with the discreet praise of being "the most readable history we have." He carefully hints to Leland that "he had never read his works, nor looked into his translations; but what he has *heard* of his writings makes him think favourably of him." Thus he teases the rhetorical professor by mentioning the "elegant translation which, *they say*, you have made of Demosthenes!" And he understands that he is "a scholar, who, *they say*, employs himself in works of learning and taste."

Lowth seems to have discovered this secret art of Warburton; for he says, "You have a set of names always at hand, a kind of infamous list, or black calendar, where every offender is sure to find a niche ready to receive him; nothing so easy as the application, and slight provocation is sufficient."

* Sometimes Warburton left his battles to be fought by subaltern genius; a circumstance to which Lowth, with keen pleasantry, thus alludes:—"Indeed, my lord, I was afterwards much surprised, when, having been with great civility dismissed from your presence. I found *your footman at your door, armed with his master's cane, and falling upon me without mercy*, yourself looking on and approving, and having probably put the weapon with proper orders into his hands. You think, it seems, that I ought to have taking my beating quietly and patiently, in respect to the livery which he wore. I was not of so tame a dis-

To establish this new government in the literary world,
this great Revolutionist was favoured by Fortune with
two important aids; the one was a *Machine*, by which

position: I wrested the weapon from him, and broke it. Your lordship, it seems, by an oblique blow, got an unlucky rap on the knuckles;
though you may thank yourself for it, you lay the blame on me."—
Lowth's *Letter to W.*, p. 11.

Warburton and Hurd frequently concerted together on the manner
of attack and defence. In one of those letters of Hurd's it is very
amusing to read—"Taylor is a more creditable dunce than Webster.
What do you think to do with the Appendix against Tillard and Sykes?
Why might not Taylor rank with them," &c. The Warburtonians had
also a system of *espionage*. When Dr. Taylor was accused by one of
them of having *said* that Warburton was no scholar, the learned
Grecian replied that he did not recollect ever *saying* that Dr. Warburton was no scholar, but that indeed he had always *thought* so.
Hence a tremendous quarrel! Hurd, the Mercury of our Jupiter, cast
the first light shaft against the doctor, then Chancellor of Lincoln, by
alluding to the Preface of his work on Civil Law as " *a certain thing
prefatory to a learned work*, intituled 'The Elements of Civil Law:' "
but at length Jove himself rolled his thunder on the hapless chancellor.
The doctor had said in his work, that "the Roman emperors persecuted the first Christians, not so much from a dislike of their tenets as
from a jealousy of their nocturnal assemblies." Warburton's doctrine
was, that "they held nocturnal assemblies because of the persecution
of their enemies." One was the fact, and the other the consequence.
But the Chancellor of Lincoln was to be outrageously degraded among
the dunces! that was the real motive; the "nocturnal assemblies"
only the ostensible one. A pamphleteer, in defence of the chancellor
in reply, thought that in "this literary persecution" it might be
dangerous "if Dr. Taylor should be provoked to *prove in print* what
he only *dropped in conversation*" How innocent was this gentleman
of the arts and stratagems of logomachy, or book wars! The *proof*
would not have altered the cause: Hurd would have disputed it tooth
and nail; Warburton was running greater risks, every day of his life,
than any he was likely to receive from this flourish in the air. The
great purpose was to make the Chancellor of Lincoln the butt of his
sarcastic pleasantry: and this object was secured by Warburton's forty
pages of preface, in which the chancellor stands to be buffeted like an
ancient quintain, "a mere lifeless block." All this came upon him
for only *thinking* that Warburton was no *scholar!*

he could wield public opinion ; and the other a *Man*, who seemed born to be his minister or his viceroy.

The *machine* was nothing less than the immortal works of Pope; as soon as Warburton had obtained a royal patent to secure to himself the sole property of Pope's works, the public were compelled, under the disguise of a Commentary on the most classical of our Poets, to be concerned with all his literary quarrels, and have his libels and lampoons perpetually before them; all the foul waters of his anger were deposited here as in a common reservoir. *

* See what I have said at the close of the note, pp. 52, 53. In a collection entitled " Verses occasioned by Mr. Warburton's late Edition of Mr. Pope's Works," 1751, are numerous epigrams, parodies, and similes on it. I give one :—

> " As on the margin of Thames' silver flood
> Stand little *necessary* piles of wood,
> So Pope's fair page appears with *notes* disgraced :
> Put down the nuisances, ye men of taste !"

Lowth has noticed the use Warburton made of his patent for vending Pope. " I thought you might possibly whip me at the cart's-tail in a note to the ' Divine Legatio n,' the ordinary place of your literary executions; or *pillory me in the Dunciad*, another engine which, as legal proprietor, you have very ingeniously and judiciously applied to the same purpose; or, perhaps, have ordered me a kind of Bridewell correction, by one of your beadles, in a pamphlet."—Lowth's *Letter to Warburton,*" p. 4.

Warburton carried the licentiousness of the pen in all these notes to the *Dunciad* to a height which can only be paralleled in the gross logomachies of Schioppius, Gronovius, and Scaliger, and the rest of that snarling crew. But his wit exceeded even his grossness. He was accused of not sparing—

> " Round-house wit and Wapping choler."
> [Verses occasioned by Mr. W.'s late Edition of Pope.]

And one of his most furious assailants thus salutes him :—" Whether you are a wrangling Wapping attorney, a pedantic pretender to criticism, an impudent paradoxical priest, or an animal yet stranger, an heterogeneous medley of all three, as your farraginous style seems to

Fanciful as was the genius of Warburton, it delighted
too much in its eccentric motions, and in its own solitary
confess."—An Epistle to the Author of a Libel entitled " A Letter to
the Editor of Bolingbroke's Works," &c.—See Nichols, vol. v. p. 651.
I have ascertained that Mallet was the author of this furious epistle.
He would not acknowledge what he dared not deny. Warburton
treated Mallet. in this instance, as he often did his superiors—he never
replied! The silence seems to have stung this irascible and evil spirit:
he returned again to the charge, with another poisoned weapon. His
rage produced " A Familiar Epistle to the Most Impudent Man Living,"
1749. The style of this second letter has been characterised as " bad
enough to disgrace even gaols and garrets." Its virulence could not
well exceed its predecessor. The oddness of its title has made this
worthless thing often inquired after. It is merely personal. It is
curious to observe Mallet, in this pamphlet. treat Pope as an object of
pity, and call him " this poor man." [David Mallet was the son of an
innkeeper, who, by means of the party he wrote for, obtained lucrative
appointments under Government, and died rich. He was unscrupu-
lous in his career, and ready as a writer to do the most unworthy
things. The death of Admiral Byng was hastened by the unscrupu-
lous denunciations of Mallet, who was pensioned in consequence.]
Orator Henley took some pains, on the first appearance of this catching title, to assure his friends that it did not refer to him. The
title proved contagious; which shows the abuse of Warburton was
very agreeable. Dr. Z. Grey, under the title of " A Country Curate,"
published " A Free and Familiar Letter to the Great Refiner of Pope
and Shakspeare," 1750; and in 1753, young Cibber tried also at " A
Familiar Epistle to Mr. William Warburton, from Mr. Theophilus
Cibber," prefixed to the " Life of Barton Booth." Dr Z. Grey's
" freedom and familiarity " are designed to show Warburton that he
has no wit; but unluckily, the doctor having none himself, his arguments against Warburton's are not decisive. " The familiarity " of
Mallet is that of a scoundrel, and the younger Cibber's that of an idiot:
the genius of Warburton was secure. Mallet overcharged his gun
with the fellest intentions, but found his piece, in bursting, annihilated nimself. The popgun of the little Theophilus could never have
been heard!
[Warburton never lost a chance of giving a strong opinion against
Mallet ; and Dr. Johnson says, " When Mallet undertook to write the
' Life of Marlborough,' Warburton remarked that he might perhaps
forget that Marlborough was a general, as he had forgotten that Bacon
was a philosopher."]

greatness, amid abstract and recondite topics, to have
strongly attracted the public attention, had not a party

But Warburton's rage was only a part of his *secret principle;* for can
anything be more witty than his attack on poor Cooper, the author of
" The Life of Socrates?" Having called his book "a late worthless
and now forgotten thing, called 'The Life of Socrates,' " he adds,
" where the head of the author has just made a shift to do the office of a
camera obscura, and represents things in an inverted order, himself *above,*
and Rollin, Voltaire, and every other author of reputation, *below.*" When
Cooper complained of this, and of some severer language, to Warburton, through a friend, Warburton replied that Cooper had attacked him,
and that he had only taken his revenge " with a slight joke." Cooper
was weak and vain enough to print a pamphlet, to prove that this was
a serious accusation, and no joke ; and if it was a joke, he shows it
was not a correct one. In fact, Cooper could never comprehend how
his head was like a *camera obscura!* Cooper was of the Shaftesburian
school—philosophers who pride themselves on "the harmony" of
their passions, but are too often in discords at a slight disturbance.
He equalled the virulence of Warburton, but could not attain to the
wit. " I found," says Cooper, "previous to his pretended witticism
about the *camera obscura,* such miserable spawn of wretched malice,
as nothing but the inflamed brain of a rank monk could conceive, or
the oyster-selling maids near London Bridge could utter." One would
not suppose all this came from the school of Plato, but rather from the
tub of Diogenes. Something must be allowed for poor Cooper, whose
"Life of Socrates " had been so positively asserted to be "a late worthless and forgotten thing." It is curious enough to observe Cooper declaring, after this sally, that Warburton " has very unfortunately used
the word *impudent* (which epithet Warburton had applied to him), as
it naturally reminds every reader that the pamphlet published about
two years ago, addressed ' to the most impudent man living,' was universally acknowledged to be dedicated to our commentator." Warburton had always the *Dunciad* in his head when a new quarrel was rising,
which produced an odd blunder on the side of Edwards, and provoked
that wit to be as dull as Cooper. Warburton said, in one of his notes
on Edwards, who had entitled himself "a gentleman of Lincoln's Inn,"
—" This gentleman, as he is pleased to call himself, is in reality a gentleman only of the *Dunciad* or, to speak him better, in the plain language
of our honest ancestors to such mushrooms, a *gentleman of the last edition.*"
Edwards misunderstood the allusion, and sore at the personal attack
which followed, of his having 'eluded the solicitude of his careful
father," considered himself "degraded of his gentility," that it was "a

been formed around him, at the head of which stood the
active and subtle Hurd; and amid the gradations of the
votive brotherhood, the profound Balguy,* the spirited
Brown,† till we descend—

reflection on his birth," and threatened to apply to "Mr. Warburton's
Masters of the Bench, for degrading a 'barrister of their house.'" This
afforded a new triumph to Warburton, in a new note, where he explains his meaning of these "mushrooms," whom he meant merely
as literary ones; and assures "Fungoso and his friends, who are all
gentlemen, that he meant no more than that Edwards had become a
gentleman *of the last edition of the Dunciad!*" Edwards and his fungous
friends had understood the phrase as applied to new-fangled gentry.
One of these wits, in the collection of verses cited above, says to Warburton:—

> "This mushroom has made sauce for you.
> He's meat; thou'rt poison—plain enough—
> If he's a *mushroom*, thou'rt a *puff!*"

Warburton had the full command over the *Dunciad*, even when Pope
was alive, for it was in consequence of Warburton's being refused a
degree at Oxford, that the poet, though one had been offered to himself, produced the celebrated lines of "Apollo's Mayor and Aldermen,"
in the fourth *Dunciad*. Thus it is that the personal likes and dislikes
of witty men come down to posterity, and are often mistaken as just
satire, when, after all, they are nothing but LITERARY QUARRELS
seldom founded on truth, and very often complete falsehoods!

* Dr. Thomas Balguy was the son of a learned father, at whose rectory of Northallerton he was born; he was appointed Archdeacon of
Salisbury in 1759, and afterwards Archdeacon of Winchester. He
died at the prebendal house of the latter city in 1795, at the age of 74.
His writings are few—chiefly on church government and authority,
which brought him into antagonism with Dr. Priestly and others, who
objected to the high view he took of its position. With Hurd and
Warburton he was always intimate; his sermon on the consecration
of the former was one of the sources of adverse attack; the latter
notes his death as that of "an old and esteemed friend."—ED.

† Dr. Brown was patronised and "pitied" by Warburton for years.
He used him, but spoke of him disparagingly, as "a helpless creature
in the ways of the world." Nichols speaks of him as an "elegant, ingenious, and unhappy author." His father was a native of Scotland;
his son was born at Rothbury, in Northumberland, educated at Cambridge, made minor canon at Carlisle, but resigned it in disgust, living

To his tame jackal, parson Towne.*
Verses on Warburton's late Edition.

This Warburtonian party reminds one of an old custom among our elder poets, who formed a kind of freemasonry among themselves, by adopting younger poets by the title of their *sons.*—But that was a domestic society of poets; this, a revival of the Jesuitic order instituted by its founder, that—

By him supported with a proper pride,
They might hold all mankind as fools beside.
Might, like himself, teach each adopted son,
' Gainst all the world, to quote a Warburton. †
Churchill's " Fragment of a Dedication."

in obscurity in that city several years, till the Rebellion of 1745, when he acted as a volunteer at the siege of the Castle, and behaved with great intrepidity. His publication of an " Essay on Satire," on the death of Pope, led to his acquaintance with Warburton, who helped him to the rectory of Horksley, near Colchester; but he quarrelled with his patron, as he afterwards quarrelled with others. He then settled down to the vicarage of St. Nicholas, Newcastle, but not for long, as an educational scheme of the Empress of Russia offered him inducements to leave England: but his health failed him before he could carry out his intentions, irritability succeeded, and his disappointments, real and imaginary, led him to commit suicide in the fifty-first year of his age. He seems to have been a continual trouble to Warburton, who often alludes to his unsettled habits—and schooled him occasionally after his own fashion. Thus he writes in 1777:—" Brown is here ; I think rather faster than ordinary, but no wiser. You cannot imagine the tenderness they all have of his tender places, and with how unfeeling a hand I probe them."—ED.

* Towne is so far " unknown to fame " that his career is unrecorded by our biographers; he was content to work for, and under the guidance of Warburton. as a literary drudge.—ED.

† Warburton, indeed, was always looking about for fresh recruits : a circumstance which appears in the curious Memoirs of the late Dr. Heathcote, written by himself. Heathcote, when young, published anonymously a pamphlet in the Middletonian controversy. By the desire of Warburton, the bookseller transmitted his compliments to the anonymous author. " I was greatly surprised," says Heathcote, " but

The character of a literary sycophant was never more perfectly exhibited than in Hurd. A Whig in principle, yet he had all a courtier's arts for Warburton; to him he devoted all his genius, though that, indeed, was moderate; aided him with all his ingenuity, which was exquisite; and lent his cause a certain delicacy of taste and cultivated elegance, which, although too prim and artificial, was a vein of gold running through his mass of erudition; it was Hurd who aided the usurpation of Warburton in the province of criticism above Aristotle and Longinus.*

soon after perceived that Warburton's state of authorship being a state of war. *it was his custom to be part cularly attentive to all young authors, in hopes of enlisting tnem into his service.* Warburton was more than civil. when necessary, on these occasions, and would procure such adventurers some slight patronage."—Nichols's "Literary Anecdotes," vol. v. p. 536.

* We are astonished at the boldness of the minor critic, when, even after the fatal edition of Warburton's Shakspeire, he should still venture, in the life of his great friend. to assert that "this fine edition must ever be highly valued by men of sense and taste; a spirit congenial to that of the author breathing throughout!"

Is it possible that the man who wrote this should ever have read the "Canons of Criticism?" Yet is it to be supposed that he who took so lively an interest in the literary fortunes of his friend should *not* have read them? The Warburtonians appear to have adopted one of the principles of the Jesuits in their controversies, which was to repeat arguments which had been confuted over and over again; to insinuate that they had not been so! But this was not too much to risk by him who, in his dedication of "Horace's Epistle to Augustus," with a Commentary, had hardily and solemnly declared that "Warburton, in his *enlarjed view of things,* had not only revived the two models of Aristotle and Longinus, but had rather struck out *a new orignal plan of criticism,* which should unite the virtues of each of them. This experiment was made on the two greatest of our own poets— Shakspeare and Pope. Still (he adds, addressing Warburton) *you went farther,* by joining to those powers a perfect insight into human nature; and so ennobling the exercise of literary by the justest moral censure, *you have now. at length, advanced criticism to its full glory."*

A perpetual intercourse of mutual adulation animated the sovereign and his viceroy, and, by mutual support, each obtained the same re-

Hurd is justly characterised by Warton, in his Spenser, vol. ii. p. 36, as "the *most sensible* and *ingenious* of modern critics."—He was a lover of his studies; and he probably was sincere, when he once told a friend of the literary antiquary Cole, that he would have chosen not to quit the university, for he loved retirement; and on that principle Cowley was his favourite poet, which he afterwards showed by his singular edition of that poet. He was called from the cloistered shades to assume the honourable dignity of a Royal Tutor. Had he devoted his days to literature, he would have still enriched its stores. But he had other more supple and more serviceable qualifications. Most adroit was he in all the archery of controversy: he had the subtlety that can evade

ward: two mitres crowned the greater and the minor critic. This intercourse was humorously detected by the lively author of "Confusion Worse Confounded."—"When the late Duke of R.," says he, "kept wild beasts, it was a common diversion to make two of his bears drunk (not metaphorically with flattery, but literally with strong ale), and then daub them over with honey. It was excellent sport to see how lovingly (like a couple of critics) they would lick and claw one another." It is almost amazing to observe how Hurd, who naturally was of the most frigid temperament, and the most subdued feelings, warmed, heated, and blazed in the progressive stages "of that pageantry of praise spread over the Rev. Mr. Warburton, when the latter was advancing fast towards a bishoprick," to use the words of Dr. Parr, a sagacious observer of man. However, notwithstanding the despotic mandates of our Pichrocole and his dapper minister, there were who did not fear to meet the greater bear of the two so facetiously described above. And the author of "Confusion Worse Confounded" tells a familiar story, which will enliven the history of our great critic. "One of the bears mentioned above happened to get loose, and was running along the street in which a tinker was gravely walking. The people all cried, 'Tinker! tinker! beware of the bear!' Upon this Magnano faced about with great composure; and raising his staff, knocked down Bruin, then setting his arms a-kimbo, walked off very sedately; only saying, 'Let the bear beware of the tinker,' which is now become a proverb in those parts."—"Confusion Worse Confounded," p. 75.

the aim of the assailant, and the slender dexterity, sub
stituted for vigour, that struck when least expected
The subaltern genius of Hurd required to be animated
by the heroic energy of Warburton; and the careless
courage of the chief wanted one who could maintain
the unguarded passages he left behind him in his
progress.

Such, then, was Warburton, and such the quarrels of
this great author. He was, through his literary life, an
adventurer, guided by that secret principle which opened
an immediate road to fame. By opposing the common
sentiments of mankind, he awed and he commanded them;
and by giving a new face to all things, he surprised, by
the appearances of discoveries. All this, so pleasing to
his egotism, was not, however, fortunate for his ambition. To sustain an authority which he had usurped;
to substitute for the taste he wanted a curious and daz
zling erudition; and to maintain those reckless decisions
which so often plunged him into perils, Warburton
adopted his *system of Literary Quarrels*. These were
the illegitimate means which raised a sudden celebrity,
and which genius kept alive, as long as that genius
lasted; but Warburton suffered that literary calamity,
too protracted a period of human life: he outlived himself and his fame. This great and original mind sacrificed all his genius to that secret principle we have endeavoured to develope—it was a self-immolation!

The learned Selden, in the curious little volume of his
" Table-Talk," has delivered to posterity a precept for
the learned, which they ought to wear, like the Jewish
phylacteries, as " a frontlet between their eyes." *No
man is the wiser for his learning: it may administer
matter to work in, or objects to work upon ; but wit and
wisdom are born with a man.* Sir Thomas Hanmer, who
was well acquainted with Warburton, during their co•

respondence about Shakspeare, often said of him :—" The only use he could find in Mr. Warburton was *starting the game ;* he was not to be trusted in *running it down.*" A just discrimination! His fervid curiosity was absolutely creative; but his taste and his judgment, perpetually stretched out by his system, could not save him from even inglorious absurdities!

Warburton, it is probable, was not really the character he appears. It mortifies the lovers of genius to discover how a natural character may be thrown into a convulsed unnatural state by some adopted system: it is this system, which, carrying it, as it were, beyond itself, communicates a more than natural, but a self-destroying energy. All then becomes reversed! The arrogant and vituperative Warburton was only such in his assumed character; for in still domestic life he was the creature of benevolence, touched by generous passions. But in public life the artificial or the acquired character prevails over the one which nature designed for us; and by that all public men, as well as authors, are usually judged by posterity.

POPE,

AND HIS MISCELLANEOUS QUARRELS.

POPE adopted a system of literary politics—collected with extraordinary care everything relative to his Quarrels—no politician ever studied to obtain his purposes by more oblique directions and intricate stratagems—some of his manœuvres—his systematic hostility not practised with impunity—his claim to his own works contested—Cibber's facetious description of Pope's feelings, and Welsted's elegant satire on his genius—Dennis's account of Pope's Introduction to him—his political prudence further discovered in the

Collection of all the Pieces relative to the *Dunciad*, in which he employed Savage—the Theobaldians and the Popeians: an attack by a
Theobaldian—The *Dunciad* ingeniously defended, for the grossness
of its imagery, and its reproach of the poverty of the authors, supposed by Pope himself, with some curious specimens of literary
personalities—the Literary Quarrel between Aaron Hill and Pope
distinguished for its romantic cast—a Narrative of the extraordinary
transactions respecting the publication of Pope's Letters; an example of Stratagem and Conspiracy, illustrative of his character.

POPE has proudly perpetuated the history of his
Literary Quarrels; and he appears to have been
among those authors, surely not forming the majority,
who have delighted in, or have not been averse to pro-
voke, hostility. He has registered the titles of every
book, even to a single paper, or a copy of verses, in
which their authors had committed treason against his
poetical sovereignty.* His ambition seemed gratified in

* Pope collected these numerous literary libels with extraordinary
care. He had them bound in volumes of all sizes; and a range of
twelves, octavos, quartos, and folios were marshalled in portentous
order on his shelves. He wrote the names of the writers, with remarks on these *Anonymiana*. He prefixed to them this motto, from
Job: "Behold, my desire is, that mine adversary had written a
book: surely I would take it upon my shoulder, and bind it as a
crown to me." xxxi. 35. Ruffhead, who wrote Pope's Life under the
eye of Warburton, who revised every sheet of the volume, and suffered
this mere lawyer and singularly wretched critic to write on, with far
inferior taste to his own—offered "the entire collection to any public
library or museum, whose search is after *curiosities*, and may be desirous of enriching their common treasure with it: it will be freely at
the service of that which asks first." Did no one accept the invitation?
As this was written in 1769, it is evidently pointed towards the
British Museum; but there I have not heard of it. This collection
must have contained much of the Secret Memoirs of Grub-street: it
was always a fountain whence those " waters of bitterness," the notes
in the *Dunciad*, were readily supplied. It would be curious to discover by what stratagem Pope obtained all that secret intelligence
about his Dunces, with which he has burthened posterity, for his own
particular gratification. Arbuthnot, it is said, wrote some notes

heaping these trophies to his genius, while his meaner
passions could compile one of the most voluminous of

merely literary; but Savage, and still humbler agents, served him as
his *Espions de Police*. He pensioned Savage to his last day, and never
deserted him. In the account of "the phantom Moore," Scriblerus
appeals to Savage to authenticate some story. One curious instance
of the fruits of Savage's researches in this way he has himself preserved, in his memoirs of "An Author to be Let, by Iscariot Hackney."
This portrait of "a perfect Town-Author" is not deficient in spirit:
the hero was one Roome, a man only celebrated in the *Dunciad* for
his "funereal frown." But it is uncertain whether this fellow had
really so dismal a countenance; for the epithet was borrowed from
his profession, being the son of an undertaker! Such is the nature of
some satire! Dr. Warton is astonished, or mortified, for he knew not
which, to see the pains and patience of Pope and his friends in compil-
ing the Notes to the *Dunciad*, to trace out the lives and works of such
paltry and forgotten scribblers. "It is like walking through the
darkest alleys in the dirtiest part of St. Giles's." Very true! But
may we not be allowed to detect the vanities of human nature at St.
Giles's as well as St. James's? Authors, however obscure, are always
an amusing race to authors. The greatest find their own passions in
the least, though distorted, or cramped in too small a compass.

It is doubtless from Pope's great anxiety for his own literary celebrity that we have been furnished with so complete a knowledge of the
grotesque groups in the *Dunciad*. "Give me a shilling," said Swift,
facetiously, "and I will insure you that posterity shall never know
one single enemy, excepting those whose memory you have preserved."
A very useful hint for a man of genius to leave his wretched assailants
to dissolve away in their own weakness. But Pope, having written a
Dunciad, by accompanying it with a commentary, took the only method
to interest posterity. He felt that Boileau's satires on bad authors
are liked only in the degree the objects alluded to are known. But he
loved too much the subject for its own sake. He abused the powers
genius had conferred on him, as other imperial sovereigns have done.
It is said that he kept the whole kingdom in awe of him. In "the
frenzy and prodigality of vanity," he exclaimed—

> "——— Yes, I am proud to see
> Men, not afraid of God, afraid of me!"

Tacitus Gordon said of him, that Pope seemed to persuade the
nation that all genius and ability were confined to him and his
friends.

the scandalous chronicles of literature. We are mortified on discovering so fine a genius in the text humbling
itself through all the depravity of a commentary full of
spleen, and not without the fictions of satire. The unhappy influence his *Literary Quarrels* had on this great
poet's life remains to be traced. He adopted a system
of literary politics abounding with stratagems, conspiracies, manœuvres, and factions.

Pope's literary quarrels were the wars of his poetical
ambition, more perhaps than of the petulance and strong
irritability of his character. They were some of the
artifices he adopted from the peculiarity of his situation.

Thrown out of the active classes of society from a
variety of causes sufficiently known,* concentrating his
passions into a solitary one, his retired life was passed in
the contemplation of his own literary greatness. Re-
viewing the past, and anticipating the future, he felt he
was creating a new era in our literature, an event which
does not always occur in a century : but eager to secure
present celebrity, with the victory obtained in the open
field, he combined the intrigues of the cabinet : thus,
while he was exerting great means, he practised little
artifices. No politician studied to obtain his purposes by
more oblique directions, or with more intricate stratagems ; and Pope was at once the lion and the fox of
Machiavel. A book might be written on the Stratagems

---

* Pope, in his energetic Letter to Lord Hervey, that "masterpiece
of invective," says Warton, which Tyers tells us he kept long back
from publishing, at the desire of Queen Caroline, who was fearful her
counsellor would become insignificant in the public esteem, and at last
in her own, such was the power his genius exercised :—has pointed out
one of these causes. It describes himself as "a private person under
penal laws, and many other disadvantages, not for want of honesty or
conscience ; yet it is by these alone I have hitherto lived *excluded from
all posts of profit or trust.* I can interfere with the views of no man."

of Literature, as Frontinus has composed one on War,
and among its subtilest heroes we might place this great
poet.

To keep his name alive before the public was one of
his early plans. When he published his "Essay on
Criticism," anonymously, the young and impatient poet
was mortified with the inertion of public curiosity : he
was almost in despair.* Twice, perhaps oftener, Pope
attacked Pope;† and he frequently concealed himself

* The first publisher of the " Essay on Criticism" must have been a
Mr. Lewis, a Catholic bookseller in Covent-garden ; for, from a de-
scendant of this Lewis, I heard that Pope, after publication, came every
day, persecuting with anxious inquiries the cold impenetrable bookseller, who, as the poem lay uncalled for, saw nothing but vexatious
importunities in a troublesome youth. One day, Pope, after nearly a
month's publication, entered, and in despair tied up a number of the
poems, which he addressed to several who had a reputation in town, as
judges of poetry. The scheme succeeded, and the poem, having
reached its proper circle, soon got into request.

† He was the author of "The Key to the Lock," written to show
that "The Rape of the Lock" was a political poem, designed to ridicule
the Barrier Treaty; [so called from the arrangement made at the
Peace of Utrecht between the ministers of Great Britain and the
States General, as to the towns on the frontiers of the Dutch, which
were to be permanently strengthened as barrier fortresses. Pope, in
the mask of Esdras Barnivelt, apothecary, thus makes out his poem to
be a political satire. " Having said that by the *lock* is meant the *Barrier
Treaty*—first then I shall discover, that Belinda represents Great
Britain, or (which is the same thing) her late Majesty. This is plainly
seen in the description of her,

"On her white breast a sparkling cross she wore."

Alluding to the ancient name of Albion, from her white cliffs, and to
the cross which is the ensign of England. The baron who cuts off the
lock, or Barrier Treaty, is the Earl of Oxford. Clarissa, who lent the
scissors, my Lady Masham. Thalestris, who provokes Belinda to
resent the loss of the lock or treaty, the Duchess of Marlborough ; and
Sir Plume, who is moved by Thalestris to re-demand it of Great Britain,
Prince Eugene, who came hither for that purpose." He concludes 32
pages of similar argument by saying, "I doubt not if the persons most

under the names of others, for some particular design. Not to point out his dark familiar " Scriblerus," always at hand for all purposes, he made use of the names of several of his friends. When he employed Savage in 'a collection of all the pieces, in verse and prose, published on occasion of the *Dunciad*," he subscribed his name to an admirable dedication to Lord Middlesex, where he minutely relates the whole history of the *Dunciad*, "and the weekly clubs held to consult of hostilities against the author ;" and, for an express introduction to that work, he used the name of Cleland, to which is added a note, expressing surprise that the world did not believe that Cleland was the writer !* Wanting a pretext for the publication of his letters, he delighted Curll by conveying to him some printed surreptitious

concerned would but order Mr. Bernard Lintott, the printer and publisher of this dangerous piece, to be taken into custody and examined, many further discoveries might be made both of this poet's and his abettors secret designs, which are doubtless of the utmost importance to Government." Such is a specimen of Pope's chicanery.] Its innocent extravagance could only have been designed to increase attention to a work, which hardly required any such artifice. [In the preface to this production, " the uncommon sale of this book" is stated as one reason for the publication: " above six thousand of them have been already vended."] In the same spirit he composed the "Guardian,' in which Phillips's Pastorals were insidiously preferred to his own. Pope sent this ironical. panegyrical criticism on Phillips anonymously to the "Guardian," and Steele not perceiving the drift, hesitated to publish it, till Pope advised it. Addison detected it. I doubt whether we have discovered all the *supercheries* of this kind. After writing the finest works of genius, he was busily employed in attracting the public attention to them. In the antithesis of his character, he was so great and so little ! But he knew mankind ! and present fame was the great business of his life.

* Cleland was the son of Colonel Cleland. an old friend of Pope ; he and his son had served in the East Indian army ; but the latter returned to London. and became a sort of literary jackal to Pope, and a hack author for the booksellers. He wrote several moral and useful works ; but as they did not pay well, he wrote an immoral one, for which he

copies, who soon discovered that it was but a fairy
treasure which he could not grasp; and Pope, in his own
defence, had soon ready the authentic edition.* Some
lady observed that Pope "hardly drank tea without a
stratagem!" The female genius easily detects its own
peculiar faculty, when it is exercised with inferior delicacy.

But his systematic hostility did not proceed with equal
impunity: in this perpetual war with dulness, he discovered that every one he called a dunce was not so; nor did he
find the dunces themselves less inconvenient to him; for
many successfully substituted, for their deficiencies in
better qualities, the lie that lasts long enough to vex a
man; and the insolence that does not fear him: they
attacked him at all points, and not always in the spirit
of legitimate warfare.† They filled up his asterisks,

obtained a better price, and a pension of 100l. a-year, on condition
that he never wrote in that manner again. This was obtained for him
by Lord Granville, after Cleland had been cited before the Privy
Council, and pleaded poverty as the reason for such authorship.—ED.

* The narrative of this dark transaction, which seems to have been
imperfectly known to Johnson, being too copious for a note, will be
found at the close of this article.

† A list of all the pamphlets which resulted from the *Dunciad* would
occupy a large space. Many of them were as grossly personal as the
celebrated poem. The poet was frequently ridiculed under the names
of "Pope Alexander" (from his dictatorial style), and "Sawney." In
"an heroic poem occasioned by the *Dunciad*," published in 1728, the
poet's snug retreat at Twickenham is thus alluded to:—

> "Sawney! a mimic sage of huge renown,
> To Twick'nam bow'rs retir'd, enjoys his wealth,
> His malice and his muse: in grottoes cool,
> And cover'd arbours, dreams his hours away."

A fragment of Pope's celebrated grotto still remains; the house is
destroyed. Pope spent all his spare cash over his Twickenham villa.
"I never save anything," he said once to Spence; and the latter has
left a detailed account of what he meant to do in the further decoration
of his garden if he had lived. As he gained a sum of money, he
regularly spent it in this way.—ED.

and accused him of treason. They asserted that the
panegyrical verses prefixed to his works (an obsolete
mode of recommendation, which Pope condescended to
practise), were his own composition, and to which he had
affixed the names of some dead or some unknown writers.
They published lists of all whom Pope had attacked;
placing at the head, "God Almighty; the King;" descending to the "lords and gentlemen."* A few suspect-

* Pope is, perhaps, the finest *character-painter* of all satirists.
Atterbury, after reading the portrait of Atticus, advised him to proceed
in a way which his genius had pointed out; but Arbuthnot, with his
dying breath, conjured him "to reform, and not to chastise;" that is,
not to spare the vice, but the person. It is said, Pope answered, that,
to correct the world with due effect, they become inseparable; and
that, deciding by his own experience, he was justified in his opinion.
Perhaps, at first, he himself wavered; but he strikes bolder as he
gathers strength. The two first editions of the *Dunciad*, now before
me, could hardly be intelligible: they exhibit lines after lines gaping
with an hiatus, or obscured with initial letters: in subsequent editions,
the names stole into their places. We are told, that the personalities in,
his satires quickened the sale: the portraits of Sporus, Bufo, Clodius,
Timon, and Atossa, were purchased by everybody; but when he once
declared, respecting the *characters* of one of his best satires, that no
real persons were intended, it checked public curiosity, which was felt
in the sale of that edition. Personality in his satires, no doubt, accorded with the temper and the talent of Pope; and the malice of mankind
afforded him all the conviction necessary to indulge it. Yet Young
could depend solely on abstract characters and pure wit; and I believe
that his "Love of Fame" was a series of admirable satires, which did
not obtain less popularity than Pope's   Cartwright, one of the poetical
sons of Ben Jonson, describes, by a beautiful and original image, the
office of the satirist, though he praises Jonson for exercising a virtue
he did not always practise; as Swift celebrates Pope with the same
truth, when he sings:—

"Yet malice never was his aim;
He lash'd the vice, but spared the name."

Cartwright's lines are:—

"———— 'tis thy skill
To strike the vice, and spare the person still;

ed his skill in Greek; but every hound yelped in the halloo against his Homer.* Yet the more extraordinary circumstance was, their hardy disputes with Pope respecting his claim to his own works, and the difficulty he more than once found to establish his rights. Sometimes they divided public opinion by even indicating the real authors; and witnesses from White's and St. James's were ready to be produced. Among these literary coteries, several of Pope's productions, in their anonymous, and even in their MS. state, had been appropriated by several pseudo authors; and when Pope called for restitution, he seemed to be claiming nothing less than their lives. One of these gentlemen had enjoyed a very fair reputation for more than two years on the "Memoirs of a Parish-Clerk;" another, on "The Messiah!" and there were many other vague claims. All this was vexatious; but not so much as the ridiculous attitude in which Pope was sometimes placed by his enraged adversaries.† He must have found himself in a more perilous

> As he who, when he saw the serpent wreath'd
> About his sleeping son, and as he breathed,
> Drink in his soul, did so the shot contrive,
> To kill the beast, but keep the child alive."

* Cooke, the translator of Hesiod, published a letter in Mist's Journal, insisting that Pope had *mistaken the whole character of Thersites*, from ignorance of the language. I regret I have not drawn some notes from that essay. The subject might be made curious by a good Greek scholar, if Pope has really erred in the degree Cooke asserts. Theobald, who seems to have been a more classical scholar than has been allowed, besides some versions from the Greek tragic bards, commenced a translation of the *Odyssey* as soon as Pope's *Iliad* appeared.

† In one of these situations, Pope issued a very grave, but very ludicrous advertisement. They had the impudence to publish an account of Pope having been flagellated by two gentlemen in Ham Walks, during his evening promenade. This was avenging Dennis for what he had undergone from the narrative of his madness. In "The Memoirs of Grub-street," vol. i. p. 96, this tingling narrative appears to have been

situation when he hired a brawny champion, or borrowed
the generous courage of some military friend.* To all
these troubles we may add, that Pope has called down on
himself more lasting vengeance; and the good sense of
Theobald, the furious but often acute remarks of Dennis;
the good humoured yet keen remonstrance of Cibber;
the silver shaft, tipped with venom, sent from the injured
but revengeful Lady Mary; and many a random shot,
that often struck him, inflicted on him many a sleepless

the ingenious forgery of Lady Mary! On this occasion, Pope thought
it necessary to publish the following advertisement in the *Daily Post*,
June 14. 1728:—

"Whereas, there has been a scandalous paper cried aloud about the
streets, under the title of 'A Pop upon Pope,' insinuating that I was
whipped in Ham Walks on Thursday last:—This is to give notice, that
I did not stir out of my house at Twickenham on that day; and the
same is a malicious and ill-founded report.—A. P."

[Spence, on the authority of Pope's half-sister, says: "When some
of the people that he had put into the *Dunciad* were so enraged against
him, and threatened him so highly, he loved to walk alone to Richmond,
only he would take a large faithful dog with him, and pistols in his
pocket. He used to say to us when we talked to him about it, that
"with pistols the least man in England was above a match for the
largest."]

It seems that Phillips hung up a birchen-rol at Button's. Pope, in
one of his letters, congratulates himself that he never attempted to use
it. [His half-sister, Mrs. Rackett, testifies to Pope's courage; she
says, "My brother never knew what fear was."]

* According to the scandalous chronicle of the day, Pope, shortly
after the publication of the *Dunciad*, had a tall Irishman to attend him
Colonel Duckett threatened to cane him, for a licentious stroke aimed
at him, which Pope recanted. Thomas Bentley, nephew to the doctor,
for the treatment his uncle had received, sent Pope a challenge. The
modern, like the ancient Horace, was of a nature liable to panic at
such critical moments. Pope consulted some military friends, who
declared that his *person* ought to protect him from any such redundance
of valour as was thus formally required; however, one of them accepted the challenge for him, and gave Bentley the option either of fighting or apologising: who, on this occasion, proved, what is usual, that
the easiest of the two was the quickest done.

night.* The younger Richardson has recorded the
personal sufferings of Pope when, one day, in taking up
Cibber's letter, while his face was writhing with agony,
he feebly declared that "these things were as good as

* I shall preserve one specimen, so classically elegant, that Pope
himself might have composed it. It is from the pen of that Leonard
Welsted whose "Aganippe" Pope has so shamefully characterised—

"Flow, Welsted, flow, like thine inspirer, beer!"

Can the reader credit, after this, that Welsted, who was clerk in ordinary at the Ordnance Office, was a man of family and independence,
of elegant manners and a fine fancy, but who considered poetry only
as a passing amusement? He has, however, left behind, amid the
careless productions of his muse, some passages wrought up with equal
felicity and power. There are several original poetical views of nature
scattered in his works, which have been collected by Mr. Nichols, that
would admit of a comparison with some of established fame.

Welsted imagined that the spirit of English poetry was on its decline
in the age of Pope, and allegorises the state of our poetry in a most
ingenious comparison. The picture is exquisitely wrought, like an
ancient gem: one might imagine Anacreon was turned critic:—

    " A flask I rear'd whose sluice began to fail,
    And told, from Phærus, this facetious tale:—
      Sabina, very old and very dry,
    Chanced, on a time, an EMPTY FLASK to spy:
    The flask but lately had been thrown aside,
    With the rich grape of Tuscan vineyards dyed;
    But lately, gushing from the slender spout,
    Its life, in purple streams, had issued out.
    The costly flavour still to sense remain'd,
    And still its sides the violet colour stain'd:
    A sight so sweet taught wrinkled age to smile;
    Pleased, she imbibes the generous fumes awhile,
    Then, downwards turn'd, the vessel gently props,
    And drains with patient care the lucid drops:
    O balmy spirit of Etruria's vine!
    O fragrant flask, she said, too lately mine!
    If such delights, THOUGH EMPTY, *thou canst yield.*
    What wondrous raptures hadst thou given if fill'd!"
      Palæmon to Cælia at Bath, or the Triumvirate.

"The empty flask" only retaining "the costly flavour," was **the**
verse of Pope.

hartshorn to him;" but he appeared at that moment
rather to want a little. And it is probably true, what
Cibber facetiously says of Pope, in his second letter:—
" Everybody tells me that I have made you as uneasy as
a rat in a hot kettle, for a twelvemonth together." *

Pope was pursued through life by the insatiable vengeance of Dennis. The young poet, who had got introduced
to him, among his first literary acquaintances, could
not fail, when the occasion presented itself, of ridiculing
this uncouth son of Aristotle. The blow was given in
the character of Appius, in the " Art of Criticism ;" and
it is known Appius was instantaneously recognised by the
fierce shriek of the agonised critic himself. From that
moment Dennis resolved to write down every work of
Pope's. How dangerous to offend certain tempers, verg-
ing on madness ! † Dennis, too, called on every one to

* Pope was made to appear as ridiculous as possible, and often
nicknamed " Poet Pug." from the frontispiece to an attack in reply
to his own, termed " Pope Alexander's Supremacy and Infallibility
examined." It represents Pope as a misshapen monkey leaning on a
pile of books, in the attitude adopted by Jervas in his portrait of the
poet.—ED.

† Dennis tells the whole story. " At his first coming to town he
was importunate with Mr. Cromwell to introduce him to me. The
recommendation engaged me to be about thrice in company with him ·
after which I went to the country. till 1 found myself most insolently
attacked in his very superficial 'Essay on Criticism,' by which he
endeavoured to destroy the reputation of a man who had published
pieces of criticism, and to set up his own. I was moved with indignation to that degree, that I immediately writ remarks on that essay. I
also writ upon part of his translation of ' Homer,' his ' Windsor
Forest,' and his infamous ' Temple of Fame.' " In the same pamphlet
he says:—" Pope writ his ' Windsor Forest' in envy of Sir John
Denham's ' Cooper's Hill;' his infamous ' Temple of Fame.' in envy of
Chaucer's poem upon the same subject; his ' Ode on St. Cecilia's Day,'
in envy of Dryden's ' Feast of Alexander.' " In reproaching Pope with,
his peculiar rhythm. that monotonous excellence, which soon became
mechanical, he has an odd attempt at a pun:—" Boileau's Pegasus

join him in the common cause; and once he retaliated
on Pope in his own way. Accused by Pope of being the
writer of an account of himself, in Jacob's "Lives of the
Poets," Dennis procured a letter from Jacob, which he
published, and in which it appears that Pope's own character in this collection, if not written by him, was by him
very carefully corrected on the proof-sheet; so that he
stood in the same ridiculous attitude into which he had
thrown Dennis, as his own trumpeter. Dennis, whose
brutal energy remained unsubdued, was a rhinoceros of a
critic, shelled up against the arrow of wit. This monster of criticism awed the poet; and Dennis proved to
be a Python, whom the golden shaft of Apollo could not
pierce.

The political prudence of Pope was further discovered
in the "Collection of all the Pieces relative to the *Dunciad*," on which he employed Savage : these exemplified
the justness of the satire, or defended it from all attacks.
The precursor of the *Dunciad* was a single chapter in
"The Bathos; or, the Art of Sinking in Poetry;" where
the humorous satirist discovers an analogy between flying-fishes, parrots, tortoises, &c., and certain writers,
whose names are designated by initial letters. In this
unlucky alphabet of dunces, not one of them but was
applied to some writer of the day; and the loud clam-
ours these excited could not be appeased by the simplicity of our poet's declaration, that the letters were
placed at random; and while his oil could not smooth
so turbulent a sea, every one swore to the flying-fish or
the tortoise, as he had described them. It was still
more serious when the *Dunciad* appeared. Of that
class of authors who depended for a wretched existence

has all his paces; the Pegasus of Pope, like a *Kentish post-horse*, is
always upon the *Canterbury*."—"Remarks upon several Passages in
the Preliminaries to the *Dunciad*," 1729.

on their wages, several were completely ruined, for no
purchasers were to be found for the works of some
authors, after they had been inscribed in the chronicle
of our provoking and inimitable satirist.*

It is in this collection by Savage I find the writer's

---

* Two parties arose in the literary republic, the *Theobaldians* and
the *Popeians*. The "Grub-street Journal," a kind of literary gazette
of some campaigns of the time, records the skirmishes with tolerable
neutrality, though with a strong leaning in favour of the prevailing
genius.

The *Popeians* did not always do honour to their great leader; and
the *Theobaldians* proved themselves, at times, worthy of being engaged,
had fate so ordered it, in the army of their renowned enemy. When
Young published his "Two Epistles to Pope, on the Authors of the
Age," there appeared "One Epistle to Mr. A. Pope, in Answer to two
of Dr. Young's." On this, a Popeian defends his master from some
extravagant accusations in "The Grub-street Memoirs." He insists,
as his first principle, that all accusations against a man's character
without an attestor are presumed to be slanders and lies, and in this
case every gentleman, though "Knight of the Bathos," is merely a
liar and scoundrel.

"You assure us he is not only a bad poet, but a stealer from bad
poets: if so, you have just cause to complain of invasion of property.
You assure us he is not even a versifier, but steals the *sound* of his
verses; now, to *steal a sound* is as ingenious as to *print an echo*. You
cannot bear *gentlemen* should be treated as vermin and reptiles: now,
to be impartial, you were compared to *flying-fishes*, *dippers*, *tortoises*,
and *parrots*, &c., not vermin, but curious and beautiful creatures "—
alluding to the abuse, in this "Epistle," on such authors as Atterbury,
Arbuthnot, Swift, the Duke of Buckingham, &c. The Popeian concludes:—

After all, *your poem*, to comfort you, is more innocent than the
Dunciad; for in the one there's no man abused but is very well pleased
to be abused in such company; whereas in the other there's no man so
much as named, but is extremely affronted to be ranked with such
people as style each other the *dullest of men*."

The publication of the *Dunciad*, however, drove the *Theobaldians* out
of the field. Guerillas, such as the "One Epistle," sometimes appeared, but their heroes struck and skulked away. A *Theobaldian*, in
an epigram, compared the *Dunciad* of Pope to the offspring of the
celebrated Pope Joan. The neatness of his wit is hardly blunted by a

admirable satire on the class of literary prostitutes. It is entitled "An Author to be Let, by Iscariot Hackney." It has been ably commended by Johnson in his "Life of Savage," and on his recommendation Thomas Davies inserted it in his "Collection of Fugitive Pieces;" but such is the careless curiosity of modern re-publishers, that often, in preserving a decayed body, they are apt to drop a limb: this was the case with Davies; for he has dropped the preface, far more exquisite than the work itself. A morsel of such poignant relish betrays the hand of the master who snatched the pen for a moment.

This preface defends Pope from the two great objections justly raised at the time against the *Dunciad:* one is, the grossness and filthiness of its imagery; and the other, its reproachful allusions to the poverty of the authors.

The *indelicacies* of the *Dunciad* are thus wittily apologised for:—

"They are suitable to the subject; a subject composed, for the most part, of authors whose writings are the refuse of wit, and who in life are the very excrement of

pun. He who talks of Pope's "stealing a sound," seems to have practised that invisible art himself, for the verse is musical as Pope's.

TO THE AUTHOR OF THE DUNCIAD.

"With rueful eyes thou view'st thy wretched race,
  The child of guilt, and destined to disgrace.
  Thus when fam'ed Joan usurp'd the Pontiff's chair,
  With terror she beheld her new-born heir:
  Ill-starr'd, ill-favour'd into birth it came;
  In vice begotten, and brought forth with shame!
  In vain it breathes, a lewd abandon'd hope!
  And calls in vain, the unhallow'd father—Pope!"

The answers to this epigram by the Popeians are too gross. The "One Epistle" is attributed to James Moore Smyth, in alliance with Welsted and other unfortunate heroes.

Nature. Mr. Pope has, too, used dung; but he disposes
that dung in such a manner that it becomes rich manure,
from which he raises a variety of fine flowers. He
deals in rags; but like an artist, who commits them to
a paper-mill, and brings them out useful sheets. The
chemist extracts a fine cordial from the most nauseous
of all dung; and Mr. Pope has drawn a sweet poetical
spirit from the most offensive and unpoetical objects
of the creation—unpoetical, though eternal writers of
poetry."

The reflections on the *poverty* of its heroes are thus
ingeniously defended :—"Poverty, not proceeding from
folly, but which may be owing to virtue, sets a man in
an amiable light; but when our wants are of our own
seeking, and prove the motive of every ill action (for
the poverty of bad authors has always a bad heart for
its companion), is it not a vice, and properly the subject
of satire?" The preface then proceeds to show how
"all these *said writers* might have been *good mechanics.*"
He illustrates his principles with a most ungracious
account of several of his contemporaries. I shall give a
specimen of what I consider as the polished sarcasm and
caustic humour of Pope, on some favourite subjects.

"Mr. Thomas *Cooke.*—His enemies confess him not
without merit. To do the man justice, he might have
made a tolerable figure as a *Tailor.* 'Twere too pre-
sumptuous to affirm he could have been a *master* in any
profession; but, dull as I allow him, he would not have
been despicable for a third or a fourth hand journeyman.
Then had his wants have been avoided; for, he would at
least have learnt to *cut his coat according to his cloth.*

" Why would not Mr. *Theobald* continue an attorney?
Is not *Word-catching* more serviceable in splitting a
cause, than explaining a fine poet?

" When Mrs. *Haywood* ceased to be a strolling-actress,

why might not the lady (though once a theatrical queen)
have subsisted by turning *washerwoman?* Has not the
fall of greatness been a frequent distress in all ages?
She might have caught a beautiful bubble, as it arose
from the suds of her tub, blown it in air, seen it glitter,
and then break! Even in this low condition, she had
played with a bubble; and what more is the vanity of
human greatness?

"Had it not been an honester and more decent live-
lihood for Mr. *Norton* (Daniel De Foe's son of love by a
lady who vended oysters) to have dealt in a *fish-market,*
than to be dealing out the dialects of Billingsgate in the
Flying-post?

"Had it not been more laudable for Mr. *Roome,* the
son of an *undertaker,* to have borne a link and a mourn-
ing-staff, in the long procession of a funeral—or even
been more decent in him to have sung psalms, according
to education, in an Anabaptist meeting, than to have
been altering the *Jovial Crew, or Merry Beggars,* into a
wicked imitation of the *Beggar's Opera?*"

This satire seems too exquisite for the touch of Savage,
and is quite in the spirit of the author of the *Dunciad.*
There is, in Ruffhead's "Life of Pope," a work to which
Warburton contributed all his care, a passage which
could only have been written by Warburton. The
strength and coarseness of the imagery could never
have been produced by the dull and feeble intellect of
Ruffhead: it is the opinion, therefore, of Warburton
himself, on the *Dunciad.* "The *good purpose* intended
by this satire was, to the *herd* in general, of less efficacy
than our author hoped; for *scribblers* have not the common sense of *other vermin,* who usually abstain from
mischief, when they see any of their kind *gibbeted* or
nail'd up, as terrible examples."—Warburton employed
the same strong image in one of his threats.

One of Pope's Literary Quarrels must be distinguished for its romantic cast.

In the Treatise on the *Bathos*, the initial letters of the bad writers occasioned many heartburns; and, among others, Aaron Hill suspected he was marked out by the letters A. H. This gave rise to a large correspondence between Hill and Pope. Hill, who was a very amiable man, was infinitely too susceptible of criticism; and Pope, who seems to have had a personal regard for him, injured those nice feelings as little as possible. Hill had published a panegyrical poem on Peter the Great, under the title of "The Northern Star;" and the bookseller had conveyed to him a criticism of Pope's, of which Hill publicly acknowledged he mistook the meaning. When the Treatise of "The Bathos" appeared, Pope insisted he had again mistaken the initials A. H.—Hill gently attacked Pope in "a paper of very pretty verses," as Pope calls them. When the *Dunciad* appeared, Hill is said "to have published pieces, in his youth, bordering upon the bombast." This was as light a stroke as could be inflicted; and which Pope, with great good-humour, tells Hill, might be equally applied to himself; for he always acknowledged, that when a boy, he had written an Epic poem of that description; would often quote absurd verses from it, for the diversion of his friends; and actually inserted some of the most extravagant ones in the very Treatise on "The Bathos." Poor Hill, however, was of the most sickly delicacy, and produced "The Caveat," another gentle rebuke, where Pope is represented as "sneakingly to approve, and want the worth to cherish or befriend men of merit." In the course of this correspondence, Hill seems to have projected the utmost stretch of his innocent malice; for he told Pope, that he had almost finished "An Essay on Propriety and Impropriety in Design, Thought, and

Expression, illustrated by examples in both kinds, from the writings of Mr. Pope;" but he offers, if this intended work should create the least pain to Mr. Pope, he was willing, with all his heart, to have it run thus:—" An Essay on Propriety and Impropriety, &c., illustrated by Examples of the first, from the writings of Mr. Pope, and of the rest, from those of the author."—To the romantic generosity of this extraordinary proposal, Pope replied, " I acknowledge your generous offer, to give *examples of imperfections* rather out of *your own works* than mine: I consent, with all my heart, to your confining them to *mine*, for two reasons: the one, that I fear your sensibility that way is greater than my own: the other is a better; namely, that I intend to correct the faults you find, if they are such as I expect from Mr. Hill's cool judgment." *

Where, in literary history, can be found the parallel of such an offer of self-immolation ? This was a literary quarrel like that of lovers, where to hurt each other would have given pain to both parties. Such skill and desire to strike, with so much tenderness in inflicting a wound; so much compliment, with so much complaint; have perhaps never met together, as in the romantic hostility of this literary chivalry.

A NARRATIVE

OF THE EXTRAORDINARY TRANSACTIONS RESPECTING THE PUBLICATION OF POPE'S LETTERS.

JOHNSON observes, that " one of the passages of Pope's life which seems to deserve some inquiry, was the publication of his letters by Curll, the rapa-

---

* The six Letters are preserved in Ruffhead's Appendix, No. 1.

cious bookseller."* Our great literary biographer has
expended more research on this occasion than his usual
penury of literary history allowed; and yet has only
told the close of the strange transaction—the previous
parts are more curious, and the whole cannot be separated. Joseph Warton has only transcribed Johnson's
narrative. It is a piece of literary history of an uncommon complexion; and it is worth the pains of telling, if
Pope, as I consider him to be, was the subtile weaver of
a plot, whose texture had been close enough for any
political conspiracy. It throws a strong light on the
portrait I have touched of him. He conducted all his
literary transactions with the arts of a Minister of State;
and the genius which he wasted on this literary stratagem, in which he so completely succeeded, might have
been perhaps sufficient to have organised rebellion.

It is well known that the origin of Pope's first letters
given to the public, arose from the distresses of a cast-
off mistress of one of his old friends (H. Cromwell),†

* Curll was a bookseller, from whose shop issued many works of
an immoral class, yet he chose for his sign "The Bible and Dial,"
which were displayed over his shop in Fleet-street. The satire of
Pope's Dunciad seems fairly to have been earned, as we may judge
from the class of books still seen in the libraries of curious collectors,
and which are certainly unfitted for more general circulation. For
these publications he was fined by the Court of King's Bench, and on
one occasion stood in the pillory as a punishment. Yet himself and
Lintot were the chief booksellers of the era, until Tonson arose, and
by taking a more enlarged view of the trade, laid the foundation of
the great publishing houses of modern times.—ED.

† Cromwell was one of the gay young men who frequented coffee-
houses and clubs when Pope, also a young man, did the same, and
corresponded freely with him for a few years, when the intimacy almost entirely ceased. The lady was a Mrs. Thomas, who became a
sort of literary hack to Curll, and is celebrated in the Dunciad under
the name of Corinna. Roscoe, in his edition of Pope, says, "Of Henry
Cromwell little is known, further than what is learnt from this correspondence, from which he appears to have been a man of respect-

who had given her the letters of Pope, which she knew
how to value: these she afterwards sold to Curll, who
preserved the originals in his shop, so that no suspicions
could arise of their authenticity. This very collection is
now deposited among Rawlinson's MSS. at the Bodleian.*

This single volume was successful; and when Pope, to
do justice to the memory of Wycherley, which had been
injured by a posthumous volume, printed some of their
letters, Curll, who seemed now to consider that all he
could touch was his own property, and that his little
volume might serve as a foundation-stone, immediately
announced *a new edition* of it, with *Additions*, meaning
to include the letters of Pope and Wycherly. Curll
now became so fond of *Pope's Letters*, that he advertised
for any: "no questions to be asked." Curll was willing
to be credulous: having proved to the world he had
some originals, he imagined these would sanction even
spurious ones. A man who, for a particular purpose,
sought to be imposed on, easily obtained his wish: they
translated letters of Voiture to Mademoiselle Rambouil-
let, and despatched them to the eager Bibliopolist to
print, as Pope's to Miss Blount. He went on increasing
his collection; and, skilful in catering for the literary
taste of the town, now inflamed their appetite by digni-
fying it with "Mr. Pope's Literary Correspondence!"

But what were the feelings of Pope during these successive surreptitious editions? He had discovered that
his genuine letters were liked; the grand experiment

able connections, talents, and education, and to have intermingled
pretty freely in the gallantries of fashionable life." He seems to have
been somewhat eccentric, and the correspondence of Pope only lasted
from 1708 to 1711.—ED.

* Pope, in his conversations with Spence, says, "My letters to
Cromwell were written with a design that does not generally appear:
they were not written in sober sadness."—ED.

with the public had been made for him, while he was
deprived of the profits; yet for he himself to publish his
own letters, which I shall prove he had prepared, was a
thing unheard of in the nation.   All this was vexatious:
and to stop the book-jobber and open the market for
himself, was a point to be obtained.

While Curll was proceeding, wind and tide in his
favour, a new and magnificent prospect burst upon him.
A certain person, masked by the initials P. T., understanding Curll was preparing *a Life of Pope*, offered
him "divers Memoirs gratuitously;" hinted that he was
well known to Pope; but the poet had lately "treated
him as a stranger."   P. T. desires an answer from E. C. by
the *Daily Advertiser*, which was complied with.   There
are passages in this letter which, I think, prove Pope to
be the projector of it: his family is here said to be allied
to Lord Downe's; his father is called a merchant.   Pope
could not bear the reproach of Lady Mary's line:—

> Hard as thy heart, and as *thy birth obscure.*

He always hinted at noble relatives; but Tyers tells us,
from the information of a relative, that "his father turns
out, at last, to have been a linen-draper in the Strand;"
therefore P. T. was at least telling a story which Pope
had no objection should be repeated.

The second letter of P. T., for the first was designed
only to break the ice, offers Curll "a large Collection of
Letters from the early days of Pope to the year 1727."
He gives an excellent notion of their value: "They will
open very many scenes new to the world, and make the
most authentic Life and Memoirs that could be."   He
desires they may be announced to the world immediately,
in Curll's precious style, that he "might not appear himself to have set the whole thing a-foot, and afterwards
he might plead he had only sent some letters to complete

the Collection." He asks nothing, and the originals were offered to be deposited with Curll.

Curll, secure of this promised addition, but still craving for more and more, composed a magnificent announcement, which, with P. T.'s entire correspondence, he enclosed in a letter to Pope himself. The letters were now declared to be a "Critical, Philological, and Historical Correspondence."—His own letter is no bad specimen of his keen sense; but after what had so often passed, his impudence was equal to the better quality.

"Sir,—To convince you of my readiness to oblige you, the inclosed is a demonstration. You have, as he says, disobliged a gentleman, the initial letters of whose name are P. T. I have some other papers in the same hand, relating to your *family*, which I will show, if you desire a sight of them. Your letters to Mr. Cromwell are out of print; and I intend to print them very beautifully, in an octavo volume. I have more to say than is proper to write; and if you will give me a meeting, I will wait on you with pleasure, and close all differences between you and yours,

"E. Curll."

Pope, surprised, as he pretends, at this address, consulted with his friends; everything evil was suggested against Curll. They conceived that his real design was "to get Pope to look over the former edition of his 'Letters to Cromwell,' and then to print it, as *revised* by Mr. Pope; as he sent an *obscene book* to a *Bishop*, and then advertised it as *corrected* and *revised* by him;" or perhaps to extort money from Pope for suppressing the MS. of P. T., and then publish it, saying P. T. had kept another copy. Pope thought proper to answer only by this public advertisement :—

"Whereas A. P. hath received a letter from E. C.,

bookseller, pretending that a person, the initials of whose
name are P. T., hath offered the said E. C. to print a
large Collection of Mr. P.'s letters, to which E. C. required an answer: A. P. having never had, nor intend-
ing to have, any private correspondence with the said
E. C., gives it him in this manner. That he knows no
such person as P. T.; that he believes he hath no such
collection; and that he thinks the whole a forgery, and
shall not trouble himself at all about it."

Curll replied, denying he had endeavoured to *corre-
spond* with Mr. Pope, and affirms that he had written to
him by *direction*.

It is now the plot thickens. P. T. suddenly takes
umbrage, accuses Curll of having " betrayed him to
' Squire Pope,' but you and he both shall soon be convinced it was no forgery. Since you would not comply
with my proposal to advertise, I have printed them at
my own expense." He offers the books to Curll for sale.

Curll on this has written a letter, which takes a full
view of the entire transaction. He seems to have grown
tired of what he calls " such jealous, groundless, and
dark negotiations." P. T. now found it necessary to
produce something more than a shadow—an agent appears. whom Curll considered to be a clergyman, who
assumed the name of R. Smith. The first proposal was,
that P. T.'s letters should be returned, that he might
feel secure from all possibility of detection; so that P.
T. terminates his part in this literary freemasonry as a
nonentity.

Here Johnson's account begins.—" Curll said, that one
evening a man in a clergyman's gown, but with a lawyer's band, brought and offered to sale a number of
printed volumes, which he found to be Pope's Epistolary
Correspondence; that he asked no name, and was told
none, but gave the price demanded, and thought himself

authorised to use his purchase to his own advantage."
Smith, the clergyman, left him some copies, and promised
more.

Curll now, in all the elation of possession, rolled his
thunder in an advertisement still higher than ever.—
"Mr. Pope's Literary Correspondence regularly digested,
from 1704 to 1734:" to lords, earls, baronets, doctors,
ladies, &c., with their respective answers, and whose
names glittered in the advertisement. The original MSS.
were also announced to be seen at his house.

But at this moment Curll had not received many
books, and no MSS. The advertisement produced the
effect designed; it roused public notice, and it alarmed
several in the House of Lords. Pope doubtless instigated his friends there. The Earl of Jersey moved, that
to publish letters of Lords was a breach of privilege;
and Curll was brought before the House.

This was an unexpected incident; and P. T. once
more throws his dark shadow across the path of Curll
to hearten him, had he wanted courage to face all the
lords. P. T. writes to instruct him in his answers to
their examination; but to take the utmost care to conceal P. T.; he assures him that the lords could not touch
a hair of his head if he behaved firmly; that he should
only answer their interrogatories by declaring he received the letters from different persons; that some were
given, and some were bought. P. T. reminds one, on this
occasion, of Junius's correspondence on a like threat
with his publisher.

"Curll appeared at the bar," says Johnson, "and
knowing himself in no great danger, spoke of Pope with
very little reverence. 'He has,' said Curll, 'a knack at
versifying; but in prose I think myself a match for him.'
When the Orders of the House were examined, none
of them appeared to have been infringed: Curll went

away triumphant, and Pope was left to seek some other remedy." The fact, not mentioned by Johnson, is, that though Curll's flourishing advertisement had announced *letters written by lords*, when the volumes were examined not one written by a lord appeared.

The letter Curll wrote on the occasion to one of these dark familiars, the pretended clergyman, marks his spirit and sagacity. It contains a remarkable passage. Some readers will be curious to have the productions of so celebrated a personage, who appears to have exercised considerable talents.

" 15th *May*, 1735.

"DEAR SIR,—I am just again going to the Lords to finish Pope. I desire you to send me the *sheets* to *perfect* the first fifty books, and likewise the *remaining three hundred books;* and pray be at the Standard Tavern this evening, and I will pay you twenty pounds more. My defence is right; I only told the lords I did not know from whence the books came, and that my wife received them. This was strict truth, and prevented all further inquiry. *The lords declared they had been made Pope's tools.* I put myself on this single point, and insisted, as there was not any Peer's letter in the book, I had not been guilty of any breach of privilege. I depend that the *books* and the *imperfections* will be sent; and believe of P. T. what I hope he believes of me.

" For the Rev. Mr. SMITH."

The reader observes that Curll talks of a great number of *books not received*, and of *the few* which he has received, as *imperfect*. The fact is, the whole bubble is on the point of breaking. He, masked in the initial letters, and he, who wore the masquerade dress of a clergyman's gown with a lawyer's band, suddenly picked a quarrel with the duped bibliopolist: they now accuse him of a design he had of betraying them to the Lords!

The tantalized and provoked Curll then addressed the following letter to "The Rev. Mr. Smith," which, both as a specimen of this celebrated personage's "prose," in which he thought himself "a match for Pope," and exhibiting some traits of his character, will entertain the curious reader.

"*Friday*, 16 *May*, 1735.

"SIR,—1st, I am falsely accused. 2. I value not any man's change of temper; I will never change my VERACITY for falsehood, in owning a fact of which I am innocent. 3. I did not own the books came from *across the water*, nor ever *named you;* all I said was, that the books came *by water*. 4. When the books were seized, I sent my son to convey a letter to you; and as you told me everybody knew you in Southwark, I bid him make a strict inquiry, as I am sure you would have done in such an exigency. 5. Sir, *I have acted justly* in this affair, and that is what I shall always think wisely. 6. I will be kept no longer in the dark; P. T. is *Will o' the Wisp;* all the books I have had are imperfect; the first fifty had no titles nor prefaces; the last five bundles seized by the Lords contained but thirty-eight in each bundle, which amounts to one hundred and ninety, and fifty, is in all but two hundred and forty books. 7. As to the loss of a future copy, I despise it, nor will I be concerned with any more such dark suspicious dealers. But now, sir, I'll tell you what I will do: when I have the *books perfected* which I have already received, and *the rest of the impression*, I will pay you for them. But what do you call this usage? First take a note for a month, and then want it to be changed for one of Sir Richard Hoare's. My note is as good, for any sum I give it, as the Bank, and shall be as punctually paid. I always say, *gold is better than paper*. But if this dark converse goes on, I will instantly reprint the whole book; and, as a supple-

ment to it, all the letters P. T. ever sent me, of which I
have exact copies, together with all your originals, and
give them in upon oath to my Lord Chancellor. You
talk of *trust*—P. T. has not reposed any in me, for he has
my money and notes for imperfect books. Let me see,
sir, either P. T. or yourself, or you'll find the Scots proverb verified, *Nemo me impune lacessit.*

"Your abused humble servant,

"E. CURLL.

"P. S. Lord —— I attend this day. Lord Delawar
I SUP WITH TO-NIGHT. Where *Pope* has one lord, I have
twenty."

After this, Curll announced "Mr. Pope's Literary
Correspondence, with the *initial correspondence* of P. T.,
R. S., &c." But the shadowy correspondents now publicly declared that they could give *no title* whatever to
Mr. Pope's letters, with which they had furnished Curll,
and never pretended any ; that therefore any bookseller
had the same right of printing them : and, in respect to
money matters between them, he had given them notes
not negotiable, and had never paid them fully for the
copies, perfect and imperfect, which he had sold.

Thus terminated this dark transaction between Curll
and his *initial* correspondents. He still persisted in
printing several editions of the letters of Pope, which
furnished the poet with a modest pretext to publish an
authentic edition—the very point to which the whole of
this dark and intricate plot seems to have been really
directed.*

Were Pope not concerned in this mysterious transaction, how happened it that the letters which P. T. actually printed were genuine? To account for this, Pope

---

* Pope's victory over Curll is represented by Hogarth in a print os-
tentatiously hung in the garret of his "Distressed Poet."—ED.

promulgated a new fact. Since the first publication of his letters to his friend Cromwell, wrenched from the distressed female who possessed them, our poet had been advised to collect his letters; and these he had preserved by inserting them in two books; either the originals or the copies. For this purpose an amanuensis or two were employed by Pope when these books were in the country, and by the Earl of Oxford when they were in town. Pope pretended that Curll's letters had been extracted from these two books, but sometimes imperfectly transcribed, and sometimes interpolated. Pope, indeed, offered a reward of twenty pounds to "P. T." and "R. Smith, who passed for a clergyman," if they would come forward and discover the whole of this affair; or "if they had acted, as it was reported, by the *direction* of any other person." They never appeared. Lintot, the son of the great rival of Curll, told Dr. Johnson, that his father had been offered the same parcel of printed books, and that Pope knew better than anybody else how Curll obtained the copies.

Dr. Johnson, although he appears not to have been aware of the subtle intricacy of this extraordinary plot, has justly drawn this inference: "To make the copies perfect was the only purpose of Pope, because the numbers offered for sale by the private messengers, showed that hope of gain could not have been the motive of the impression. It seems that Pope, being desirous of printing his letters, and not knowing how to do, without imputation of vanity, what has in this country been done very rarely, contrived an appearance of compulsion; when he could complain that his letters were surreptitiously printed, he might decently and defensively publish them himself."

I have observed, how the first letter of P. T. pretending to be written by one who owed no kindness to Pope,

bears the evident impression of his own hand; for it
contains matters not exactly true, but exactly what Pope
wished should appear in his own life. That he had prepared his letters for publication, appears by the story of
the two MS. books—that the printed ones came by water,
would look as if they had been sent from his house at
Twickenham; and, were it not absurd to pretend to de-
cipher initials, P. T. might be imagined to indicate the
name of the owner, as well as his place of abode.

Worsdale, an indifferent painter, was a man of some
humour in personating a character, for he performed Old
Lady Scandal in one of his own farces. He was also a
literary adventurer, for, according to Mrs. Pilkington's
Memoirs, wishing to be a poet as well as a mimic, he got
her and her husband to write all the verses which passed
with his name ; such a man was well adapted to be this
clergyman with the lawyer's band, and Worsdale has
asserted that he was really employed by his friend Pope
on this occasion.

Such is the intricate narrative of this involved transaction. Pope completely succeeded, by the most subtile
manœuvres imaginable; the incident which perhaps was
not originally expected, of having his letters brought
before the examination at the House of Lords, most
amply gratified his pride, and awakened public curiosity.
"He made the House of Lords," says Curll, " his tools."
Greater ingenuity, perplexity, and secrecy have scarcely
been thrown into the conduct of the writer, or writers,
of the Letters of Junius.

POPE AND CIBBER;

CONTAINING

A VINDICATION OF THE COMIC WRITER.

POPE attacked Cibber from personal motives—by dethroning Theobald, in the *Dunciad*, to substitute Cibber, he made the satire not apply—Cibber's facetious and serious remonstrance—Cibber's inimitable good-numour—an apology for what has been called his "effrontery" —perhaps a modest man, and undoubtedly a man of genius—his humorous defence of his deficiency in Tragedy, both in acting and writing—Pope more hurt at being exposed as a ridiculous lover than as a bad man—an account of "The Egotist, or Colley upon Cibber," a kind of supplement to the "Apology for his Life," in which he has drawn his own character with great freedom and spirit.

POPE'S quarrel with Cibber may serve to check the haughtiness of genius; it is a remarkable instance how good-humour can gently draw a boundary round the arbitrary power, whenever the wantonness of satire would conceal calumny. But this quarrel will become even more interesting, should it throw a new light on the character of one whose originality of genius seems little suspected. Cibber showed a happy address in a very critical situation, and obtained an honourable triumph over the malice of a great genius, whom, while he complained of he admired, and almost loved the cynic.

Pope, after several "flirts," as Cibber calls them, from slight personal motives, which Cibber has fully opened,* at length from "peevish weakness," as Lord

* Johnson says, that though "Pope attacked Cibber with acrimony, the provocation is not easily discoverable." But the statements of Cibber, which have never been contradicted, show sufficient motives to exc'te the poetic irascibility. It was Cibber's "fling" at the unowned and condemned comedy of the triumvirate of wits, Pope,

Orford has happily expressed it, closed his insults by
dethroning Theobald, and substituting Cibber; but as
he would not lose what he had already written, this
change disturbed the whole decorum of the satiric fiction. Things of opposite natures, joined into one, became the poetical chimera of Horace. The hero of the
Dunciad is neither Theobald nor Cibber; Pope forced a

Gay, and Arbuthnot, *Three Hours after Marriage,* when he performed
Bayes in the *Rehearsal,* that incurred the immortal odium. There was
no malice on Cibber's side ; for it was then the custom to restore the
zest of that obsolete dramatic satire, by introducing allusions to any
recent theatrical event. The plot of this ridiculous comedy hinging
on the deep contrivance of two lovers getting access to the wife of a
virtuoso, "one curiously swathed up like an Egyptian mummy, and
the other slily covered in the pasteboard skin of a crocodile," was an
incident *so extremely natural,* that it seemed congenial with the high
imagination and the deep plot of a Bayes! Poor Cibber, in the gaiety
of his *impromptu,* made the "fling;" and, unluckily, it was applauded
by the audience! The irascibility of Pope too strongly authenticated
one of the three authors. "In the swelling of his heart, after the
play was over, he came behind the scenes with his lips pale and his
voice trembling, to call me to account for the insult ; and accordingly
fell upon me with all the foul language that a wit out of his senses
would be capable of, choked with the foam of his passion." Cibber
replied with dignity, insisted on the privilege of the character, and
that he would repeat the same jest as long as the public approved of
it. Pope would have certainly approved of Cibber's manly conduct,
had he not been the author himself. To this circumstance may be
added the reception which the town and the court bestowed on Cibber's "Nonjuror," a satire on the politics of the jacobite faction; Pope
appears, under the assumed name of *Barnevelt,* to have published "an
odd piece of wit, proving that the Nonjuror, in its design, its characters, and almost every scene of it, was a closely-couched jacobite libel
against the Government." Cibber says that "this was so shrewdly
maintained, that I almost liked the jest myself." Pope seems to have
been fond of this new species of irony; for, in the Pastorals of Phillips, he showed the same sort of ingenuity, and he repeated the same
charge of political mystery against his own finest poem; for he proved
by many "merry inuendoes," that "The Rape of the Lock," was as
audacious a libel as the pretended Barnevelt had made out the Nonjuror to be. See note, p. 75.

dunce to appear as Cibber; but this was not making
Cibber a dunce. This error in Pope emboldened Cibber
in the contest, for he still insisted that the satire did not
apply to him;* and humorously compared the libel "to a
purge with a wrong label," and Pope "to an apothecary
who did not mind his business."†

Cibber triumphed in the arduous conflict—though
sometimes he felt that, like the Patriarch of old, he was
wrestling, not with an equal, but one of celestial race,

---

* Cibber did not obtrude himself in this contest. Had he been
merely a poor vain creature, he had not preserved so long a silence.
His good-temper was without anger, but he remonstrates with no little
dignity, when he chooses to be solemn; though to be playful was
more natural to him. "If I have lain so long stoically silent, or un-
mindful of your satirical favours, it was not so much for want of a
proper reply, as that I thought there never needed a public one; for
all people of sense would know what truth or falsehood there was in
what you said of me, without my wisely pointing it out to them. Nor
did I choose to follow your example, of being so much a self-tormentor, as to be concerned at whatever opinion of me any published
invective might infuse into people unknown to me. Even the malicious, though they may like the libel, don't always believe it." His
reason for reply is, that his silence should not be further reproached
"as a plain confession of my being a bankrupt in wit, if I don't
immediately answer those bills of discredit you have drawn upon me."
There is no doubt that Cibber perpetually found instigators to encourage these attacks; and one forcible argument he says was, that "a
disgrace, from such a pen, would stick upon me to posterity." He
seems to be aware that his acquaintance cheer him to the lists "for
their particular amusement."

† "His edition of Shakspeare proved no better than a foil to set off
the superiority of Theobald's; and Cibber bore away the palm from
him in the drama. We have an account of two attempts of Pope's,
one in each of the two principal branches of this species of poetry,
and both unsuccessful. The fate of the comedy has been already mentioned (in page 300), and the tragedy was saved from the like fate by
one not less ignominious, being condemned and burnt by his own
hands. It was called *Cleone*, and formed upon the same story as a
late one wrote and published by Mr. Dodsley with the same title in
1759. See Dodsley's Preface."—*Biographia Britannica*, 1760.

"and the hollow of his thigh was out of joint." Still,
however, he triumphed, by that singular felicity of character, that inimitable *quieté de cœur*, that honest simplicity of truth, from which flowed so warm an admiration of the genius of his adversary; and that exquisite
tact in the characters of men, which carried down this
child of airy humour to the verge of his ninetieth year,
with all the enjoyments of strong animal spirits, and all
that innocent egotism which became frequently a source
of his own raillery.* He has applied to himself the epithet "impenetrable," which was probably in the mind of
Johnson when he noticed his "impenetrable impudence."
A critic has charged him with "effrontery."† Critics

---

* Armstrong, who was a keen observer of man, has expressed his
uncommon delight in the company of Cibber. "Beside his abilities as
a writer (as a writer of comedies, Armstrong means), and the singular
variety of his powers as an actor, he was to the last one of the most
agreeable, cheerful, and best-humoured men you would ever wish to
converse with."—Warton's *Pope*, vol. iv. 160.

Cibber was one of those rare beings whose dispositions Hume
describes "as preferable to an inheritance of 10,000*l.* a year."

† Dr. Aikin, in his Biographical Dictionary, has thus written on
Cibber: "It cannot be doubted, that, at the time, the contest was more
painful to Pope than to Cibber. But Pope's satire is immortal, whereas Cibber's sarcasms are no longer read. *Cibber may therefore be
represented to future times with less credit for abilities than he really
deserves;* for he was certainly no dunce, though not, in the higher
sense of the word, a man of genius. *His effrontery and vanity* could
not be easily overcharged, even by a foe. Indeed, they are striking
features in the portrait drawn by himself." Dr. Aikin's political
morality often vented its indignation at the successful injustice of
great power! Why should not the same spirit conduct him in the
Literary Republic? With the just sentiments he has given on Cibber,
it was the duty of an intrepid critic to raise a moral feeling against the
despotism of genius, and to have protested against the arbitrary
power of Pope. It is participating in the injustice to pass it by, without even a regret at its effect.

As for Cibber himself, he declares he was *not impudent*, and I am

are apt to admit too much of traditional opinion into their own; it is necessary sometimes to correct the knowledge we receive. For my part, I can almost believe that Cibber was a *modest man!** as he was most

disposed to take his own word, for he *modestly* asserts this, in a remark on Pope's expression,

"'Cibberian forehead,'

"by which I find you modestly mean *Cibberian impudence*, as a sample of the strongest.—Sir, your humble servant—but pray, sir, in your 'Epistle to Dr. Arbuthnot' (where, by the way, in your ample description of a great Poet, you slily hook in a whole hat-full of virtues to your own character) have not you this particular line?

'And thought a *Lie*, in verse or prose, the same—'"

Cibber laments it is not so, for "any accusation in smooth verse will always sound well, though it is not tie l down to have a tittle of truth in it, when the strongest defence in poor humble prose, not having that harmonious advantage, takes nobody by the ear—very hard upon an innocent man! For suppose in prose, now, I were as confidently to insist that you were an *honest, good-natured, inoffensive creature,* would my barely saying so be any proof of it? No sure. Why then, might it not be supposed an equal truth, that both our assertions were equally false? *Yours*, when you call me *impudent; mine,* when I call you *modest,* &c. While my superiors suffer me occasionally to sit down with them, I hope it will be thought that rather the *Papal* than the *Cibberian* forehead ought to be out of countenance." I give this as a specimen of Cibber's serious reasonings—they are poor; and they had been so from a greater genius; for ridicule and satire, being only a mere abuse of eloquence, can never be effectually opposed by truisms. Satire must be repelled by satire; and Cibber's *sarcasms* obtained what Cibber's *reasonings* failed in.

* Vain as Cibber has been called, and vain as he affects to be, he has spoken of his own merits as a comic writer,—and he was a very great one,—with a manly moderation, very surprising indeed in a vain man. Pope has sung in his *Dunciad,* most harmoniously inhuman,

" How, with less reading than makes felons scape,
    Less human genius than God gives an ape,
    Small thanks to France, and none to Rome or Greece,
    A patch'd, vamp'd, future, old, revived new piece;
    'Twixt Plautus, Fletcher, Congreve, and Corneille,
    Can make a Cibber, Johnson, and Ozell."

certainly a man of genius. Cibber had lived a dissipated
life, and his philosophical indifference, with his careless
gaiety, was the breastplate which even the wit of Pope
failed to pierce. During twenty years' persecution for

Blasting as was this criticism, it could not raise the anger of the gay
and careless Cibber. Yet what could have put it to a sharper test?
Johnson and Ozell are names which have long disappeared from the
dramatic annals, and could only have been coupled with Cibber to give
an idea of what the satirist meant by "the human genius of an ape."
But listen to the mild, yet the firm tone of Cibber—he talks like
injured innocence, and he triumphs over Pope, in all the dignity of
truth.—I appeal to Cibber's posterity!

"And pray, sir, why my name under this scurvy picture? I flatter
myself, that if you had not put it there, nobody else would have
thought it like me; nor can I easily believe that you yourself do: but
perhaps you imagined it would be a laughing ornament to your verse,
and had a mind to divert other people's spleen with it as well as your
own. Now let me hold up my head a little, and then we shall see how
the features hit me." He proceeds to relate, how "many of those
plays have lived the longer for my meddling with them." He mentions several, which "had been dead to the stage out of all memory,
which have since been in a constant course of acting above these
thirty or forty years." And then he adds: "Do those altered plays
at all take from the merit of those *more successful pieces*, which were
entirely my own?—When a man is abused, he has a right to speak even
laudable truths of himself, to confront his slanderer. Let me therefore add, that my first Comedy of *The Fool in Fashion* was as much
(though not so valuable) an original, as any work Mr. Pope himself has produced. It is now forty-seven years since its first appearance on the stage, where it has kept its station, to this very day,
without ever lying one winter dormant. Nine years after this, I
brought on *The Careless Husband*, with still greater success; and was
that too

'A patch'd, vamp'd, future, old, revived new piece?'

Let the many living spectators of these plays, then, judge between us,
whether the above verses came from the honesty of a satirist, who
would be thought, like you, the upright censor of mankind. Sir, this
libel was below you! Satire, without truth, recoils upon its author,
and must, at other times, render him suspected of prejudice, even
where he may be just; as frauds, in religion, make more atheists than

his unlucky Odes, he never lost his temper; he would read to his friends the best things pointed against them, with all the spirit the authors could wish; and would himself write epigrams for the pleasure of hearing them repeated while sitting in coffee-houses; and whenever they were applauded as "Palpable hits!"—"Keen!"— "Things with a spirit in them!"—he enjoyed these attacks on himself by himself.* If this be vanity, it is at least " *Cibberian.*"

It was, indeed, the singularity of his personal character which so long injured his genius, and laid him open to the perpetual attacks of his contemporaries,† who were mean enough to ridicule undisguised foibles, but dared not be just to the redeeming virtues of his genius. Yet his genius far exceeded his literary frailties. He knew he was no poet, yet he would string wretched rhymes, even when not salaried for them; and once

converts; and the bad heart. Mr. Pope, that points an injury with verse, makes it the more unpardonable, as it is not the result of sudden passion, but of an indulged and slowly-meditating ill-nature. What a merry mixed mortal has nature made you, that can debase that strength and excellence of genius to the lowest human weakness, that of offering unprovoked injuries, at the hazard of your being ridiculous too, when the venom you spit falls short of your aim!" I have quoted largely, to show that Cibber was capable of exerting a dignified remonstrance, as well as pointing the lightest, yet keenest, shafts of sarcastic wit.

* Ayre's "Memoirs of Pope," vol. ii. p. 82.
† Even the "Grub-street Journal" had its jest on his appointment to the laureateship. In No. 52 was the following epigram:—

"Well, said Apollo, still 'tis mine
To give the real laurel:
For that my Pope, my son divine,
Of rivals ends the quarrel.
But guessing who would have the luck
To be the birth-day fibber,
I thought of Dennis, Tibbald, Duck,
But never dreamt of Cibber!"—ED.

wrote an Essay on Cicero's character, for which his
dotage was scarcely an apology ;—so much he preferred
amusement to prudence.* Another foible was to act
tragedies with a squeaking voice,† and to write them

* It may be reasonably doubted, however, if vanity had not something to do with this—the vanity of appearing as a philosophical
writer, and astonishing the friends who had considered him only as a
good comedian. The volume was magnificently printed in quarto on
fine paper, "for the author," in 1747. It is entitled 'The Character
and Conduct of Cicero Considered, from the History of his Life by the
Rev. Dr. Middleton ; with occasional Essays and Observations upon
the most Memorable Facts and Persons during that Period." The
entire work is a series of somewhat too-familiar notes on the various
passages of "Cicero's Life and Times," as narrated by Middleton. He
terms the unsettled state after the death of Sylla "an uncomfortable
time for those sober citizens who had a mind and a right to be quiet."
His professional character breaks forth when he speaks of Roscius
instructing Cicero in acting ; and in the very commencement of his
grave labour he rambles back to the theatre to quote a scene from
Vanbrugh's *Relapse*. as a proof how little fashionable readers *think*
while they *read*. Colley's well-meaning but free-and-easy reflections
on the gravities of Roman history, in the progress of his work, are
remarkable, and have all the author's coarse common-sense, but very
little depth or refinement.—ED.

† With what good-humour he retorts a piece of sly malice of Pope's ;
who, in the notes to the *Dunciad*, after quoting Jacob's account of
Cibber's talents. adds—" Mr. Jacob omitted to remark that he is particularly admirable in tragedy." To which Cibber rejoins—" Ay, sir,
and your remark has omitted, too, that (with all his commendations) I
can't dance upon the rope. or make a saddle, nor play upon the organ.
My dear, dear Mr. Pope, how could a man of your stinging capacity
let so tame, so low a reflection escape him ? Why, this hardly rises
above the petty malice of Miss Molly. 'Ay, ay, you may think my
sister as handsome as you please, but if you were to see her legs !'
If I have made so many crowded theatres laugh, and in the right
place, too. for above forty years together. am I to make up the number
of your dunces, because I have not the equal talent of making them
cry too ? Make it your own case. Is what you have excelled in at all
the worse for your having so dismally dabbled in the farce of *Three
Hours after Marriage?* What mighty reason will the world have to
laugh at my weakness in tragedy, more than at yours in comedy?"

with a genius about the same size for the sublime; but
the malice of his contemporaries seemed to forget that
he was creating new dramatic existences in the exquisite
personifications of his comic characters; and was producing some of our standard comedies, composed with
such real genius, that they still support the reputation
of the English stage.

In the "Apology for his Life," Cibber had shown
himself a generous and an ill-treated adversary, and at all
times was prodigal of his eulogiums, even after the death
of Pope; but, when remonstrance and good temper
failed to sheathe with their oil the sharp sting of the
wasp, as his weakest talent was not the ludicrous, he
resolved to gain the laughers over, and threw Pope into

I will preserve one anecdote of that felicity of temper—that undisturbed good-humour which never abandoned Cibber in his most dis-
tressful moments. When he brought out, in 1724, his *Cæsar in Egypt*,
at a great expense, and "a beggarly account of empty boxes" was the
result, it raised some altercations between the poet and his brother
managers, the bard still struggling for another and another night. At
length he closed the quarrel with a pun, which confessed the misfortune,
with his own good-humour. In a periodical publication of the times I
find the circumstance recorded in this neat epigram:—

On the Sixth Night of CIBBER's *"Cæsar in Egypt."*

When the pack'd audience from their posts retired,
And Julius in a general hiss expired;
Sage Booth to Cibber cried, "Compute our gains!
These dogs of Egypt, and their dowdy queins,
But ill requite these habits and these scenes,
To rob Corneille for such a motley piece:
His geese were swans; but zounds! thy swans are geese!"
Rubbing his firm invulnerable brow,
The bard replied—"The critics must allow
'Twas ne'er in *Cæsar's destiny* TO RUN!"
Wilks bow'd, and bless'd the gay pacific pun.

a very ridiculous attitude.*   It was extorted from Cibber
by this insulting line of Pope's:—

> And has not Colley, too, his Lord and w—e ?

It seems that Pope had once the same!   But a ridiculous
story, suited to the taste of the loungers, nettled Pope
more than the keener remonstrances and the honest
truths which Cibber has urged.   Those who write libels,
invite imitation.

Besides the two letters addressed by Cibber to Pope,
this quarrel produced a moral trifle, or rather a philosophical curiosity, respecting Cibber's own character,
which is stamped with the full impression of all its
originality.

The title, so expressive of its design, and the whim
and good-humour of the work, which may be considered
as a curious supplement to the "Apology for his Life,"
could scarcely have been imagined, and most certainly
could not have been executed, but by the genius who

---

* A wicked wag of a lord had enticed Pope into a tavern, and laid
a love-plot against his health. Cibber describes his resolute interfer-
ence by snatching "our little Homer by the heels. This was done
for the honour of our nation. Homer would have been too serious a
sacrifice to our evening's amusement." He has metamorphosed our
Apollo into a "Tomtit;" but the Ovidian warmth, however ludicrous,
will not *now* admit of a narrative. This story, by our comic writer,
was accompanied by a print, that was seen by more persons, probably,
than read the *Dunciad.* In his second letter, Cibber, alluding to the
vexation of Pope on this ridiculous story, observes—"To have been
exposed as *a bad man*, ought to have given thee thrice the concern of
being shown a *ridiculous lover.*" And now that he had discovered that
he could touch the nerves of Pope, he throws out one of the most
ludicrous analogies to the figure of our bard:—"When crawling in
thy dangerous deed of darkness, I gently, with a finger and a thumb,
picked off thy small round body by thy long legs, like a spider making
love in a cobweb."

dared it. I give the title in the note.* It is a curious
exemplification of what Shaftesbury has so fancifully
described as "self-inspection." This little work is a
conversation between "Mr. Frankly and his old acquaintance, Colley Cibber." Cibber had the spirit of making
this Mr. Frankly speak the bitterest things against himself; and he must have been an attentive reader of all
the keenest reproaches his enemies ever had thrown out.
This caustic censor is not a man of straw, set up to be
easily knocked down. He has as much vivacity and wit
as Cibber himself, and not seldom has the better of the
argument. But the gravity and the levity blended in
this little piece form admirable contrasts : and Cibber,
in this varied effusion, acquires all our esteem for that
open simplicity, that unalterable good-humour which
flowed from nature, and that fine spirit that touches
everything with life; yet, as he himself confesses, the
main accusation of Mr. Frankly, that "his philosophical
air will come out at last mere vanity in masquerade,"
may be true.

I will attempt to collect some specimens of this extraordinary production, because they harmonise with the
design of the present work, and afford principles, in regard to preserving an equability of temper, which may
guide us in Literary Quarrels.

Frankly observes, on Cibber's declaration that he is
not uneasy at Pope's satire, that "no blockhead is so
dull as not to be sore when he is called so ; and (you'll
excuse me) if that were to be your own case, why should

* "The EGOTIST, or Colley upon Cibber ; being his own picture retouched to so *plain* a likeness that no one *now* would have the face to
own it BUT HIMSELF.

'But one stroke more, and that shall be my last.'

London, 1743.   DRYDEN."

we believe you would not be as uneasy at it as another
blockhead ?

Author. This is pushing me pretty home indeed; but I
wont give out. For as it is not at all inconceivable,
that a blockhead of my size may have a particular knack
of doing some useful thing that might puzzle a wiser
man to be master of, will not that blockhead still have
something in him to be conceited of? If so, allow me
but the vanity of supposing I may have had some such
possible knack, and you will not wonder (though in
many other points I may still be a blockhead) that I
may, notwithstanding, be contented with my condition.

Frankly. Is it not commendable, in a man of parts, to
be warmly concerned for his reputation ?

Author. In what regards his honesty or honour, I will
make some allowance; but for the reputation of his
parts, not one tittle.

Frankly. How! not to be concerned for what half the
learned world are in a continual war about.

Author. So are another half about religion; but neither Turk or Pope, swords or anathemas, can alter truth!
There it stands! always visible to reason, self-defended
and immovable! Whatever it *was*, or *is*, it ever *will be!*
As no attack can alter, so no defence can add to its
proportion.

Frankly. At this rate, you pronounce all controversies
in wit to be either needless or impertinent.

Author. When one in a hundred happens *not* to be so,
or to make amends for being either by its pleasantry,
we ought in justice to allow it a great rarity. A reply to a just satire or criticism will seldom be thought
better of.

Frankly. May not a reply be a good one ?

Author. Yes, but never absolutely necessary; for as
your work (or reputation) must have been good or bad,

before it was censured, your reply to that censure could not alter it: it would still be but what it was. If it was good, the attack could not hurt it: if bad, the reply could not mend it.*

Frankly. But slander is not always so impotent as you seem to suppose it; men of the best sense may be misled by it, or, by their not inquiring after truth, may never come at it; and the vulgar, as they are less apt to be good than ill-natured, often mistake malice for wit, and have an uncharitable joy in commending it. Now, when this is the case, is not a tame silence, upon being satirically libelled, as liable to be thought guilt or stupidity, as to be the result of innocence or temper?— Self-defence is a very natural and just excuse for a reply.

Author. Be it so! But still that does not always make it necessary; for though slander, by their not

---

* How many good authors might pursue their studies in quiet, would they never reply to their critics but on matters of fact, in which their honour may be involved. I have seen very tremendous criticisms on some works of real genius, like serpents on marble columns, wind and dart about, and spit their froth, but they die away on the pillars that enabled them to erect their malignant forms to the public eye. They fall in due time; and weak must be the substance of that pillar which does not stand, and look as beautiful, when the serpents have crawled over it, as before. Dr. Brown, in his " Letter to Bishop Lowth," has laid down an axiom in literary criticism :—" *A mere literary attack,* however well or ill-founded, would not easily have drawn me into a *public expostulation ;* for every man's true literary character is best seen in his own writings. Critics may rail, disguise, insinuate, or pervert; yet still the object of their censures lies equally open to all the world. Thus the world becomes a competent judge of the merits of the work animadverted on. Hence, the mere *author* hath a fair chance for a fair decision, at least among the judicious; and it is of no mighty consequence what opinions the *injudicious* form concerning mental abilities. For this reason, I have never replied to any of those numerous critics who have on different occasions honoured me with their regard."

weighing it, may pass upon some few people of sense for
truth, and might draw great numbers of the vulgar into
its party, the mischief can never be of long duration. *A
satirical slander, that has no truth to support it, is
only a great fish upon dry land: it may flounce and
fling, and make a fretful pother, but it wont bite you;
you need not knock it on the head; it will soon lie still,
and die quietly of itself.*

Frankly. The single-sheet critics will find you employ-
ment.

Author. Indeed they wont. I'm not so mad as to
think myself a match for the invulnerable.

Frankly. Have a care; there's Foulwit; though he
can't feel, he can bite.

Author. Ay, so will bugs and fleas; but that's only
for sustenance: everything must feed, you know; and
your creeping critics are a sort of vermin, that if they
could come to a king, would not spare him; yet, whenever they can persuade others to laugh at their jest upon
me, I will honestly make one of the number; but I must
ask their pardon, if that should be all the reply I can
afford them."

This " boy of seventy odd," for such he was when he
wrote " The Egotist," unfolds his character by many
lively personal touches. He declares he could not have
" given the world so finished a coxcomb as Lord Fop-
pington, if he had not found a good deal of the same
stuff in himself to make him with." He addresses " A
Postscript, To those few unfortunate Readers and
Writers who may not have more sense than the
Author:" and he closes, in all the fulness of his spirit,
with a piece of consolation for those who are so cruelly
attacked by superior genius.

" Let us then, gentlemen. who have the misfortune to
lie thus at the mercy of those whose natural parts hap-

pen to be stronger than our own—let us, I say, make the most of our sterility! Let us double and treble the ranks of our thickness, that we may form an impregnable phalanx, and stand every way in front to the enemy! or, would you still be liable to less hazard, lay but yourselves down, as I do, flat and quiet upon your faces, when Pride, Malice, Envy, Wit, or Prejudice let fly their formidable shot at you, what odds is it they don't all whistle over your head? Thus, too, though we may want the artillery of missive wit to make reprisals, we may at least in security bid them kiss the tails we have turned to them. Who knows but, by this our supine, or rather prone serenity, their disappointed valour may become their own vexation? Or let us yet, at worst, but solidly stand our ground, like so many defensive stone-posts, and we may defy the proudest Jehu of them all to drive over us. Thus, gentlemen, you see that Insensibility is not without its comforts; and as I give you no worse advice than I have taken myself, and found my account in, I hope you will have the hardness to follow it, for your own good and the glory of

"Your impenetrable humble servant,

"C. C."

After all, one may perceive, that though the good-humour of poor Cibber was real, still the immortal satire of Pope had injured his higher feelings. He betrays his secret grief at his close, while he seems to be sporting with his pen; and though he appears to confide in the falsity of the satire as his best chance for saving him from it, still he feels that the caustic ink of such a satirist must blister and spot wherever it falls. The anger of Warburton, and the sternness of Johnson, who seem always to have considered an actor as an inferior being among men of genius, have degraded Cibber. They never suspected that "a blockhead of his size could do

what wiser men could not," and, as a fine comic genius,
command a whole province in human nature.

POPE AND ADDISON.

THE quarrel between Pope and Addison originated in one of the infirmities of genius—a subject of inquiry even after their death, by
Sir William Blackstone—Pope courts Addison—suspects Addison
of jealousy—Addison's foible to be considered a great poet—interview between the rivals, of which the result was the portrait of Atticus, for which Addison was made to sit.

AMONG the Literary Quarrels of Pope one acquires
dignity and interest from the characters of both
parties. It closed by producing the severest, but the
most masterly portrait of one man of genius, composed
by another, which has ever been hung on the satiric
Parnassus for the contemplation of ages. Addison must
descend to posterity with the dark spots of Atticus
staining a purity of character which had nearly proved
immaculate.

The friendship between Pope and Addison was interrupted by one of the infirmities of genius. Tempers of
watchful delicacy gather up in silence and darkness
motives so shadowy in their origin, and of such minute
growth, that, never breaking out into any open act, they
escape all other eyes but those of the parties themselves.
These causes of enmity are too subtle to bear the touch;
they cannot be inquired after, nor can they be described;
and it may be said that the minds of such men have
rather quarrelled than they themselves: they utter no
complaints, but they avoid each other. All the world

perceived that two authors of the finest genius had separated from motives on which both were silent, but which had evidently operated with equal force on both. Their admirers were very general, and at a time when literature divided with politics the public interest, the best feelings of the nation were engaged in tracking the obscure commencements and the secret growth of this literary quarrel, in which the amiable and moral qualities of Addison, and the gratitude and honour of Pope, were equally involved. The friends of either party pretended that their chiefs entertained a reciprocal regard for each other, while the illustrious characters themselves were living in a state of hostility. Even long after these literary heroes were departed, the same interest was general among the lovers of literature; but those obscure motives which had only influenced two minds—those imperceptible events, which are only events as they are watched by the jealousy of genius—eluded the most anxious investigation. Yet so lasting and so powerful was the interest excited by this literary quarrel, that within a few years, the elegant mind of Sir William Blackstone withdrew from the severity of profounder studies to inquire into the causes of a quarrel which was still exciting the most opposite opinions. Blackstone has judged and summed up; but though he evidently inclines to favour Addison, by throwing into the balance some explanation for the silence of Addison against the audible complaints of Pope; though sometimes he pleads as well as judges, and infers as well as proves; yet even Blackstone has not taken on himself to deliver a decision. His happy genius has only honoured literary history by the masterly force and luminous arrangement of investigation, to which, since the time of Bayle, it has been too great a stranger.*

* Sir William Blackstone's Discussion on the Quarrel between

At this day, removed from all personal influence and
affections, and furnished with facts which contemporaries
could not command, we take no other concern in this
literary quarrel but as far as curiosity and truth delight
us in the study of human nature. We are now of no
party—we are only historians!

Pope was a young writer when introduced to Addison
by the intervention of that generously-minded friend of
both, Steele. Addison eulogised Pope's "Essay on
Criticism;" and this fine genius covering with his wing
an unfledged bardling, conferred a favour which, in the
estimation of a poet, claims a life of indelible gratitude.

Pope zealously courted Addison by his poetical aid on
several important occasions; he gave all the dignity that
fine poetry could confer on the science of medals, which
Addison had written on, and wrote the finest prologue
in the language for the Whig tragedy of his friend.
Dennis attacked, and Pope defended *Cato*.* Addison

Addison and Pope was communicated by Dr. Kippis in his "Biographia Britannica," vol. i. p. 56. Blackstone is there designated as ''a
gentleman of considerable rank, to whom the public is obliged for
works of much higher importance."

* Dennis asserts in one of his pamphlets that Pope, fermenting
with envy at the success of Addison's *Cato*, went to Lintot, and persuaded him to engage this redoubted critic to write the remarks on
Cato—that Pope's gratitude to Dennis for having complied with his
request was the well-known narrative of Dennis ''being placed as a
lunatic in the hands of Dr. Norris, a curer of mad people, at his house
in Hatton-garden, though at the same time I appeared publicly every
day, both in the park and in the town.'' Can we suppose that Dennis
tells a falsehood respecting Pope's desiring Lintot to engage Dennis to
write down *Cato?* If true, did Pope wish to see Addison degraded,
and at the same time take an opportunity of ridiculing the critic, without, however, answering his arguments? The secret history of
literature is like that of politics!

[Dennis took a strong dislike to Addison's *Cato*, and his style of
criticism is thus alluded to in the humorous account of his frenzy
written by Pope: ''On all sides of his room were pinned a great many
sheets of a tragedy called *Cato*, with notes on the margin by his ow-

might have disapproved both of the manner and the matter of the defence; but he did more—he insulted Pope by a letter to Dennis, which Dennis eagerly published as Pope's severest condemnation. An alienation of friendship must have already taken place, but by no overt act on Pope's side.

Not that, however, Pope had not found his affections weakened: the dark hints scattered in his letters show that something was gathering in his mind. Warburton, from his familiar intercourse with Pope, must be allowed to have known his literary concerns more than any one; and when he drew up the narrative,* seems to me to have stated uncouthly, but expressively, the progressive state of Pope's feelings. According to that narrative, Pope "reflected," that after he had first published "The Rape of the Lock," then nothing more than a hasty *jeu d'esprit*, when he communicated to Addison his very original project of the whole sylphid machinery, Addison chilled the ardent bard with his coldness, advised him against any alteration, and to leave it as "a delicious little thing, *merum sal*." It was then, says Warburton, "Mr. Pope began to *open his eyes* to Addison's character." But when afterwards he discovered that Tickell's Homer was opposed to his, and judged, as Warburton says, "by *laying many odd circumstances* together," that Addison,† and not Tickell, was the author—the

hand. The words *absurd, monstrous, execrable*, were everywhere written in such large characters, that I could read them without my spectacles." Warton says that "Addison highly disapproved of this bitter satire on Dennis, and Pope was not a little chagrined at this disapprobation; for the narrative was intended to court the favour of Addison, by defending his *Cato*: in which seeming defence Addison was far from thinking our author sincere."]

* In the notes to the Prologue to the Satires.

† Pope's conjecture was perfectly correct. Dr. Warton confirms it from a variety of indisputable authorities.—Warton's "Pope," vol. iv. p. 34.

alienation on Pope's side was complete. No open breach indeed had yet taken place between the rival authors, who, as jealous of dominion as two princes, would still demonstrate, in their public edicts, their inviolable regard; while they were only watching the advantageous moment when they might take arms against each other.

Still Addison publicly bestowed great encomiums on Pope's *Iliad*, although he had himself composed the rival version, and in private preferred his own.* He did this with the same ease he had continued its encouragement while Pope was employed on it. We are astonished to discover such deep politics among literary Machiavels! Addison had certainly raised up a literary party. Sheridan, who wrote nearly with the knowledge of a contemporary, in his " Life of Swift," would naturally use the language and the feelings of the time ; and in describing Ambrose Phillips, he adds, he was "one of Mr. Addison's little senate."

But in this narrative I have dropt some material parts. Pope believed that Addison had employed Gildon to write against him, and had encouraged Phillips to asperse his character.† We cannot, now, quite demonstrate these alleged facts; but we can show that Pope believed them, and that Addison does not appear to have refuted them.‡

* In the " Freeholder," May. 1716.

† Pope himself thus related the matter to Spence: " Phillips seemed to have been encouraged to abuse me in coffee-houses and conversations: and Gildon wrote a thing about Wycherly, in which he had abused both me and my relations very grossly. Lord Warwick himself told me one day that it was in vain for me to endeavour to be well with Mr. Addison : that his jealous temper would never admit of a settled friendship between us, and to convince me of what he had said, assured me that Addison had encouraged Gildon to publish those scandals, and had given him ten guineas after they were published."—ED.

‡ The strongest parts of Sir William Blackstone's discussion turn on certain inaccurate dates of Ruffhead, in his statements, which show them to be inconsistent with the times when they are alleged to have

Such tales, whether entirely false or partially true, may be considered in this inquiry of little amount. The greater events must regulate the lesser ones.*

Was Addison, then, jealous of Pope? Addison, in every respect, then, his superior; of established literary fame when Pope was yet young; preceding him in age

happened. These erroneous dates had been detected in an able article in the Monthly Review on that work, April, 1769. Ruffhead is a tasteless, confused, and unskilful writer—Sir William has laid great stress on the incredible story of Addison paying Gildon to write against Pope, "a man so amiable in his moral character." It is possible that the Earl of Warwick, who conveyed the information, might have been a malicious, lying youth; but then Pope had some knowledge of mankind—he believed the story, for he wrote instantly, with honest though heated feelings, to Addison, and sent him, at that moment, the first sketch of the character of Atticus. Addison used him very civilly ever after—but it does not appear that Addison ever contradicted the tale of the officious Earl. All these facts, which Pope repeated many years after to Spence, Sir William was not acquainted with, for they were transcribed from Spence's papers by Johnson, after Blackstone had written. [This is fully in accordance with his previous conduct, as he described it to Spence; on the first notification of the Earl of Warwick's news, "the next day when I was heated with what I had heard, I wrote a letter to Mr. Addison, to let him know that I was not unacquainted with this behaviour of his; that if I was to speak severely of him, in return for it, it should not be in such a dirty way; and that I should rather tell himself freely of his faults, and allow his good qualities: and that it should be something in the following manner: I then adjoined the first sketch of what has since been called my Satire on Addison. Mr. Addison used me very civilly ever after, and never did me any injustice that I know of from that time to his death, which was about three years after.]"

* That Addison did occasionally divert Pope's friends from him, appears from the advice which Lady Mary Wortley Montague says he gave to her—"Leave him as soon as you can, he will certainly play you some devilish trick else: he has an appetite to satire." Malone thinks this may have been said under the irritation produced by the verses on Addison, which Pope sent to him, as described above. Pope's love of satire, and unflinching use of it, was as conspicuous as Addison's nervous dislike to it.—ED.

and rank; and fortunate in all the views of human ambition.   But what if Addison's foible was that of being
considered a great poet ?   His political poetry had raised
him to an undue elevation, and the growing celebrity of
Pope began to offend him, not with the appearance of a
meek rival, with whom he might have held divided empire, but as a master-spirit, that was preparing to reign
alone.   It is certain that Addison was the most feeling
man alive at the fate of his poetry.   At the representa-
tion of his *Cato*, such was his agitation, that had *Cato*
been condemned, the life of Addison might, too, have
been shortened.   When a wit had burlesqued some lines
of this dramatic poem, his uneasiness at the innocent
banter was equally oppressive ; nor could he rest, till, by
the interposition of a friend, he prevailed upon the author
to burn them.*

To the facts already detailed, and to this disposition in
Addison's temper, and to the quick and active suspicions
of Pope, irritable, and ambitious of all the sovereignty
of poetry, we may easily conceive many others of those
obscure motives, and invisible events, which none but
Pope, alienated every day more and more from his affections for Addison, too acutely perceived, too profoundly
felt, and too unmercifully avenged.   These are alluded
to when the satirist sings—

>Damn with faint praise; assent with civil leer;
>And, without sneering, teach the rest to sneer;
>Willing to wound, and yet afraid to strike ;
>Just hint a fault, and hesitate dislike, &c.

Accusations crowded faster than the pen could write
them down.   Pope never composed with more warmth.
No one can imagine that Atticus was an ideal personage,
touched as it is with all the features of an extraordinary

* From Lord Egmont's MS. Collections.—See the "Addenda to
Kippis's Biographia Britannica."

individual. In a word, it was recognised instantly by
the individual himself; and it was suppressed by Pope
for near twenty years, before he suffered it to escape to
the public.

It was some time during their avowed rupture, for the
exact period has not been given, that their friends promoted a meeting between these two great men. After a
mutual lustration, it was imagined they might have expiated their error, and have been restored to their original purity. The interview did take place between the
rival wits, and was productive of some very characteristic ebullitions, strongly corroborative of the facts as they
have been stated here. This extraordinary interview
has been frequently alluded to. There can be no doubt
of the genuineness of the narrative; but I know not on
what authority it came into the world.*

* The earliest and most particular narrative of this remarkable
interview I have hitherto only traced to "Memoirs of the Life and
Writings of A. Pope, Esq., by William Ayre, Esq.," 1745, vol. i. p.
100. This work comes in a very suspicious form; it is a huddled
compilation, yet contains some curious matters; and pretends, in the
title-page, to be occasionally drawn from "original MSS. and the testimonies of persons of honour." He declares, in the preface, that he
and his friends "had means and some helps which were never public."
He sometimes appeals to several noble friends of Pope as his authorities. But the mode of its publication, and that of its execution, are
not in its favour. These volumes were written within six months of
the decease of our poet; have no publisher's name; and yet the
author, whoever he was, took out "a patent, under his majesty's
royal signet," for securing the copyright. This Ayre is so obscure an
author, though a translator of Tasso's "Aminta," that he seems to
have escaped even the minor chronicles of literature. At the time of
its publication there appeared "Remarks on Squire Ayre's Memoirs of
Pope." The writer pretends he has discovered him to be only one of
the renowned Edmund Curll's "squires," who, about that time, had created an order of literary squires, ready to tramp at the funeral of every
great personage with his life. The "Remarker" then addresses Curll,
and insinuates he speaks from personal knowledge of the man:—"You
have an adversaria of title-pages of your own contrivance, and which

The interview between Addison and Pope took place
in the presence of Steele and Gay. They met with cold
civility. Addison's reserve wore away, as was usual
with him, when wine and conversation imparted some
warmth to his native phlegm. At a moment the generous Steele deemed auspicious, he requested Addison
would perform his promise in renewing his friendship
with Pope. Pope expressed his desire : he said he was
willing to hear his faults, and preferred candour and
severity rather than forms of complaisance; but he spoke
in a manner as conceiving Addison, and not himself, had
been the aggressor. So much like their humblest in-
feriors do great men act under the influence of common
passions: Addison was overcome with anger, which cost
him an effort to suppress; but, in the formal speech he
made, he reproached Pope with indulging a vanity that
far exceeded his merit; that he had not yet attained to
the excellence he imagined; and observed, that his verses
had a different air when Steele and himself corrected
them; and, on this occasion, reminded Pope of a particular line which Steele had improved in the "Messiah."*

your authors are to write books to. Among what you call *the occasional, or black list*, I have seen Memoirs of Dean Swift, Pope, &c."
Curll, indeed, was then sending forth many pseudo squires, with lives
of "Congreve," "Mrs. Oldfield," &c.; all which contained some
curious particulars, picked up in coffee-houses, conversations, or
pamphlets of the day. This William Ayre I accept as "a squire of
low degree," but a real personage. As for this interview, Ayre was
certainly incompetent to the invention of a single stroke of the conversations detailed: where he obtained all these interesting particulars, I
have not discovered. Johnson alludes to this interview, states some
of its results, but refers to no other authority than floating rumours.

* The line stood originally, and nearly literally copied from Isaiah—

"He wipes the tears for ever from our eyes;"

which Steele retouched, as it now stands—

"From every face he wipes off every tear."

Dr. Warton prefers the rejected verse. The latter, he thinks, has

Addison seems at that moment to have forgotten that he
had trusted, for the last line of his own dramatic poem,
rather to the inspiration of the poet he was so contemptuously lecturing than to his own.* He proceeded
with detailing all the abuse the herd of scribblers had
heaped on Pope; and by declaring that his Homer was
"an ill-executed thing," and Tickell's had all the spirit.
We are told, he concluded "in a low hollow voice of
feigned temper," in which he asserted that he had ceased
to be solicitous about his own poetical reputation since
he had entered into more public affairs; but, from friendship for Pope, desired him to be more humble, if he
wished to appear a better man to the world.

When Addison had quite finished schooling his little
rebel, Gay, mild and timid (for it seems, with all his love
for Pope, his expectations from the court, from Addison's
side, had tethered his gentle heart), attempted to say
something. But Pope, in a tone far more spirited than
all of them, without reserve told Addison that he appealed from his judgment, and did not esteem him able
to correct his verses; upbraided him as a pensioner from
early youth, directing the learning which had been obtained by the public money to his own selfish desire of
power, and that he "had always endeavoured to cut
down new-fledged merit." The conversation now became a contest, and was broken up without ceremony
Such was the notable interview between two rival wits,

too much of modern quaintness. The difficulty of choice lies between
that naked simplicity which scarcely affects, and those strokes of art
which are too apparent.

* The last line of Addison's tragedy read originally--

"And oh! 'twas this that ended Cato's life."

A very weak line, which was altered at the suggestion of Pope as it
stands at present:—

"And robs the guilty world of Cato's life."—ED.

which only ended in strengthening their literary quarrel;
and sent back the enraged satirist to his inkstand, where
he composed a portrait, for which Addison was made to
sit, with the fine *chiar' oscuro* of Horace, and with as
awful and vindictive features as the sombre hand of
Juvenal could have designed.

BOLINGBROKE AND MALLET'S POST-HUMOUS QUARREL WITH POPE.

LORD BOLINGBROKE affects violent resentment for Pope's pretended
breach of confidence in having printed his "Patriot King"—War
burton's apology for Pope's disinterested intentions—Bolingbroke
instigates Mallet to libel Pope, after the poet's death—The real motive for libelling Pope was Bolingbroke's personal hatred of Warburton, for the ascendancy the latter had obtained over the poet—
Some account of their rival conflicts—Bolingbroke had unsettled
Pope's religious opinions, and Warburton had confirmed his faith—
Pope, however, refuses to abjure the Catholic religion—Anecdote
of Pope's anxiety respecting a future state—Mallet's intercourse
with Pope : anecdote of "The Apollo Vision," where Mallet mistook
a sarcasm for a compliment—Mallet's character—Why Leonidas
Glover declined writing the Life of Marlborough—Bolingbroke's
character hit off—Warburton, the concealed object of this posthumous quarrel with Pope.

ON the death of Pope, 1500 copies of one of Lord
Bolingbroke's works, "The Patriot King," were
discovered to have been secretly printed by Pope, but
never published. The honest printer presented the
whole to his lordship, who burned the edition in his
gardens at Battersea. The MS. had been delivered to
our poet by his lordship, with a request to print a few

copies for its better preservation, and for the use of a few
friends.

Bolingbroke affected to feel the most lively resentment
for what he chose to stigmatise as "a breach of confidence." "His thirst of vengeance," said Johnson, "in-
cited him to blast the memory of the man over whom he
had wept in his last struggles; and he employed Mallet,
another friend of Pope, to tell the tale to the public with
all its aggravations. Warburton, whose heart was warm
with his legacy, and tender by the recent separation,"
apologised for Pope. The irregular conduct which Bolingbroke stigmatised as a breach of trust, was attributed
to a desire of perpetuating the work of his friend, who
might have capriciously destroyed it. Our poet could
have no selfish motive; he could not gratify his vanity
by publishing the work as his own, nor his avarice by
its sale, which could never have taken place till the death
of its author; a circumstance not likely to occur during
Pope's lifetime.*

The vindictive rage of Bolingbroke; the bitter invective he permitted Mallet to publish, as the editor of
his works; and the two anonymous pamphlets of the
latter, which I have noticed in the article of Warburton;
are effects much too disproportionate to the cause which
is usually assigned. Johnson does not develope the secret motives of what he has energetically termed "Bolingbroke's thirst of vengeance." He and Mallet carried

* At the time, to season the tale for the babble of Literary Tattlers,
it was propagated that Pope intended, on the death of Bolingbroke, to
sell this eighteenpenny pamphlet at a guinea a copy; which would
have produced an addition of as many hundreds to the thousands
which the poet had honourably reaped from his Homer. This was
the ridiculous lie of the day, which lasted long enough to obtain its
purpose, and to cast an odium on the shade of Pope. Pope must have
been a miserable calculator of *survivorships*, if ever he had reckoned
on this.

their secret revenge beyond all bounds: the lordly stoic
and the irritated bardling, under the cloak of anonymous
calumny, have but ill-concealed the malignity of their
passions. Let anonymous calumniators recollect, in the
midst of their dark work, that if they escape the detection of their contemporaries, their reputation, if they
have any to lose, will not probably elude the researches
of the historian;—a fatal witness against them at the
tribunal of posterity.

The preface of Mallet to the "Patriot King" of Bolingbroke, produced a literary quarrel: and more pamphlets
than perhaps I have discovered were published on this
occasion.

Every lover of literature was indignant to observe
that the vain and petulant Mallet, under the protection
of Pope's

Guide, philosopher, and friend!

should have been permitted to have aspersed Pope with
the most degrading language. Pope is here always
designated as "This Man." Thus " *This Man* was no
sooner dead than Lord Bolingbroke received information
that an entire edition of 1500 copies of these papers had
been printed; that this very *Man* had corrected the
press, &c." Could one imagine that this was the Tully
of England, describing our Virgil? For Mallet was but
the mouthpiece of Bolingbroke.

After a careful detection of many facts concerning the
parties now before us, I must attribute the concealed
motive of this outrage on Pope to the election the dying
poet made of Warburton as his editor. A mortal hatred
raged between Bolingbroke and Warburton. The philosophical lord had seen the mighty theologian ravish the
prey from his grasp. Although Pope held in idolatrous
veneration the genius of Bolingbroke, yet had this literary superstition been gradually enlightened by the

energy of Warburton. They were his good and his evil genii in a dreadful conflict, wrestling to obtain the entire possession of the soul of the mortal. Bolingbroke and Warburton one day disputed before Pope, and parted never to meet again. The will of Pope bears the trace of his divided feelings: he left his MSS. to Bolingbroke as his executor, but his works to Warburton as his editor. The secret history of Bolingbroke and Warburton with Pope is little known: the note will supply it.*

* Splendid as was the genius of Bolingbroke, the gigantic force of Warburton obtained the superiority. Had the contest solely depended on the effusions of genius, Bolingbroke might have prevailed; but an object more important than human interests induced the poet to throw himself into the arms of Warburton.

The "Essay on Man" had been reformed by the subtle aid of Warburton, in opposition to the objectionable principles which Boling-broke had infused into his system of philosophy: this, no doubt, had vexed Bolingbroke. But another circumstance occurred of a more mortifying nature. When Pope one day showed Warburton Boling-broke's "Letters on the Study and Use of History," printed, but not published, and concealing the name of the author, Warburton not only made several very free strictures on that work, but particularly attacked a digression concerning the authenticity of the Old Testament Pope requested him to write his remarks down as they had occurred, which he instantly did; and Pope was so satisfied with them, that he crossed out the digression in the printed book, and sent the animadversions to Lord Bolingbroke, then at Paris. The style of the great dogmatist, thrown out in heat, must no doubt have contained many fiery particles, all which fell into the most inflammable of minds. Popo soon discovered his officiousness was received with indignation. Yet when Bolingbroke afterwards met Warburton he dissimulated: he used the language of compliment, but in a tone which claimed homage. The two most arrogant geniuses who ever lived, in vain exacted submission from each other: they could allow of no divided empire, and they were born to hate each other. Bolingbroke suppressed his sore feelings, for at that very time he was employed in collecting matter to refute the objections; treasuring up his secret vengeance against Pope and Warburton, which he threw out immediately on the death of Pope. I collect these particulars from Ruffhead, p. 527, and when-ever, in that volume, Warburton's name is introduced, it must be con-sidered as coming from himself.

But how did the puny Mallet stand connected with these great men? By the pamphlets published during this literary quarrel he appears to have enjoyed a more intimate intercourse with them than is known. In one of them he is characterised "as a fellow who, while Mr. Pope lived, was as diligent in licking his feet, as he is now in licking your lordship's; and who, for the sake of giving himself an air of importance, in being joined with you, and for the vanity of saying 'the Author and I,'— 'the Editor and me,'—has sacrificed all his pretensions to friendship, honour, and humanity."* An anecdote in this pamphlet assigns a sufficient motive to excite some wrath in a much less irritable animal than the self-important editor of Bolingbroke's Works. The anecdote may be distinguished as

THE APOLLO VISION.

"The editor (Mallet) being in company with the per-

The reasonings of Bolingbroke appear at times to have disturbed the religious faith of our poet, and he owed much to Warburton in having that faith confirmed. But Pope rejected, with his characteristic good sense, Warburton's tampering with him to abjure the Catholic religion. On the belief of a future state, Pope seems often to have meditated with great anxiety; and an anecdote is recorded of his latest hours, which shows how strongly that important belief affected him. A day or two before his death he was at times delirious, and about four o'clock in the morning he rose from bed and went to the library, where a friend who was watching him found him busily writing. He persuaded him to desist, and withdrew the paper he had written. The subject of the thoughts of the delirious poet was a new theory on the "Immortality of the Soul," in which he distinguished between those material objects which tended to strengthen his conviction, and those which weakened it. The paper which contained these disordered thoughts was shown to Warburton, and surely has been preserved.

* "A letter to the Lord Viscount B——ke, occasioned by his treatment of a deceased friend." Printed for A. Moore, without date. This pamphlet either came from Warburton himself, or from one of his intimates. The writer, too, calls Pope his friend.

son to whom Mr. Pope has consigned the care of his works (Warburton), and who, he thought, had some intention of writing Mr. Pope's life, told him he had an anecdote, which he believed nobody knew but himself. I was sitting one day (said he) with Mr. Pope, in his last illness, who coming suddenly out of a reverie, which you know he frequently fell into at that time, and fixing his eyes steadfastly upon me; 'Mr. M. (said he), I have had an odd kind of vision. Methought I saw my own head open, and Apollo came out of it; I then saw your head open, and Apollo went into it; after which our heads closed up again.' The gentleman (Warburton) could not help smiling at his vanity; and with some humour replied, ' Why, sir, if I had an intention of writing *your* life, this might perhaps be a proper anecdote; but I don't see, that in Mr. Pope's it will be of any consequence at all.' " P. 14.

This exhibits a curious instance of an author's egotism, or rather of Mallet's conceit, contriving, by some means, to have his name slide into the projected Life of Pope by Warburton, who appears, however, always to have treated him with the contempt Pope himself evidently did.* What opinion could the poet have

---

* We find also the name of Mallet closely connected with another person of eminence, the Patriot-Poet, Leonidas Glover. I take this opportunity of correcting a surmise of Johnson's in his Life of Mallet, respecting Glover, and which also places Mallet's character in a true light.

A minute life of Mallet might exhibit a curious example of mediocrity of talent, with but suspicious virtues, brought forward by the accident of great connexions, placing a bustling intriguer much higher in the scale of society than "our philosophy ever dreamt of." Johnson says of Mallet, that "It was remarkable of him, that he was the only Scot whom Scotchmen did not commend." From having been accidentally chosen as private tutor to the Duke of Montrose, he wound himself into the favour of the party at Leicester House; he wrote tragedies conjointly with Thomson, and was appointed, with

entertained of the taste of that weak and vain critic,
who, when Pope published anonymously "The Essay on
Man," being asked if anything new had appeared, replied that he had looked over a thing called an "Essay
on Man," but, discovering the utter want of skill and
knowledge in the author, had thrown it aside. Pope
mortified him by confiding to him the secret.

Glover, to write the Life of the Duke of Marlborough. Yet he had
already shown to the world his scanty talent for biography in his
"Life of Lord Bacon," on which Warburton so acutely animadverted.

According to Johnson's account, the Duchess of Marlborough assigned the task of writing the life of the Duke to Glover and to
Mallet, with a remuneration of a thousand pounds. She must, however, have mortified the poets by subjoining the sarcastic prohibition
that "no verses should be inserted." Johnson adds, "Glover, *I suppose, rejected with disdain the legacy,* and devolved the whole work
upon Mallet."

The cause why Glover declined this work could not, indeed, be
known to Johnson: it arose from a far more dignified motive than the
petty disdain of the legacy, which our great literary biographer has
surmised. It can now be told in his own words, which I derive f om
a very interesting extract communicated to me by my friend Mr. Duppa,
from that portion of the MS. Memoirs of Glover not yet published

I shall first quote the remarkable codicil from the original will of
her Grace, which Mr. Duppa took the pains to consult. She assigns
her reasons for the choice of her historians, and discriminates between
the two authors. After bequeathing the thousand pounds for them,
she adds: "I believe Mr. Glover is a very honest man, who wishes,
as I do, all the good that can happen, to preserve the liberties and
laws of England. Mr. Mallet was recommended to me by the late
Duke of Montrose, whom I admired extremely for his great steadiness
and behaviour in all things that related to the preservation of our laws
and the public good."—Thus her Grace has expressed a personal
knowledge and confidence in Glover, distinctly marked from her
"recommended" acquaintance Mallet.

Glover refused the office of historian, not from "disdain of the
legacy," nor for any deficient zeal for the hero whom he admired.
He refused it with sorrowful disappointment: for, besides the fantastical restrictions of "not writing any verses;" and the cruel one of
yoking such a patriot with the servile Mallet, there was one which

"The Apollo Vision" was a stinging anecdote, and it came from Warburton either directly or indirectly. This was followed up by "A Letter to the Editor of the Letters on the Spirit of Patriotism, the Idea of a Patriot King," &c., a dignified remonstrance of Warburton himself; but "The Impostor Detected and Convicted, or the Principles and Practices of the Author of the Spirit

placed the revision of the work in the hands of the Earl of Chesterfield: this was the *circumstance* at which the dignified genius of Glover revolted. Chesterfield's mean political character had excited his indignation; and he has drawn a lively picture of this polished nobleman's "eager prostitution," in his printed Memoirs, recently published under the title of "Memoirs of a celebrated Literary and Political Character," p. 24.

In the following passage, this great-minded man, for such he was, "unburthens his heart in a melancholy digression from his plain narrative."

"Composing such a narrative (alluding to his own Memoirs) and endeavouring to establish such a temper of mind, I cannot at intervals refrain from regret that the *capricious restrictions* in the Duchess of Marlborough's will, appointing me to write the life of her illustrious husband, compelled me to reject the undertaking. There, conduct, valour, and success abroad; prudence, perseverance, learning, and science, at home; would have shed some porticu of their graces on their historian's page: a mediocrity of talent would have felt an unwonted elevation in the bare attempt of transmitting so splendid a period to succeeding ages." Such was the dignified regret of Glover!

Doubtless, he disdained, too, his colleague; but Mallet reaped the whole legacy, and still more, a pension: pretending to be always occupied on the Life of Marlborough, and every day talking of the great discoveries he had made, he contrived to make this nonentity serve his own purposes. Once hinting to Garrick, that, in spite of chronology, by some secret device of anticipation, he had reserved a niche in this great work for the Roscius of his own times, the gratitude of Garrick was instant. He recollected that Mallet was a tragedy-writer; and it also appeared that our dramatic bardling had one ready. As for the pretended Life of Marlborough, not a line appears ever to have been written!

Such was the end of the ardent solicitude and caprice of the Duchess of Marlborough, exemplified in the last solemn act of life, where she

of Patriotism (Lord Bolingbroke) set forth in a clear light,
in a Letter to a Member of Parliament in Town, from his
Friend in the Country, 1749," is a remarkable production.
Lord Bolingbroke is the impostor and the concealed Jacobite. Time, the ablest critic on these party productions,
has verified the predictions of this seer. We discover
here, too, a literary fact, which is necessary to complete
our present history. It seems that there were omissions
and corrections in the edition Pope printed of " The Patriot King," which his caution or his moderation prompted, and which such a political demagogue as Bolingbroke
never forgave. They are thus alluded to: "Lord B.
may remember " (from a conversation held, at which the
writer appears to have been present), "that a difference
in opinion prevailed, and a few points were urged by
that gentleman (Pope) in opposition to some particular
tenets which related to the limitation of the English
monarchy, and to the ideal doctrine of a patriot king.
These were Mr. P.'s reasons for the emendations he
made; and which, together with the consideration that
both their lives were at that time in a declining state,
was the true cause, and no other, of his care to preserve
those letters, by handing them to the press, with the

betrayed the same warmth of passion, and the same arrogant caprice
she had always indulged, at the cost of her judgment, in what Pope
emphatically terms "the trade of the world." She was

" The wisest fool much time has ever made."

Even in this darling project of her last ambition, to immortalise her
name, she had incumbered it with such arrogant injunctions, mixed
up such contrary elements, that they were certain to undo their own
purpose. Such was the barren harvest she gathered through a life of
passion, regulated by no principle of conduct. One of the most
finished portraits of Pope is the Atossa, in his " Epistle on Woman."
How admirably he shows what the present instant proves, that she
was one who, always possessing the *means*, was sure to lose the
ends

precaution mentioned by the author." Indeed the cry
raised against the *dead man* by Bolingbroke and Mallet,
was an artificial one: that it should ever have tainted
the honour of the bard, or that it should ever have been
excited by his "Philosopher and Friend," are equally
strange; it is possible that the malice of Mallet was more
at work than that of Bolingbroke, who suffered himself
to be the dupe of a man held in contempt by Pope, by
Warburton, and by others. But the pamphlet I have
just noticed might have enraged Bolingbroke, because
his true character is ably drawn in it. The writer says
that "a person in an eminent station of life abroad, when
Lord B—— was at Paris to transact a certain affair,
said, *C'est certainement un homme d'esprit, mais un co-
quin sans probité.*" This was a very disagreeable truth!

In one of these pamphlets, too, Bolingbroke was mortified at his dignity being lessened by the writer, in comparing his lordship with their late friend Pope.—"I
venture to foretell, that the name of Mr. Pope, in spite
of your unmanly endeavours, shall revive and blossom
in the dust, from his own merits; and presume to remind you, that *yours*, had it not been for *his* genius, *his*
friendship, *his* idolatrous veneration for *you*, might, in
a short course of years, have died and been forgotten."
Whatever the degree of genius Bolingbroke may claim,
doubtless the verse of Pope has embalmed his fame. I
have never been able to discover the authors of these
pamphlets, who all appear of the first rank, and who
seem to have written under the eye of Warburton. The
awful and vindictive Bolingbroke, and the malignant
and petulant Mallet, did not long brood over their anger:
he or they gave it vent on the head of Warburton, in
those two furious pamphlets, which I have noticed in
the Quarrels of Warburton." All these pamphlets were
published in the same year, 1749, so that it is now

difficult to arrange them according to their priority.
Enough has been shown to prove, that the loud outcry
of Bolingbroke and Mallet, in their posthumous attack
on Pope, arose from their unforgiving malice against him,
for the preference by which the poet had distinguished
Warburton; and that Warburton, much more than Pope,
was the real object of this masked battery.

LINTOT'S ACCOUNT-BOOK.

A N odd sort of literary curiosity has fallen in my
way. It throws some light on the history of the
heroes of the *Dunciad ;* but such *minutiæ literariæ* are
only for my bibliographical readers.

It is a book of accounts, which belonged to the renowned Bernard Lintot, the bookseller, whose character
has been so humorously preserved by Pope, in a dialogue
which the poet has given as having passed between them
in Windsor Forest. The book is entitled " *Copies, when
Purchased.*" The power of genius is exemplified in the
ledger of the bookseller as much as in any other book;
and while I here discover, that the moneys received even
by such men of genius as Gay, Farquhar, Cibber, and
Dr. King, amount to small sums, and such authors as
Dennis, Theobald, Ozell, and Toland, scarcely amount
to anything, that of Pope much exceeds 4000*l.*

I am not in all cases confident of the nature of these
"Copies purchased ;" those works which were originally
published by Lintot may be considered as purchased at
the sums specified : some few might have been subsequent
to their first edition. The guinea, at that time, passing
for twenty-one shillings and sixpence, has occasioned the
fractions.

I transcribe Pope's account. Here it appears that he sold "The Key to the Lock" and "Parnell's Poems." The poem entitled, "To the Author of a Poem called *Successio*," appears to have been written by Pope, and has escaped the researches of his editors. The smaller poems were contributed to a volume of Poetical Miscellanies, published by Lintot. *

MR. POPE.

	£	s.	d
19 *Feb.* 1711-12.			
Statius, First Book			
Vertumnus and Pomona	16	2	6
21 *March,* 1711-12.			
First Edition Rape	7	0	0
9 *April,* 1712.			
To a Lady presenting Voiture			
Upon Silence	3	16	6
To the Author of a Poem called *Successio* .			
23 *Feb.* 1712-13.			
Windsor Forest	32	5	0
23 *July,* 1713.			
Ode on St. Cecilia's day	15	0	0
20th *Feb.* 1713-14.			
Additions to the Rape	15	0	0
1 *Feb.* 1714-15.			
Temple of Fame	32	5	0
30 *April,* 1715.			
Key to the Lock	10	15	0
17 *July,* 1716.			
Essay on Criticism †	15	0	0
13 *Dec.* 1721.			
Parnell's Poems	15	0	0
23 *March,* 1713.			
Homer, vol. i.	215	0	0
650 books on royal paper . . .	176	0	0

* "Miscellaneous Poems and Translations, by several Hands," 1712. The second edition appeared in 1714; and in the title-page are enumerated the poems mentioned in this account, and Pope's name affixed, as if he were the actual editor—an idea which Mr. Nichols thought he affected to discountenance. It is probable that Pope was the editor. We see, by this account, that he was paid for his contributions.

† This was a new edition, published conjointly by Lintot and Lewis,

9 *Feb.* 1715-16. £ *s.* *d.*
Homer, vol. ii. 215 0 0
7 *May*, 1716.
650 royal paper 150 0 0
This article is repeated to the sixth volume of
Homer. To which is to be added another
sum of 810*l*, paid for an assignment of all the
copies. The whole of this part of the account
amounting to 3203 4 0
Copy-moneys for the Odyssey, vols. i. ii. iii, and
750 of each vol. royal paper, 4to. . . . 615 6 0
Ditto for the vols. iv. v. and 750 do. . . . 425 18 7½
                                          ──────────
                                          £4244 8 7½
                                          ══════════

MR. GAY.

12 *May*, 1713. £ *s.* *d.*
Wife of Bath 25 0 0
11 *Nov.* 1714.
Letter to a Lady 5 7 6
14 *Feb.* 1714.
The What d'ye ye call it ? 16 2 6
22 *Dec.* 1715.
Trivia 43 0 0
Epistle to the Earl of Burlington 10 15 0
4 *May*, 1717.
Battle of the Frogs 16 2 6
8 *Jan.* 1717.
Three Hours after Marriage 43 2 6
The Mohocks, a Farce. 2*l.* 10*s.*
(Sold the Mohocks to him again. *)
Revival of the Wife of Bath 75 0 0
                                          ──────────
                                          £234 10 0
                                          ══════════

the Catholic bookseller and early friend of Pope, of whom, and of the
first edition, 1711, I have preserved an anecdote. p. 75.

* The late Isaac Reed, in the Biog. Dramatica, was uncertain
whether Gay was the author of this unacted drama. It is a satire on
the inhuman frolics of the bucks and bloods of those days, who imitated the savageness of the Indians whose name they assumed.[1] Why

────────

[1] The brutal amusements of these "Mohocks," and the helpless
terror of London, is scarcely credible in modern days. Wild bands

MR. DENNIS.

		£	s.	d.
Feb. 24, 1703–4.				
Liberty Asserted, one half share* . . .		7	3	0
10 *Nov.* 1708.				
Appius and Virginia		21	10	0
25 *April,* 1711.				
Essay on Public Spirit		2	12	6
6 *Jan.* 1711.				
Remarks on Pope's Essay		2	12	6

Dennis must have sold himself to criticism from ill-nature, and not for pay. One is surprised that his two tragedies should have been worth a great deal more than

Gay repurchased "The Mohocks," remains to be discovered. Was it another joint production with Pope?—The literary co-partnership between Pope and Gay has never been opened to the curious. It is probable that Pope was consulted, if not concerned, in writing "The What d'yo call it?" which, Jacob says in his "Poetical Register," "exposes several of our eminent poets." Jacob published while Gay was living, and seems to allude to this literary co-partnership; for, speaking of Gay, he says: "that having an inclination to poetry, by the strength of his own genius, and the *conversation* of Mr. Pope, he has made some progress in poetical writings."

This tragi-comical farce of "The Mohocks" is satirically dedicated to Dennis, "as a *horrid* and *tremendous* piece, formed on the mo el of his own 'Appius and Virginia.'" This touch seems to come from the finger of Pope. It is a mock-tragedy, for the Mohocks themselves rant in blank verse; a feeble performance, far inferior to its happier predecessor, "The What d'ye call it?"

---

of drunken men nightly infested the streets, attacking and ill-using every passer-by. A favourite pastime was to surround their victim with drawn swords, pricking him on every side as he endeavoured to escape. Many persons were maimed and dangerously wounded. Gay, in his *Trivia.*, has noted some of their more innocent practical jokes; and asks—

> "Who has not trembled at the Mohock's name ?
> Was there a watchman took his hourly rounds,
> Safe from their blows or new invented wounds?"

Swift, in his notes to Stella, had expressed his dread, while in London, of being maimed, or perhaps killed, by them.—ED.

* Bought of Mr. George Strahan, bookseller.

his criticism. Criticism was then worth no more than too frequently it deserves; Dr. Sewel, for his "Observations on the Tragedy of *Jane Shore*," received only a guinea.

I had suggested a doubt whether Theobald attempted to translate from the original Greek : one would suppose he did by the following entry, which has a line drawn through it, as if the agreement had not been executed. Perhaps Lintot submitted to pay Theobald for *not doing* the Odyssey when Pope undertook it

MR. THEOBALD.

		£	s.	d.
23 *May*, 1713.				
Plato's Phædon	. . . . . .	5	7	6
For *Æsculus's* Trag.	. . . . . .	1	1	6
being part of Ten Guineas.				
12 *June*, 1714.				
La Motte's Homer	. . . . . .	3	4	6

April 21, 1714. Articles signed by Mr. Theobald, to translate for B. Lintot the 24 books of Homer's Odyssey into English blank verse. Also the four Tragedies of Sophocles, called Œdipus Tyrannus, Œdipus Colonens, Trachiniæ, and Philoctetes, into English blank verse, with Explanatory Notes to the twenty-four Books of the Odyssey, and to the four Tragedies. To receive, for translating every 450 Greek verses, with Explanatory Notes thereon, the sum of 2*l*. 10*s*.

To translate likewise the Satires and Epistles of Horace into English rhyme. For every 120 Latin lines so translated, the sum of 1*l*. 1*s*. 6*d*.

These Articles to be performed, according to the time specified, under the penalty of fifty pounds, payable by either party's default in performance.

Paid in hand, 2*l*. 10*s*.

It appears that Toland never got above 5*l*., 10*l*., or 20*l*., for his publications. See his article in "Calamities of Authors," p. 238. I discovered the humiliating conditions that attended his publications, from an examination of his original papers. All this author seems to have reaped from a life devoted to literary enterprise, and

philosophy, and patriotism, appears not to have exceeded
200*l*.

Here, too, we find that the facetious Dr. King threw
away all his sterling wit for five miserable pounds,
though "The Art of Cookery," and that of "Love,"
obtained a more honourable price. But a mere school-
book probably inspired our lively genius with more real
facetiousness than any of those works which communicate so much to others.

DR. KING.

18 *Feb.* 1707–8.	£	s.	d.
Paid for Art of Cookery	32	5	0
16 *Feb.* 1708–9.			
Paid for the First Part of Transactions . .	5	0	0
Paid for his Art of Love	32	5	0
23 *June.* 1709.			
Paid for the Second Part of the Transactions* .	5	0	0
4 *March,* 1709–10.			
Paid for the History of Cajamai	5	0	0
10 *Nov.* 1710.			
Paid for King's Gods	50	0	0
1 *July.* 1712.			
Useful Miscellany, Part I.	1	1	6
Paid for the Useful Miscellany	3	0	0

Lintot utters a groan over "The Duke of Buckingham's Works" (Sheffield), for "having been *jockeyed* of
them by Alderman Barber and Tonson." Who can
ensure literary celebrity? No bookseller would *now*
regret being *jockeyed* out of his Grace's works!

The history of plays appears here somewhat curious :—
tragedies, then the fashionable dramas, obtained a considerable price; for though Dennis's luckier one reached
only to 21*l.*, Dr. Young's *Busiris* acquired 84*l.* Smith's
Phædra and Hippolytus, 50*l.* ; Rowe's *Jane Shore*, 50*l.*

* For an account of these humorous pieces, see the following article
on 'The Royal Society."

15*s.*; and *Jane Gray*, 75*l.* 5*s.* Cibber's *Nonjuror* obtained 105*l.* for the copyright.

Is it not a little mortifying to observe, that among all
these customers of genius whose names enrich the ledger
of the bookseller, Jacob, that "blunderbuss of law,"
while his law-books occupy in space as much as Mr.
Pope's works, the amount of his account stands next in
value, far beyond many a name which has immortalised
itself!

POPE'S EARLIEST SATIRE.

WE find by the first edition of Lintot's "Miscellaneous Poems," that the anonymous lines "To the
Author of a Poem called *Successio*," was a literary satire
by Pope, written when he had scarcely attained his
fourteenth year. This satire, the first probably he wrote
for the press, and in which he has succeeded so well,
that it might have induced him to pursue the bent of his
genius, merits preservation. The juvenile composition
bears the marks of his future excellences: it has the
tune of his verse, and the images of his wit. Thirty
years afterwards, when occupied by the *Dunciad*, he
transplanted and pruned again some of the original
images.

The hero of this satire is Elkanah Settle. The subject
is one of those Whig poems, designed to celebrate the
happiness of an uninterrupted "Succession" in the
Crown, at the time the Act of Settlement passed, which
transferred it to the Hanoverian line. The rhymer and
his theme were equally contemptible to the juvenile
Jacobite poet.

The hoarse and voluminous Codrus of Juvenal aptly
designates this eternal verse-maker;—one who has written

with such constant copiousness, that no bibliographer
has presumed to form a complete list of his works.*

When Settle had outlived his temporary rivalship with
Dryden, and was reduced to mere Settle, he published
party-poems, in folio, composed in Latin, accompanied
by his own translations. These folio poems, uniformly
bound, except that the arms of his patrons, or rather
his purchasers, richly gilt, emblazon the black morocco,
may still be found. These presentation-copies were sent
round to the chiefs of the party, with a mendicant's
petition, of which some still exist. To have a clear
conception of the *present views* of some politicians, it is
necessary to read their history backwards. In 1702, when
Settle published "Successio," he must have been a Whig.
In 1685 he was a Tory, commemorating, by a heroic
poem, the coronation of James II., and writing period-
ically against the Whigs. In 1680 he had left the Tories
for the Whigs, and conducted the whole management of
burning the Pope, then a very solemn national ceremony.†
A Whig, a pope-burner, and a Codrus, afforded a full
draught of inspiration to the nascent genius of our youth-
ful satirist.

* The fullest account we have of Settle, a busy scribe in his day, is
in Mr. Nichols's "Literary Anecdotes," vol. i. p. 41.

† It was the custom when party feeling ran high on the subject of
papacy, towards the close of the reign of Charles the Second, to get
up these solemn mock-processions of the Pope and Cardinals, accompanied with figures to represent Sir Edmundbury Godfrey, and other
subjects well adapted to heat popular feelings, and parade them through
the streets of London. The day chosen for this was the anniversary
of the Coronation of Queen Elizabeth (Nov. 17), and when the procession reached Temple-bar, the figure of the Pope was tossed from his
chair by one dressed as the Devil into a great bonfire made opposite
the statue of Queen Elizabeth, on the city side of Temple-bar. Two
rare tracts describe these "solemn mock-processions," as they are
termed, in 1679 and 1680. Prints were also published depicting the
whole proceedings, and descriptive pamphlets from the pen of Settle,
who arranged these shows.—ED.

Settle, in his latter state of wretchedness, had one
standard *elegy* and *epithalamium* printed off with *blanks*.
By the ingenious contrivance of inserting the name of
any considerable person who died or was married, no
one who had gone out of the world or was entering into
it but was equally welcome to this dinnerless livery-man
of the draggled-tailed Muses. I have elsewhere noticed
his last exit from this state of poetry and of pauperism,
when, leaping into a green dragon which his own creative genius had invented, in a theatrical booth, Codrus,
in hissing flames and terrifying-morocco folds, discovered
" the fate of talents misapplied !"

TO THE AUTHOR OF A POEM ENTITLED " SUCCESSIO."

Begone, ye critics, and restrain your spite;
Codrus writes on, and will for ever write.
The heaviest Muse the swiftest course has gone,
As clocks run fastest when most lead is on.*
What though no bees around your cradle flew,
Nor on your lips distill'd their golden dew;
Yet have we oft discover'd in their stead,
A swarm of drones that buzz'd about your head.
When you, like Orpheus, strike the warbling lyre,
Attentive blocks stand round you, and admire.
Wit past through thee no longer is the same,
As meat digested takes a different name ; †

---

* Thus altered in the *Dunciad*, book i., ver. 183—
    " As clocks to weight their nimble motions owe,
    The wheels above urged by the load below."

† This original image a late caustic wit (Horne Tooke), who probably had never read this poem, employed on a certain occasion. God-
win, who had then distinguished himself by his genius and by some
hardy paradoxes, was pleading for them as hardily, by showing that
they did not originate in him—that they were to be found in Helvetius, in Rousseau, and in other modern philosophers. "Ay," retorted
the cynical wit; "so you eat at my table venison and turtle, but from
you the same things come quite changed!" The original, after all, is
in Donne, long afterwards versified by our poet. See Warton's edition,
vol. iv. p. 257. Pope must have been an early reader of Donne.

But sense must sure thy safest plunder be,
Since no reprisals can be made on thee.
Thus thou mayst rise, and in thy daring flight
(Though ne'er so weighty) reach a wondrous height:
So, forced from engines, lead itself can fly,
And pond'rous slugs move nimbly through the sky.*
Sure Bavius copied Mævius to the full,
And Chærilus† taught Codrus to be dull;
Therefore, dear friend, at my advice give o'er
This needless labour, and contend no more
To prove a *dull Succession* to be true,
Since 'tis enough we find it so in you.

THE ROYAL SOCIETY.

THE ROYAL SOCIETY at first opposed from various quarters—their Experimental Philosophy supplants the Aristotelian methods—suspected of being the concealed Advocates of Popery, Arbitrary Power, and Atheism—disappointments incurred by their promises—the simplicity of the early Inquirers—ridiculed by the Wits and others—Narrative of a quarrel between a Member of the Royal Society and an Aristotelian—Glanvill writes his "Plus Ultra," to show the Improvements of Modern Knowledge—Character of Stubbe of Warwick—his Apology, from himself—opposes the "Plus Ultra" by the "Plus Ultra reduced to a Nonplus"—his "Campanella revived" —the Political Projects of Campanella—Stubbe persecuted, and menaced to be publicly whipped; his Roman spirit—his "Legends no Histories"—his "Censure on some Passages of the History of the Royal Society" —Harvey's ambition to be considered the Discoverer of the Circulation of the Blood, which he demonstrates—Stubbe

* Thus altered in the *Dunciad*, book i. ver. 181—

" As, forced from wind-guns, lead itself can fly,
And pond'rous slugs cut swiftly through the sky."

† Perhaps, by *Chærilus*, the juvenile satirist designated *Flecknoe*, or *Shadwell*, who had received their immortality of dulness from his master, catholic in poetry and opinions, Dryden.

describes the Philosophy of Science—attacks Sprat's Dedication to
the King—The Philosophical Transactions published by Sir Hans
Sloane ridiculed by Dr. King—his new Species of Literary Burlesque
—King's character—these attacks not ineffectually renewed by Sir
John Hill.

THE ROYAL SOCIETY, on its first establishment, at the
era of the Restoration, encountered fierce hostilities ;
nor, even at later periods, has it escaped many wanton
attacks. A great revolution in the human mind was
opening with that establishment ; for the spirit which had
appeared in the recent political concussion, and which
had given freedom to opinion, and a bolder scope to
enterprise, had now reached the literary and philosophical
world; but causes of the most opposite natures operated
against this institution of infant science.

In the first place, the new experimental philosophy,
full of inventions and operations, proposed to supplant
the old scholastic philosophy, which still retained an obscure jargon of terms, the most frivolous subtilties, and all
those empty and artificial methods by which it pretended
to decide on all topics. Too long it had filled the ear
with airy speculation, while it starved the mind that
languished for sense and knowledge. But this emanci-
pation menaced the power of the followers of Aristotle,
who were still slumbering in their undisputed authority,
enthroned in our Universities. For centuries the world
had been taught that the philosopher of Stagira had
thought on every subject; Aristotle was quoted as equal
authority with St. Paul, and his very image has been
profanely looked on with the reverence paid to Christ.
Bacon had fixed a new light in Europe, and others were
kindling their torches at his flame. When the great usurper of the human understanding was once fairly opposed
to Nature, he betrayed too many symptoms of mere
humanity. Yet this great triumph was not obtained

without severe contention; and upon the Continent even
blood has been shed in the cause of words. In our country, the University of Cambridge was divided by a party
who called themselves *Trojans*, from their antipathy to
the *Greeks*, or the Aristotelians; and once the learned
Richard Harvey, the brother of Gabriel, the friend of
Spenser, stung to madness by the predominant powers, to
their utter dismay set up their idol on the school-gates,
with his heels upwards, and ass's ears on his head. But
at this later period, when the Royal Society was established, the war was more open, and both parties more
inveterate. Now the world seemed to think, so violent
is the reaction of public opinion, that they could reason
better without Aristotle than with him : that he had often
taught them nothing more than self-evident propositions,
or had promoted that dangerous idleness of maintaining
paradoxes, by quibbles and other captious subtilties. The
days had closed of the "illuminated," the "profound,"
and the "irrefragable," titles, which the scholastic heroes
had obtained; and the Aristotelian four modes, by
which all things in nature must exist, of *materialiter*,
formaliter, *fundamentaliter*, and *eminenter*, were now
considered as nothing more than the noisy rattles, or
chains of cherry-stones, which had too long detained us
in the nursery of the human mind.* The world had been

* Some may be curious to have these monkish terms defined.
Causes are distinguished by Aristotle into four kinds:—The material
cause, *ex qua*, out of which things are made; the formal cause, *per quam*,
by which a thing is that which it is, and nothing else; the efficient
cause, *a qua*, by the agency of which anything is produced; and the
final cause, *propter quam*, the end for which it is produced. Such are his
notions in his Phys. l. ii. c. iii., referred to by Brucker and Formey in
their Histories of Philosophy. Of the Scholastic Metaphysics. *Sprat*,
the historian of the Royal Society, observes, "that the lovers of that
cloudy knowledge boast that it is an excellent instrument to refine and
make subtle the minds of men. But there may be *a greater excess in
the subtlety of men's wits* than in their *thickness; as* we see those

cheated with words instead of things; and the new experimental philosophy insisted that men should be less loquacious, but more laborious.

Some there were, in that unsettled state of politics and religion, in whose breasts the embers of the late Revolution were still hot: they were panic-struck that the advocates of popery and arbitrary power were returning on them, disguised as natural philosophers. This new

threads, which are of too fine a spinning, are found to be more useless than those which are homespun and gross."—*History of the Royal Society*, p. 326.

In the histo¬y of human folly, often so closely connected with that of human knowledge, some of the schoolmen (the commentators on Aquinas and others) prided themselves, and were even admired for their impenetrable obscurity! One of them, and our countryman, is singularly commended by Cardin. for that "only one of his arguments was enough to puzzle all posterity; and that, when he had grown old, he wept because he could not understand his own books." Baker, in his Reflections upon Learning, who had examined this schoolman, declares that his obscurity is such, as if he never meant to be understood. The extravagances of the schoolmen are, however, not always those of Aristotle. Pope, and the wits of that day, like these early members of the Royal Society, decried Aristotle, who did not probably fall in the way of their studies. His great imperfections are in natural philosophy; but he still preserves his eminence for his noble treatises of Ethics, and Politics, and Poetics, notwithstanding the imperfect state in which these have reached us. Dr. Copleston and Dr. Gillies have given an energetic testimony to their perpetual value. Pope, in satirising the University as a nest of dunces, considered the followers of Aristotle as so many stalled oxen, "*fat bulls of Basan.*"

"A hundred head of Aristotle's friends."
DUNCIAD.

Swift has drawn an allegorical personage of Aristotle, by which he describes the nature of his works. "He stooped much, and made use of a staff: his visage was meagre, his hair lank and thin, and his voice hollow;" descriptive of his abrupt conciseness, his harsh style, the obscurities of his dilapidated text, and the deficiency of feeling which his studied compression, his deep sagacity, and his analytical genius, so frequently exhibit.

terror had a very ludicrous origin:—it arose from some casual expressions, in which the Royal Society at first delighted, and by which an air of mystery was thrown over its secret movements: such was that "Universal Correspondence" which it affected to boast of; and the vaunt to foreigners of its "Ten Secretaries," when, in truth, all these magnificent declarations were only objects of their wishes. Another fond but singular expression, which the illustrious Boyle had frequently applied to it in its earliest state, when only composed of a few friends, calling it "The Invisible College," all concurred to make the Royal Society wear the appearance of a conspiracy against the political freedom of the nation. At a time, too, when, according to the historian of the Royal Society, "almost every family was widely disagreed among themselves on matters of religion," they believed that this "new experimental philosophy was subversive of the Christian faith!"* and many mortally hated the newly-invented optical glasses, the telescope and the microscope, as atheistical inventions, which perverted our sight, and made everything appear in a new and false light! Sprat wrote his celebrated "History of the Royal Society," to show that experimental philosophy was neither designed for the extinction of the Universities, nor of the Christian religion, which were really imagined to be in danger.

Others, again, were impatient for romantic discoveries; miracles were required, some were hinted at, while

* Sprat makes an ingenious observation on the notion of those who declared that "the most learned ages are still the most atheistical, and the ignorant the most devout." He says this had become almost proverbial, but he shows that piety is little beholden to those who make this distinction. "The Jewish law forbids us to offer up to God a sacrifice that has a blemish; but these men bestow the most excellent of men on the devil, and only assign to religion those men and those times which have the greatest blemish of human nature, even a defect in their knowledge and understanding."—History of the Royal Society, p. 356.

some were promised. In the ecstasy of imagination, they lost their soberness, forgetting that they were but the historians of nature, and not her prophets.* But amid these dreams of hope and fancy, the creeping ex-

---

* Science, at its birth, is as much the child of imagination as curiosity; and, in rapture at the new instrument it has discovered, it impatiently magnifies its power. To the infant, all improvements are wonders; it chronicles even its dreams, and has often described what it never has seen, delightfully deceived; the cold insults of the cynics, the wits, the dull, and the idle, maliciously mortify the infant in its sports, till it returns to slow labour and patient observation. It is rather curious, however, that when science obtains a certain state of maturity, it is liable to be attacked by the same fits of the marvellous which affected its infancy;—and the following extract from one of the enthusiastic *Virtuosi* in the infancy of science, rivals the visions of "the perfectibility of man" of which we hear so much at this late period. Some, perhaps, may consider these strong tendencies of the imagination, breaking out at these different periods in the history of science, to indicate results, of which the mind feels a consciousness, which the philosopher should neither indulge nor check.

"Should these heroes go on (the Royal Society) as they have happily begun, they will fill the world with wonders; and posterity will find many things that are now but *rumours*, verified into practical *realities*. It may be, some ages hence, a *voyage* to the southern unknown tracts, yea, possibly the *Moon*, will not be more strange than one to America. To them that come after us, it may be as ordinary to *buy a pair of wings* to fly into remotest regions, as now *a pair of boots* to ride a journey. And to confer at the distance of the Indies, by *sympathetic conveyances*, may be as usual to future times, as to us in a literary correspondence. The restoration of *grey hairs to juvenility*, and renewing the *exhausted marrow*, may at length be effected without a miracle; and the turning the now comparative *desert world* into a *paradise*, may not improbably be expected from late *agriculture*.

"Those that judge by the narrowness of former principles and successes, will smile at these paradoxical expectations. But the great inventions of latter ages, which altered the face of all things, in their naked proposals and mere suppositions, were to former times as ridiculous. To have talked of a new earth to have been discovered, had been a romance to antiquity; and to sail without sight of stars or shores, by the guidance of a mineral, a story more absurd than the flight of Dædalus. That men should speak after their tongues were

perimentalist was still left boasting of improvements, so
slow that they were not perceived, and of novelties so
absurd that they too often raised the laugh against their
grave and unlucky discoverers. The philosophers themselves seemed to have been fretted into the impatient
humour which they attempted to correct; and the
amiable Evelyn becomes an irritated satirist, when he
attempts to reply to the repeated question of that day,
" What have they done?" *

But a source of the ridicule which was perpetually
flowing against the Royal Society, was the almost infantine simplicity of its earliest members, led on by their
honest zeal; and the absence of all discernment in many
trifling and ludicrous researches, which called down the

ashes, or communicate with each other in differing hemispheres, before
the invention of letters, could not but have been thought a fiction.
Antiquity would not have believed the almost incredible force of our
cannons, and would as coldly have entertained the wonders of the
telescope."—Glanvill, *Scepsis Scientifica*, p. 133.

* Evelyn, whose elegant mind, one would have imagined, had been
little susceptible of such vehement anger, in the preface to his " Sylva,"
scolds at no common rate : " Well-meaning people are led away by the
noise of a few ignorant and comical buffoons, who, with an insolence
suitable to their understanding, are still crying out, *What have the
Society done?*" He attributes all the opposition and ridicule the
Society encountered to a personage not usual to be introduced into a
philosophical controversy—" The Enemy of Mankind." But it was
well to denounce the devil himself, as the Society had nearly lost the
credit of fearing him. Evelyn insists that "next to the propagation
of our most holy faith," that of the new philosophy was desirable
both for the king and the nation ; " for," he adds, " it will survive
the triumphs of the proudest conquerors ; since, when all their pomp
and noise is ended, they are those *little things in black*, whom now in
scorn they term philosophers and fops, to whom they must be obliged
for making their names outlast the pyramids, whose founders are as
unknown as the heads of the Nile." Why Evelyn designates the
philosophers as *little things in black*, requires explanation. Did they
affect a dress of this colour in the reign of Charles II., or does he allude
to the dingy appearance of the chemists?

malice of the wits;* there was, too, much of that unjust
contempt between the parties, which students of opposite
pursuits and tastes so liberally bestow on each other.
The researches of the Antiquarian Society were sneered at

* It is not easy to credit the simplicity of these early inquirers. In
a Memorial in Sprat's History, entitled, "Answers returned by Sir
Philliberto Vernatti to certain Inquiries sent by order of the Royal
Society;" among some of the most extraordinary questions and descriptions of nonentities, which must have fatigued Sir Philliberto, who
then resided in Batavia, I find the present:—"Qy. 8. What ground
there may be for that relation concerning *horns taking root, and growing
about Goa?*" It seems the question might as well have been asked at
London, and answered by some of the members themselves; for Sir
Philliberto gravely replied—"Inquiring about this, a friend laughed,
and told me it was a jeer put upon the Portuguese, because the women
of Goa are counted none of the chastest." Inquiries of this nature, and
often the most trivial objects set off with a singular minuteness of
description, tempted the laugh of the scoffers. Their great adversary,
Stubbe, ridiculing their mode of giving instructions for inquiries, re-
grets that the paper he received from them had been lost, otherwise
he would have published it. "The great Mr. Boyle, when he brought
it, tendered it with blushing and disorder," at the simplicity of the
Royal Society! And indeed the royal founder himself, who, if he was
something of a philosophe, was much more of a wit, set the example.
The Royal Society, on the day of its creation, was the whetstone of
the wit of their patron. When Charles II. dined with the members on
the occasion of constituting them a Royal Society, towards the close
of the evening he expressed his satisfaction in being the first English
monarch who had laid a foundation for a society who proposed that
their sole studies should be directed to the investigation of the arcana
of nature; and added with that peculiar gravity of countenance he
usually wore on such occasions, that among such learned men he now
hoped for a solution to a question which had long perplexed him. The
case he thus stated:—"Suppose two pails of water were fixed in two
different scales that were equally poised, and which weighed equally
alike, and that two live bream, or small fish, were put into either of
these pails, he wanted to know the reason why that pail, with such
addition, should not weigh more than the other pail which stood
against it." Every one was ready to set at quiet the royal curiosity;
but it appeared that every one was giving a different opinion. One, at
length, offered so ridiculous a solution, that another of the members

by the Royal, and the antiquaries avenged themselves
by their obstinate incredulity at the prodigies of the
naturalists; the student of classical literature was equally
slighted by the new philosophers; who, leaving the study
of words and the elegancies of rhetoric for the study
merely of things, declared as the cynical ancient did of
metaphors, "Poterimus vivere sine illis"—We can do
very well without them! The ever-witty South, in his
oration at Oxford, made this poignant reflection on the
Royal Society—"Mirantur nihil nisi pulices, pediculos,
et seipsos." They can admire nothing except fleas, lice,
and themselves! And even Hobbes so little comprehended the utility of these new pursuits, that he considered the Royal Society merely as so many labourers,
who, when they had washed their hands after their
work, should leave to others the polishing of their discourses. He classed them, in the way they were proceeding, with apothecaries, and gardeners, and mechanics,
who might now "all put in for, and get the prize." Even
at a later period, Sir William Temple imagined the virtuosi to be only so many Sir Nicholas Gimcracks; and
contemptuously called them, from the place of their first
meeting, "the Men of Gresham!" doubtless considering
them as wise as "the Men of Gotham!" Even now,
men of other tempers and other studies are too apt to
refuse the palm of philosophy to the patient race of
naturalists.* Wotton, who wrote so zealously at the

could not refrain from a loud laugh: when the King, turning to him,
insisted that he should give his sentiments as well as the rest. This
he did without hesitation, and told his majesty, in plain terms, that he
denied the fact! On which the King, in high mirth, exclaimed—
"Odds fish, brother, you are in the right!" The jest was not ill
designed. The story was often useful, to cool the enthusiasm of the
scientific visionary, who is apt often to account for what never has
existed.

* Pope was severe in his last book of the *Dunciad* on the students

commencement of the last century in favour of modern
knowledge, is alarmed lest the effusions of wit, in his
time, should "deaden the industry of the philosophers
of the next age; for," he adds, "nothing wounds so
effectually as a jest: and when men once become ridiculous, their labours will be slighted, and they will find
few imitators." The alarm shows his zeal, but not his
discernment: since curiosity in hidden causes is a passion which endures with human nature. "The philosophers of the next age" have shown themselves as persevering as their predecessors, and the wits as malicious.
The contest between men of meditation and men of experiment, is a very ancient quarrel; and the "divine"
Socrates was no friend to, and even a ridiculer of, those
very pursuits for which the Royal Society was established.*

of insects, flowers, &c.: and R. O. Cambridge followed out the idea of
a mad virtuoso in his "Scribleriad," which he has made up from the
absurd or trifling parts of natural history and philosophy. His hero
is—

> " A much-enduring man, whose curious soul
> Bore him with ceaseless toil from pole to pole ;
> Insatiate endless knowledge to obtain,
> Thro' woes by land, thro' dangers on the main."

He collects curiosities from all parts of the world: studies occult and
natural sciences; and is at last beatified by electrical glories at a
meeting of hermetical philosophers. This poem is elucidated by notes,
which point the allusions to the works or doings of the old philosophers.—ED.

   * Evelyn, who could himself be a wit occasionally, was, however,
much annoyed by the scorners. He applies to these wits a passage in
Nehemiah ii. 19, which describes those who laughed at the *builders of
Jerusalem.* "These are the Sanballats, the Horonites, who disturb
our men upon the wall; but *let us rise up and build!*" He describes
these Horonites of wit as "magnificent fops, whose talents reach but
to the adjusting of their perukes." But the Royal Society was attacked
from other quarters, which ought to have assisted them. Evelyn, in

In founding this infant empire of knowledge, a memorable literary war broke out between Glanvill, the author of the treatise on " Witches," &c., and Stubbe, a physician, a man of great genius. It is the privilege of genius that its controversies enter into the history of the human mind ; what is but temporary among the vulgar of mankind, with the curious and the intelligent become monuments of lasting interest. The present contest, though the spark of contention flew out of a private quarrel, at length blazed into a public controversy.

The obscure individual who commenced the fray, is forgotten in the boasted achievements of his more potent ally ; he was a clergyman named Cross, the Vicar of Great Chew, in Somersetshire, a stanch Aristotelian.

Glanvill, a member of the Royal Society, and an enthusiast for the new philosophy, had kindled the anger of the peripatetic, who was his neighbour, and who had the reputation of being the invincible disputant of his county.* Some, who had in vain contended with Glan-

his valuable treatise on forest-trees, had inserted a new project for making cider ; and Stubbe insisted, that in consequence " much cider had been spoiled within these three years, by following the directions published by the commands of the Royal Society." They afterwards announced that they never considered themselves as answerable for their own memoirs, which gave Stubbe occasion to boast that he had forced them to deny what they had written. A passage in Hobbes's " Considerations upon his Reputation, &c.," is as remarkable for the force of its style as for that of sense, and may be applicable to *some* at this day, notwithstanding the progress of science, and the importance attached to their busy idleness.

" Every man that hath spare money can get furnaces, and buy coals Every man that hath spare money can be at the charge of making great moulds, &c., and so may have the best and greatest telescopes. They can get engines made, recipients made, and try conclusions ; but they are never the more philosophers for all this. 'Tis laudable to bestow money on curious or useful delights, but that is none of the praises of a philosopher." p. 53.

* Glanvill was a learned man, but evidently superstitious, particu-

vill, now contrived to inveigle the modern philosopher into an interview with this redoubted champion.

When Glanvill entered the house, he perceived that he was to begin an acquaintance in a quarrel, which was not the happiest way to preserve it. The Vicar of Great Chew sat amid his congregated admirers. The peripatetic had promised them the annihilation of the new-fashioned virtuoso, and, like an angry boar, had already been preluding by whetting his tusks. Scarcely had the first cold civilities passed, when Glanvill found himself involved in single combat with an assailant armed with the ten categories of Aristotle. Cross, with his *Quodam modo*, and his *Modo quodam*, with his *Ubi* and his *Quando*, scattered the ideas of the simple experimentalist, who, confining himself to a simple recital of *facts* and a description of *things*, was referring, not to the logic of Aristotle, but to the works of nature. The imperative Aristotelian was wielding weapons, which, says Glanvill, "were nothing more than like those of a cudgel-player, or fencing-master."*

larly in all that related to witchcraft and apparitions; the reality of both being insisted on by him in a series of books which he published at various periods of his life, and which he continually worked upon with new arguments and instances, in spite of all criticism or opposition. He was a member of the Royal Society, prebend of Worcester, and rector of Bath, where he died, October 4, 1680.—ED.

* The ninth chapter in the "Plus Ultra," entitled "The Credit of Optic Glasses vindicated against a disputing man, who is afraid to believe his eyes against Aristotle," gives one of the ludicrous incidents of this philosophical visit. The disputer raised a whimsical objection against the science of optics, insisting that the newly-invented glasses, the telescope, the microscope, &c., were all deceitful and fallacious; for, said the Aristotelian, "take two spectacles, use them at the same time, and you will not see so well as with one singly—*ergo*, your microscopes and telescopes are impostors." How this was forced into a syllogism does not appear; but still the conclusion ran, "We can see better through one pair than two, therefore all perspectives are fallacious!"

The last blow was still reserved, when Cross asserted
that Aristotle had more opportunities to acquire knowledge than the Royal Society, or all the present age had,
or could have, for this definitive reason, " because Aristotle did, *totam peragrare Asiam.*" Besides, in the Chew
philosophy, where novelty was treason, improvements or
discoveries could never exist. Here the Aristotelian
made his stand; and at length, gently hooking Glanvill
between the horns of a dilemma, the entrapped virtuoso
threw himself into an unguarded affirmation; at which
the Vicar of Great Chew, shouting in triumph, with a
sardonic grin, declared that Glanvill and his Royal Society had now avowed themselves to be atheistical!
This made an end of the interview, and a beginning of
the quarrel.*

> One proposition for sense,
> And t'other for convenience,

will make a tolerable syllogism for a logician in despair. The Aristotelian was, however, somewhat puzzled by a problem which he had
himself raised—"Why we cannot see with two pair of spectacles
better than with one singly?" for the man of axioms observed, "*Vis
unita fortior,*" "United strength *is stronger.*" It is curious enough,
in the present day, to observe the sturdy Aristotelian denying these
discoveries, and the praises of optics, and "the new glasses," by
Glanvill. "If this philosopher," says the member of the Royal Society, "had spared some of those thoughts to the profitable doctrino
of optics which he hath spent upon *genus* and *species*, we had never
heard of this objection." And he replies to the paradox which the
Aristotelian had raised by "Why cannot he write better with *two pens*
than with a *single one*, since *Vis unita fortior?* When he hath answered this *Quære*, he hath resolved his own. The reason he gave why it
should be so, is the reason why 'tis not." Such are the squabbles
of infantine science, which cannot as yet discover causes, although it
has ascertained effects.

   * This appears in chap. xviii. of the "Plus Ultra." With great
simplicity Glanvill relates :—"At this period of the conference, the
disputer lost all patience, and with sufficient spite and rage told me
'that I was an atheist!—that he had indeed desired my acquaintance,

Glanvill addressed an expostulatory letter to the in-human Aristotelian, who only replied by calling it a recantation, asserting that the affair had finished with the conviction.

On this, Glanvill produced his " Plus Ultra,"* on the modern improvements of knowledge. The quaint title referred to that Asian argument which placed the bound-aries of knowledge at the ancient limits fixed by Aris-totle, like the pillars of Hercules, on which was inscribed *Ne plus ultra*, to mark the extremity of the world. But Glanvill asserted we might advance still further—*plus ultra !* To this book the Aristotelian replied with such rancour, that he could not obtain a licence for the invec-tive either at Oxford or London. Glanvill contrived to get some extracts, and printed a small number of copies for his friends, under the sarcastic title of "The Chew Gazette,"—a curiosity, we are told, of literary scolding, and which might now, among literary trinkets, fetch a Roxburgh prize.

but would have no more on't,' and so turned his back and went away, giving me time only to answer that ' I had no great reason to lament the loss of an acquaintance that could be so easily forfeited.'" The following chapter vindicates the Royal Society from the charge of atheism ! to assure the world they were not to be ranked "among the black conspirators against Heaven !" We see the same objections again occurring in the modern system of geology.

* This book was so scarce in 1757, that the writer in the " Bio-graphia Britannica " observes that this "small but elegant treatise is still very much esteemed by the curious, being become so scarce as not to be met with in other hands." Oldys, in 1738, had, in his "British Librarian," selected this work among the scarce and valuable books of which he has presented us with so many useful analyses.

The history of books is often curious. At one period a book is scarce and valuable, and at another is neither one nor the other. This does not always depend on the caprice of the public, or what may be called literary fashions. Glanvill's " Plus Ultra" is probably now of easy occurrence ; like a prophecy fully completed, the uncertain event being verified, the prophet has ceased to be remembered.

Cross, maddened that he could not get his bundle of peripatetic ribaldries printed, wrote ballads, which he got sung as it chanced. But suppressed invectives and eking rhymes could but ill appease so fierce a mastiff: he set on the poor F.R.S. an animal as rabid, but more vigorous than himself—both of them strangely prejudiced against the modern improvements of knowledge; so that, like mastiffs in the dark, they were only the fiercer.

This was Dr. Henry Stubbe, a physician of Warwick—one of those ardent and versatile characters, strangely made up of defects as strongly marked as their excellences. He was one of those authors who, among their numerous remains, leave little of permanent value; for their busy spirits too keenly delight in temporary controversy, and they waste the efforts of a mind on their own age, which else had made the next their own. Careless of worldly opinions, these extraordinary men, with the simplicity of children, are mere beings of sensation; perpetually precipitated by their feelings, with slight powers of reflection, and just as sincere when they act in contradiction to themselves, as when they act in contradiction to others. In their moral habits, therefore, we are often struck with strange contrasts; their whole life is a jumble of actions; and we are apt to condemn their versatility of principles as arising from dishonest motives; yet their temper has often proved more generous, and their integrity purer, than those who have crept up in one unvarying progress to an eminence which they quietly possess, without any of the ardour of these original, perhaps whimsical, minds. The most tremendous menace to a man of this class would be to threaten to write the history of his life and opinions. When Stubbe attacked the Royal Society, this threat was held out against him. But menaces never startled his intrepid genius; he roved in all his wild greatness;

and, always occupied more by present views than interested by the past events of his life, he cared little for
his consistency in the high spirit of his independence.

The extraordinary character of Stubbe produced as
uncommon a history. Stubbe had originally been a
child of fortune, picked up at Westminster school by
Sir Henry Vane the younger, who sent him to Oxford;
where this effervescent genius was, says Wood, " kicked,
and beaten, and whipped."* But if these little circumstances marked the irritability and boldness of his youth,
it was equally distinguished by an entire devotion to his
studies. Perhaps one of the most anomalous of human
characters was that of his patron, Sir Henry Vane the
younger (whom Milton has immortalised in one of the
noblest of sonnets), the head of the Independents, who
combined with the darkest spirit of fanaticism the clear

* His early history is given by Wood in his usual style. His father
had been a Lincolnshire parson, who was obliged to leave his poor
curacy, because " anabaptistically inclined," and fled to Ireland, whence
his mother and her children were obl'ged to return on the breaking
out of the rebellion of 1641, and landed at Liverpool; afterward, says
Wood, " they all beated it on the hoof thence to London, where she,
gaining a comfortable subsistence by her needle, sent her son Henry,
being then ten years of age, to the collegiate school at Westminster.
At that time Mr. Richard Busbie was the chief master, who finding
the boy have pregnant parts to a miracle, did much favour and encourage him. At length Sir Henry Vane, junior (the same who was
beheaded on Tower Hill, 1662), coming casually into the school with
Dr. Lambert Osbaldiston, he did, at the master's motion, take a kindness to the said boy, and gave him the liberty to resort to his house,
and to fill that belly which otherwise had no sustenance but what one
penny could purchase for his dinner: and as for his breakfast, he had
none, except he got it by making somebody's exercise. Soon after,
Sir Henry got him to be a king's scholar; and his master perceiving
him to be beyond his years in proficiency, he gave him money to buy
books, clothes, and his teaching for nothing." Such was the humble
beginning of a learned man, who lived to be a formidable opponent to
the whole body of the Royal Society.—ED.

views of the most sagacious politician. The gratitude of Stubbe lasted through all the changeful fortunes of the chief of a faction—a long date in the records of human affection! Stubbe had written against monarchy, the church, the university, &c.; for which, after the Restoration, he was accused by his antagonists. He exults in the reproach; he replies with all that frankness of simplicity, so beautiful amid our artificial manners. He denies not the charge; he never trims, nor glosses over, nor would veil, a single part of his conduct. He wrote to serve his patrons, but never himself. I preserve the whole of this noble passage in the note.* Wood bears

* When Sprat and Glanvill, and others, had threatened to write his life, Stubbe draws this apology for it, while he shows how much, in a time of revolutions, the Royal Society might want one for themselves.

"I was so far from being daunted at these rumours and threats, that I enlarged much this book thereupon, and resolved to charge the enemy home when I saw how weak a resistance I should meet with. I knew that recriminations were no answers. I understood well that the passages of a life like mine, spent in different places with much privacy and obscurity, was unknown to them; that even those actions they would fix their greatest calumnies upon, were such as that they understood not the grounds, nor had they learning enough and skill to condemn. I was at Westminster School when the late king was beheaded. I never took covenant nor engagement. In sum, *I served my patron.* I endeavoured to express my *gratitude* to him who had relieved me, being a *child*, and in great poverty (the rebellion in Ireland having deprived my parents of all means wherewith to educate me); who made me a king's scholar; preferred me to Christchurch College, Oxon.; and who often supplied me with money when my tender years gave him little hopes of any return; and who protected me amidst the *Presbyterians*, and *Independents*, and other *sects*. With none thereof did I contract any relation or acquaintance; my familiarity never engaged me with ten of that party; and my genius and humour inclined me to fewer. I neither enriched, nor otherwise advanced myself, during the late troubles; and shared the common *odium* and *dangers*, not *prosperity*, with my *benefactor*. I believe no generous man, who hath the least sense of bravery, will condemn me; and I profess I am ashamed rather to have done so little, than that I

witness to his perfect disinterestedness. He never par
took of the prosperity of his patron, nor mixed with any
parties, loving the retirement of his private studies; and
if he scorned and hated one party, the Presbyterians, it
was, says Wood, because his high generous nature de-
tested men " void of generous souls, sneaking, snivelling,
&c." Stubbe appears to have carried this philosophical
indifference towards objects of a higher interest than
those of mere profit; for, at the Restoration, he found
no difficulty in conforming to the Church* and to the
Government. The king bestowed on him the title of

have done so much, for him that so frankly obliged a *stranger* and a
child. When Gracchus was put to death for sedition, that faithful
friend and accomplice of his was dismissed, and mentioned with honour by all posterity, who, when he was impeached, *justified his treason*
by the avowing a *friendship* so great that, whatever Gracchus had
commanded him, he would not have declined it. And being further
questioned, whether he would have burned the capitol at his bidding?
he replied again, that he should have done it; but Gracchus would
not bid such a thing. They that knew me heretofore, know I have a
thousand times thus apologised for myself; adding, that in *rassals* and
slaves, and persons *transcendently obliged,* their fidelity exempted them
from all ignominy, though the principal *lords, masters,* and *patrons,* might
be accounted *traitors.* My youth and other circumstances incapaci-
tated me from rendering him any great services; but *all that I did,* and
all that I writ, had no other aim than *his interest;* nor do I care how
much any man can inodiate my former writings, as long as they were
subservient to him.

"Having made this declaration, let them (or more able men than
they) write the life of a man who hath some virtues of the most celebrated times, and hath preserved himself free from the vices of these.
My reply shall be a scornful silence."—Preface to Stubbe's "Legends
no Histories," 1670.

* His reasons for conformity on these important objects are given
with his usual simplicity. "I have at length removed all the um-
brages I ever lay under. I have joined myself to the Church of England, not only upon account of its being *publicly imposed* (which in *th ngs
indifferent* is no small consideration, as I learned from the Scottish
transactions at Perth), but because it is *the least defining,* and consequently *the most comprehensive and fitting to be national.*"

his physician; yet, for the sake of making philosophical experiments, Stubbe went to Jamaica, and intended to have proceeded to Mexico and Peru, pursuing his profession, but still an adventurer. At length Stubbe returned home; established himself as a physician at Warwick, where, though he died early, he left a name celebrated.* The fertility of his pen appears in a great number of philosophical, political, and medical publications. But all his great learning, the facility of his genius, his poignant wit, his high professional character, his lofty independence, his scorn of practising the little mysterious arts of life, availed nothing; for while he was making himself popular among his auditors, he was eagerly depreciated by those who would not willingly allow merit to a man who owned no master, and who feared no rival.

Literary coteries were then held at coffee-houses;† and there presided the voluble Stubbe, with "a big and magisterial voice, while his mind was equal to it," says the characterising Wood; but his attenuated frame seemed too delicate to hold long so unbroken a spirit. It was an accident, however, which closed this life of toil and hurry and petulant genius. Going to a patient at night, Stubbe was drowned in a very shallow river, "his head (adds our cynic, who had generously paid the

* He died at Bath in 1676, where he had gone in attendance upon several of his patients from the neighbourhood of Warwick, where he for a long time practised as a physician. His old antagonist Glanvill was at that time rector of the Abbey Church in which he was buried, and so became the preacher of his funeral sermon. Wood says he "said no great matter of him."—ED.

† Pope said to Spence, "It was Dryden who made Will's coffee-house the great resort for the wits of his time. After his death Addison transferred it to Button's, who had been a servant of his." Will's coffee-house was at the corner of Bow-street, Covent-garden, and Button's close by in Russell-street.—ED.

tribute of his just admiration with his strong peculiarity of style) being then intoxicated with bibbing, but more with talking and snuffing of powder."

Such was the adversary of the Royal Society! It is quite in character that, under the government of Cromwell, he himself should have spread a taste for what was then called "The New Philosophy" among our youth and gentlemen, with the view of rendering the clergy contemptible; or, as he says, "to make them appear egregious fools in matters of common discourse." He had always a motive for his actions, however opposite they were; pretending that he was never moved by caprice, but guided by principle. One of his adversaries, however, has reason to say, that judging him by his "printed papers, he was a man of excellent contradictory parts." After the Restoration, he furnished as odd, but as forcible a reason, for opposing the Royal Society. At that time the nation, recent from republican ardours, was often panic-struck by papistical conspiracies, and projects of arbitrary power; and it was on this principle that he took part against the Society. Influenced by Dr. Fell and others, he suffered them to infuse these extravagant opinions into his mind. No private ends appear to have influenced his changeable conduct; and in the present instance he was sacrificing his personal feelings to his public principles; for Stubbe was then in the most friendly correspondence with the illustrious Boyle, the father of the Royal Society, who admired the ardour of Stubbe, till he found its inconvenience.*

---

* "Some years after the king's restoration he took pet against the Royal Society, (for which before he had a great veneration,) and being encouraged by Dr. Jo. Fell, ι o admirer of that society, became in his writings an inveterate enemy against it for several pretended reasons: among which were, first, that the members thereof intended to bring a contempt upon ancient and solid learning, upon Aristotle, to under-

Stubbe opened his formidable attacks, for they form a series, by replying to the " Plus Ultra " of Glanvill, with a title as quaint, " The *Plus Ultra* reduced to a *Non-plus*, in animadversions on Mr. Glanvill and the Virtuosi." For a pretence for this violent attack, he strained a passage in Glanvill; insisting that the honour of the whole faculty of which he was a member was deeply concerned to refute Glanvill's assertion, that "the ancient physicians could not cure a cut finger."—This Glanvill denied he had ever affirmed or thought ; * but war once resolved

mine the universities, and reduce them to nothing, or at least to be very inconsiderable. Secondly, that at long running to destroy the established religion, and involve the nation in popery, and I know not what, &c. So dexterous was his pen, whether *pro* or *con*, that few or none could equal, answer, or come near him. He was a person of most admirable parts, had a most prodigious memory, though his enemies would not acknowledge it, but said he read indexes; was the most noted Latinist and Grecian of his age; and after he had been put upon it, was so great an enemy to the *virtuosi* of his time, I mean those of the Royal Society, that, as he saith, they alarmed him with dangers and troubles even to the hazard of his life and fortunes."— *Wood.*

* The aspersed passage in Glanvill is this: "The philosophers of elder times, though their wits were excellent, yet the way they took was not like to bring much advantage to knowledge, or any of the uses of human life, being, for the most part, that of *Notion* and *Dispute*, which still runs round in a labyrinth of talk, but advanceth nothing. *These methods*, in so many centuries, *never brought the world so much practical beneficial knowledge as could help towards the cure of a cut finger.*" Plus Ultra, p. 7.—Stubbe, with all the malice of a wit, drew his inference. and turned the point unfairly against his adversary!

I shall here observe how much some have to answer, in a literary court of conscience, when they unfairly depreciate the works of a contemporary ; and how idly the literary historian performs his task, whenever he adopts the character of a writer from another who is his adversary. This may be particularly shown in the present instance.

Morhoff, in his *Polyhistor Litteraria*, censures the *Plus Ultra* of Glanvill, conceiving that he had treated with contempt all ages and nations but his own. The German bibliographer had never seen the book, but took its character from Stubbe and Meric Casaubon. The

on, a pretext as slight as the present serves the purpose; and so that an odium be raised against the enemy, the end is obtained before the injustice is acknowledged. This is indeed the history of other wars than those of words. The present was protracted with an hostility unsubduing and unsubdued. At length the malicious ingenuity, or the heated fancy, of Stubbe, hardly sketched a political conspiracy, accusing the ROYAL SOCIETY of having adopted the monstrous projects of Campanella; —an anomalous genius, who was confined by the Inquisition the greater part of his life, and who, among some political reveries, projected the establishment of a universal empire, though he was for shaking off the yoke of authority in the philosophical world. He was for one government and one religion throughout Europe, but in other respects he desired to leave the minds of men quite free. Campanella was one of the new lights of the age; and his hardy, though wild genius much more resembled our Stubbe, who denounced his extravagancies, than any of the Royal Society, to whom he was so artfully compared.

The tremendous attack appeared in Stubbe's " Campanella Revived, or an Enquiry into the History of the Royal Society; whether the Virtuosi there do not pursue the projects of Campanella, for reducing England into Popery; relating the quarrel betwixt H. S. and the R. S., &c. 1670." *

design of the *Plus Ultra*, however, differs little from the other works of G.anvill, which Morhoff had seen, and has highly commended.

* The political reverie of Campanella was even suspected to cover very opposite designs to those he seemed to be proposing to the world. He attempted to turn men's minds from all inquiries into politics and religion, to mere philosophical ones. He wished that the passions of mankind might be so directed, as to spend their force in philosophical discussions, and in improvements in science. He therefore insisted on a uniformity on those great subjects which have so long agitated

Such was the dread which his reiterated attacks caused the Royal Society, that they employed against him all the petty persecutions of power and intrigue. "Thirty legions," says Stubbe, alluding to the famous

modern Europe; for the ancients seem to have had no wars merely for religion, and perhaps none for modes of government. One may discover an enlightened principle in the project; but the character of Campanella was a jumble of sense, subtlety, and wildness. He probably masked his real intentions. He appears an advocate for the firm establishment of the papal despotism; yet he aims to give an enlightened principle to regulate the actions of mankind. The intentions of a visionary are difficult to define. If he were really an advocate for despotism, what occasioned an imprisonment for the greater part of his days? Did he lay his project much deeper than the surface of things? Did Campanella imagine that, if men were allowed to philosophise with the utmost freedom, the despotism of religion and politics would dissolve away in the weakness of its quiescent state?

The project is a chimera—but, according to the projector, the political and religious freedom of *England* formed its greatest obstacle. Part of his plan, therefore, includes the means of weakening the Insular heretics by intestine divisions—a mode not seldom practised by the continental powers of France and Spain.

The political project of this fervid genius was, that his "Prince," the Spanish king, should be the mightiest sovereign in Europe. For this, he was first to prohibit all theological controversies from the Transalpine schools, those of Germany, &c. "A controversy," he observes, "always shows a kind of victory, and may serve as an authority to a bad cause." He would therefore admit of no commentaries on the Bible, to prevent all diversity of opinion. He would have revived the ancient philosophical sects, instead of the modern religious sects.

The *Greek* and the *Hebrew* languages were not to be taught! for the republican freedom of the ancient Jews and Grecians had often proved destructive of monarchy. Hobbes, in the bold scheme of his *Leviathan*, seems to have been aware of this fatality. Campanella would substitute for these ancient languages the study of the *Arabic* tongue! The troublesome Transalpine wits might then employ themselves in confuting the Turks, rather than in vexing the Catholics; so closely did sagacity and extravagance associate in the mind of this wild genius. But *Mathematical* and *Astronomical* schools, and other institutions for the encouragement of the *mechanical arts*, and particularly those to

reply of the philosopher, who would not dispute with a
crowned head, " were to be called to aid you against a
young country physician, who had so long discontinued
studies of this nature." However, he announces that
he has finished three more works against the Royal

which the northern genius is most apt, as navigation, &c., were to occupy the studies of the people, divert them from exciting fresh troubles,
and withdraw them from theological factions. Campanella thus would
make men great in science, having first made them slaves in politics;
a philosophical people were to be the subjects of despots—not an impossible event!

His plan, remarkable enough, of *weakening the English*, I give in
his words:—"No better way can possibly be found than by causing
divisions and dissensions among them, and by continually keeping up
the same; which will furnish the Spaniard and the French with advantageous opportunities. As for their religion, which is a mo lerated
Calvinism, that cannot be so easily extinguished and rooted out there,
unless there were some schools set up in Flanders, where the English
have great commerce, by means of which there may be scattered abroad
the seeds of schism and division. These people being of a nature which
is still desirous of novelties and change, they are easily wrought over
to anything." These *schools* were tried at Douay in Flanders, and at
Valladolid in Spain, and other places. They became nests of rebellion
for the English Catholics; or for any one, who, being discontented
with government, was easily converted to any religion which aimed to
overturn the British Constitution. The *secret history* of the Roman
Catholics in England remains yet to be told: they indeed had their
martyrs and their heroes; but the *public effects* appear in the frequent
executions which occurred in the reigns of Elizabeth and James.

Stubbe appears to have imagined that the ROYAL SOCIETY was
really formed on the principle of Campanella: to withdraw the people
from intermeddling with *politics* and *religion*, by engaging them merely
in philosophical pursuits.—The reaction of the public mind is an object
not always sufficiently indicated by historians. The vile hypocrisy and
mutual persecutions of the numerous fanatics occasioned very relaxed
and tolerant principles of religion at the Restoration; as, the democratic
fury having spent itself, too great an indulgence was now allowed to
monarchy. Stubbe was alarmed that, should Popery be established,
the crown of England would become feudatory to foreign power, and
embroil the nation in the restitution of all the abbey lands, of which,
at the Reformation, the Church had so zealously been plundered. He

Society, and has a fourth nearly ready, if it be necessary
to prove that the rhetorical history of the Society by
Sprat must be bad, because " no eloquence can be complete if the subject-matter be foolish !" His adversaries
not only threatened to write his life, * but they represented him to the king as a libeller, who ought to be whipped
at a cart's tail ; a circumstance which Stubbe records
with the indignation of a Roman spirit. † They stopped

was still further alarmed that the *virtuosi* would influence the education of our youth to these purposes; "an evil," says he, "which has
been guarded against by our ancestors in foun ling *free-schools*, by uniformity of instruction cementing men's minds." We now smile at
these terrors; perhaps they were sometimes real. The absolute necessity of strict conformity to the prevalent religion of Europe was
avowed in that unrivalled scheme of depotism, which menaced to
efface every trace of popular freedom, and the independence of nations,
under the dominion of Napoleon.

* To this threat of writing his life, we have already noticed the
noble apology he has drawn up for the versatility of his opinions. See
p. 161. At the moment of the Restoration it was unwise for any of
the parties to reproach another for their opinions or their actions. In
a national revolution, most men are implicated in the general reproach;
and Stubbe said, on this occasion, that "he had observed worse faces
in the society than his own." Waller, and Sprat, and Cowley had
equall.· commemorated the protectorship of Cromwell and the restoration of Charles. Our satirist insidiously congratulates himself that "he
had never compared Oliver the regicide to Moses. or his son to Joshua;"
nor that he had ever written any Pindaric ode. "dedicated to the happy
memory of the most renowned Prince Oliver, Lord Protector:" nothing
to recommend "the sacred urn of that blessed spirit to the veneration
of posterity; as if

"His *fame*, like men. the elder it doth grow,
Will of itself turn *whiter* too,
Without what needle-s art can do "

These lines were. I think, taken from Sprat himself! Stubbe adds, it
would be "imprudent in them to look beyond the act of idemnity and
oblivion, which was more necessary to the Royal Society than to me,
who joined with no party, &c."—*Preface to " Legends no Histories."*

† He has described this intercourse of his enemies at court with the
king, where, when this punishment was suggested, "a generous per-

his work several times, and by some stratagem they
hindered him from correcting the press; but nothing
could impede the career of his fearless genius. He
treated with infinite ridicule their trivial or their marvellous discoveries in his "Legends no Histories," and his
"Censure on some Passages of the History of the Royal
Society." But while he ridiculed, he could instruct them;
often contributing new knowledge, which the Royal
Society had certainly been proud to have registered in
their history. In his determination of depreciating the
novelties of his day, he disputes even the honour of
Harvey to the discovery of the circulation of the blood:
he attributes it to Andreas Cæsalpinus, who not only
discovered it, but had given it the name of *Circulatio
Sanguinis.**

sonage, altogether unknown to me, being present, bravely and frankly
interposed, saying, that ' whatever I was. I was a Roman; that Englishmen were not s) precipitously to be condemned to so exemplary a punishment: that representing that book to be a libel against the king
was too remote a consequence to be admitted of in a nation free-born,
and governed by laws, and tender of ill precedents.'" It was a noble
speech, in the relaxed politics of the court of Charles II. He who
made it deserved to have had his name more explicitly told: he is
designated as "that excellent Englishman, the great ornament of this
age nation. and House of Commons; he whose single worth balanceth
much of the debaucheries, follies. and impertinences of the kingdom."
—*A Reply unto the Letter written to Mr. Henry Stubbe, Oxford, 1671*,
p. 20.

    * Stubbe gives some curious information on this subject. Harvey
published his Treatise at Frankfort, 1628. but Cæsalpinus's work had
appeared in 1593. Harvey adopted the notion. and more fully and
perspicuously proved it. I shall give what Stubbe says. "Harvey,
in his two Answers to Riolan, nowhere asserts the invention so to
himself, as to deny that he had the intimation or notion from Cæsalpinus; and his silence I take for a tacit confession. His *ambition of
glory* made him *willing to be thought the author of a paradox* he had so
illustrated. and brought upon the stage, where *it lay unregarded*, and
in all probability buried in oblivion; yet such was his modesty, as not

Stubbe was not only himself a man of science, but a caustic satirist, who blends much pleasantry with his bitterness. In the first ardour of philosophical discovery, the Society, delighted by the acquisition of new facts, which, however, rarely proved to be important, and were often ludicrous in their detail, appear to have too much neglected the arts of reasoning; they did not even practise common discernment, or what we might term philosophy in its more enlarged sense. * Stubbe, with no

to vindicate it to himself by telling a lie."—Stubbe's *Censure*, &c., p. 112.

I give this literary anecdote, as it enters into the history of most discoveries, of which the *improvers*, rather than the *inventors*, are usually the most known to the world. Bayle, who wrote much later than Stubbe, asserts the same, and has preserved the entire passage, art. *Cæsalpinus*. It is said Harvey is more expressly indebted to a passage in Servetus, which Wotton has given in the preface to his "Reflections on Ancient and Modern Learning," edition 1725. The notion was probably then afloat, and each alike contributed to its development. Thus it was disputed with Copernicus, whether his great discovery of a fixed sun, and the earth wheeling round that star, was his own; others had certainly observed it; yet the invention was still Copernican: for that great genius alone corrected, extended, and gave perfection to a hint, till it expanded to a system.

So gradual have often been the great inventions of genius. What others *conjectured*, and some *discovered*, Harvey *demonstrated*. The fate of Harvey's discovery is a curious instance of that patience and fortitude which genius must too often exert in respect to itself. Though Harvey lived to his eightieth year, he hardly witnessed his great discovery established before he died; and it has been said, that he was the only one of his contemporaries who lived to see it in some repute. No physician adopted it; and when it got into vogue, they then disputed whether he was the inventor! Sir William Temple denied not only the discovery, but the doctrine of the Circulation of the Blood. "Sense can hardly allow it; which," says he, "in this dispute must be satisfied as well as reason, before mankind will concur."

* Stubbe has an eloquent passage, which describes the philosophy of science. The new Experimental School had perhaps too wholly rejected some virtues of the old one; the cultivation of the human under-

respect for "a Society," though dignified by the addition
of "Royal," says, "a cabinet of virtuosi are but pitiful
reasoners. Ignorance is infectious; and 'tis possible for
men to grow fools by contact. I will speak to the virtuosi in the language of the Romish Saint Francis (who,
in the wilderness, so humbly addressed his only friends),
'*Salvete, fratres asini! Salvete, fratres lupi!*'" As
for their Transactions and their History, he thinks
"they purpose to grow famous, as the Turks do to gain
Paradise, *by treasuring up all the waste paper they meet
with.*" He rallies them on some ridiculous attempts,
such as "An Art of Flying;" an art, says Stubbe, in
which they have not so much as effected the most facile
part of the attempt, which is to break their necks!

Sprat, in his dedication to the king, had said that "the
establishment of the Royal Society was an enterprise
equal to the most renowned actions of the best princes."
One would imagine that the notion of a monarch found-

standing, as well as the mere observation on the facts that they collected ; an error which has not been entirely removed.

"That art of reasoning by which the prudent are discriminated from
fools, which methodiseth and facilitates our discourses, which informs
us of the validity of consequences and the probability of arguments,
and manifests the fallacies of impostors : that art which gives life to
solid eloquence, and which renders Statesmen. Divines. Physicians,
and Lawyers accomplished : how is this cried down and vilified by the
ignoramuses of these days! What contempt is there raised upon the
disputative Ethics of Aristotle and the Stoics; and those moral instructions. which have produced the Alexanders and the Ptolemies,
the Pompeys and the Ciceroes, are now slighted in comparison of *day-
labouring!* Did we live at Sparta, where the daily employments were
the exercises of substantial virtue and gallantry, and *men,* like *setting
dogs.* were rather *bred up* unto, than *taught* reason and worth, it were
a more tolerable proposal (though the different policy of these times
would not admit of it); but this *working. so* recommended, is but the
feeding of corp in the air, &c. As for the study of Politics. and all
critical learning. these are either pedantical, or tedious. to those who
have *a shorter way of studying men.*"—*Preface to "Legends no Histories."*

ing a society for the cultivation of the sciences could hardly be made objectionable; but, in literary controversy, genius has the power of wresting all things to its purpose by its own peculiar force, and the art of placing every object in the light it chooses, and can thus obtain our attention in spite of our conviction. I will add the curious animadversion of Stubbe on Sprat's compliment to the king :—

" Never Prince acquired the fame of great and good by any knicknacks—but by actions of political wisdom, courage, justice," &c.

Stubbe shows how Dionysius and Nero had been depraved by these *mechanic philosophers*—that

" An Aristotelian would never pardon himself if he compared *this* heroical enterprise with the actions of our Black Prince or Henry V.; or with Henry VIII. in demolishing abbeys and rejecting the papal authority; or Queen Elizabeth's exploits against Spain; or her restoring the Protestant religion, putting the Bible into English, and supporting the Protestants beyond sea. But the reason he (Sprat) gives why the establishment of the Royal Society of experimentators equals the most renowned actions of the best princes, is such a pitiful one as Guzman de Alfarache never met with in the whole extent of the *Hospital of Fools*—' To increase the power, by new arts, of conquered nations !' These consequences are twisted like the *cordage of Ocnus*, the God of Sloth, in hell, which are fit for nothing but to *fodder asses with*. If our historian means by *every little invention to increase the powers of mankind*, as an enterprise of such renown, he is deceived ; this glory is not due to such as go about with a dog and a hoop, nor to the practicers of legerdemain, or upon the high or low rope; not to every mountebank and his man Andrew; all which, with many other mechanical and experimental philosophers,

do in some sort increase the powers of mankind, and
differ no more from some of the virtuosi, than *a cat in a
hole* doth from *a cat out of a hole;* betwixt which that
inquisitive person Asdryasdust Tossoffacan found a very
great resemblance. 'Tis not the increasing of the *powers
of mankind* by a pendulum watch, nor spectacles whereby divers may see under water, nor the new ingenuity
of apple-roasters, nor every petty discovery or instrument, must be put in comparison, much less preferred,
before the *protection and enlargement of empires.*" *

Had Stubbe's death not occurred, this warfare had
probably continued. He insisted on a complete victory.
He had forced the Royal Society to disclaim their own
works, by an announcement that they were not answerable, as a body, for the various contributions which they
gave the world : an advertisement which has been more
than once found necessary to be renewed. As for their
historian Sprat, our intrepid Stubbe very unexpectedly
offered to manifest to the parliament that this courtly
adulator, by his book, was chargeable with high treason ;
if they believed that the Royal Society were really engaged so deeply as he averred in the portentous Cæsarean Popery of Campanella. Glanvill, who had "insulted all university learning," had been immolated at the
pedestal of Aristotle. " I have done enough," he adds,
"since my animadversions contain more than they all
knew; and that these have shown that the *virtuosi* are
very great impostors, or men of little reading;" alluding
to the various discoveries which they promulgated as
novelties, but which Stubbe had asserted were known to
the ancients and others of a later period. This forms a
perpetual accusation against the inventors and discoverers, who may often exclaim, "Perish those who have

---

* "Legends no Histories," p. 5.

done our good works before us!" "The Discoveries of the Ancients and Moderns" by Dutens, had this book been then published, might have assisted our keen investigator; but our combatant ever proudly met his adversaries single-handed.

The "Philosophical Transactions" were afterwards accused of another kind of high treason, against grammar and common sense. It was long before the collectors of facts practised the art of writing on them; still later before they could philosophise, as well as observe: Bacon and Boyle were at first only imitated in their patient industry. When Sir Hans Sloane was the secretary of the Royal Society, he, and most of his correspondents, wrote in the most confused manner imaginable. A wit of a very original cast, the facetious Dr. King,* took advantage of their perplexed and often unintelligible descriptions; of the meanness of their style, which humbled even the great objects of nature; of their credulity that heaped up marvels, and their vanity that prided itself on petty discoveries, and invented a new

---

* Dr. King was allied to the families of Clarendon and Rochester; he took a degree as Doctor of Civil Law, and soon got into great practice. "He afterwards went with the Earl of Pembroke, Lord-Lieutenant, to Ireland, where he became Judge Advocate, Sole Commissioner of the Prizes, Keeper of the Records, Vicar-General to the Lord Primate of Ireland; was countenanced by persons of the highest rank, and might have made a fortune. But so far was he from heaping up riches, that he returned to England with no other treasure than a few merry poems and humorous essays, and returned to his student's place in Christ Church."—*Enc. Brit*. He was assisted by Bolingbroke; but when his patronage failed, Swift procured him the situation of editor to "Barber's Gazette." He ultimately took to drinking; Lintot the bookseller, told Pope, "I remember Dr. King could write verses in a tavern three hours after he could not speak." His last patron was Lord Clarendon, and he died in apartments he had provided for him in London, Dec. 25, 1712, and was buried in the cloisters of Westminster Abbey at the expense of his lordship.—ED.

species of satire. Sloane, a name endeared to posterity, whose life was that of an enthusiast of science, and who was the founder of a national collection; and his numerous friends, many of whose names have descended with the regard due to the votaries of knowledge, fell the victims. Wit is an unsparing leveller.

The new species of literary burlesque which King seems to have invented, consists in selecting the very expressions and absurd passages from the original he ridiculed, and framing out of them a droll dialogue or a grotesque narrative, he adroitly inserted his own remarks, replete with the keenest irony, or the driest sarcasm.* Our arch wag says, "The bulls and blunders which Sloane and his friends so naturally pour forth cannot be

* Sloane describes Clark, the famous posture-master, " Phil. Trans." No. 242, certainly with the wildest grammar. but with many curious particulars; the gentleman in one of Dr. King's Dialogues inquires the secretary's opinion of the causes of this man's wonderful pliability of limbs; a question which Sloane had thus solved, with colloquial ease: it depended upon "bringing the body to it. by using himself to it."

In giving an account of "a child born without a brain"—"Had it lived long enough," said King, "it would have made an excellent publisher of Philosophical Transactions!"

Sloane presented the Royal Society with "a figure of a Chinese, representing one of that nation using an ear-picker, and expressing great satisfaction therein."—"Whatever pleasure," said that learned physician, "the Chinese may take in thus picking their ears, I am certain most people in these parts, who have had their hearing impaired, have had such misfortune first come to them by picking their ears too much."—He is so *curious*, says King, that the secretary took as much satisfaction in looking upon the ear-picker, as the Chinese could do in picking their ears!

But " What drowning is"—that " Hanging is only apoplexy!" that "Men cannot swallow when they are dead!" that "No fish die of fevers!" that "Hogs s—t soap, and cows s—t fire?" that the secretary had "Shells, called *Blackmoor's-teeth*, I suppose from their *wh tene-s!*" and the learned Ray's, that grave naturalist, incredible description of "a very curious little instrument!" I leave to the reader and Dr. King.

misrepresented, so careful I am in producing them."
King still moves the risible muscles of his readers. "The
Voyage to Cajamai," a travestie of Sloane's valuable
"History of Jamaica," is still a peculiar piece of humour;
and it has been rightly distinguished as "one of the
severest and merriest satires that was ever written in
prose."* The author might indeed have blushed at the
labour bestowed on these drolleries; he might have
dreaded that humour so voluminous might grow tedious;
but King, often with a Lucianic spirit, with flashes of
Rabelais, and not seldom with the causticity of his friend
Swift, dissipated life in literary idleness, with parodies
and travesties on most of his contemporaries; and he
made these little things often more exquisite at the cost
of consuming on them a genius capable of better. A
parodist or a burlesquer is a wit who is perpetually on
the watch to catch up or to disguise an author's words,
to swell out his defects, and pick up his blunders—to
amuse the public! King was a wit, who lived on the
highway of literature, appropriating, for his own purpose,
the property of the most eminent passengers, by a dex-

---

* Sir Hans Sloane was unhappily not insensible to these ludicrous
assaults, and in the preface to his "History of Jamaica," 1707, a work
so highly prized for its botanical researches, absolutely anticipated
this fatal facetiousness, for thus he delivers himself:—"Those who
strive to make ridiculous anything of this kind, and think themselves
great wits, but are very ignorant, and understand nothing of the
argument, these, if one were afraid of them, and consulted his own
ease, might possibly hinder the publication of any such work, the
efforts to be expected from them, making possibly some impression
upon persons of equal dispositions: but considering that I have the
approbation of others, whose judgment, knowledge, &c., I have great
reason to value; and considering that these sorts of men have been in
all ages ready to do the like, not only to ordinary persons and their
equals, but even to abuse their prince and blaspheme their Maker, I
shall, as I have ever since I seriously considered this matter, think of
and treat them with the greatest contempt."

trous mode no other had hit on. What an important
lesson the labours of King offer to real genius! Their
temporary humour lost with their prototypes becomes
like a paralytic limb, which, refusing to do its office,
impedes the action of the vital members.

Wotton, in summing up his "Reflections upon Ancient
and Modern Learning," was doubtful whether knowledge
would improve in the next age proportionably as it had
done in his own. "The humour of the age is visibly
altered," he says, "from what it had been thirty years
ago. Though the Royal Society has weathered the rude
attacks of Stubbe," yet "the sly insinuations of the *Men
of Wit*," with "the *public ridiculing* of all who spend
their time and fortunes in scientific or curious researches,
have so taken off the edge of those who have opulent
fortunes and a love to learning, that these studies begin
to be contracted amongst physicians and mechanics."—
He treats King with good-humour. " A man is got but
a very little way (in philosophy) that is concerned as
often as such a merry gentleman as Dr. King shall think
fit to make himself sport."*

* Dr. King's dispersed works have fortunately been collected by Mr.
Nichols, with ample illustrations, in three vols. 8vo, 1776. The
"Useful Transactions in Philosophy and other sorts of Learning,"
form a collection of ludicrous dissertations of Antiquarianism, Natural
Philosophy, Criticism, &c, where his own peculiar humour combines
with his curious reading. [In this he burlesqued the proceedings of
the Royal and Antiquarian Societies with some degree of spirit and
humour. By turning vulgar lines into Greek, Latin, and Anglo-Saxon,
a learned air is given to some papers on childish subjects. One learned
doctor communicates to another "an Essay proving, by arguments
philosophical, that millers, falsely so reputed, are not thieves, with an
interesting argument that taylors likewise are not so." A Welsh
schoolmaster sends some "natural observations" made in Wales, in
direct imitation of the "Philosophical Transactions" for 1707, and
with humorous love for genealogy, reckons that in his school, "since
the flood, there have been 466, and I am the 467th master: before the

SIR JOHN HILL,

WITH

THE ROYAL SOCIETY, FIELDING, SMART, &c.

A PARALLEL between Orator Henley and Sir John Hill—his love of the Science of Botany, with the fate of his "Vegetable System"—ridicules scientific Collectors; his "Dissertation on Royal Societies," and his "Review of the Works of the Royal Society"—compliments himself that he is NOT a Member—successful in his attacks on the Experimentalists, but loses his spirit in encountering the Wits—"The Inspector"—a paper war with Fielding—a literary stratagem—battles with Smart and Woodward—Hill appeals to the Nation for the Office of Keeper of the Sloane Collection—closes his life by turning Empiric—Some Epigrams on Hill—his Miscellaneous Writings.

IN the history of literature we discover some who have opened their career with noble designs, and

flood, they living long, there were but two—Rice ap Evan Dha the good, and Davie ap Shones Gonnah the naught, in whose time the flood came." The first paper of the collection is an evident jest on John Bagford and his gatherings for the history of printing, now preserved among the manuscripts of the British Museum. It purports to be "an Essay on the invention of samplers, communicated by Mrs. Judith Bagford, with an account of her collections for the same," and written in burlesque of a paper in the "Philosophical Transactions" for April, 1697. It is a most elaborate performance, deducing with mock-seriousness the origin of samplers from the ancient tales of Arachne, who "set forth the whole story of her wrongs in needlework, and sent it to her sister;" and our author adds, with much humour, "it is very remarkable that the memory of this story does at present continue, for there are no samplers, which proceed in any measure beyond the first rudiments, but have a tree and a nightingale sitting on it." Such were the jests of the day against the Royal philosophers.] He also invented *satirical and humorous indexes*, not the least facetious parts of his volumes. King had made notes on more than 20,000 books and MSS., and his *Adversaria*, of which a portion has been preserved, is not inferior in curiosity to the literary journals of Gibbon, though it wants the investigating spirit of the modern philosopher.

with no deficient powers, yet unblest with stoic virtues,
having missed, in their honourable labours, those rewards
they had anticipated, they have exhibited a sudden
transition of character, and have left only a name proverbial for its disgrace.

Our own literature exhibits two extraordinary characters, indelibly marked by the same traditional odium.
The wit and acuteness of Orator Henley, and the science
and vivacity of the versatile Sir John Hill, must separate
them from those who plead the same motives for abjuring all moral restraint, without having ever furnished the
world with a single instance that they were capable of
forming nobler views.

This *orator* and this *knight* would admit of a close
parallel;* both as modest in their youth as afterwards
remarkable for their effrontery. Their youth witnessed
the same devotedness to study, with the same inventive
and enterprising genius. Hill projected and pursued a
plan of botanical travels, to form a collection of rare
plants: the patronage he received was too limited, and
he suffered the misfortune of having anticipated the
national taste for the science of botany by half a century.
Our young philosopher's valuable "Treatise on Gems,"
from Theophrastus, procured for him the warm friendship
of the eminent members of the Royal Society. To this
critical period of the lives of Henley and of Hill, their
resemblance is striking; nor is it less from the moment
the surprising revolution in their characters occurred.

Pressed by the wants of life, they lost its decencies.
Henley attempted to poise himself against the University; Hill against the Royal Society. Rejected by these
learned bodies, both these Cains of literature, amid their
luxuriant ridicule of eminent men, still evince some

* The moral and literary character of Henley has been developed in
"Calamities of Authors."

claims to rank among them. The one prostituted his
genius in his "Lectures;" the other, in his "Inspectors."
Never two authors were more constantly pelted with
epigrams, or buffeted in literary quarrels. They have
met with the same fate; covered with the same odium.
Yet Sir John Hill, this despised man, after all the fertile
absurdities of his literary life, performed more for the
improvement of the "Philosophical Transactions," and
was the cause of diffusing a more general taste for the
science of botany, than any other contemporary. His
real ability extorts that regard which his misdirected
ingenuity, instigated by vanity, and often by more
worthless motives, had lost for him in the world.*

* The twenty-six folios of his "Vegetable System," with many
others, testify his love and his labour. It contains 1600 plates, representing 26,000 different figures of plants *from nature only.* This publication ruined the author, whose widow (the sister of Lord Ranelagh)
published "An Address to the Public, by the Hon. Lady Hill, setting
forth the consequences of the late Sir John Hill's acquaintance with
the Earl of Bute," 1787. I should have noticed it in the "Calamities
of Authors." It offers a sad and mortifying lesson to the votary of
science who aspires to a noble enterprise. Lady Hill complains of the
patron; but a patron, however great, cannot always raise the public
taste to the degree required to afford the only true patronage which
can animate and reward an author. Her detail is impressive:—

"Sir John Hill had just wrote a book of great elegance—I think it
was called 'Exotic Botany'—which he wished to have presented to the
king, and therefore named it to Lord Bute. His lordship waived that,
saying that 'he had a greater object to propose;' and shortly after
laid before him a plan of the most voluminous, magnificent, and costly
work that ever man attempted. I tremble when I name its title—
because I think the severe application which it required killed him;
and I am sure the expense ruined his fortune—'The Vegetable System.' This work was to consist of twenty-six volumes folio, containing sixteen hundred copper-plates, the engraving of each cost four
guineas; the paper was of the most expensive kind; the drawings by
the first hands. The printing was also a very weighty concern; and
many other articles, with which I am unacquainted. Lord Bute said
that 'the expense had been considered, and that Sir John Hill might

At the time that Hill was engaged in several large
compilations for the booksellers, his employers were desirous that the honours of an F.R.S. should ornament
his title-page. This versatile genius, however, during
these graver works, had suddenly emerged from his
learned garret, and, in the shape of a fashionable lounger,
rolled in his chariot from the Bedford to Ranelagh; was
visible at routs; and sate at the theatre a tremendous ar-
biter of taste, raising about him tumults and divisions;*
and in his " Inspectors," a periodical paper which he published in the *London Daily Advertiser*, retailed all the
great matters relating to himself, and all the little matters he collected in his rounds relating to others.
Among other personalities, he indulged his satirical
fluency on the scientific collectors. The Antiquarian
Society were twitted as medal-scrapers and antediluvian
knife-grinders; conchologists were turned into cockle-
shell merchants; and the naturalists were made to re-

rest assured his circumstances should not be injured.' Thus he
entered upon and finished his destruction. The sale bore no proportion to the expense. After 'The Vegetable System' was completed,
Lord Bute proposed another volume to be added, which Sir John
strenuously opposed; but his lordship repeating his desire, Sir John
complied, lest his lordship should find a pretext to cast aside repeated
promises of ample provision for himself and family. But this was the
crisis of his fate—he died." Lady Hill adds:—" He was a character
on which every virtue was impressed." The domestic partiality of
the widow cannot alter the truth of the narrative of " The Vegetable
System." and its twenty-six tomes.

* His apologist forms this excuse for one then affecting to be a
student and a rake:—" Though engaged in works which required the
attention of a whole life, he was so exact an economist of his time that
he scarcely ever missed a public amusement for many years; and
this, as he somewhere observes, was of no small service to him; as,
without indulging in these respects, he could not have undergone the
fatigue and study inseparable from the execution of his vast designs."
—Short account of the " Life, Writings, and Character of the late Sir
John Hill, M. D." Edinburgh: 1779.

cord pompous histories of stickle-backs and cock-chafers.
Cautioned by Martin Folkes, President of the Royal
Society,* not to attempt his election, our enraged comic
philosopher, who had preferred his jests to his friends,
now discovered that he had lost three hundred at once.
Hill could not obtain three signatures to his recommendation. Such was the real, but, as usual, not the ostensible,
motive of his formidable attack on the Royal Society.
He produced his " Dissertation on Royal Societies, in a
letter from a Sclavonian nobleman to his friend," 1751 ;
a humorous prose satire, exhibiting a ludicrous description of a tumultuous meeting at the Royal Society,
contrasted with the decorum observed in the French
Academy ; and moreover, he added a *conversazione* in a
coffee-house between some of the members.

Such was the declaration of war, in a first act of hostility ; but the pitched-battle was fought in " A Review
of the Works of the Royal Society, in eight parts," 1751.
This literary satire is nothing less than a quarto volume,
resembling, in its form and manner, the Philosophical
Transactions themselves ; printed as if for the convenience of members to enable them to bind the " Review "
with the work reviewed. Voluminous pleasantry incurs
the censure of that tedious trifling which it designs to
expose. In this literary facetia, however, no inconsiderable knowledge is interspersed with the ridicule. Perhaps Hill might have recollected the successful attempts
of Stubbe on the Royal Society, who contributed that
curious knowledge which he pretended the Royal So-

* Hogarth has painted a portrait of Folkes, which is still hanging
in the rooms of the Royal Society. He was nominated vice-president
by the great Sir Isaac Newton, and succeeded him as president. He
wrote a work on the " English Silver Coinage," and died at the age of
sixty-four, 1754.—ED.

ciety wanted; and with this knowledge he attempted to combine the humour of Dr. King.*

Hill's rejection from the Royal Society, to another man would have been a puddle to step over; but he tells a story, and cleanly passes on, with impudent adroitness. †

* Hill planned his Review with good sense. He says:—"If I am merry in some places, it ought to be considered that the subjects are too ridiculous for serious criticism. That the work, however, might not be without its *real use*, an *Error* is nowhere exposed without establishing a *Truth* in its place." He has incidentally thrown out much curious knowledge—such as his plan for forming a *Hortus Siccus*, &c. The Review itself may still be considered both as curious and entertaining.

† In exposing their deficiencies, as well as their redundancies, Hill only wishes, as he tells us, that the Society may by this means become ashamed of what it has been, and that the world may know that *he is* NOT *a member of it till it is an honour to a man to be so!* This was telling the world, with some ingenuity, and with no little impudence, that the Royal Society would not admit him as a member. He pretends to give a secret anecdote to explain the cause of this rejection. Hill, in every critical conjuncture of his affairs, and they were frequent ones, had always a story to tell, or an evasion, which served its momentary purpose. When caned by an Irish gentleman at Ranelagh, and his personal courage, rather than his stoicism, was suspected, he published a story of *his* having once caned a person whom he called Mario; on which a wag, considering Hill as a Prometheus, wrote—

" To beat one man great Hill was fated.
What man?—a man whom he created!"

We shall see the story he turned to his purpose, when pressed hard by Fielding. In the present instance, in a letter to a foreign correspondent, who had observed his name on the list of the *Corre pon lents* of the Royal Society, Hill said—"You are to know that *I have the honour* NOT *to be a member of the Royal Society of London.*"—This letter lay open on his table when a member, upon his accustomed visit, came in, and in his absence read it. " And we are not to wonder," says Hill, " that he who could obtain intelligence in this manner could also divulge it. *Hinc illæ lachrymæ!* Hence all the animosities that have since disturbed this philosophic world." While Hill insolently congratulates himself that he is *not* a member of the Royal Society, he

Hill, however, though he used all the freedom of a

has most evidently shown that he had no objection to be the member of any society which would enrol his name among them. He obtained his medical degree from no honourable source; and another title, which he affected, he mysteriously contracted into barbaric dissonance. Hill entitled himself—

Acad. Reg. Scient. Burd. &c. Soc.

To which Smart, in the "Hilliad." alludes—

" While *Jorgon* gave his titles on a *block*,
And styled him M.D. Acad. Budig. Soc."

His personal attacks on Martin Folkes, the president, are caustic, but they may not be true; and on Baker, celebrated for his microscopical discoveries, are keen. He reproaches Folkes, in his severe dedication of the work, in all the dignity of solemn invective—"The manner in which you represented me to a noble friend, while to myself you made me much more than I deserved; the ease with which you had excused yourself, and the solemnity with which, in the face of Almighty God, you excused yourself again ; when we remember that the whole was done within the compass of a day ; these are surely virtues in a patron that I, of all men, ought not to pass over in silence." Baker, in his early days, had unluckily published a volume of lusory poems. Some imitations of Prior's loose tales Hill makes use of to illustrate *his* "Philosophical Transactions." All is food for the malicious digestion of Wit!

His anecdote of Mr. Baker's *Louse* is a piece of secret scientific history sufficiently ludicrous.

"The Duke of Montague was famous for his love to the whole animal creation, and for his being able to keep a very grave face when not in the most serious earnest. Mr. Baker, a distinguished member of the Royal Society, had one day entertained this nobleman and several other persons with the sight of the peristaltic motion of the bowels in a louse, by the microscope. When the observation was over, he was going to throw the creature away; but the Duke, with a face that made him believe he was perfectly in earnest, told him it would be not only cruel, but ungrateful, in return for the entertainment that creature had given them, to destroy it. He ordered the boy to be brought in from whom it was procured, and after praising the smallness and delicacy of Mr. Baker's fingers, persuaded him carefully to replace the animal in its former territories, and to give the boy a shilling not to disturb it for a fortnight."—"A Review of the Works of the Royal Society," by John Hill, M.D., p. 5.

satirist, by exposing many ridiculous papers, taught the
Royal Society a more cautious selection. It could, however, obtain no forgiveness from the parties it offended;
and while the respectable men whom Hill had the audacity to attack, Martin Folkes, the friend and successor
of Newton, and Henry Baker, the naturalist, were above
his censure,—his own reputation remained in the hands
of his enemies. While Hill was gaining over the laughers on his side, that volatile populace soon discovered
that the fittest object to be laughed at was our literary
Proteus himself.

The most egregious egotism alone could have induced
this versatile being, engaged in laborious works, to venture to give the town the daily paper of *The Inspector*
which he supported for about two years. It was a light
scandalous chronicle all the week, with a seventh-day
sermon. His utter contempt for the genius of his contemporaries, and the bold conceit of his own, often rendered the motley pages amusing. *The Inspector* became,
indeed, the instrument of his own martyrdom; but his
impudence looked like magnanimity; for he endured,
with undiminished spirit, the most biting satires, the most
wounding epigrams, and more palpable castigations.* His

* These papers had appeared in the London *Daily Advertiser*, 1754.
At their close he gleaned the best. and has preserved them in two
volumes. But as Hill will never rank as a classic, the original nonsense will be considered as most proper for the purposes of a true collector. Woodward, the comedian. in his lively attack on Hill, has
given "a mock Inspector," an exquisite piece of literary ridicule,
in which he has hit off the egotisms and slovenly ease of the real
ones. Never, like "The Inspector," flamed such a provoking prodigy
in the cloudy skies of Grub-street; and Hill seems studiously to have
mortified his luckless rivals by a perpetual embroidery of his adventures in the "Walks at Marybone." the "Rotunda at Ranelagh,"
spangled over with "my domestics," and "my equipage." [One of
his adventures at Ranelagh was sufficiently unfortunate to obtain for
him the unenviable notoriety of a caricature print representing him

vein of pleasantry ran more freely in his attacks on the
Royal Society than in his other literary quarrels. When
Hill had not to banter ridiculous experimentalists, but
to encounter wits, his reluctant spirit soon bowed its
head. Suddenly even his pertness loses its vivacity; he
becomes drowsy with dulness, and, conscious of the du-
biousness of his own cause, he skulks away terrified: he
felt that the mask of quackery and impudence which he
usually wore was to be pulled off by the hands now extended against him.

A humorous warfare of wit opened between Fielding,
in his *Covent-Garden Journal*, and Hill, in his *Inspector*.
The Inspector had made the famous lion's head, at the
Bedford, which the genius of Addison and Steele had
once animated, the receptacle of his wit; and the wits
asserted, of this now *inutile lignum*, that it was reduced
to a mere state of *blockheadism*. Fielding occasionally
gave a facetious narrative of a paper war between the
forces of Sir Alexander Draweansir, the literary hero of
the *Covent-Garden Journal*, and the army of Grub-
street; it formed an occasional literary satire. Hill's
lion, no longer Addison's or Steele's, is not described
without humour. Draweansir's "troops are kept in awe
by a strange mixed monster, not much unlike the famous
chimera of old. For while some of our Reconnoiterers
tell us that this monster has the appearance of a lion,

enduring a castigation at the Rotunda gate from an Irish gentleman
named Brown, with whose character he had made far too free in one
of his "Inspectors." Hill showed much pusillanimity in the affair,
took to his bed, and gave out that the whole thing was a conspiracy
to murder him. This occasioned the publication of another print, in
which he is represented in bed, surrounded by medical men, who treat
him with very little respect. One insists on his fee, because Hill has
never been acknowledged as one of themselves; and another, to his
plea of want of money, responds, "Sell your sword, it is only an en-
cumbrance."]

others assure us that his ears are much longer than those
of that generous beast."

Hill ventured to notice this attack on his "blockhead;"
and, as was usual with him, had some secret history to
season his defence with.

"The author of 'Amelia,' whom I have only once seen,
told me, at that accidental meeting, he held the present
set of writers in the utmost contempt; and that, in his
character of Sir Alexander Drawcansir, he should treat
them in the most unmerciful manner. He assured me he
had always excepted me; and after honouring me with
some encomiums, he proceeded to mention a conduct
which would be, he said, useful to both; this was, the
amusing our readers with a mock fight; giving blows
that would not hurt, and sharing the advantage in silence."*

Thus, by reversing the fact, Hill contrived to turn
aside the frequent stories against him by a momentary
artifice, arresting or dividing public opinion. The truth
was, more probably, as Fielding relates it, and the story,
as we shall see, then becomes quite a different affair. At
all events, Hill incurred the censure of the traitor who
violates a confidential intercourse.

> And if he lies not, must at least betray.
> POPE.

* It is useful to remind the public that they are often played upon
in this manner by the artifices of *political writers*. We have observed
symptoms of this deception practised at present. It is an old trick of
the craft, and was greatly used at a time when the nation seemed
maddened with political factions. In a pamphlet of "A View of London and Westminster, or the Town-Spy," 1725, I find this account:—
"The *seeming quarrel*, formerly, between *Mist's Journal* and the *Flying Post* was *secretly concerted* between themselves, in order to decoy
the eyes of all the parties on both their papers; and the project succeeded beyond all expectation; for I have been told that the former
narrowly missed getting an estate by it."—p. 32.

Fielding lost no time in reply. To have brought down the *Inspector* from his fastnesses into the open field, was what our new General only wanted: a battle was sure to be a victory. Our critical Drawcansir has performed his part, with his indifferent puns, but his natural facetiousness.

"It being reported to the General that a *hill* must be levelled, before the Bedford coffee-house could be taken, orders were given; but this was afterwards found to be a mistake; for this *hill* was only a little paltry *dunghill*, and had long before been levelled with the dirt. The General was then informed of a report which had been spread by his *lowness*, the Prince of Billingsgate, in the Grub-street army, that his Excellency had proposed, by a *secret treaty* with that Prince, to carry on the war only in appearance, and so to betray the common cause; upon which his Excellency said with a smile:—'If the betrayer of a private treaty could ever deserve the least credit, yet his Lowness here must proclaim himself either a liar or a fool. None can doubt but that he is the former, if he hath feigned this treaty; and I think few would scruple to call him the latter, if he had rejected it.' The General then declared the fact stood thus:—'His Lowness came to my tent on an affair of his own. I treated him, though a commander in the enemy's camp, with civility, and even kindness. I told him, with the utmost good-humour, I should attack his Lion; and that he might, if he pleased, in the same manner defend him; from which, said I, no great loss can happen on either side—'"

The Inspector slunk away, and never returned to the challenge.

During his inspectorship, he invented a whimsical literary stratagem, which ended in his receiving a castigation more lasting than the honours performed on him

at Ranelagh by the cane of a warm Hibernian. Hill
seems to have been desirous of abusing certain friends
whom he had praised in the *Inspectors;* so volatile, like
the loves of coquettes, are the literary friendships of the
"Scribleri." As this could not be done with any propriety there, he published the first number of a new
paper, entitled *The Impertinent.* Having thus relieved
his private feelings, he announced the cessation of this
new enterprise in his *Inspectors,* and congratulated the
public on the ill reception it had given to the *Impertinent,* applauding them for their having shown by this
that "their indignation was superior to their curiosity."
With impudence all his own, he adds—"It will not be
easy to say too much in favour of the candour of the
town, which has despised a piece that cruelly and unjustly attacked Mr. Smart the poet." What innocent
soul could have imagined that *The Impertinent* and *The
Inspector* were the same individual? The style is a
specimen of *persiflage;* the thin sparkling thought; the
pert vivacity, that looks like wit without wit; the glittering bubble, that rises in emptiness;—even its author
tells us, in *The Inspector,* it is "the most pert, the most
pretending," &c.*

* Isaac Reed, in his "Repository of Fugitive Pieces of Wit and
Humour," vol. iv., in republishing "The Hilliad," has judiciously preserved the offending " Impertinent " and the abjuring " Inspector." The
style of " The Impertinent " is volatile and poignant. His four classes
of authors are not without humour. "There are men who write because they have wit; there are those who write because they are
hungry; there are some of the modern authors who have a constant
fund of both these causes; and there are who will write, although
they are not instigated either by the one or by the other. The first
are all spirit; the second are all earth; the third disclose more life, or
more vapidity, as the one or the other cause prevails; and for the last,
having neither the one nor the other principle for the cause, they show
neither the one nor the other character in the effect; but begin, continue, and end, as if they had neither begun, continued, nor ended at

Smart, in return for our Janus-faced critic's treatment, balanced the amount of debtor and creditor with a pungent Dunciad *The Hilliad*. Hill, who had heard of the rod in pickle, anticipated the blow, to break its strength; and, according to his adopted system, introduced himself and Smart, with a story of his having recommended the bard to his bookseller, "who took him into salary on my approbation. I betrayed him into the profession, and having starved upon it, he has a right to abuse me." This story was formally denied by an advertisement from Newbery, the bookseller.

"The Hilliad" is a polished and pointed satire. The hero is thus exhibited on earth, and in heaven.

On earth, "a tawny sibyl," with "an old striped curtain—"

> And tatter'd tapestry o'er her shoulders hung—
> Her loins with patchwork cincture were begirt,
> That more than spoke diversity of dirt.
> Twain were her teeth, and single was her eye—
> Cold palsy shook her head——

with "moon-struck madness," awards him all the wealth and fame she could afford him for sixpence; and closes her orgasm with the sage admonition—

> The chequer'd world's before thee; go, farewell!
> Beware of Irishmen; and learn to spell!

all." The first class he instances by Fielding; the second by Smart. Of the third he says:—"The mingled wreath belongs to Hill," that is himself; and the fourth he illustrates by the absurd Sir William Browne.

"Those of the first rank are the most capricious and lazy of all animals. The monkey genius would rarely exert itself, if even idleness innate did not give way to the superior love of mischief. The ass (that is Smart), which characters the second, is as laborious as he is empty; he wears a ridiculous comicalness of aspect (which was, indeed, the physiognomy of the poor poet), that makes people smile when they see him at a distance. His mouth opens, because he must be fed, while we laugh at the insensibility and obstinacy that make him prick his lips with thistles."

But in heaven, among the immortals, never was an unfortunate hero of the vindicative Muses so reduced into
nothingness! Jove, disturbed at the noise of this thing
of wit, exclaims, that nature had never proved productive in vain before, but now,

> On mere privation she bestow'd a frame,
> And dignified a nothing with a name;
> A wretch devoid of use, of sense, of grace,
> The insolvent tenant of incumber'd space!

Pallas hits off the style of Hill, as

> The neutral nonsense, neither false nor true—
> Should Jove himself, in calculation mad,
> Still negatives to blank negations add:
> How could the barren ciphers ever breed;
> But nothing still from nothing would proceed.
> Raise, or depress, or magnify, or blame,
> Inanity will ever be the same.

But Phœbus shows there may still be something produced from inanity.

> E'en blank privation has its use and end—
> From emptiness, how sweetest music flows!
> How absence, to possession adds a grace,
> And modest vacancy, to all gives place.
> So from Hillario, some effect may spring;
> E'en him—that slight penumbra of a thing!

The careless style of the fluent Inspectors, beside their
audacity, brought Hill into many scrapes. He called
Woodward, the celebrated harlequin, "the meanest of
all characters." This Woodward resented in a pamphlet-
battle, in which Hill was beaten at all points.* But Hill,

---

* Woodward humorously attributes Hill's attack on him to his
jealousy of his successful performance of *Harlequin*, and opens some
of the secret history of Hill, by which it appears that early in life he
trod the theatrical boards. He tells us of the extraordinary pains the
prompter had taken with Hill, in the part of Oroonoko; though, "if

or the Monthly Reviewer, who might be the same person, for that journal writes with the tenderness of a brother of whatever relates to our hero, pretends that the Inspector only meant, that "the character of Harlequin (if a thing so unnatural and ridiculous ought to be called a character) was the *meanest* on the stage !" *

I will here notice a characteristic incident in Hill's literary life, of which the boldness and the egotism is scarcely paralleled, even by Orator Henley. At the time

he had not quite forgotten it, to very little purpose." He reminds Hill of a dramatic anecdote, which he no doubt had forgotten. It seems he once belonged to a strolling company at May-fair, where, in the scene between Altamont and Lothario, the polite audience of that place all chorused, and agreed with him, when dying he exclaimed, "Oh, Altamont, thy genius is the stronger." He then shows him off as the starved apothecary in *Romeo and Juliet*, in one of his botanic peregrinations to Chelsea Garden ; from whence, it is said, he was expelled for "culling too many rare plants"—

> " I do remember an apothecary,
> Culling of simples——."

Hill, who was often so brisk in his attack on the wits, had no power of retort ; so that he was always buffeting and always buffeted.

* He was also satirised in a poem termed "The Pasquinade," published in 1752, in which the goddesses of Pertness and Dulness join to praise him as their favourite reflex.

> " Pertness saw her form distinctly shine
> In none, immortal Hill so full as thine."

Dulness speaks of him thus rapturously:—

> " See where my son, who gratefully repays
> Whate'er I lavish'd on his younger days ;
> Whom still my arm protects to brave the town
> Secure from Fielding, Machiavel, or Brown ;
> Whom rage nor sword e'er mortally shall hurt,
> Chief of a hundred chiefs o'er all the pert !
> Rescued an orphan babe from common sense,
> I gave his mother's milk to Confidence ;
> She with her own ambrosia bronz'd his face,
> And changed his skin to monumental brass."

the Sloane Collection of Natural History was purchased, to form a part of our grand national establishment, the British Museum, Hill offered himself, by public advertisement, in one of his *Inspectors*, as the properest person to be placed at its head. The world will condemn him for his impudence. The most reasonable objection against his mode of proceeding would be, that the thing undid itself; and that the very appearance, by public advertisement, was one motive why so confident an offer should be rejected. Perhaps, after all, Hill only wanted to *advertise himself*.

But suppose that Hill was the man he represents himself to be, and he fairly challenges the test, his conduct only appears eccentric, according to routine. Unpatronised and unfriended men are depressed, among other calamities, with their quiescent modesty; but there is a rare spirit in him who dares to claim favours, which he thinks his right, in the most public manner. I preserve, in the note, the most striking passages of this extraordinary appeal.*

* Hill addresses the Lord Chancellor, Archbishop of Canterbury, and the Speaker, on Sir Hans Sloane's Collection of Natural History, proposing himself as a candidate for nomination in the principal office, by whatever name that shall be called:—"I deliver myself with humility; but conscious also that I possess the liberties of a British subject, I shall speak with freedom." He says that the only means left for a Briton is to address his sovereign and the public. "That foreigners will resort to this collection is certain, for it is the most considerable in the world; and that our own people will often visit it is as sure, because it may be made the means of much useful as well as curious knowledge One and the other will expect a person in that office who has sufficient knowledge: he must be able to give account of every article, freely and fluently, not only in his own, but in the Latin and French languages.

"This the world, and none in it better than your lordship, sees is not a place that any one can execute: it requires knowledge in a peculiar and uncommon kind of study—knowledge which very few

At length, after all these literary quarrels, Hill survived his literary character. He had written himself
down to so low a degree, that whenever he had a work
for publication, his employers stipulated, in their contracts, that the author should conceal his name; a circumstance not new among a certain race of writers.* But

possess; and in which, my lord, the bitterest of my enemies (and I
have thousands, although neither myself nor they know why) will not
say I am deficient——.

"My lord, the eyes of all Europe are upon this transaction. What
title I have to your lordship's favour, those books which I have published, and with which (pardon the necessary boast) all Europe is
acquainted, declare. Many may dispute by interest with me; but if
there be one who would prefer himself, by his abilities, I beg the
matter may be brought to trial. The collection is at hand; and I request, my lord, such person and myself may be examined by that test,
together. It is an amazing store of knowledge; and he has most, in
this way, who shall slow himself most acquainted with it.

"What are my own abilities it very ill becomes me thus to boast;
but did they not qualify me for the trust, my lord, I would not ask it.
As to those of any other, unless a man be conjured from the dead. I
shall not fear to say there is not any one whoever that is able so
much as to call the parts of the collection by their names.

"I know I shall be accused of ostentation in giving to myself this
preference; and I am sorry for it: but those who have candour will
know it could not be avoided.

"Many excel, my lord, in other studies: it is my chance to have bestowed the labour of my life on this: those labours may be of some
use to others. This appears the only instance in which it is possible
that they should be rewarded——."

In a subsequent *Inspector*, he treated on the improvement of botany
by raising plants, and reading lectures on them at the British Museum,
with the living plants before the lecturer and his auditors. Poor Sir
John! he was born half a century too early!—He would, in this day,
have made his lectures fashionable; and might have secured at the
opera every night an elegant audience for the next morning in the
gardens of the Museum.

* It would be difficult to form a list of his anonymous works or
compilations, among which many are curious. Tradition has preserved
his name as the writer of Mrs. Glasse's Cookery, and of several

the genius of Hill was not annihilated by being thrown down so violently on his mother earth; like Antæus, it

novels. There is a very curious work, entitled "Travels in the East," 2 vols. 8vo, of which the author has been frequently and in vain inquired after. These travels are attributed to a noble lord; but it now appears that they are a very entertaining narrative manufactured by Hill. Whiston, the bookseller, had placed this work in his MS. catalogue of Hill's books.

There is still another production of considerable merit, entitled "Observations on the Greek and Roman Classics," 1753. A learned friend recollects, when young, that this critical work was said to be written by Hill. It excels Blackwell and Fenton; and aspires to the numerous composition of prose. The sentimental critic enters into the feelings of the great authors whom he describes with spirit, delicacy of taste, and sometimes with beautiful illustration. It only wants a chastening hand to become a manual for the young classical student, by which he might acquire those vivid emotions, which many college tutors may not be capable of communicating.

I suspect, too, he is the author of this work, from a passage which Smart quotes, as a specimen of Hill's puffing himself, and of those smart short periods which look like wit, without being witty. In a letter to himself, as we are told, Hill writes:—"You have discovered many of the beauties of the ancients—they are obliged to you; we are obliged to you: were they alive, they would thank you; we who are alive do thank you." If Hill could discriminate the most hidden beauties of the ancients, the *tact* must have been formed at his leisure—in his busy hours he never copied them; but when had he leisure?

Two other works, of the most contrasted character, display the versatility and dispositions of this singular genius, at different eras. When "The Inspector" was rolling in his chariot about the town, appeared "Letters from the Inspector to a Lady." 1752. It is a pamphlet, containing the amorous correspondence of Hill with a reigning beauty, whom he first saw at Ranelagh. On his first ardent professions he is contemptuously rejected; he perseveres in high passion, and is coldly encouraged; at length he triumphs; and this proud and sullen beauty, in her turn, presents a horrid picture of the passions. Hill then becomes the reverse from what he was; weary of her jealousy, sated with the intercourse, he studiously avoids, and at length rejects her; assigning for his final argument his approaching marriage. The work may produce a moral effect, while it exhibits a

rose still fresh; and like Proteus, it assumed new forms.* Lady Hill and the young Hills were claimants on his industry far louder than the evanescent epigrams which darted around him: these latter, however, were more numerous than ever dogged an author in his road to literary celebrity.† His science, his ingenuity, and his

striking picture of all the misery of illicit connexions: but the scenes are coloured with Ovidian warmth. The original letters were shown at the bookseller's: Hill's were in his own handwriting, and the lady's in a female hand. But whether Hill was the publisher, as an attempt at notoriety—or the lady admired her own correspondence, which is often exquisitely wrought, is not known.

Hill, in his serious hours, published a large quarto volume, entitled "Thoughts Concerning God and Nature," 1755. This work, the result of his scientific knowledge and his moral reasoning, was never undertaken for the purpose of profit. He printed it with the certainty of a considerable loss, from its abstract topics, not obvious to general readers; at a time, too, when a guinea quarto was a very hazardous enterprise. He published it purely from conscientious and religious motives; a circumstance mentioned in that Apology of his Life which we have noticed. The more closely the character of Hill is scrutinised, the more extraordinary appears this man, so often justly contemned, and so often unjustly depreciated.

* Through the influence of Lord Bute he became connected with the Royal Gardens at Kew; and his lordship also assisted him in publishing his botanical works. See note, p. 181.

† It would occupy pages to transcribe epigrams on Hill. One of them alludes to his philosophical as well as his literary character:—

> "Hill puffs himself; forbear to chide!
> An insect vile and mean
> Must first, he knows, be magnified
> Before it can be seen."

Garrick's happy lines are well known on his farces:—

> "For physic and farces his equal there scarce is—
> His farces are physic, his physic a farce is."

Another said—

> "The worse that we wish thee, for all thy vile crimes,
> Is to take thy own physic, and read thy own rhymes."

impudence once more practised on the credulity of the
public, with the innocent quackery of attributing all
medicinal virtues to British herbs. He made many walk
out, who were too sedentary: they were delighted to
cure headaches by feverfew tea; hectic fevers by the
daisy; colics by the leaves of camomile, and agues by
its flowers. All these were accompanied by plates of the
plants, with the Linnæan names.* This was preparatory
to the *Essences* of Sage, *Balsams* of Honey, and *Tinc-
tures* of Valerian. Simple persons imagined they were
scientific botanists in their walks, with Hill's plates in
their hands. But one of the newly-discovered virtues
of British herbs was, undoubtedly, that of placing the
discoverer in a chariot.

In an Apology for the character of Sir John Hill, published after his death, where he is painted with much
beauty of colouring, and elegance of form, the eruptions
and excrescences of his motley physiognomy, while they
are indicated—for they were too visible to be entirely
omitted in anything pretending to a resemblance—are
melted down, and even touched into a grace. The
Apology is not unskilful, but the real purpose appears in
the last page; where we are informed that Lady Hill,
fortunately for the world, possesses all his valuable
recipes and herbal remedies!

The rejoinder would reverse the wish—

> " For, if he takes his physic first,
> He'll never read his rhymes."

---

* Hill says, in his pamphlet on the "Virtues of British Herbs":—
"It will be happy if, by the same means, the knowledge of plants also
becomes more general. The study of them is pleasant, and the exercise
of it healthful. He who seeks the herb for its cure, will find it half
effected by the walk; and when he is acquainted with the useful
kinds, he may be more people's, besides his own, physician."

BOYLE AND BENTLEY.

A Faction of Wits at Oxford the concealed movers of this Controversy
—Sir William Temple's opinions the ostensible cause: Editions of
classical Authors by young Students at Oxford the probable one—
Boyle's first attack in the Preface to his "Phalaris"—Bentley,
after a silence of three years, betrays his feelings on the literary
calumny of Boyle—Boyle replies by the "Examination of Bentley's
Dissertation"—Bentley rejoins by enlarging it—the effects of a
contradictory Narrative at a distant time—Bentley's suspicions of
the origin of the "Phalaris," and "The Examination," proved by
subsequent facts—Bentley's dignity when stung at the ridicule of
Dr. King—applies a classical pun, and nicknames his facetious and
caustic Adversary—King invents an extraordinary Index to dissect
the character of Bentley—specimens of the Controversy; Boyle's
menace, anathema, and ludicrous humour—Bentley's sarcastic reply
not inferior to that of the Wits.

THE splendid controversy between Boyle and Bentley was at times a strife of gladiators, and has
been regretted as the opprobrium of our literature; but
it should be perpetuated to its honour; for it may be
considered, on one side at least, as a noble contest of
heroism.

The ostensible cause of the present quarrel was inconsiderable; the concealed motive lies deeper; and the
party feelings of the haughty Aristarchus of Cambridge,
and a faction of wits at Oxford, under the secret influence of Dean Aldrich, provoked this fierce and glorious
contest.

Wit, ridicule, and invective, by cabal and stratagem,
obtained a seeming triumph over a single individual, but
who, like the Farnesian Hercules, personified the force
and resistance of incomparable strength. "The Bees of
Christchurch," as this conspiracy of wits has been called,

so musical and so angry, rushed in a dark swarm about
him, but only left their fine stings in the flesh they could
not wound. He only put out his hand in contempt,
never in rage. The Christchurch men, as if doubtful
whether wit could prevail against learning, had recourse
to the maliciousness of personal satire. They amused
an idle public, who could even relish sense and Greek,
seasoned as they were with wit and satire, while Boyle was
showing how Bentley wanted wit, and Bentley was
proving how Boyle wanted learning.

To detect the origin of the controversy, we must find
the seed-plot of Bentley's volume in Sir William Temple's
"Essay upon Ancient and Modern Learning," which
he inscribed to his alma mater, the University of Cambridge. Sir William, who had caught the contagion of
the prevalent literary controversy of the times, in which
the finest geniuses in Europe had entered the lists, imagined that the ancients possessed a greater force of
genius, with some peculiar advantages—that the human
mind was in a state of decay—and that our knowledge
was nothing more than scattered fragments saved out of
the general shipwreck. He writes with a premeditated
design to dispute the improvements or undervalue the
inventions of his own age. Wotton, the friend of Bentley, replied by his curious volume of "Reflections on
Ancient and Modern Learning." But Sir William, in
his ardour, had thrown out an unguarded opinion, which
excited the hostile contempt of Bentley. "The oldest
books," he says, "we have, are still in their kind the
best: the two most ancient that I know of, in prose, are
'Æsop's Fables' and 'Phalaris's Epistles.'"—The "Epistles," he insists, exhibit every excellence of "a statesman, a
soldier, a wit, and a scholar." That ancient author, who
Bentley afterwards asserted was only "some dreaming
pedant, with his elbow on his desk."

Bentley, bristled over with Greek, perhaps then considered that to notice a vernacular and volatile writer ill assorted with the critic's *Fastus*. But about this time Dean Aldrich had set an example to the students of Christchurch of publishing editions of classical authors. Such juvenile editorships served as an easy admission into the fashionable literature of Oxford. Alsop had published the " Æsop;" and Boyle, among other " young gentlemen," easily obtained the favour of the dean, " to *desire* him to undertake an edition of the 'Epistles of Phalaris.'" Such are the modest terms Boyle employs in his reply to Bentley, after he had discovered the unlucky choice he had made of an author.

For this edition of "Phalaris" it was necessary to collate a MS. in the king's library; and Bentley, about this time, had become the royal librarian. Boyle did not apply directly to Bentley, but circuitously, by his bookseller, with whom the doctor was not on terms. Some act of civility, or a Mercury more " formose," to use one of his latinisms, was probably expected. The MS. was granted, but the collator was negligent; in six days Bentley reclaimed it, " four hours" had been sufficient for the purpose of collation.

When Boyle's " Phalaris" appeared, he made this charge in the preface, that having ordered the Epistles to be collated with the MS. in the king's library, the collator was prevented perfecting the collation by the *singular humanity* of the library-keeper, who refused any further use of the MS.; *pro singulari suâ humanitate negavit:* an expression that sharply hit a man marked by the haughtiness of his manners.*

* Haughtiness was the marking feature of Bentley's literary character; and his Wolseyan style and air have been played on by the wits. Bentley happened to express himself on the King's MS. of Phalaris in a manner their witty malice turned against him. " 'Twas a surprise

Bentley, on this insult, informed Boyle of what had
passed. He expected that Boyle would have civilly cancelled the page; though he tells us he did not require this,
because, "to have insisted on the cancel, might have
been forcing a gentleman to too low a submission;"—a
stroke of delicacy which will surprise some to discover in
the strong character of Bentley. But he was also too
haughty to ask a favour, and too conscious of his superiority to betray a feeling of injury. Boyle replied, that
the bookseller's account was quite different from the
doctor's, who had spoken slightingly of him. Bentley
said no more.

Three years had nearly elapsed, when Bentley, in a
new edition of his friend Wotton's book, published "A
Dissertation on the Epistles of the Ancients;" where,
reprehending the false criticism of Sir William Temple, he
asserted that the "Fables of Æsop" and the "Epistles of
Phalaris" were alike spurious. The blow was levelled at
Christchurch, and all "the bees" were brushed down
in the warmth of their summer-day.

It is remarkable that Bentley kept so long a silence;
indeed, he had considered the affair so trivial, that he
had preserved no part of the correspondence with Boyle,
whom no doubt he slighted as the young editor of a
spurious author. But Boyle's edition came forth, as
Bentley expresses it, "with a sting in its mouth." This,
at first, was like a cut finger—he breathed on it, and
would have forgotten it; but the nerve was touched, and
the pain raged long after the stroke. Even the great

(he said) to find that OUR MS. was not perused."—"OUR MS. (they
proceed) that is, his Majesty's and mine! He speaks out now; 'tis no
longer the King's, but OUR MS., i. e. Dr. Bentley's and the King's in
common. *Ego et Rex meus*—much too familiar for a library-keeper!"—It
has been said that Bentley used the same Wolseyan egotism on Pope's
publications:—"This man is always abusing *me* or the *King!*"

mind of Bentley began to shrink at the touch of literary calumny, so different from the vulgar kind, in its extent and its duration. He betrays the soreness he would wish to conceal, when he complains that "the false story has been spread all over England."

The statement of Bentley produced, in reply, the famous book of Boyle's "Examination of Bentley's Dissertation." It opens with an imposing narrative, highly polished, of the whole transaction, with the extraordinary furniture of documents, which had never before entered into a literary controversy—depositions—certificates—affidavits—and private letters. Bentley now rejoined by his enlarged "Dissertation on Phalaris," a volume of perpetual value to the lovers of ancient literature, and the memorable preface of which, itself a volume, exhibits another Narrative, entirely differing from Boyle's. These produced new replies and new rejoinders. The whole controversy became so perplexed, that it has frightened away all who have attempted to adjust the particulars. With unanimous consent they give up the cause, as one in which both parties studied only to contradict each other. Such was the fate of a Narrative, which was made out of the recollections of the parties, with all their passions at work, after an interval of three years. In each, the memory seemed only retentive of those passages which best suited their own purpose, and which were precisely those the other party was most likely to have forgotten. What was forgotten, was denied ; what was admitted, was made to refer to something else ; dialogues were given which appear never to have been spoken ; and incidents described which are declared never to have taken place; and all this, perhaps, without any purposed violation of truth. Such were the dangers and misunderstandings which attended a Narrative framed out of the broken or passionate recollec-

tions of the parties on the watch to confound one another.*

Bentley's Narrative is a most vigorous production: it
heaves with the workings of a master-spirit; still reasoning with such force, and still applying with such happiness the stores of his copious literature, had it not been
for this literary quarrel, the mere English reader had lost
this single opportunity of surveying that commanding
intellect.

Boyle's edition of "Phalaris" was a work of parade,
designed to confer on a young man, who bore an eminent
name, some distinction in the literary world.   But

---

* Bentley, in one place, having to give a positive contradiction to
the statement of the bookseller, rising in all his dignity and energy,
exclaims, " What can be done in this case?   Here are two contrary
affirmations; and the matter being done in private, neither of us have
any witness, I might plead, as Æmilius did against one Varius, of Sucro.
Varius Surronensis ait, Æmilius Scaurus negat.   Utri creditis Quirites?"
p. 21.—The story is told by Valerius Maximus, lib. iii. c. 7. Scaurus
was insolently accused by one Varius, a Sucronian, that he had taken
bribes from Mithridates: Scaurus addressed the Roman people.   " He
did not think it just that a man of his age should defend himself against
accusations, and before those who were not born when he filled the
offices of the republic, nor witnessed the actions he had performed.
Varius, the Sucronian, says that Scaurus, corrupted by gold, would
have betrayed the republic: Scaurus replies, It is not true.   Whom
will you believe, fellow-Romans?"—This appeal to the people produced
all the effect imaginable, and the ridiculous accuser was silenced.
Bentley points the same application, with even more self-conscious-
ness of his worth, in another part of his preface.   It became necessary
to praise himself, to remove the odium Boyle and his friends had
raised on him—it was a difficulty overcome.   " I will once more borrow the form of argument that Æmilius Scaurus used against Varius
Sucronensis.   Mr. Spanheim and Mr. Grævius give a high character
of Dr. B.'s learning: Mr. Boyle gives the meanest that malice can
furnish himself with.   *Utri creditis, Quirites?*   Whether of the characters will the present age or posterity believe?"—p. 82.   It was only
a truly great mind which could bring itself so close to posterity.

Bentley seems to have been well-informed of the secret
transactions at Christchurch. In his first attack he
mentions Boyle as "the young gentleman of great hopes,
whose name is set to the edition;" and asserts that the
editor, no more than his own "Phalaris," has written
what was ascribed to him. He persists in making a plu-
rality of a pretended unity, by multiplying Boyle into a
variety of little personages, of "new editors," our "an-
notators," our "great geniuses." * Boyle, touched at
these reflections, declared "they were levelled at a
learned society, in which I had the happiness to be educated; as if 'Phalaris' had been made up by contributions from several hands." Pressed by Bentley to
acknowledge the assistance of Dr. John Freind, Boyle
confers on him the ambiguous title of "The Director of
Studies." Bentley links the Bees together—Dr. Freind
and Dr. Alsop. "The Director of Studies, who has
lately set out Ovid's 'Metamorphoses,' with a paraphrase
and notes, is of the same size for learning with the late
editor of the Æsopian Fables. They bring the nation
into contempt abroad, and themselves into it at home;"

* It was the fashion then to appear very unconcerned about one's
literary reputation; but then to be so tenacious about it when once
obtained as not to suffer, with common patience, even the little finger
of criticism to touch it. Boyle, after defending what he calls his
"honesty," adds, " the rest *only* touches my learning. This will give me
no concern, though it may put me to some little trouble. I shall enter
upon this with *the indifference of a gamester who plays but for a trifle.*"
On this affected indifference, Bentley keenly observes:—"This was
entering on his work a little ominously; for a gamester who plays
with indifference never plays his game well. Besides that, by this odd
comparison, he seems to give warning, and is as good as his word,
that he will put the dice upon his readers as often as he can. But
what is worse than all, this comparison puts one in mind of a general
rumour, that there's another set of gamesters who *play him* in his dispute while themselves are safe behind the curtain."—Bentley's *Dissertation on Phalaris*, p. 2.

and adds to this magisterial style, the mortification of his criticism on Freind's Ovid, as on Alsop's Æsop.

But Boyle assuming the honours of an edition of "Phalaris," was but a venial offence, compared with that committed by the celebrated volume published in its defence.

If Bentley's suspicions were not far from the truth, that "the 'Phalaris' had been *made up by contributions*," they approached still closer when they attacked "The Examination of his Dissertation." Such was the assistance which Boyle received from all "the Bees," that scarcely a few ears of that rich sheaf fall to his portion. His efforts hardly reach to the mere narrative of his transactions with Bentley. All the varied erudition, all the Attic graces, all the inexhaustible wit, are claimed by others; so that Boyle was not materially concerned either in his "Phalaris," or in the more memorable work.*

* Rumours and conjectures are the lot of contemporaries; truth seems reserved only for posterity; and, like the fabled Minerva, she is born of age at once. The secret history of this volume, which partially appeared, has been more particularly opened in one of Warburton's letters, who received it from Pope, who had been "let into the secret." Boyle wrote the Narrative, "which, too, was corrected for him." Freind, who wrote the entire Dissertation on Æsop in that volume, wrote also, with Atterbury, the body of the Criticisms; King, the droll argument, proving that Bentley was not the author of his own Dissertation, and the extraordinary index which I shall shortly notice. In Atterbury's "Epistolary Correspondence" is a letter, where, with equal anger and dignity, Atterbury avows his having written *about half, and planned the whole* of Boyle's attack upon Bentley! With these facts before us, we can read without surprise, if not without indignation, the passage I shall now quote from the book to which the name of Boyle is prefixed. In raising an artful charge against Bentley, of appropriating to himself some MS. notes of Sir Edward Sherburn, Boyle, replying to the argument of Bentley, that "Phalaris" was the work of some sophist, says:—"The sophists are everywhere pelted by Dr. Bentley, for putting out what they wrote in other men's names; but I did not expect to hear so loudly of it from one that has

The Christchurch party now formed a literary conspiracy against the great critic; and as treason is infectious so far outdone them; for *I think 'tis much worse to take the honour of another man's book to one's self*, than to entitle one's own book to another man."—p. 16.

I am surprised Bentley did not turn the point of his antagonist's sword on himself, for this flourish was a most unguarded one. But Bentley could not then know so much of the book, "made up by contributions," as ourselves.

Partial truths flew about in rumours at the time; but the friends of a young nobleman, and even his fellow-workmen, seemed concerned that his glory should not be diminished by a ruinous division. Rymer, in his "Essay concerning Curious and Critical Learning." judiciously surmised its true origin. " I fancy this book was written (as most compositions in that college are) by a *select club*. Every one seems to have thrown in a repartee or so in his turn; and the most ingenious Dr. Aldrich (he does not deserve the epithet in its most friendly sense) no doubt at their head, smoked and punned plentifully on this occasion." The arrogance of Aldrich exceeded even that of Bentley. Rymer tells further, that Aldrich was notorious for thus employing his " young inexperienced students;" that he " *betrayed* Mr. Boyle into the controversy, and is still involving others in the quarrel." Thus he points at the rival chieftains; one of whom never appeared in public, but was the great mover behind the curtain. These lively wits, so deeply busied among the obscurest writers of antiquity, so much against their will, making up a show of learning against the formidable array of Bentley, exhilarated themselves in their dusty labours by a perpetual stimulus of keen humour. playful wit, and angry invective. No doubt they were often enraged at bearing the yoke about their luxuriant manes, ploughing the darkest and heaviest soil of antiquity. They had been reared—

"Insultare solo, et gressus glomerare superbos."
"Georg." Lib. iii. 117.

"To insult the ground, and proudly pace the plain."
TRAPP.

Swift, in "The Battle of the Books," who under his patron. Sir William Temple, was naturally in alliance with "the Bees," with ingenious ambiguity alludes to the glorious manufacture. "Boyle, clad in a suit of armour, *which had been given him by all the* Gods." Still the truth was only floating in rumours and surmises; and the little that Boyle had done was not yet known. Lord Orrery, his son, had a diffi-

when the faction is strong, they were secretly engaging
new associates. Whenever any of the party published
anything themselves, they had sworn to have always
"a fling at Bentley," and intrigued with their friends to
do the same.

They procured Keil, the professor of astronomy, in so
grave a work as "The Theory of the Earth," to have a
fling at Bentley's boasted sagacity in conjectural criticism. Wotton, in a dignified reproof, administered a
spirited correction to the party-spirit; while his love of
science induced him generously to commend Keil, and
intimate the advantages the world may derive from his
studies, "as he grows older." Even Garth and Pope
struck in with the alliance, and condescended to pour out
rhymes more lasting than even the prose of "the
Bees."

But of all the rabid wits who, fastening on their prey,
never drew their fangs from the noble animal, the facetious Dr. King seems to have been the only one who
excited Bentley's anger. Persevering malice, in the
teasing shape of caustic banter, seems to have affected
the spirit even of Bentley.

culty to overcome to pass lightly over this allusion. The literary
honour of the family was at stake, and his filial piety was exemplary
to a father, who had unfortunately, in passion, deprived his lordship
of the family library—a stroke from which his sensibility never recovered, and which his enemies ungenerously pointed against him.
Lord Orrery, with all the tenderness of a son, and the caution of a
politician, observes on "the armour given by the Gods"—"I shall not
d spute about the *gift* of the armour. The Gods never bestowed celestial armour except upon heroes, whose courage and superior strength
distinguished them from the rest of mankind." Most ingeniously ho
would seem to convert into a classical fable what was designed as a
plain matter of fact!

It does credit to the discernment of Bentley, whose taste was not
very lively in English composition, that he pronounced Boyle was *not
the author* of the "Examination," from *the variety of styles in it.*—p. 107.

At one of those conferences which passed between Bentley and the bookseller, King happened to be present; and being called on by Boyle to bear his part in the drama, he performed it quite to the taste of " the Bees." He addressed a letter to Dean Aldrich, in which he gave one particular : and, to make up a sufficient dose, dropped some corrosives. He closes his letter thus :—" That scorn and contempt which I have naturally for pride and insolence, makes me remember that which otherwise I might have forgotten." Nothing touched Bentley more to the quick than reflections on "his pride and insolence." Our defects seem to lose much of their character, in reference to ourselves, by habit and natural disposition ; yet we have always a painful suspicion of their existence ; and he who touches them with no tenderness is never pardoned. The invective of King had all the bitterness of truth. Bentley applied a line from Horace ; which showed that both Horace and Bentley could pun in anger : —

Proscripti *Regis Rupili* pus atque venenum.*—*Sat.* i. 7.
The filth and venom of *Rupilius King*.

The particular incident which King imperfectly recollected, made afterwards much noise among the wits, for giving them a new notion of the nature of ancient MSS. King relates that Dr. Bentley said—" If the MS. were collated, it would be worth nothing for the future." Bentley, to mortify the pertness of the bookseller, who would not send his publications to the Royal Library, had said that he ought to do so, were it but to make

---

* This short and pointed satire of Horace is merely a pleasant story about a low wretch of the name of King; and Brutus, under whose command he was, is entreated to get rid of him, from his hereditary hatred to *all kings*. I suppose this pun must be considered legitimate, otherwise Horace was an indifferent punster.

amends for the damage the MS. would sustain by his
printing the various readings; "for," added Bentley,
"after the various lections were once taken and printed,
*the MS. would be like a squeezed orange, and little worth
for the future."* This familiar comparison of a MS. with
a squeezed orange provoked the epigrammatists. Bentley, in retorting on King, adds some curious facts concerning the fate of MSS. after they have been printed;
but is aware, he says, of what little relish or sense the
Doctor has of MSS., who is better skilled in "the catalogue of ales, his Humty-Dumty, Hugmatee,Three-threads,
and the rest of that glorious list, than in the catalogue
of MSS." King, in his banter on Dr. Lister's journey to
Paris, had given a list of these English beverages. It
was well known that he was in too constant an intercourse with them all. Bentley nicknames King through
the progress of his Controversy, for his tavern-pleasures,
Humty-Dumty, and accuses him of writing more in a
tavern than in a study. He little knew the injustice of
his charge against a student who had written notes on
22,000 books and MSS.; but they were not Greek ones.

All this was not done with impunity. An irritated
wit only finds his adversary cutting out work for him.
A second letter, more abundant with the same pungent
qualities, fell on the head of Bentley. King says of the
arch-critic—"He thinks meanly, I find, of my reading;
yet for all that, I dare say I have read more than any
man in England besides *him* and *me;* for I have read
his book all over." * Nor was this all; "Humty-Dumty"

---

* A keen repartee! Yet King could read this mighty volume as "a
vain confused performance." but the learned Dodwell declared to
"the Bees of Christchurch," who looked up to him. that "he had
never learned so much from any book of the size in his life." King was
as unjust to Bentley, as Bentley to King. Men of genius are more subject to "unnatural civil war" than even the blockheads whom Pope sar

published eleven "Dialogues of the Dead," supposed to
be written by a student at Padua, concerning "one Ben-
tivoglio, a very troublesome critic in the world;" where,
under the character of "Signior Moderno," Wotton falls
into his place. Whether these dialogues mortified Bentley, I know not: they ought to have afforded him very
high amusement. But when a man is at once tickled
and pinched, the operation requires a gentler temper
than Bentley's. "Humty-Dumty," indeed, had Bentley
too often before him. There was something like invet-
eracy in his wit; but he who invented the remarkable
index to Boyle's book, must have closely studied Bentley's character. He has given it with all its protuberant
individuality.*

castically reproaches with it. The great critic's own notion of his
volume seems equally modest and just. "To undervalue this dispute
about 'Phalaris,' because it does not suit one's own studies, is to
quarrel with a circle because it is not a square. If the question be not
of vulgar use, it was writ therefore for a few; for even the greatest
performances, upon the most important subjects, are no entertainment
at all to *the many of the world*."—p. 107.

* This index, a very original morsel of literary pleasantry, is at
once a satirical character of the great critic, and what it professes to
be. I preserve a specimen among the curiosities I am collecting. It
is entitled—

"*A Short Account of* Dr. Bentley, *by way of Index.*

"Dr. Bentley's true story proved false, by the testimonies of, &c., p.—
        "His civil language, p. —
        "His nice taste,
                in wit, p. —
                in style, p. —
                in Greek, p. —
                in Latin, p. —
                in English, p. —
        "His modesty and decency in contradicting great
                men"—a very long list of authors, concluding
                with '*Everybody*,' p. —
        "His familiar acquaintance with books he never
                saw," p. —

Bentley, with his peculiar idiom, had censured "all
the stiffness and stateliness, and operoseness of style,
quite alien from the character of 'Phalaris,' a man of
business and despatch." Boyle keenly turns his own
words on Bentley. "*Stiffness and stateliness, and operoseness of style*, is indeed quite *alien from the character
of a man of business ;* and being but a *library-keeper*, it
is not over-modestly done, to oppose his judgment and
taste to that of Sir William Temple, who knows more of
these things than Dr. Bentley does of Hesychius and
Suidas. Sir William Temple has spent a good part of
his life in transacting affairs of state : he has written to
kings, and they to him; and this has qualified him to
judge how kings should write, much better than the
library-keeper at St. James's."—This may serve as a
specimen of the Attic style of the controversy. Hard
words sometimes passed. Boyle complains of some of
the *similes* which Bentley employs, more significant than
elegant. For the new readings of "Phalaris," "he
likens me to a bungling tinker mending old kettles."
Correcting the faults of the version, he says, "The first
epistle cost me four pages in scouring;" and, "by the
help of a Greek proverb, he calls me downright ass."
But while Boyle complains of these sprinklings of ink,
he himself contributes to Bentley's "Collection of Asi-
nine Proverbs," and "throws him in one out of Aristophanes," of "an ass carrying mysteries:" "a proverb,"
says Erasmus, (as 'the Bees' construe him,) "applied to
those who were preferred to some place they did not deserve, as when a *dunce* was made a *library-keeper.*"

Some ambiguous threats are scattered in the volume,
while others are more intelligible. When Bentley, in

And lastly, "his profound skill in criticism—from
beginning to THE END."
Which thus terminates the volume.

his own defence, had referred to the opinions which some learned foreigners entertained of him—they attribute these to "the foreigners, because they are foreigners—we, that have the happiness of a nearer conversation with him, know him better; and we may perhaps take an opportunity of setting these mistaken strangers right in their opinions." They threaten him with his character, "in a tongue that will last longer, and go further, than their own;" and, in the imperious style of Festus, add:—"Since Dr. Bentley has appealed to foreign universities, to foreign universities he must go." Yet this is light, compared with the odium they would raise against him by the menace of the resentments of a whole society of learned men.

"*Single adversaries* die and drop off; but *societies* are immortal: their resentments are sometimes delivered down from hand to hand; and when once they have begun with a man, there is no knowing when they will leave him."

In reply to this literary anathema, Bentley was furnished, by his familiarity with his favourite authors, with a fortunate application of a term, derived from Phalaris himself. Cicero had conveyed his idea of Cæsar's cruelty by this term, which he invented from the very name of the tyrant.*

"There is a certain temper of mind that Cicero calls *Phalarism;* a spirit like Phalaris's. One would be apt to imagine that a portion of it had descended upon some of his translators. The gentleman has given a broad hint more than once in his book, that if I proceed further against Phalaris, I may draw, perhaps, a duel, or a stab upon myself; a generous threat to a divine, who neither carries arms nor principles fit for that sort of contro-

* Cicero ad Atticum, Lib. vii., Epist. xii.

versy. I expected such usage from the spirit of Phalarism."

In this controversy, the amusing fancy of "the Bees" could not pass by Phalaris without contriving to make some use of that brazen bull by which he tortured men alive. Not satisfied in their motto, from the Earl of Roscommon, with wedging "the great critic, like Milo, in the timber he strove to rend," they gave him a second death in their finis, by throwing Bentley into Phalaris's bull, and flattering their vain imaginations that they heard him "bellow."

" He has defied Phalaris, and used him very coarsely, under the assurance, as he tells us, that 'he is out of his reach.' Many of Phalaris's enemies thought the same thing, and repented of their vain confidence afterwards in his *bull*. Dr. Bentley is perhaps, by this time, or will be suddenly, satisfied that he also has presumed a little too much upon his distance; but it will be too late to repent when he begins to bellow."*

Bentley, although the solid force of his mind was not favourable to the lighter sports of wit, yet was not quite destitute of those airy qualities; nor does he seem insensible to the literary merits of "that odd work," as he calls Boyle's volume, which he conveys a very good notion of:—"If his book shall happen to be preserved anywhere as an useful commonplace book for ridicule, banter, and all the topics of calumny." With equal dignity and sense he observes on the ridicule so freely used by both parties—"I am content that what is the greatest virtue of his book should be counted the greatest fault of mine."

---

* No doubt this idea was the origin of that satirical Capriccio, which closed in a most fortunate pun—a literary caricature, where the doctor is represented in the hands of Phalaris's attendants, who are putting him into the tyrant's bull, while Bentley exclaims, "I had rather be *roasted* than *Boyled*."

His reply to "Milo's fate," and the tortures he was supposed to pass through when thrown into Phalaris's bull, is a piece of sarcastic humour which will not suffer by comparison with the volume more celebrated for its wit.

"The facetious examiner seems resolved to vie with Phalaris himself in the science of *Phalarism ;* for his revenge is not satisfied with one single death of his adversary, but he will kill me over and over again. He has slain me twice by two several deaths! one, in the first page of his book; and another, in the last. In the title-page I die the death of Milo, the Crotonian :—

—— Remember Milo's end,
Wedged in that timber which he strove to rend.

"The application of which must be this:—That as Milo, after his victories at six several Olympiads, was at last conquered and destroyed in wrestling with a *tree*, so I, after I had attained to some small reputation in letters, am to be quite baffled and run down by *wooden antagonists.* But in the end of his book he has got me into Phalaris's bull, and he has the pleasure of fancying that he hears me *begin to bellow.* Well, since it is certain that I am in the bull, I have performed the part of a sufferer. For as the cries of the tormented in old Phalaris's bull, being conveyed through pipes lodged in the machine, were turned into music for the entertainment of the tyrant, so the complaints which my torments express from me, being conveyed to Mr. Boyle by this answer, are all dedicated to his pleasure and diversion. But yet, methinks, when he was setting up to be *Phalaris junior*, the very omen of it might have deterred him. As the old tyrant himself at last bellowed in his own bull, his imitators ought to consider that at long run their own actions may chance to overtake them."—p. 43.

Wit, however, enjoyed the temporary triumph; not but that some, in that day, loudly protested against the award.* "The Episode of Bentley and Wotton," in "The Battle of the Books," is conceived with all the caustic imagination of the first of our prose satirists. There Bentley's great qualities are represented as " tall, without shape or comeliness ; large, without strength or proportion." His various erudition, as " armour patched up of a thousand incoherent pieces;" his book, as " the sound " of that armour, " loud and dry, like that made by the fall of a sheet of lead from the roof of some steeple;" his haughty intrepidity, as " a vizor of brass, tainted by his breath, corrupted into copperas, nor wanted gall from the same fountain ; so that, whenever provoked by anger or labour, an atramentous quality of most malignant nature was seen to distil from his lips." Wotton is " heavy-armed and slow of foot, lagging behind." They perish together in one ludicrous death. Boyle, in his celestial armour, by a stroke of his weapon, transfixes both " the lovers," " as a cook trusses a brace of woodcocks, with iron skewer piercing the tender sides of both.   Joined in their lives, joined in their death,

* Sir Richard Blackmore, in his bold attempt at writing "A Satire against Wit." in utter defiance of it, without any, however, conveys some opinions of the times.   He there paints the great critic, "crowned with applause," seated amidst "the spoils of ruined wits:"

> " Till his rude strokes had thresh'd the empty sheaf,
>   Methought there had been something else than chaff."

Boyle, not satisfied with the undeserved celebrity conceded to his volume, ventured to write poetry, in which no one appears to have suspected the aid of "The Bees "—

> " See a fine scholar sunk by wit in Boyle!
>   After his foolish rhymes, both friends and foes
>   Conclude they know *who did not write his prose.*"
>
> *A Satire against Wit.*

so closely joined, that Charon would mistake them both for one, and waft them over Styx for half his fare." Such is the candour of wit! The great qualities of an adversary, as in Bentley, are distorted into disgraceful attitudes; while the suspicious virtues of a friend, as in Boyle, not passed over in prudent silence, are ornamented with even spurious panegyric.

Garth, catching the feeling of the time, sung—

> And to a Bentley 'tis we owe a Boyle.

Posterity justly appreciates the volume of Bentley for its stores of ancient literature; and the author, for that peculiar sagacity in emending a corrupt text, which formed his distinguishing characteristic as a classical critic; and since his book but for this literary quarrel had never appeared, reverses the names in the verse of the "Satirist."

PARKER AND MARVELL.

MARVELL the founder of "a newly-refined art of jeering buffoonery "— his knack of nicknaming his adversaries—Parker's Portrait—Parker suddenly changes his principles—his declamatory style—Marvell prints his anonymous letter as a motto to "The Rehearsal Trans-prosed"—describes him as an "At-all"—Marvell's ludicrous de-scription of the whole posse of answers summoned together by Parker—Marvell's cautious allusion to Milton—his solemn invective against Parker—anecdote of Marvell and Parker—Parker retires after the second part of "The Rehearsal Transprosed"—The Re-creant, reduced to silence, distils his secret vengeance in a posthu-mous libel.

ONE of the legitimate ends of satire, and one of the proud triumphs of genius, is to unmask the false zealot; to beat back the haughty spirit that is treading down all; and if it cannot teach modesty, and raise a blush, at least to inflict terror and silence. It is then that the satirist does honour to the office of the executioner.

> As one whose whip of steel can with a lash
> Imprint the characters of shame so deep,
> Even in the brazen forehead of proud Sin,
> That not eternity shall wear it out.*

The quarrel between Parker and Marvell is a striking example of the efficient powers of genius, in first humbling, and then annihilating, an unprincipled bravo, who had placed himself at the head of a faction.

Marvell, the under-secretary and the bosom-friend of Milton, whose fancy he has often caught in his verse, was one of the greatest wits of the luxuriant age of Charles II.; he was a master in all the arts of ridicule; and his inexhaustible spirit only required some permanent subject to have rivalled the causticity of Swift, whose style, in neatness and vivacity, seems to have been modelled on his.† But Marvell placed the oblation of genius on a temporary altar, and the sacrifice sunk with it; he wrote to the times, and with the times his writings have passed away; yet something there is incorruptible in wit, and wherever its salt has fallen, that part is still preserved.

Such are the vigour and fertility of Marvell's writings, that our old Chronicler of Literary History, Anthony Wood, considers him as the founder of "the then newly-refined art (though much in mode and fashion almost ever since) of sportive and jeering buffoonery;"‡ and

---

* Randolph's *Muses' Looking-glass.* Act 1, Scene 4.

† Swift certainly admired, if he did not imitate Marvell: for in his "Tale of a Tub" he says, "We still read Marvell's answer to Parker with pleasure, though the book it answers be sunk long ago."

‡ This is a curious remark of Wood's: How came raillery and

the crabbed humorist describes "this pen-combat as
briskly managed on both sides; a jerking flirting way
of writing entertaining the reader, by seeing two such
right cocks of the game so keenly engaging with sharp
and dangerous weapons."—Burnett calls Marvell "the
liveliest droll of the age, who writ in a burlesque strain,
but with so peculiar and entertaining a conduct, that
from the king to the tradesman, his books were read with
great pleasure." Charles II. was a more polished judge
than these uncouth critics; and, to the credit of his im-
partiality,—for that witty monarch and his dissolute

satire to be considered as "a newly-refined art?" Has it not, at all
periods, been prevalent among every literary people? The remark
is, however, more founded on truth than it appears, and arose from
Wood's own feelings. Wit and Raillery had been so strange to us
during the gloomy period of the fanatic Commonwealth, that honest
Anthony, whose prejudices did not run in favour of Marvell, not only
considers him as the "restorer of this newly-refined art," but as one
" hugely versed in it," and acknowledges all its efficacy in the complete
discomfiture of his haughty rival. Besides this, *a small book* of controversy, such as Marvell's usually are, was another novelty—the
" aureoli libelli," as one fondly calls his precious books, were in the
wretched taste of the times, rhapsodies in folio. The reader has
doubtless heard of Caryll's endless " Commentary on Job," consisting of 2400 folio pages! in small type. Of that monument of human
perseverance, which commenting on Job's patience, inspired what
few works do to whoever read them, the exercise of the virtue it
inculcated, the publisher, in his advertisement in Clavel's Catalogue of
Books, 1681, announces the two folios in 600 sheets each! these were
a republication of the first edition, in twelve volumes quarto! he
apologises "that it hath been *so long a doing*, to the great vexation and
loss of the proposer." He adds, "indeed, *some few lines*, no more than
what may be contained *in a quarto page*, are expunged, *they not relating
to the Exposition*, which nevertheless some, by malicious prejudice,
have so unjustly aggravated, as if the whole work had been disordered."
He apologises for curtailing *a few lines* from 2400 folio pages! and he
considered that these few lines were the only ones that did not relate
to the Exposition! At such a time, the little books of Marvell must
have been considered as relishing morsels after such indigestible surfeits.

court were never spared by Marvell, who remained
inflexible to his seduction—he deemed Marvell the best
prose satirist of the age.   But Marvell had other qualities than the freest humour and the finest wit in this
" newly-refined art," which seems to have escaped these
grave critics—a vehemence of solemn reproof, and an
eloquence of invective, that awes one with the spirit of
the modern Junius,* and may give some notion of that
more ancient satirist, whose writings are said to have so
completely answered their design, that, after perusal,
their victim hanged himself on the first tree; and in the
present case, though the delinquent did not lay violent
hands on himself, he did what, for an author, may be
considered as desperate a course, "withdraw from the
town, and cease writing for some years."†

* The severity of his satire on Charles's court may be well understood by the following lines:—

> "A colony of French possess the court,
> Pimps, priests, buffoons, in privy-chamber sport;
> Such slimy monsters ne'er approached a throne
> Since Pharaoh's days, nor so defil'd a crown;
> In sacred ear tyrannick arts they croak,
> Pervert his mind, and good intentions choak."

"The Historical Poem," given in the poems on State affairs, is so
personal in its attacks on the vices of Charles, that it is marvellous
how its author escaped punishment.   "Hodge's Vision from the
Monument" is equally strong, while the "Dialogue between two
Horses" (that of the statue of Charles I. at Charing-cross, and
Charles II., then in the city), has these two strong lines of regret:—

> "—— to see *Deo Gratias* writ on the throne,
> And the king's wicked life say God there is none."

The satire ends with the question:—

> "But canst thou devise when things will be mended?"

Which is thus answered:—

> "When the reign of the line of the Stuarts is ended?"—ED.

† So Burnet tells us.

The celebrated work here to be noticed is Marvell's "Rehearsal Transprosed;" a title facetiously adopted from Bayes in "The Rehearsal Transposed" of the Duke of Buckingham. It was written against the works and the person of Dr. Samuel Parker, afterwards Bishop of Oxford, whom he designates under the character of Bayes, to denote the incoherence and ridiculousness of his character. Marvell had a peculiar knack of calling names,—it consisted in appropriating a ludicrous character in some popular comedy, and dubbing his adversaries with it. In the same spirit he ridiculed Dr. Turner, of Cambridge, a brother-genius to Parker, by nicknaming him "Mr. Smirk, the Divine in Mode," the name of the Chaplain in Etherege's "Man of Mode," and thus, by a stroke of the pen, conveyed an idea of "a neat, starched, formal, and forward divine." This application of a fictitious character to a real one, this christening a man with ridicule, though of no difficult invention, is not a little hazardous to inferior writers; for it requires not less wit than Marvell's to bring out of the real character the ludicrous features which mark the factitious prototype.

Parker himself must have his portrait, and if the likeness be justly hit off, some may be reminded of a resemblance. Mason applies the epithet of "Mitred Dullness" to him: but although he was at length reduced to railing and to menaces, and finally mortified into silence, this epithet does not suit so hardy and so active an adventurer.

The secret history of Parker may be collected in Marvell,* and his more public one in our honest chronicler, Anthony-Wood. Parker was originally educated in strict sectarian principles; a starch Puritan, "fasting and pray-

* See "The Rehearsal Transprosed, the second part," p. 76.

ing with the Presbyterian students weekly, and who, for
their refection feeding only on thin broth made of oat-
meal and water, were commonly called *Gruellers.*"
Among these, says Marvell, "it was observed that he
was wont to put more graves than all the rest into his
porridge, and was deemed one of the *preciousest** young
men in the University." It seems that these mortified
saints, both the brotherhood and the sisterhood, held
their chief meetings at the house of " Bess Hampton, an
old and crooked maid that drove the trade of laundry,
who, being from her youth very much given to the godly
party, as they call themselves, had frequent meetings, especially for those that were her customers." Such is the
dry humour of honest Anthony, who paints like the Ostade
of literary history.

But the age of sectarism and thin gruel was losing all
its coldness in the sunshine of the Restoration; and this
" preciousest young man," from praying and caballing
against episcopacy, suddenly acquainted the world, in
one of his dedications, that Dr. Ralph Bathurst had
" rescued him from the chains and fetters of an unhappy
education," and, without any intermediate apology, from
a sullen sectarian turned a flaming highflyer for the
" supreme dominion" of the Church.†

---

* One of the canting terms used by the saints of those days, and
not obsolete in the dialect of those who still give themselves out to be
saints in the present.

† Marvell admirably describes Parker's journey to London at the Restoration. where " he spent a considerable time in creeping into all corners and companies, horoscoping up and down concerning the duration
of the government." This term. so expressive of his political doubts
is from " Judicial Astrology." then a prevalent study. " Not considering anything as best, but as most lasting and most profitable : and after
having many times cast a figure, he at last satisfied himself that the
episcopal government would endure as long as this king lived, and from
thenceforwards cast about to find the highway to preferment. To do

It is the after-conduct of Parker that throws light on this rapid change. On speculative points any man may be suddenly converted; for these may depend on facts or arguments which might never have occurred to him before. But when we watch the weathercock chopping with the wind, so pliant to move, and so stiff when fixed—when we observe this "preciousest grueller" clothed in purple, and equally hardy in the most opposite measures—become a favourite with James II., and a furious advocate for arbitrary power; when we see him railing at and menacing those, among whom he had committed as many extravagances as any of them;* can we hesitate

---

this, he daily enlarged not only his conversation but his conscience, and was made free of some of the town vices; imagining, like Mule-asses, King of Tunis (for I take witness that on all occasions I treat him rather above his quality than otherwise), that by hiding himself among the onions he should escape being traced by his perfumes." The narrative proceeds with a curious detail of all his sycophantic attempts at seducing useful patrons, among whom was the Archbishop of Canterbury. Then began "those pernicious books," says Marvell, "in which he first makes all that he will to be law, and then whatsoever is law, to be divinity." Parker, in his "Ecclesiastical Polity," came at length to promulgate such violent principles as these, "He openly declares his submission to the government of a Nero and a Caligula, rather than suffer a dissolution of it." He says, "it is absolutely necessary to set up a more severe government over men's consciences and religious persuasions than over their vices and immoralities;" and that "men's vices and debaucheries may be more safely indulged than their consciences." Is it not difficult to imagine that this man had once been an Independent, the advocate for every congregation being independent of a bishop or a synod?

* Parker's father was a lawyer, and one of Oliver's most submissive sub-committee men, who so long pillaged the nation and spilled its blood, "not in the hot and military way (which diminishes always the offence), but in the cooler blood and sedentary execution of an high court of justice." He wrote a very remarkable book (after he had been petitioned against for a misdemeanour) in defence of that usurped irregular state called "The Government of the People of England." It had "a most hieroglyphical title" of several emblems: two

to decide that this bold, haughty, and ambitious man was
one of those who, having neither religion nor morality for
a casting weight, can easily fly off to opposite extremes?
and whether a puritan or a bishop, we must place his
zeal to the same side of his religious ledger—that of the
profits of barter!

The quarrel between Parker and Marvell originated in
a preface,* written by Parker, in which he had poured
down his contempt and abuse on his old companions,
the Nonconformists.   It was then Marvell clipped his
wings with his "Rehearsal Transprosed;" his wit and
humour were finely contrasted with Parker's extravagances, set off in his declamatory style; of which Marvell wittily describes "the volume and circumference of
the periods, which, though he takes always to be his
chiefest strength, yet, indeed, like too great a line,
weakens the defence, and requires too many men to
make it good."   The tilt was now opened, and certain
masqued knights appeared in the course; they attempted
to grasp the sharp and polished weapon of Marvell, to
turn it on himself.†   But Marvell, with malicious inge-

hands joined, and beneath a sheaf of arrows, stuffed about with half-a-
dozen mottoes, "enough," says Marvell, "to have supplied the mant-
lings and achievement of this (godly) family."   An anecdote in this
secret history of Parker is probably true.   "He shortly afterwards did
inveigh against his father's memory, and in his mother's presence, before witnesses, for a couple of whining fanatics."—*Rehearsal Transprosed,* second part, p. 75

   * This preface was prefixed to Bishop Bramhall's "Vindication of
the Bishops from the Presbyterian Charge of Popery."

   † As a specimen of what old Anthony calls "a jerking flirting way
of writing." I transcribe the titles of these answers which Marvell
received.   As Marvell had nicknamed Parker, Bayes, the quaint
humour of one entitled his reply, "Rosemary and Bayes;" another,
"The Transproser Rehearsed, or the Fifth Act of Mr. Bayes's Play;"
another, "Gregory Father Greybeard, with his Vizard off;" another
f:rmed "a Commonplace Book out of the Rehearsal, digested under

nnity, sees Parker in them all—they so much resembled
their master! "There were no less," says the wit,
"than six scaramouches together on the stage, all of
them of the same gravity and behaviour, the same tone,
the same habit, that it was impossible to discern which
was the true author of the 'Ecclesiastical Polity.' I believe he imitated the wisdom of some other princes, who
have sometimes been persuaded by their servants to disguise several others in the regal garb, that the enemy
might not know in the battle whom to single." Parker,
in fact, replied to Marvell anonymously, by "A Reproof
to the Rehearsal Transprosed," with a mild exhortation
to the magistrate to crush with the secular arm the pestilent wit, the servant of Cromwell, and the friend of
Milton. But this was not all; something else, anonymous too, was despatched to Marvell: it was an extraordinary letter, short enough to have been an epigram,
could Parker have written one; but short as it was, it
was more in character, for it was only a threat of assassination! It concluded with these words : "If thou
darest to print any lie or libel against Dr. Parker, by
the Eternal God I will cut thy throat." Marvell replied
to "the Reproof," which he calls a printed letter, by the
second part of "the Rehearsal Transprosed ;" and to
the unprinted letter, by publishing it on his own title-
page.

Of two volumes of wit and broad humour, and of the
most galling invective, one part flows so much into another, that the volatile spirit would be injured by an
analytical process. But Marvell is now only read by the
curious lovers of our literature, who find the strong,
luxuriant, though not the delicate, wit of the wittiest

heads;" and lastly, "Stoo him Bayes, or some Animadversions on the
Humour of writing Rehearsals."—*Biog. Brit.* p. 3055.
This was the very Bartlemy-fair of wit!

age, never obsolete : the reader shall not, however, part from Marvell without some slight transplantations from a soil whose rich vegetation breaks out in every part.

Of the pleasantry and sarcasm, these may be considered as specimens. Parker was both author and licenser of his own work on " Ecclesiastical Polity;" * and it appears he got the licence for printing Marvell's first *Rehearsal* recalled. The Church appeared in danger when the doctor discovered he was so furiously attacked. Marvell sarcastically rallies him on his dual capacity :—

" He is such an *At-all*, of so many capacities, that he would excommunicate any man who should have presumed to intermeddle with any one of his provinces. Has he been an author? he is too the licenser. Has he been a father? he will stand too for godfather. Had he acted *Pyramus*, he would have been *Moonshine* too, and the *Hole in the Wall*. That first author of ' Ecclesiastical Polity,' (such as his) Nero, was of the same temper. He could not be contented with the Roman empire, unless he were too his own precentor; and lamented only the detriment that mankind must sustain at his death, in losing so considerable a fiddler."

The satirist describes Parker's arrogance for those whom Parker calls the vulgar, and whom he defies as " a rout of wolves and tigers, apes and buffoons;" yet his personal fears are oddly contrasted with his self-importance : " If he chance but to sneeze, he prays that the *foundations of the earth* be not shaken.—Ever since he crept up to be but the *weathercock of a steeple*, he trembles and cracks at every puff of wind that blows

* The title will convey some notion of its intolerant principles : "A Discourse of Ecclesiastical Polity, wherein the authority of the Civil Magistrate *over the Consciences of Subjects*, in matters of external Religion, is asserted."

about him, as if the *Church of England* were falling."
Parker boasted, in certain philosophical "Tentamina,"
or essays of his, that he had confuted the atheists: Marvell declares, "If he had reduced any atheist by his
book, he can only pretend to have converted them (as in
the old Florentine wars) by mere tiring them out, and
perfect weariness." A pleasant allusion to those mock
fights of the Italian mercenaries, who, after parading all
day, rarely unhorsed a single cavalier.

Marvell blends with a ludicrous description of his answerers great fancy :—

"The whole *Posse Archidiaconatus* was raised to re-
press me; and great rising there was, and sending post
every way to pick out the ablest ecclesiastical droles to
prepare an answer. Never was such a hubbub made
about a sorry book. One flattered himself with being
at least a surrogate; another was so modest as to set
up with being but a paritor; while the most generous hoped only to be graciously smiled upon at a good
dinner; but the more hungry starvelings generally looked
upon it as an immediate call to a benefice; and he that
could but write an answer, whatsoever it were, took it
for the most dexterous, cheap, and legal way of simony.
As is usual on these occasions, there arose no small com-
petition and mutiny among the pretenders."

It seems all the body had not impudence enough,
and had too nice consciences, and could not afford an
extraordinary expense in wit for the occasion. It was
then

"The author of the 'Ecclesiastical Polity' altered his
lodgings to a calumny-office, and kept open chamber for
all comers, that he might be supplied himself, or supply
others, as there was occasion. But the information came
in so slenderly, that he was glad to make use of anything
rather than sit out; and there was at last nothing so

slight, but it grew material; nothing so false, but he
resolved it should go for truth; and what wanted in
matter, he would make out with invention and artifice.
So that he and his remaining comrades seemed to have
set up a glass-house, the model of which he had observed
from the height of his window in the neighbourhood, and
the art he had been initiated into ever since from the
manufacture (he will criticise because not orifacture) of
soap-bubbles, he improved by degrees to the mystery of
making *glass-drops*, and thence, in running leaps, mounted
by these virtues to be Fellow of the Royal Society, Doctor of Divinity, Parson, Prebend, and Archdeacon. The
furnace was so hot of itself, that there needed no coals,
much less any one to blow them. One burnt the weed,
another calcined the flint, a third melted down that mix-
ture; but he himself fashioned all with his breath, and
polished with his style, till, out of a mere jelly of sand
and ashes, he had furnished a whole cupboard of things,
so brittle and incoherent, that the least touch would
break them again in pieces, and so transparent, that
every man might see through them."

Parker had accused Marvell with having served Cromwell, and being the friend of Milton, then living, at a
moment when such an accusation not only rendered a
man odious, but put his life in danger.* Marvell, who
now perceived that Milton, whom he never looked on
but with the eyes of reverential awe, was likely to be
drawn into his quarrel, touches on this subject with in-

---

* Milton had become acquainted with Marvell when travelling in
Italy, where he had gone to perfect his studies. He returned to
England in 1653, and was connected with the Cromwellian party,
through the introduction of Milton, in 1657. The great poet was at
that time secretary to Cromwell, and he became his assistant-secre-
tary. He afterwards represented his native town of Hull in Parliament.—ED.

finite delicacy and tenderness, but not with diminished
energy against his malignant adversary, whom he shows
to have been an impertinent intruder in Milton's house,
where indeed he had first known him. He cautiously
alludes to our English Homer by his initials: at that
moment the very name of Milton would have tainted
the page!

" J. M. was, and is, a man of great learning and sharp-
ness of wit, as any man. It was his misfortune, living in
a tumultuous time, to be tossed on the wrong side ; and
he writ, *flagrante bello*, certain dangerous treatises. But
some of his books, upon which you take him at advantage were of no other nature than that one writ by your
own father; only with this difference, that your father's,
which I have by me, was written with the same design,
but with much less wit or judgment, for which there
was no remedy, unless you will supply his judgment
with his high Court of Justice. At his Majesty's happy
return, J. M. did partake, even as you yourself did, for all
your huffing, of his royal clemency, and has ever since
expiated himself in a retired silence. Whether it were
my foresight, or my good fortune, I never contracted
any friendship or confidence with you ; but then it was
you frequented J. M. incessantly, and haunted his house
day by day. What discourses you there used, he is too
generous to remember. But for you to insult over his
old age, to traduce him by your scaramouches, and in
your own person, as a schoolmaster, who was born and
hath lived more ingenuously and liberally than yourself!"

Marvell, when he lays by his playful humour and fertile fancy for more solemn remonstrances, assumes a
loftier tone, and a severity of invective, from which, indeed, Parker never recovered.

Accused by Parker of aiming to degrade the clerical

character, Marvell declares his veneration for that holy
vocation, and that he reflected even on the failings of
the men, from whom so much is expected, with indulgent
reverence :—

"Their virtues are to be celebrated with all encouragement; and if their vices be not notoriously palpable, let
the eye, as it defends its organ, so conceal the object by
connivance." But there are cases when even to write
satirically against a clergyman may be not only excus-
able, but necessary :—"The man who gets into the church
by the belfry or the window, ought never to be borne in
the pulpit; and so the man who illustrates his own corrupt doctrines with as ill a conversation, and adorns the
lasciviousness of his life with an equal petulancy of style
and language."—In such a concurrence of misdemeanors,
what is to be done? The example and the consequence
so pernicious! which could not be, "if our great pastors
but exercise the wisdom of common shepherds, by part-
ing with one to stop the infection of the whole flock,
when his rottenness grows notorious. Or if our clergy
would but use the instinct of other creatures, and chastise the blown deer out of their herd, such mischiefs
might easily be remedied. In this case it is that I think
a clergyman is laid open to the pen of any one that
knows how to manage it; and that every person who
has either wit, learning, or sobriety, is licensed, if debauched, to curb him; if erroneous, to catechise him;
and if foul-mouthed and biting, to muzzle him. Such an
one would never have come into the church, but to take
sanctuary; rather wheresoever men shall find the footing
of so wanton a satyr out of his own bounds, the neighbourhood ought, notwithstanding all his pretended caper-
ing divinity, to hunt him through the woods, with hounds
and horse, home to his harbour."

And he frames an ingenious apology for the freedom

of his humour, in this attack on the morals and person
of his adversary :—

"To write against him (says Marvell) is the odiousest
task that ever I undertook, and has looked to me all the
while like the cruelty of a living dissection; which, however it may tend to public instruction, and though I
have picked out the noxious creature to be anatomised,
yet doth scarce excuse the offensiveness of the scent and
fouling of my fingers: therefore, I will here break off
abruptly, leaving many a vein not laid open, and many
a passage not searched into. But if I have undergone
the drudgery of the most loathsome part already (which
is his personal character), I will not defraud myself of
what is more truly pleasant, the conflict with, if it may
be so called, his reason."

It was not only in these "pen-combats" that this
Literary Quarrel proceeded; it seems also to have
broken out in the streets; for a tale has been preserved
of a rencontre, which shows at once the brutal manners
of Parker, and the exquisite wit of Marvell. Parker
meeting Marvell in the streets, the bully attempted to
shove him from the wall: but, even there, Marvell's
agility contrived to lay him sprawling in the kennel; and
looking on him pleasantly, told him to "lie there for a
son of a whore!" Parker complained to the Bishop of
Rochester, who immediately sent for Marvell, to repri-
mand him; but he maintained that the doctor had so
called himself, in one of his recent publications; and pointing to the preface, where Parker declares "he is 'a true
son of his mother, the Church of England;' and if you
read further on, my lord, you find he says: 'The Church
of England has spawned two bastards, the Presbyterians
and the Congregationists;' ergo, my lord, he expressly
declares that he is the *son of a whore!*"

Although Parker retreated from any further attack,

after the second part of "The Rehearsal Transprosed,"
he in truth only suppressed passions to which he was
giving vent in secrecy and silence. That, indeed, was
not discovered till a posthumous work of his appeared,
in which one of the most striking parts is a most dis-
gusting caricature of his old antagonist. Marvell was,
indeed, a republican, the pupil of Milton, and adored his
master: but his morals and his manners were Roman—
he lived on the turnip of Curtius, and he would have
bled at Philippi. We do not sympathise with the fierce
republican spirit of those unhappy times that scalped
the head feebly protected by a mitre or a crown. But
the private virtues and the rich genius of such a man are
pure from the taint of party. We are now to see how
far private hatred can distort, in its hideous vengeance,
the resemblance it affects to give after nature. Who
could imagine that Parker is describing Marvell in these
words?—

"Among these insolent revilers of great fame for
ribaldry was one Marvell. From his youth he lived in
all manner of wickedness; and thus, with a singular
petulancy from nature, he performed the office of a
satirist for the faction, not so much from the quickness
of his wit, as from the sourness of his temper. A vaga-
bond, ragged, hungry poetaster, beaten at every tavern,
where he daily received the rewards of his impudence in
kicks and blows.* By the interest of Milton, to whom
he was somewhat agreeable for his malignant wit, he
became the under-secretary to Cromwell's secretary."

And elsewhere he calls him "a drunken buffoon," and
asserts that "he made his conscience more cheap than
he had formerly made his reputation;" but the familiar

* Vanus, pannosus, et famelicus poetaster œnopolis quovis va-
pulans, fuste et calce indies petulantiæ pœnas tulit—are the words in
Parker's "De Rebus sui Temporis Commentariorum," p. 275.

anecdote of Marvell's political honesty, when, wanting a
dinner, he declined the gold sent to him by the king,
sufficiently replies to the calumniator. Parker, then in
his retreat, seems not to have been taught anything like
modesty by his silence, as Burnet conjectured; who
says, " That a face of brass must grow red when it is
burnt as his was." It was even then that the recreant,
in silence, was composing the libel, which his cowardice
dared not publish, but which his invincible malice has
sent down to posterity.

D'AVENANT
AND A CLUB OF WITS.

CALAMITIES of Epic Poets—Character and Anecdotes of D'Avenant—
attempts a new vein of invention—the Critics marshalled against
each other on the "Gondibert"—D'Avenant's sublime feelings of
Literary Fame—attacked by a Club of Wits in two books of Verses
—the strange misconception hitherto given respecting the Second
Part—various specimens of the Satires on Gondibert, the Poet, and
his Panegyrist Hobbes—the Poet's silence; and his neglect of the
unfinished Epic, while the Philosopher keenly retorts on the Club,
and will not allow of any authority in WIT.

THE memoirs of epic poets, in as far as they relate to
the history of their own epics, would be the most
calamitous of all the suitors of the Muses, whether their
works have reached us, or scarcely the names of the
poets. An epic, which has sometimes been the labour of
a life, is the game of the wits and the critics. One ridicules what is written; the other censures for what has not
been written :—and it has happened, in some eminent
instances, that the rudest assailants of him who "builds
the lofty rhyme," have been his ungenerous contempo-

raries. Men, whose names are now endeared to us, and who have left their *KTHMA ES AEI*, which Hobbes so energetically translates "a possession for everlasting," have bequeathed an inheritance to posterity, of which they have never been in the receipt of the revenue. "The first fruits" of genius have been too often gathered to place upon its tomb. Can we believe that Milton did not endure mortification from the neglect of "evil days," as certainly as Tasso was goaded to madness by the systematic frigidity of his critics? He who is now before us had a mind not less exalted than Milton or Tasso; but was so effectually ridiculed, that he has only sent us down the fragment of a great work.

One of the curiosities in the history of our poetry, is the Gondibert of D'Avenant; and the fortunes and the fate of this epic are as extraordinary as the poem itself. Never has an author deserved more copious memoirs than the fertility of this man's genius claims. His life would have exhibited a moving picture of genius in action and in contemplation. With all the infirmities of lively passions, he had all the redeeming virtues of magnanimity and generous affections; but with the dignity and the powers of a great genius, falling among an age of wits, he was covered by ridicule. D'Avenant was a man who had viewed human life in all its shapes, and had himself taken them. A poet and a wit, the creator of the English stage with the music of Italy and the scenery of France; a soldier, an emigrant, a courtier, and a politician:—he was, too, a state-prisoner, awaiting death with his immortal poem in his hand;* and at all times a philosopher!

---

* D'Avenant commenced his poem during his exile at Paris. The preface is dated from the Louvre; the postscript from Cowes Castle, in the Isle of Wight, where he was then confined, expecting his immediate execution. The poem, in the first edition, 1651, is therefore

That hardiness of enterprise which had conducted him through life, brought the same novelty, and conferred on him the same vigour in literature.

D'Avenant attempted to open a new vein of invention in narrative poetry; which not to call *epic*, he termed *heroic;* and which we who have more completely emancipated ourselves from the arbitrary mandates of Aristotle and Bossu, have since styled romantic. Scott, Southey, and Byron have taught us this freer scope of invention, but characterised by a depth of passion which is not found in D'Avenant. In his age, the title which

abruptly concluded. There is something very affecting and great in his style on this occasion. " I am here arrived at the middle of the third book. But it is high time to strike sail and cast anchor, though I have run but half my course, when at the helm I am threatened with *death ;* who, though he can visit us but once, seems troublesome; and even in the innocent may beget such a gravity, as diverts the music of verse. Even in a worthy design, I shall ask leave to desist, when I am interrupted by so great an experiment as *dying ;*—and 'tis an experiment to the most experienced; for no man (though his mortifications may be much greater than mine) can say *he has already died.*"—D'Avenant is said to have written a letter to Hobbes about this time, giving some account of his progress in the third book. " But why (said he) should I trouble you or myself with these thoughts, when I am pretty certain I shall be hanged next week ?"— A stroke of the gaiety of temper of a very thoughtful mind ; for D'Avenant, with all his wit and fancy, has made the profoundest reflections on human life.

The reader may be interested to know, that after D'Avenant's removal from Cowes to the Tower, to be tried, his life was saved by the gratitude of two aldermen of York, whom he had obliged. It is delightful to believe the story told by Bishop Newton, that D'Avenant owed his life to Milton ; Wood, indeed, attributes our poet's escape to both ; at the Restoration D'Avenant interposed, and saved Milton. Poets, after all, envious as they are to a brother, are the most generously-tempered of men : they libel, but they never hang ; they will indeed throw out a sarcasm on the man whom they saved from being hanged. " Please your Majesty," said Sir John Denham, "do not hang George Withers—that it may not be said I am the worst poet alive."

he selected to describe the class of his poetical narrative, was a miserable source of petty criticism. It was decreed that every poem should resemble another poem, on the plan of the ancient epic. This was the golden age of "the poet-apes," till they found that it was easier to produce epic writers than epic readers.

But our poet, whose manly genius had rejected one great absurdity, had the folly to adopt another. The first reformers are always more heated with zeal than enlightened by sagacity. The four-and-twenty chapters of an epic, he perceived, were but fantastical divisions, and probably, originally, but accidental; yet he proposed another form as chimerical; he imagined that by having only five he was constructing his poem on the dramatic plan of five acts. He might with equal propriety have copied the Spanish comedy which I once read, in twenty-five acts, and in no slender folio. "Sea-marks (says D'Avenant, alluding to the works of antiquity) are chiefly useful to *coasters*, and serve not those who have the ambition of *discoverers*, that love to sail in untried seas;" and yet he was attempting to turn an epic poem into a monstrous drama, from the servile habits he had contracted from his intercourse with the theatre! This error of the poet has, however, no material influence on the "Gondibert," as it has come down to us; for, discouraged and ridiculed, our adventurer never finished his voyage of discovery. He who had so nobly vindicated the freedom of the British Muse from the meanness of imitation, and clearly defined what such a narrative as he intended should be, "a perfect glass of nature, which gives us a familiar and easy view of ourselves," did not yet perceive that there is no reason why a poetical narrative should be cast into any particular form, or be longer or shorter than the interest it excites will allow.

More than a century and a half have elapsed since the

first publication of "Gondibert," and its merits are still a subject of controversy ; an indubitable proof of some inherent excellence not willingly forgotten. The critics are marshalled on each side, one against the other, while between these formidable lines stands the poet, with a few scattered readers ;* but what is more surprising in

---

* It would form a very curious piece of comparative criticism, were the opinions and the arguments of all the critics—those of the time and of the present day—thrown into the smelting-pot. The massiness of some opinions of great authority would be reduced to a thread of wire ; and even what is accepted as standard ore might shrink into "a gilt sixpence." On one side, the condemners of D'Avenant would be Rymer, Blackwall, Granger, Knox, Hurd, and Hayley; and the advocates would be Hobbes, Waller, Cowley, Dr. Aikin, Headley, &c. Rymer opened his Aristotelian text-book. He discovers that the poet's first lines do not give any light into his design (it is probable D'Avenant would have found it hard to have told it to Mr. Rymer) ; that it has neither proposition nor invocation—(Rymer might have filled these up himself) ; so that "he chooses to enter into the top of the house, because the morta's of mean and satisfied minds go in at the door;" and then "he has no hero or action so illustrious that the *name* of the poem prepared the reader for its reception." D'Avenant had rejected the marvellous from his poem—that is, the machinery of the epic : he had resolved to compose a tale of human beings for men. "This was," says Blackwall, another of the classical flock, "like lopping off a man's limb, and then putting him upon running races." Our formal critics are quite lively in their dulness on our "adventurer." But poets, in the crisis of a poetical revolution, are more legitimate judges than all such critics. Waller and Cowley applaud D'Avenant for this very omission of the epical machinery in this new vein of invention :—

> "Here no bold tales of gods or monsters swell,
> But human passions such as with us dwell ;
> *Man is thy theme*, his virtue or his rage,
> Drawn to the life in each elaborate page."
>
> WALLER.

> "Methinks heroic poesy, till now,
> Like some fantastic fairy-land did show,
> *And all but man, in man's best work had place*."
>
> COWLEY.

the history of the "Gondibert," the poet is a great poet, the work imperishable!

The "Gondibert" has poetical defects fatal for its popularity; the theme was not happily chosen; the quatrain has been discovered by capricious ears to be unpleasing, though its solemnity was felt by Dryden.* The style is sometimes harsh and abrupt, though often exquisite; and the fable is deficient in that rapid interest which the story-loving readers of all times seem most to regard. All these are diseases which would have long since proved mortal in a poem less vital; but our poet was a commanding genius, who redeemed his bold errors by his energetic originality. The luxuriancy of his fancy, the novelty of his imagery, the grandeur of his views of human life; his delight in the new sciences of his age;— these are some of his poetical virtues. But, above all, we dwell on the impressive solemnity of his philosophical reflections, and his condensed epigrammatic thoughts. The work is often more ethical than poetical; yet, while we feel ourselves becoming wiser at every page, in the fulness of our minds we still perceive that our emotions have been seldom stirred by passion. The poem falls

---

Hurd's discussion on "Gondibert," in his "Commentaries," is the most important piece of criticism: subtle, ingenious, and exquisitely analytical. But he holds out the fetter of authority, and he decides as a judge who expounds laws: not the best decision, when new laws are required to abrogate obsolete ones. And what laws invented by man can be immutable? D'Avenant was thus tried by the laws of a country, that of Greece or Rome, of which, it is said, he was not even a denizen.

It is remarkable that all the critics who condemn D'Avenant could not but be struck by his excellences, and are very particular in expressing their admiration of his genius. I mean all the critics who have read the poem: some assuredly have criticised with little trouble.

* It is written in the long four-line stanzas, which Dryden adopted for his *Anus Mirabilis;* nearly 2000 of such stanzas are severe trials for the critical reader.—ED.

from our hands! yet is there none of which we wish to
retain so many single verses.   D'Avenant is a poetical
Rochefoucault ; the sententious force of his maxims on all
human affairs could only have been composed by one
who had lived in a constant intercourse with mankind.*

A delightful invention in this poem is "the House of
Astragon," a philosophical residence.   Every great poet
is affected by the revolutions of his age.   The new experimental philosophy had revived the project of Lord
Bacon's learned retirement, in his philosophical romance
of the *Atalantis ;* and subsequently in a time of civil re-

* I select some of these lines as examples.   Of Care, who only,
"seals her eyes in cloisters," he says,
> "She visits cities, but she dwells in thrones."

Of learned Curiosity, eager, but not to be hurried—the student is
> "Hasty to know, though not by haste beguiled."

He calls a library, with sublime energy,
> "The monument of vanish'd minds."

Never has a politician conveyed with such force a most important
precept :
> ——————"The laws,
> Men from themselves, but not from power, secure."

Of the Court he says,
> "There prosperous power sleeps long, though suitors wake."
> "Be bold, for number cancels bashfulness ;
> Extremes, from which a King would blushing shrink,
> Unblushing senates act as no excess."

And these lines, taken as they occur :
> "Truth's a discovery made by travelling minds."
> "Honour's the moral conscience of the great."
> "They grow so certain as to need no hope.'
> "Praise is devotion fit for mighty minds."

I conclude with one complete stanza, of the same cast of reflection.
It may be inscribed in the library of the student, in the studio of the
artist, in every place where excellence can only be obtained by
knowledge.
> "Rich are the diligent, who can command
> Time, nature's stock! and, could his hour-glass fall,
> Would, as for seed of stars, stoop for the sand
> And by incessant labour gather all!"

pose after civil war, Milton, Cowley, and Evelyn attempted to devote an abode to science itself. These tumults of the imagination subsided in the establishment of the Royal Society. D'Avenant anticipated this institution. On an estate consecrated to philosophy stands a retired building on which is inscribed, " Great Nature's Office," inhabited by sages, who are styled " Nature's Registers," busily recording whatever is brought to them by " a throng of Intelligencers," who make " patient observations " in the field, the garden, the river, on every plant, and " every fish, and fowl, and beast." Near at hand is " Nature's Nursery," a botanical garden. We have also " a Cabinet of Death," " the Monument of Bodies," an anatomical collection, which leads to " the Monument of vanished Minds," as the poet finely describes the library. Is it not striking to find, says Dr. Aikin, so exact a model of *the school of Linnæus?*

This was a poem to delight a philosopher; and Hobbes, in a curious epistle prefixed to the work, has strongly marked its distinct beauties. " Gondibert " not only came forth with the elaborate panegyric of Hobbes, but was also accompanied by the high commendatory poems of Waller and Cowley; a cause which will sufficiently account for the provocations it inflamed among the poetical crew; and besides these accompaniments, there is a preface of great length, stamped with all the force and originality of the poet's own mind; and a postscript, as sublime from the feelings which dictated it as from the time and place of its composition.

In these, this great genius pours himself out with all that " glory of which his large soul appears to have been full," as Hurd has nobly expressed it.* Such a con-

---

* Can one read such passages as these without catching some of the sympathies of a great genius that knows itself?

" He who writes an heroic poem leaves an estate entailed, and he

scious dignity of character struck the petulant wits with a provoking sense of their own littleness.

A club of wits caballed and produced a collection of short poems sarcastically entitled "Certain Verses written by several of the Author's Friends, to be reprinted in the Second Edition of 'Gondibert,'" 1653. Two years after appeared a brother volume, entitled "The Incomparable Poem of Gondibert vindicated from the Wit-Combats of Four Esquires; Clinias, Dametas, Sancho and Jack Pudding;"* with these mottoes:

gives a greater gift to posterity than to the present age; for a public benefit is best measured in the number of receivers; and our contemporaries are but few when reckoned with those who shall succeed.

"If thou art a malicious reader, thou wilt remember my preface boldly confessed, that a main motive to the undertaking was a desire of fame; and thou mayest likewise say, I may very possibly not live to enjoy it. Truly. I have some years ago considered that Fame, like Time. only gets a reverence by long running; and that, like a river, 'tis narrowest where 'tis bred, and broadest afar off.

"If thou, reader, art one of those who have been warmed with poetic fire. I reverence thee as my judge; and whilst others tax me with vanity, I appeal to thy conscience whether it be more than such a necessary assurance as thou hast made to thyself in like undertakings? For when I observe that writers have many enemies, such inward assurance, methinks, resembles that forward confidence in men of arms, which makes them proceed in great enterprise; since the right examination of abilities begins with inquiring whether we doubt ourselves."

Such a composition is injured by mutilation. He here also alludes to his military character: "Nor could I sit idle and sigh with such as mourn to hear the drum; for if the age be not quiet enough to be taught virtue a pleasant way, the next may be at leisure; nor could I (like men that have civilly slept till they are old in dark cities) think war a novelty." Shakspeare could not have expressed his feelings, in his own style, more eloquently touching than D'Avenant.

* It is said there were four writers. The Clinias and Dametas were probably Sir John Denham and Jo. Donne: Sir Allan Broderick and Will Crofts, who is mentioned by the clubs as one of their fellows, appear to be the Sancho and Jack Pudding. Will Crofts was a favourite with Charles II.: he had been a skilful agent, as appears in Clarendon. [In the accounts of moneys disbursed for secret services in the

Κοτέει καὶ ἀοίδος ἀοίδῳ
Vatum quoque gratia, rara est.
Anglicè,
One wit-brother
Envies another.

Of these rare tracts, we are told by Anthony Wood
and all subsequent literary historians, too often mere
transcribers of title-pages, that the second was written
by our author himself. Would not one imagine that it
was a real vindication, or at least a retort-courteous on
these obliging friends. The irony of the whole volume
has escaped their discovery. The second tract is a continuation of the satire: a mock defence, where the sarcasm and the pretended remonstrance are sometimes
keener than the open attack. If, indeed, D'Avenant
were the author of a continuation of a satire on himself,
it is an act of *felo de se* no poet ever committed; a self-
flagellation by an iron whip, where blood is drawn at
every stroke, the most penitent bard never inflicted on
himself. Would D'Avenant have bantered his proud
labour, by calling it "incomparable?" And were it true,
that he felt the strokes of their witty malignity so lightly,
would he not have secured his triumph by finishing that
"Gondibert," "the monument of his mind?" It is too
evident that this committee of wits hurt the quiet of a
great mind.

As for this series of literary satires, it might have been
expected, that since the wits clubbed, this committee
ought to have been more effective in their operations.
Many of their papers were, no doubt, more blotted with

reign of Charles II., published by the Camden Society, his name appears for 200l., but that of his wife repeatedly figures for large sums,
"as of free guift." In this way she receives 700l. with great regularity for a series of years, until the death of Charles II.] Howell has
a poem "On some who, blending their brains together, plotted how to
bespatter one of the Muses' choicest sons, Sir William D'Avenant."

their wine than their ink. Their variety of attack is
playful, sarcastic, and malicious. They were then such
exuberant wits, that they could make even ribaldry and
grossness witty. My business with these wicked trifles
is only as they concerned the feelings of the great poet,
whom they too evidently hurt, as well as the great
philosopher who condescended to notice these wits, with
wit more dignified than their own.

Unfortunately for our "jeered Will," as in their usual
court-style they call him, he had met with "a foolish
mischance," well known among the collectors of our
British portraits. There was a feature in his face, or
rather no feature at all, that served as a perpetual provocative : there was no precedent of such a thing, says
Suckling, in "The Sessions of the Poets"—

> In all their records, in verse or in prose,
> There was none of a Laureat who wanted a nose.

Besides, he was now doomed—

> Nor could old Hobbes
> Defend him trom dry bobbs.

The preface of "Gondibert," the critical epistle of
Hobbes, and the poems of the two greatest poets in England, were first to be got rid of. The attack is brisk
and airy.

UPON THE PREFACE.

> Room for the best of poets heroic,
> If you'll believe two wits and a Stoic.
> Down go the *Iliads*, down go the *Æneidos :*
> All must give place to the *Gondiberteidos.*
> For to *Homer* and *Virgil* he has a just pique,
> Because one's writ in Latin, the other in Greek;
> Besides an old grudge (our critics they say so)
> With *Ovid,* because his sirname was *Naso.*
> If fiction the fame of a poet thus raises,
> What poets are you that have writ his praises ?

> But we justly quarrel at this our defeat;
> You give us a stomach, he gives us no meat.
> A preface to no book, a porch to no house;
> Here is the mountain, but where is the mouse?

This stroke, in the mock defence, is thus warded off, with a slight confession of the existence of "the mouse."

> Why do you bite, you men of fangs
> (That is, of teeth that forward hangs),
> And charge my dear Ephestion
> With want of meat? you want digestion.
> We poets use not so to do,
> To find men meat and stomach too.
> You have the book, you have the house,
> And mum, good Jack, and catch the mouse.

Among the personal foibles of D'Avenant appears a desire to disguise his humble origin; and to give it an air of lineal descent, he probably did not write his name as his father had done. It is said he affected, at the cost of his mother's honour, to insinuate that he was the son of Shakspeare, who used to bait at his father's inn.* These humorists first reduce D'Avenant to "Old Daph."

---

* The story was current in D'Avenant's time, and it is certain he encouraged the believers in its truth. Anthony Wood speaks of the lady as "a very beautiful woman, of a good wit and conversation, in which she was imitated by none of her children but by this William." He also notes Shakspeare's custom to lodge at the Crown Inn, Oxford, kept by her husband, "in his journies between Warwickshire and London." Aubrey tells the same tale, adding that D'Avenant "would sometimes, when he was pleasant over a glass of wine with his most intimate friends, e. g. Sam. Butler (author of "Hudibras, &c.,) say, that it seemed to him that he writ with the very same spirit that Shakspeare did, and was contented enough to be thought his son;" he adds that "his mother had a very light report." It was Pope who told Oldys the jesting story he had obtained from Betterton, of little Will running from school to meet Shakspeare, in one of his visits to Oxford, and being asked where he was running, by an old townsman, replied, to "see my godfather Shakspeare." "There's a good boy," said the

> Denham, come help me to laugh,
>   At old Daph,
> Whose fancies are higher than chaff.

Daph swells afterwards into " Daphne ;" a change of
sex inflicted on the poet for making one of his heroines
a man; and this new alliance to Apollo becomes a source
of perpetual allusion to the bays—

> Cheer up, small wits, now *you* shall crowned be,—
> Daphne himself is turn'd into a tree

One of the club inquires about the situation of
Avenant—

> —— where now it lies,
> Whether in Lombard,* or the skies.

Because, as seven cities disputed for the birth of Homer,
so after ages will not want towns claiming to be
Avenant—

> Some say by *Avenant* no place is meant,
> And that our Lombard is without descent;
> And as, by *Bilk*, men mean there's nothing there,
> So come from *Avenant*, means from *no where*.
> Thus *Will*, intending *D'Avenant* to grace,
> Has made a notch in's name like that in's face.

D'Avenant had been knighted for his good conduct at
the siege of Gloucester, and was to be tried by the Parliament, but procured his release without trial. This
produces the following sarcastic epigram :—

UPON FIGHTING WILL.

> The King knights Will for fighting on his side ;
> Yet when Will comes for fighting to be tried,
> There is not one in all the armies can
> Say they e'er felt, or saw, this fighting man.

---

old gentleman, "but have a care that you don't take God's name in
vain."—ED.

* The scene where the story of "Gondibert" is placed, which the
wits sometimes pronounced *Lumber* and *Lumbery*.

Strange, that the Knight should not be known i' th' field;
A face well charged, though nothing in his shield.
Sure fighting Will like *basilisk* did ride
Among the troops, and all that *saw* Will died;
Else how could Will, for fighting, be a Knight,
And none alive that ever saw Will fight?

Of the malignancy of their wit, we must preserve one specimen. They probably harassed our poet with anonymous despatches from the Club: for there appears another poem on D'Avenant's anger on such an occasion:—

A LETTER SENT TO THE GOOD KNIGHT.

Thou hadst not been thus long neglected,
But we, thy four best friends, expected,
Ere this time, thou hadst stood corrected.
But since that planet governs still,
That rules thy tedious fustain quill
'Gainst nature and the Muses' will;
When, by thy friends' advice and care,
'Twas hoped, in time, thou wouldst despair
To give ten pounds to write it fair;
Lest thou to all the world would show it,
We thought it fit to let thee know it:
Thou art a damn'd insipid poet!

These literary satires contain a number of other "pasquils," burlesquing the characters, the incidents, and the stanza, of the Gondibert: some not the least witty are the most gross, and must not be quoted; thus the wits of that day were poetical suicides, who have shortened their lives by their folly.

D'Avenant, like more than one epic poet, did not tune to his ear the *names* of his personages. They have added, to show that his writings are adapted to an easy musical singer, the names of his heroes and heroines, in these verses:—

Hurgonil, Astolpho, Borgia, Goltha, Tibalt,
Astragon, Hermogild, Ulfinor, Orgo, Thula.

And "epithets that will serve for any substantives, either in this part or the next."

Such are the labours of the idlers of genius, envious of the nobler industry of genius itself!—How the great author's spirit was nourished by the restoratives of his other friends, after the bitter decoctions prescribed by these "Four," I fear we may judge by the unfinished state in which "Gondibert" has come down to us. D'Avenant seems, however, to have guarded his dignity by his silence; but Hobbes took an opportunity of delivering an exquisite opinion on this Club of Wits, with perfect philosophical indifference. It is in a letter to the Hon. Edward Howard, who requested to have his sentiments on another heroic poem of his own, "The British Princes."

"My judgment in poetry hath, you know, been once already censured, by very good wits, for commending 'Gondibert;' but yet they have not, I think, disabled my testimony. For, *what authority is there in wit?* A jester may have it; a man in drink may have it, and be fluent over-night, and wise and dry in the morning. What is it? or who can tell whether it be better to have it, or be without it, especially if it be a pointed wit? I will take my liberty to praise what I like, as well as they do to reprehend what they do not like."

The stately "Gondibert" was not likely to recover favour in the court of Charles the Second, where man was never regarded in his true greatness, but to be ridiculed; a court where the awful presence of Clarendon became so irksome, that the worthless monarch exiled him; a court where nothing was listened to but wit at the cost of sense, the injury of truth, and the violation of decency; where a poem of magnitude with new claims was a very business for those volatile arbiters of taste; an epic poem that had been travestied and epigrammed,

was a national concern with them, which, next to some
new state-plot, that occurred oftener than a new epic,
might engage the monarch and his privy council. These
were not the men to be touched by the compressed
reflections and the ideal virtues personified in this poem.
In the court of the laughing voluptuary the manners as
well as the morals of these satellites of pleasure were so
little heroic, that those of the highest rank, both in
birth and wit, never mentioned each other but with the
vulgar familiarity of nicknames, or the coarse appel-
latives of Dick, Will, and Jack! Such was the era
when the serious "Gondibert" was produced, and such
were the judges who seem to have decided its fate.

THE

PAPER-WARS OF THE CIVIL WARS.

THE "Mercuries" and "Diurnals," archives of political fictions —
"The Diurnals," in the pay of the Parliament, described by Butler
and Cleveland—Sir John Birkenhead excels in sarcasm, with specimens of his "Mercurius Aulicus"—how he corrects his own lies—
Specimens of the Newspapers on the side of the Commonwealth.

AMONG these battles of logomachy, in which so
much ink has been spilt, and so many pens have
lost their edge—at a very solemn period in our history,
when all around was distress and sorrow, stood forwards
the facetious ancestors of that numerous progeny who
still flourish among us, and who, without a suspicion of
their descent, still bear the features of their progenitors,
and inherit so many of the family humours. These were
the MERCURIES and DIURNALS—the newspapers of our
Civil Wars.

The distinguished heroes of these Paper-Wars, Sir
John Birkenhead, Marchmont Needham, and Sir Roger
L'Estrange, I have elsewhere portrayed.* We have had
of late correct lists of these works; but no one seems as
yet to have given any clear notion of their spirit and
their manner.

The London Journals in the service of the Parliament
were usually the *Diurnals.* These politicians practised
an artifice which cannot be placed among "the lost
inventions." As these were hawked about the metropolis
to spur curiosity, often languid from over-exercise, or to
wheedle an idle spectator into a reader, every paper
bore on its front the inviting heads of its intelligence.
Men placed in the same circumstances will act in the
same manner, without any notion of imitation; and the
passions of mankind are now addressed by the same
means which our ancestors employed, by those who do
not suspect they are copying them.

These *Diurnals* have been blasted by the lightnings of
Butler and Cleveland. Hudibras is made happy at the
idea that he may be

> Register'd by fame eternal
> In deathless pages of DIURNAL.

But Cleveland has left us two remarkable effusions of his
satiric and vindictive powers, in his curious character of
"A Diurnal Maker," and "A London Diurnal." He
writes in the peculiar vein of the wit of those times,
with an originality of images, whose combinations excite
surprise, and whose abundance fatigues our weaker delicacy.

"A Diurnal-Maker is the Sub-Almoner of History;
Queen Mab's Register; one whom, by the same figure
that a North-country pedler is a merchantman, you may

* "Curiosities of Literature," vol. i. p. 158 (last edition).

style an author. The silly countryman who, seeing an
ape in a scarlet coat, blessed his young worship, and
gave his landlord joy of the hopes of his house, did not
slander his compliment with worse application than he
that names this shred an historian. To call him an Historian is to knight a Mandrake; 'tis to view him through
a perspective, and, by that gross hyperbole, to give the
reputation of an engineer to a maker of mousetraps.
When these weekly fragments shall pass for history, let
the poor man's box be entitled the Exchequer, and the
alms-basket a Magazine. Methinks the Turke should
license Diurnals, because he prohibits learning and
books." He characterises the Diurnal as "a puny
chronicle, scarce pin-feathered with the wings of time;
it is a history in sippets; the English Iliads in a nut-
shell; the Apocryphal Parliament's Book of Maccabees
in single sheets."

But Cleveland tells us that these Diurnals differ from
a *Mercurius Aulicus* (the paper of his party),—"as the
Devil and his Exorcist, or as a black witch doth from a
white one, whose office is to unravel her enchantments."

The *Mercurius Aulicus* was chiefly conducted by Sir
John Birkenhead, at Oxford, "communicating the intelligence and affairs of the court to the rest of the kingdom." Sir John was a great wag, and excelled in
sarcasm and invective; his facility is equal to repartee,
and his spirit often reaches to wit: a great forger of
tales, who probably considered that a romance was a
better thing than a newspaper.* The royal party were

* There is a small poem, published in 1643, entitled "The Great
Assizes holden in Parnassus," in the manner of a later work, "The
Sessions of the Poets," in which all the Diurnals and Mercuries are
arraigned and tried. An impartial satire on them all; and by its good
sense and heavy versification, is so much in the manner of George
Wither, that some have conjectured it to be that singular author's.
Its rarity gives it a kind of value. Of such verses as Wither's, who

so delighted with his witty buffoonery, that Sir John was
recommended to be Professor of Moral Philosophy at
Oxford. Did political lying seem to be a kind of moral
philosophy to the feelings of a party? The originality
of Birkenhead's happy manner consists in his adroit use
of sarcasm : he strikes it off by means of a parenthesis.
I shall give, as a specimen, one of his summaries of what
the *Parliamentary Journals* had been detailing during
the week.

"The Londoners in print this week have been pretty
copious. They say that *a troop of the Marquess of
Newcastle's horse have submitted to the Lord Fairfax.*
(They were part of the *German* horse which came over
in the *Danish* fleet.)* That the Lord *Wilmot hath been*

has been of late extolled too highly, the chief merit is their sense and
truth; which, if he were not tedious, might be an excellence in prose.
Antiquaries, when they find a poet adapted for their purposes, conjecture that he is an excellent one. This prosing satirist, strange to
say, in some pastoral poetry, has opened the right vein.

Aulicus is well characterized :—

—————— "hee, for wicked ends,
Had the Castalian spring defiled with gall,
And changed by Witchcraft most satyricall,
The bayes of Helicon and myrtles mild,
To pricking hawthornes and to hollies wild.
—————— with slanders false,
With forged fictitious calumnies and tales—
He added fewel to the direful flame
Of civil discord; and domestic blowes,
By the incentives of malicious prose.
For whereas he should have composed his inke
Of liquors that make flames expire, and shrink
Into their cinders—
—He laboured hard for to bring in
The exploded doctrines of the Florentine,
And taught that to dissemble and to lie
Were vital parts of human policie."

* Alluding to a ridiculous rumour, that the King was to receive
foreign troops by a Danish fleet.

dead five weeks, but the Cavaliers concealed his death.
(Remember this!) That *Sir John Urrey* is dead and
buried at Oxford.* (He died the same day with the Lord
Wilmot.) That the *Cavaliers, before they have done,
will* HURREY *all men into misery.* (This quibble hath
been six times printed, and nobody would take notice
of it; now let's hear of it no more!) That *all the Cavaliers which Sir William Waller took prisoners (besides
500) tooke the National Covenant.* (Yes, all he took
(besides 500) tooke the Covenant.) That 2000 *Irish
Rebels landed in Wales.* (You called them English
Protestants till you cheated them of their money.)
That *Sir William Brereton left* 140 *good able men in
Hawarden Castle.* ('Tis the better for Sir Michael Earn-
ley, who hath taken the Castle.) That *the Queen hath
a great deafnesse.* (Thou hast a great blister on thy
tongue.) That *the Cavaliers burned all the suburbs of
Chester, that Sir William Brereton might find no shelter
to besiedge it.* (There was no hayrick, and Sir William
cares for no other shelter.)† The SCOTTISH DOVE says

---

* Col. Urrey. *alias* Hurrey. deserted the Parliament, and went over
to the King; afterwards deserted the King, and discovered to the Parliament all he knew of the King's forces.—*See Clarendon.*

† This Sir William Brereton. or. as Clarendon writes the name,
Bruerton, was the famous Cheshire knight. whom Cleveland character-
izes as one of those heroes whose courage lies in their teeth. "Was
Brereton," says the loyal satirist, "to fight with his teeth, as he in all
other things resembles the beast, he would have odds of any man at
this weapon. He's a terrible slaughterman at a Thanksgiving dinner.
Had he been cannibal enough to have eaten those he vanquished, his
gut would have made him valiant." And in "Loyal Songs" his
valiant appetite is noticed:

> "But, oh! take heed lest he do eat
> The Rump all at one dinner!"

And Aulicus, we see. accuses him of concealing his bravery in a hayrick. It is always curious and useful to confer the writers of intem-
perate times one with another. Lord Clarendon, whose great mind

(there are Doves in Scotland!) that *Hawarden Castle had but forty men in it when the Cavaliers took it.* (Another told you there were 140 lusty stout fellows in it: for shame, gentlemen! conferre Notes!) That *Colonel Norton at Rumsey took* 200 *prisoners.* (I saw them counted: they were just two millions.) Then the *Dove* hath this sweet passage: *O Aulicus, thou profane wretch, that darest scandalize* God's *saints, darest thou call that loyal subject Master Pym a traitor?* (Yes, pretty *Pigeon,** he was charged with six articles by his Majesty's

was incapable of descending to scurrility, gives a very different character to this pot-valiant and hayrick runaway; for he says. "It cannot be denied but S r William Brereton, and the other gentlemen of that party, albeit their education and course of life had been very different from their present engagements, and for the most part very unpromising in matters of war, and therefore were too much contemned enemies, executed their commands with notable sobriety and indefatigable industry (virtues not so well practised in the King's quarters), insomuch as the best soldiers who encountered with them had no cause to despise them."—*Clarendon*, vol. ii. p. 147.

* "The Scotch Dove" seems never to have recovered from this metamorphosis, but ever after, among the newsmen, was known to be only a Widgeon. His character is not very high in "The Great Assizes."

"The innocent *Scotch Dove* did then advance,
Full sober in his wit and countenance:
And, though his book contain'd not mickle scence,
Yet his endictment shew'd no great offence.
Great wits to perils great, themselves exposo
Oft-times; but the *Scotch Dove* was none of those.
In many words he little matter drest,
And did laconick brevity detest.
But while his readers did expect some Newes,
They found a Sermon—"

The Scotch Dove desires to meet the classical Aulicus in the duel of the pen:—

———————— "to turn me loose,
Scottish Dove against a *Roman Goose.*"

"The Scotch Dove" is condemned "to cross the seas, or to repasse

Atturney Generall.) Next he says, that *Master Pym died like Moses upon the Mount.* (He did not die upon the mount, but should have done.) Then he says *Master Pym died in a good old age, like Jacob in Egypt.* (Not like Jacob, yet just as those died in Egypt in the days of Pharaoh.)"*

As Sir John was frequently the propagator of false intelligence, it was necessary at times to seem scrupulous, and to correct some slight errors. He does this very adroitly, without diminishing his invectives.

"We must correct a mistake or two in our two last weeks. We advertised you of certain money speeches made by Master *John* Sedgwick: on better information, it was not *John,* but *Obadiah,* Presbyter of Bread-street, who in the pulpit in hot weather used to unbutton his doublet, which John, who wanteth a thumbe, forbears to practise. And when we told you last week of a committee of *Lawyers* appointed to put their new *Seale* in execution, we named, among others, Master George Peard. † I confess this was no small errour to reckon Master Peard among the *Lawyers,* because he now lies sicke, and so farre from being their new *Lord Keeper,* that he now despairs to become their *Door Keeper,* which office he performed heretofore. But since Master Peard has become desperately sick; and so his vote, his law, and haire have all forsook him, his corporation of Barnstable have been in perfect health and loyalty. The town of Barnstable having submitted to the King, this will no

the Tweede." They all envy him his "easy mulet," but he wofully exclaims at the hard sentence,

> " For if they knew that *home* as well as he,
> They'd rather die than there imprison'd be!"

* This stroke alludes to a rumour of the times, noticed also by Clarendon, that Pym died of the *morbus pediculosus.*

† " Peard, a bold lawyer of little note."—*Clarendon.*

doubt be a special cordial for their languishing Burgess.
And yet the man may grow hearty again when he hears
of the late defeat given to his Majesty's forces in Lincolnshire."

This paper was immediately answered by Marchmont
Needham, in his "Mercurius Britannicus," who cannot
boast the playful and sarcastic bitterness of Sir John;
yet is not the dullest of his tribe. He opens his reply
thus:

"Aulicus will needs venture his soule upon the other
half-sheet; and this week he *lies,* as completely as ever
he did in *two full sheets;* full of as many scandals and
fictions, full of as much stupidity and ignorance, full of
as many tedious untruths as ever.   And because he
would *recrute* the reputation of his wit, he falls into the
company of our *Diurnals* very furiously, and there lays
about him in the midst of our weekly pamphlets; and he
casts in the few squibs, and the little wildfire he hath,
dashing out his conceits; and he takes it ill that the
poore scribblers should tell a story for their living; and
after a whole week spent at Oxford, in inke and paper,
to as little purpose as *Maurice* spent his shot and powder
at *Plimouth,* he gets up, about Saturday, into a jingle
or two, for he cannot reach to a full jest; and I am informed that the three-quarter conceits in the last leafe
of his Diurnall cost him fourteen pence in *aqua vitæ.*"

Sir John never condescends formally to reply to Needham, for which he gives this singular reason:—"As for
this libeller, we are still resolved to take no notice till
we find him able to spell his own name, which to this
hour Britannicus never did."

In the next number of Needham, who had always
written it *Brittanicus,* the correction was silently adopted.   There was no crying down the etymology of an
Oxford malignant

I give a short narrative of the political temper of the times, in their unparalleled gazettes.

At the first breaking out of the parliament's separation from the royal party, when the public mind, full of consternation in that new anarchy, shook with the infirmity of childish terrors, the most extravagant reports were as eagerly caught up as the most probable, and served much better the purposes of their inventors. They had daily discoveries of new conspiracies, which appeared in a pretended correspondence written from Spain, France, Italy, or Denmark: they had their amusing literature, mixed with their grave politics; and a dialogue between "a Dutch mariner and an English ostler," could alarm the nation as much as the last letter from their "private correspondent." That the wildest rumours were acceptable appears from their contemporary Fuller. Armies were talked of, concealed under ground by the king, to cut the throats of all the Protestants in a night. He assures us that one of the most prevailing dangers among the Londoners was "a design laid for a mine of powder under the Thames, to cause the river to drown the city." This desperate expedient, it seems, was discovered just in time to prevent its execution; and the people were devout enough to have a public thanksgiving, and watched with a little more care that the Thames might not be blown up. However, the plot was really not so much at the bottom of the Thames as at the bottom of their purses. Whenever they wanted 100,000*l.* they raised a plot, they terrified the people, they appointed a thanksgiving-day, and while their ministers addressed to God himself all the news of the week, and even reproached him for the rumours against their cause, all ended, as is usual at such times, with the gulled multitude contributing more heavily to the adventurers who ruled them than the legal authorities had exacted in their greatest wants.

"The Diurnals" had propagated thirty-nine of these "Treasons, or new Taxes," according to one of the members of the House of Commons, who had watched their patriotic designs.

These "Diurnals" sometimes used such language as the following, from *The Weekly Accompt*, January, 1643:—

"This day afforded no newes at all, but onely what was *heavenly* and *spiritual;*" and he gives an account of the public fast, and of the grave divine Master Henderson's sermon, with his texts in the morning; and in the afternoon, another of Master Strickland, with his texts—and of their spiritual effect over the whole parliament!*

Such news as the following was sometimes very agreeable:—

"From Oxford it is informed, that on Sunday last was fortnight in the evening, Prince Rupert, accompanied with some lords, and other cavaliers, *danced through the streets openly, with music before them*, to one of the colleges; where, after they had stayed about half an houre, they returned back again, dancing with the same music; and immediately there followed *a pack of women, or curtizans*, as it may be supposed, for they were hooded, and could not be knowne; and this the party who related affirmed he saw with his own eyes."

---

* These divines were as ready with the sword as the pen; thus, we are told in "The Impartial Scout" for July, 1650—"The ministers are now as active in the military discipline as formerly they were in the gospel profession, Parson Ennis, Parson Brown, and about thirty other ministers having received commissions to be majors and captains, who now hold forth the Bible in one hand, and the sword in the other, telling the soldiery that they need not fear what man can do against them—that God is on their side—and that He hath prepared an engine in heaven to break and blast the designs of all covenant-breakers."—ED.

On this the Diurnal-maker pours out severe anathemas
—and one with a *note*, that "*dancing* and *drabbing* are
inseparable companions, and follow one another close at
the heels." He assures his readers, that the malignants,
or royalists, only fight like sensual beasts, to maintain
their dancing and drabbing!—Such was the revolutionary tone here, and such the arts of faction everywhere.
The matter was rather peculiar to our country, but the
principle was the same as practised in France. Men of
opposite characters, when acting for the same concealed
end, must necessarily form parallels.

POLITICAL CRITICISM

ON

LITERARY COMPOSITIONS.

Anthony Wood and Locke—Milton and Sprat—Burnet and his His-
tory—Prior and Addison—Swift and Steele—Wagstaffe and Steele
—Steele and Addison—Hooke and Middleton—Gilbert Wakefield—
Marvell and Milton—Clarendon and May.

VOLTAIRE, in his letters on our nation, has hit off
a marked feature in our national physiognomy.
"So violent did I find parties in London, that I was
assured by several that the Duke of Marlborough was a
coward, and Mr. Pope a fool."

A foreigner indeed could hardly expect that in collecting the characters of English authors by English authors
(a labour which has long afforded me pleasure often interrupted by indignation)—in a word, that a class of
literary history should turn out a collection of personal

quarrels. Would not this modern Baillet, in his new *Jugemens des Scavans*, so ingeniously inquisitive but so infinitely confused, require to be initiated into the mysteries of that spirit of party peculiar to our free country!

All that boiling rancour which sputters against the thoughts, the style, the taste, the moral character of an author, is often nothing more than practising what, to give it a name, we may call *Political Criticism in Literature;* where an author's literary character is attacked solely from the accidental circumstance of his differing in opinion from his critics on subjects unconnected with the topics he treats of.

Could Anthony Wood, had he not been influenced by this political criticism, have sent down Locke to us as "a man of a turbulent spirit, clamorous, and never contented, prating and troublesome?"* But Locke was the antagonist of Filmer, that advocate of arbitrary power; and Locke is described "as bred under a fanatical tutor," and when in Holland, as one of those who under the Earl of Shaftesbury "stuck close to him when discarded, and carried on the *trade of faction* beyond and within the seas several years after." In the great original genius, born, like Bacon and Newton, to create a new era in the history of the human mind, this political literary critic, who was not always deficient in his per-

---

* A forcible description of Locke may be found in the curious "Life of Wood," written by himself. I shall give the passage where Wood acknowledges his after celebrity, at the very moment the bigotry of his feelings is attempting to degrade him.

Wood belonged to a club with Locke and others, for the purpose of hearing chemical lectures. "John Locke of Christchurch was afterwards a noted writer. This John Locke was a man of a turbulent spirit, clamorous, and never contented. The club wrote and took notes from the mouth of their master, who sat at the upper end of a table, but the said John Locke scorned to do it: so that while every man besides of the club were writing, he would be prating and troublesome."

ceptions of genius, could only discover "a trader in faction," though in his honesty he acknowledges him to be
"a noted writer."

A more illustrious instance of party-spirit operating
against works of genius is presented to us in the awful
character of Milton. From earliest youth to latest age
endowed with all the characteristics of genius; fervent
with all the inspirations of study; in all changes still
the same great literary character as Velleius Paterculus
writes of one of his heroes—" Aliquando fortunâ, semper
animo maximus:" while in his own day, foreigners, who
usually anticipate posterity, were inquiring after Milton,
it is known how utterly disregarded he lived at home.
The divine author of the "Paradise Lost" was always
connected with the man for whom a reward was offered in
the *London Gazette*. But in their triumph, the lovers
of monarchy missed their greater glory, in not separating for ever the republican Secretary of State from the
rival of Homer.

That the genius of Milton pined away in solitude, and
that all the consolations of fame were denied him during
his life, from this political criticism on his works, is generally known; but not perhaps that this spirit propagated
itself far beyond the poet's tomb. I give a remarkable
instance. Bishop Sprat, who surely was capable of feeling the poetry of Milton, yet from political antipathy
retained such an abhorrence of his *name*, that when the
writer of the Latin Inscription on the poet John Philips,
in describing his versification, applied to it the term
Miltono, Sprat ordered it to be erased, as polluting a
monument raised in a church.* A mere critical opinion

---

* This anecdote deserves preservation. I have drawn it from the
MSS. of Bishop Kennet.

"In the Epitaph on John Philips occurs this line on his metre, that

on versification was thus sacrificed to political feeling:
—a stream indeed which in its course has hardly yet
worked itself clear. It could only have been the strong
political feeling of Warton which could have induced
him to censure the prose of Milton with such asperity,
while he closed his critical eyes on its resplendent passages, which certainly he wanted not the taste to feel,—
for he caught in his own pages, occasionally, some of the
reflected warmth. This feeling took full possession of
the mind of Johnson, who, with all the rage of political

> 'Uni in hoc laudis genere Miltono secundus,
> Primoque pene par.'

These lines were ordered to be razed out of the monument by Dr.
Sprat, Bishop of Rochester. The word Miltono being, as he said, not
fit to be in a Christian church : but they have since been restored by
Dr. Atterbury, who succeeded him as Bishop of Rochester, and who
wrote the epitaph jointly with Dr. Freind."—Lansdowne MSS., No.
908, p. 162.

The anecdote has appeared, but without any authority. Dr. Sym-
mons, in his "Life of Milton," observing on what he calls Dr. Johnson's "biographical libel on Milton," that Dr. Johnson has mentioned
this fact, seems to suspect its authenticity; for, if true, "it would
cover the respectable name of Sprat with eternal dishonour." Of its
truth the above gives sufficient authority; but at all events the prejudices of Sprat must be pardoned, while I am showing that minds far
greater than his have shared in the same unhappy feeling. Dr. Sym-
mons himself bears no light stain for his slanderous criticism on the
genius of Thomas Warton, from the motive we are discussing: though
Warton, as my text shows, was too a sinner! I recollect in my
youth a more extraordinary instance than any other which relates
to Milton. A woman of no education, who had retired from the business of life, became a very extraordinary reader; accident had thrown
into her way a large library composed of authors who wrote in the
reigns of the two Charleses. She turned out one of the *malignant*
party, and an abhorrer of the Commonwealth's men. Her opinion of
Cromwell and Milton may be given. She told me it was no wonder
that the rebel who had been secretary to the usurper should have
been able to have drawn so finished a character of Satan, and that the
Pandæmonium, with all the oratorical devils, was only such as he had
himself viewed at Oliver's council-board.

criticism on subjects of literature, has condemned the
finest works of Milton, and in one of his terrible parox-
ysms has demonstrated that the Samson Agonistes is " a
tragedy which ignorance has admired and bigotry applauded." Had not Johnson's religious feelings fortunately interposed between Milton and his "Paradise,"
we should have wanted the present noble effusion of his
criticism ; any other Epic by Milton had probably sunk
beneath his vigorous sophistry, and his tasteless sarcasm.
Lauder's attack on Milton was hardily projected, on a
prospect of encouragement, from this political criticism
on the literary character of Milton ; and he succeeded
as long as he could preserve the decency of the delusion.

The Spirit of Party has touched with its plague-spot
the character of Burnet ; it has mildewed the page of a
powerful mind, and tainted by its suspicions, its rumours,
and its censures, his probity as a man. Can we forbear
listening to all the vociferations which faction has thrown
out ? Do we not fear to trust ourselves amid the multi-
plicity of his facts? And when we are familiarised with
the variety of his historical portraits, are we not startled
when it is suggested that " they are tinged with his own
passions and his own weaknesses ?" Burnet has indeed
made " his humble appeal to the Great God of Truth "
that he has given it as fully as he could find it ; and he
has expressed his abhorrence of " a lie in history," so
much greater a sin than a lie in common discourse, from
its lasting and universal nature. Yet these hallowing
protestations have not saved him ! A cloud of witnesses,
from different motives, have risen up to attaint his veracity and his candour; while all the Tory wits have
ridiculed his style, impatiently inaccurate, and uncouthly
negligent, and would sink his vigour and ardour, while
they expose the meanness and poverty of his genius.

Thus the literary and the moral character of no ordinary author have fallen a victim to party-feeling.*

* I throw into this note several curious notices respecting Burnet, and chiefly from contemporaries.

Burnet has been accused, after a warm discussion, of returning home in a passion, and then writing the character of a person. But as his feelings were warm, it is probable he might have often practised the reverse. An anecdote of the times is preserved in "The Memoirs of Grub-street," vol. ii. p. 291. "A noble peer now living declares he stood with a very ill grace in the history, till he had an opportunity put into his hands of obliging the bishop, by granting a favour at court, upon which the bishop told a friend, within an hour, that he was mistaken in such a lord, and must go and alter his whole character ; and so he happens to have a pretty good one." In this place I also find this curious extract from the MS. "Memoirs of the M—— of H——." "Such a day Dr. B——t told me King William was an obstinate, conceited man, that would take no advice; and on this day King William told me that Dr. B——t was a troublesome, impertinent man, whose company he could not endure." These anecdotes are very probable, and lead one to reflect. Some political tergiversation has been laid to his charge ; Swift accused him of having once been an advocate for passive obedience and absolute power. He has been reproached with the deepest ingratitude, for the purpose of gratifying his darling passion of popularity, in his conduct respecting the Duke of Lauderdale, his former patron. If the following piece of secret history be true, he showed too much of a compliant humour, at the cost of his honour. I find it in Bishop Kennet's MSS. "Dr. Burnet having *over night* given in some important depositions against the Earl of Lauderdale to the House of Commons, was, *before morning*, by the intercession of the D——, made king's chaplain and preacher at the Rolls ; so he was bribed to hold the peace."—Lansdowne MSS., 990. This was quite a politician's short way to preferment! An honest man cannot leap up the ascent, however he may try to climb. There was something morally wrong in this transaction, because Burnet notices it, and acknowledges—"I was much blamed for what I had done." The story is by no means refuted by the *naïve* apology.

Burnet's character has been vigorously attacked, with all the nerve of satire, in "Faction Displayed," attributed to Shippen, whom Pope celebrates—

——"And pour myself as plain
As honest Shippen or as old Montaigne."

Shippen was a Tory. In "Faction Displayed," Burnet is represented

But this victim to political criticism on literature was himself criminal, and has wreaked his own party feelings with his Cabal (so some party nicknames the other), on the accession of Queen Anne, plotting the disturbance of her government. "Black Aris's fierceness," that is Burnet, is thus described:—

> "A Scotch, seditious, unbelieving priest,
> The brawny chaplain of the calves'-head feast,
> Who first his patron, then his prince betray'd,
> And does that church he's sworn to guard, invade,
> Warm with rebellious rage, he thus began," &c.

One hardly suspects the hermit Parnell capable of writing rather harsh verses, yet stinging satire : they are not in his works : but he wrote the following lines on a report of a fire breaking out in Burnet's library, which had like to have answered the purpose some wished—of condemning the author and his works to the flames—

> "He talks, and writes, that Popery will return,
> And we, and he, and all his works will burn ;
> And as of late he meant to bless the age
> With *flagrant prefaces of party rage,*
> O'ercome with passion and the subject's weight,
> Lolling he nodded in his elbow-seat :
> Down fell the candle ! Grease and zeal conspire,
> Heat meets with heat, and pamphlets burn their sire;
> Here crawls a *preface* on its half-burn'd maggots,
> And there an *introduction* brings its fagots :
> Then roars the prophet of the northern nation,
> Scorch'd by a flaming speech on moderation."

Thomas Warton smiles at Burnet for the horrors of Popery which perpetually haunted him, in his " Life of Sir T. Pope," p. 53. But if we substitute the term arbitrary power for popery, no Briton will join in the abuse Burnet has received on this account. A man of Burnet's fervid temper, whose foible was strong vanity and a passion for popularity, would often rush headlong into improprieties of conduct and language ; his enemies have taken ample advantage of his errors; but many virtues his friends have recorded; and the elaborate and spirited character which the Marquis of Halifax has drawn of Burnet may soothe his manes, and secure its repose amid all these disturbances around his tomb. This fine character is preserved in the " Biographia Britannica." Burnet is not the only instance of the motives of a man

on the *Papist* Dryden, and the *Tory* Prior; Dryden he
calls, in the most unguarded language, "a monster of im-
modesty and impurity of all sorts." There had been a
literary quarrel between Dryden and Burnet respecting
a translation of Varillas' "History of Heresies;" Burnet
had ruined the credit of the papistical author while Dryden was busied on the translation; and as Burnet says,
"he has wreaked his malice on me for spoiling his three
months' labour." In return, he kindly informs Dryden,
alluding to his poem of "The Hind and the Panther,"
"that he is the author of the *worst* poem the age has produced;" and that as for "his morals, it is scarce possible
to grow a worse man than he was"—a personal style not
to be permitted in any controversy, but to bring this
passion on the hallowed ground of history, was not
"casting away his shoe" in the presence of the divinity
of truth.* It could only have been the spirit of party

being honourable, while his actions are frequently the reverse, from
his impetuous nature. He has been reproached for a want of that
truth which he solemnly protests he scrupulously adhered to; yet, of
many circumstances which were at the time condemned as "lies,"
when Time drew aside the mighty veil. Truth was discovered beneath.
Tovey, with his usual good humour, in his "Anglia Judaica." p. 277,
notices "that pleasant copious imagination which will for ever rank
our *English Burnet* with the *Grecian Heliodorus*." Roger North, in his
"Examen," p. 413, calls him "a busy Scotch parson." Lord Orford
sneers at his hasty epithets, and the colloquial carelessness of his style,
in his "Historic Doubts," where, in a note, he mentions "*one* Burnet"
tells a ridiculous story, mimicking Burnet's chit-chat, and concludes
surprisingly with, "So the Prince of Orange mounted the throne."

After reading this note, how would that learned foreigner proceed,
who I have supposed might be projecting the "Judgments of the
Le rned" on our English authors? Were he to condemn Burnet as an
historian void of all honour and authority, he would not want for documents. It would require a few minutes to explain to the foreigner
the nature of political criticism.

* Dryden was very coarsely satirised in the political poems of his
own day; and among the rest, in "The Session of the Poets,"—a

which induced Burnet, in his History, to mention with
contempt and pretended ignorance so fine a genius as
"*one Prior*, who had been Jersey's secretary." It was
the same party-feeling in the Tory Prior, in his elegant
"Alma," where he has interwoven so graceful a wreath
for Pope, that could sneer at the fine soliloquy of the
Roman Cato of the Whig Addison :

> I hope you would not have me die
> *Like simple Cato in the play,*
> For anything that he can say.

It was the same spirit which would not allow that
Garth was the author of his celebrated poem—

> Garth did not write his own Dispensary,

as Pope ironically alludes to the story of the times:—a
contemporary wit has recorded this literary injury, by
repeating it.*   And Swift, who once exclaimed to Pope,
"The deuce take party !" was himself the greatest sinner
of them all.   He, once the familiar friend of Steele till
party divided them, not only emptied his shaft of quivers

general onslaught directed against the writers of the time, which furnishes us with many examples of unjust criticism on these literary men,
entirely originating in political feeling.   One example may suffice:

> "Then in came Denham, that limping old bard,
>   Whose fame on *the Sophy* and *Cooper's-hill* stands,
> And brought many stationers, who swore very hard
>   That nothing sold better except 'twere his lauds.
> But Apollo advised him to write something more,
>   To clear a suspicion which possessed the Court,
> That *Cooper's-hill*, so much bragg'd on before,
>   Was writ by a vicar, who had forty pounds for't."

* Dr. Wagstaffe, in his "Character of Steele," alludes to the rumour
which Pope has sent down to posterity in a single verse: "I should
have thought Mr. Steele might have the example of his *friend* before
his eyes, who *had the reputation of being the author of The Dispensary*,
till, by two or three unlucky after-claps, he proved himself incapable
of writing it."—Wagstaffe's *Misc. Works*, p. 136

against his literary character, but raised the horrid yell of the war-whoop in his inhuman exultation over the unhappy close of the desultory life of a man of genius. Bitterly has he written—

> From perils of a hundred jails,
> Withdrew to starve, and die in Wales.

When Steele published "The Crisis," Swift attacked the author in so exquisite a piece of grave irony, that I am tempted to transcribe his inimitable parallels of a triumvirate composed of the writer of the *Flying Post*, Dunton the literary projector, and poor Steele: the one, the Iscariot of hackney scribes; the other a crack-brained scribbling bookseller, who boasted he had a thousand projects, fancied he had methodised six hundred, and was ruined by the fifty he executed. The following is a specimen of that powerful irony in which Swift excelled all other writers; that fine Cervantic humour, that provoking coolness which Swift preserves while he is panegyrising the objects of his utter contempt.

"Among the present writers on the Whig side, I can recollect but *three* of any great distinction, which are the *Flying Post*, Mr. Dunton, and the Author of 'The Crisis.' The first of these seems to have been much sunk in reputation since the sudden retreat of the only true, genuine, original author, Mr. Ridpath, who is celebrated by the *Dutch Gazetteer* as one of *the best pens in England*. Mr. Dunton hath been longer and more conversant in books than any of the three, as well as more voluminous in his productions: however, having employed his studies in so great a variety of other subjects, he hath, I think, but lately turned his genius to politics. His famous tract entitled 'Neck or Nothing' must be allowed to be the shrewdest piece, and written with the most spirit of any which hath appeared from that side

since the change of the ministry. It is indeed a most
cutting satire upon the Lord Treasurer and Lord Bolingbroke; and I wonder none of our friends ever undertook
to answer it. I confess I was at first of the same opinion
with several good judges, who from the style and manner
suppose it to have issued from the sharp pen of the Earl
of Nottingham; and I am still apt to think it might
receive his lordship's last hand. The third and principal
of this triumvirate is the author of 'The Crisis,' who,
although he must yield to the *Flying Post* in knowledge
of the world and skill in politics, and to Mr. Dunton in
keenness of satire and variety of reading, hath yet other
qualities enough to denominate him a writer of a superior
class to either, provided he would a little regard the
propriety and disposition of his words, consult the grammatical part, and get some information on the subject he
intends to handle." *

So far this fine ironical satire may be inspected as a
model; the polished weapon he strikes with so gracefully,
is allowed by all the laws of war; but the political criticism on the literary character, the party feeling which de-
grades a man of genius, is the drop of poison on its point.

Steele had declared in the " Crisis " that he had always
maintained an inviolable respect for the clergy. Swift
(who perhaps was aimed at in this instance, and whose
character, since the publication of " The Tale of a Tub,"

---

* I know not how to ascertain the degree of political skill which
Steele reached in his new career—he was at least a spirited Whig,
but the ministry was then under the malignant influence of the concealed adherents to the Stuarts, particularly of Bolingbroke, and such
as Atterbury, whose secret history is now much better known than in
their own day. The terrors of the Whigs were not unfounded. Steele
in the House disappointed his friends; from his popular Essays, it was
expected he would have been a fluent orator; this was no more the
case with him than Addison. On this De Foe said he had better have
continued the *Spectator* than the *Tatler.*—Lansdowne's *MSS.* 1007.

lay under a suspicion of an opposite tendency) turns on
Steele with all the vigour of his wit, and all the causticity of retort:—

"By this he would insinuate that those papers among
the *Tatlers* and *Spectators*, where the whole order is
abused, were not his own. I will appeal to all who know
the flatness of his style, and the barrenness of his invention, whether he doth not grossly prevaricate? *Was he
ever able to walk without his leading-strings, or swim
without bladders, without being discovered by his hobbling
or his sinking?*"

Such was the attack of Swift, which was pursued in
the *Examiner*, and afterwards taken up by another writer.
This is one of the evils resulting from the wantonness of
genius: it gives a contagious example to the minor race;
its touch opens a new vein of invention, which the poorer
wits soon break into; the loose sketch of a feature or
two from its rapid hand is sufficient to become a minute
portrait, where not a hair is spared by the caricaturist.
This happened to Steele, whose literary was to be sacrificed to his political character; and this superstructure
was confessedly raised on the malicious hints we have
been noticing. That the *Examiner* was the seed-plot of
"The Character of Richard St—le, Esq.," appears by its
opening—"It will be no injury, I am persuaded, to the
Examiner to borrow *him* a little (Steele), upon promise
of returning him safe, as children do their playthings,
when their mirth is over, and they have done with them."

The author of the "Character of Richard St—le,
Esq.," was Dr. Wagstaffe, one of those careless wits *
who lived to repent a crazy life of wit, fancy, and hope,

---

* Wagstaffe's "Miscellaneous Works." 1726, have been collected
into a volume. They contain satirical pieces of humour, accompanied
by some Hogarthian prints. His "Comment upon the History of
Tom Thumb," ridicules Addison's on the old ballad of "Chevy Chase,"

and an easy, indolent one, whose genial hours force up
friends like hot-house plants, that bloom and flower in
the spot where they are raised, but will not endure the
change of place and season—this wit caught the tone of
Swift, and because, as his editor tells us, "he had some
friends in the ministry, and thought he could not take a
better way to oblige them than by showing his dislike to
a gentleman who had so much endeavoured to oppose
them," he sat down to write a libel with all the best
humour imaginable; for, adds this editor, "he was so
far from having any personal pique or enmity against
Mr. Steele, that at the time of his writing he did not so
much as know him, even by sight." This principle of
"having some friends in the ministry," and not "any
knowledge" of the character to be attacked, has proved
a great source of invention to our political adventurers;
—thus Dr. Wagstaffe was fully enabled to send down to
us a character where the moral and literary qualities of
a genius, to whom this country owes so much as the
father of periodical papers, are immolated to his political

who had declared "it was full of the majestic simplicity which we admire in the greatest of the ancient poets," and quoted passages which
he paralleled with several in the Æneid. Wagstaffe tells us he has
found "in the library of a school-boy, among other undiscovered
valuable authors, one more proper to adorn the shelves of Bodley or
the Vatican than to be confined to the obscurity of a private study."
This little Homer is the chanter of Tom Thumb. He performs his
office of "a true commentator," proving the congenial spirit of the
poet of Thumb with that of the poet of Æneas. Addison got himself
ridiculed for that fine natural taste, which felt all the witchery of our
ballad-Enniuses, whose beauties, had Virgil lived with Addison, he
would have inlaid into his mosaic. The bigotry of classical taste,
which is not always accompanied by a natural one, and rests securely
on prescribed opinions and traditional excellence, long contemned our
vernacular genius, spurning at the minstrelsy of the nation; Johnson's
ridicule of "Percy's Reliques" had its hour, but the more poetical
mind of Scott has brought us back to home feelings, to domestic manners, and eternal nature.

purpose. This severe character passed through several
editions. However the careless Steele might be willing
to place the elaborate libel to the account of party writings, if he did not feel disturbed at reproaches and accusations, which are confidently urged, and at critical
animadversions, to which the negligence of his style
sometimes laid him too open, his insensibility would
have betrayed a depravity in his morals and taste which
never entered into his character.*

* I shall content myself with referring to "The Character of
Richard St—le, Esq.," in Dr. Wagstaffe's Miscellaneous Works, 1726.
Considering that he had no personal knowledge of his victim, one may
be well surprised at his entering so deeply into his private history; but
of such a character as Steele, the private history is usually too public—
a mass of scandal for the select curious.   Poor Steele, we are told, was
" arrested for the maintenance of his bastards, and afterwards printed
a *proposal* that the public should take care of them;" got into the
House "not to be arrested;"—"his *set* speeches there, which he designs to get *extempore* to speak in the House."   For his literary character we are told that ' Steele was a jay who borrowed a feather from
the peacock, another from the bullfinch, and another from the magpye;
so that *Dick* is made up of borrowed colours; he borrowed his humour
from Estcourt, criticism of Addison, his poetry of Pope, and his politics
of Ridpath; so that his qualifications as a man of genius, like Mr.
T——s, as a member of Parliament, *lie in thirteen parishes.*"   Such are
the pillows made up for genius to rest its head on!
Wagstaffe has sometimes delicate humour; Steele, who often wrote
in haste, necessarily wrote incorrectly.   Steele had this sentence:
" And ALL, as one man, will join in a common indignation against ALL
who would perplex our obedience:" on which our pleasant critic remarks—" Whatever contradiction there is, as some suppose, in *all joining against all*, our author has good authority for what he says; and it
may be proved, in spite of Euclid or Sir Isaac, that everything consists
of *two alls*, that these *alls* are capable of being divided and subdivided
into as many *alls* as you please, and so *ad infinitum*.   The following
lines may serve for an illustration:—

> 'Three children sliding on the ice
>   Upon a summer's day;
>   As it fell out, they all fell in;
>   The rest they ran away.'

Steele was doomed even to lose the friendship of Addison amid political discords; but on that occasion Steele showed that his taste for literature could not be injured by political animosity. It was at the close of Addison's life, and on occasion of the Peerage Bill, Steele published "The Plebeian," a cry against enlarging the aristocracy Addison replied with "The Old Whig," Steele rejoined without alluding to the person of his opponent. But "The Old Whig" could not restrain his political feelings, and contemptuously described "little Dicky, whose trade it was to write pamphlets." Steele replied with his usual warmth; but indignant at the charge of "vassalage," he says, "I will end this paper, by firing every free breast with that noble exhortation of the tragedian—

> Remember, O my friends! the laws, the rights,
> The generous plan of power deliver'd down
> From age to age, &c."

Thus delicately he detects the anonymous author, and thus energetically commends, while he reproves him!

"Though this polite author does not directly say there are *two alls,* yet he implies as much; for I would ask any *reasonable* man what can be understood by *the rest they ran away,* but the *other all* we have been speaking of? The world may see that I can exhibit the beauties, as well as quarrel with the faults, of his composition, but I hope he will not value himself on his *hasty produc tions."*

Poor Steele, with the best humour, bore these perpetual attacks, nor, however, without an occasional groan, just enough to record his feelings. In one of his will, yet well-meant projects, of the invention of "a Fish-pool, or Vessel for Importing Fish Alive," 1718, he complains of calumnies and impertinent observations on him, and seems to lay some to the account of his knighthood:—"While he was pursuing what he believed might conduce to the common good, he gave the syllables *Richard Steel* to the publick, to be used and treated as they should think fit; he must go on in *the same indifference,* and allow the Town *their usual liberty with his name,* which I find they think they have much more room to sport with than formerly, as it is lengthened with the monosyllable SIR."

Hooke (a Catholic), after he had written his "Roman
History," published "Observations on Vertot, Middleton, &c., on the Roman Senate," in which he particularly treated Dr. Middleton with a disrespect for which
the subject gave no occasion: this was attributed to the
Doctor's *offensive* letter from Rome. Spelman, in replying to this concealed motive of the Catholic, reprehends
him with equal humour and bitterness for his desire of
roasting a Protestant parson.

Our taste, rather than our passions, is here concerned;
but the moral sense still more so. The malice of faction
has long produced this literary calamity; yet great
minds have not always degraded themselves; not always
resisted the impulse of their finer feelings, by hardening
them into insensibility, or goading them in the fury of
a misplaced revenge. How delightful it is to observe
Marvell, the Presbyterian and Republican wit, with that
generous temper that instantly discovers the alliance of
genius, warmly applauding the great work of Butler,
which covered his own party with odium and ridicule.
"He is one of an excellent wit," says Marvell, "and whoever dislikes the choice of his subject, cannot but commend the performance." *

Clarendon's profound genius could not expand into
the same liberal feelings. He highly commends May
for his learning, his wit and language, and for his Supplement to Lucan, which he considered as "one of the
best epic poems in the English language;" but this great
spirit sadly winces in the soreness of his feelings when he
alludes to May's "History of the Parliament;" then we
discover that this late "ingenious person" performed his
part "so meanly, that he seems to have lost his wit when
he left his honesty." Behold the political criticism in

* "Rehearsal Transprosed," p. 45.

literature! However we may incline to respect the feelings of Clarendon, this will not save his judgment nor his candour. We read May now, as well as Clarendon; nor is the work of May that of a man who "had lost his wits," nor is it " meanly performed." Warburton, a keen critic of the writers of that unhappy and that glorious age for both parties, has pronounced this " History " to be " a just composition, according to the rules of history; written with much judgment, penetration, manliness, and spirit, and with a candour that will greatly increase your esteem, when you understand that he wrote by order of his masters the Parliament."

Thus have authors and their works endured the violations of party feelings; a calamity in our national literature which has produced much false and unjust criticism.* The better spirit of the present times will main-

* The late Gilbert Wakefield is an instance where the political and theological opinions of a recluse student tainted his pure literary works. Condemned as an enraged Jacobin by those who were Unitarians in politics, and rejected because he was a Unitarian in religion by the orthodox, poor Wakefield's literary labours were usually reduced to the value of waste-paper. We smile, but half in sorrow, in reading a letter, where he says. " I meditate a beginning, during the winter, of my criticisms on all the ancient Greek and Latin authors, *by small piecemeals, on the cheapest possible paper, and at the least possible expense of printing.* As I can never do more than barely indemnify myself, I shall print only 250 copies." He half-ruined himself by his splendid edition of Lucretius, which could never obtain even common patronage from the opulent friends of classical literature. Since his death it has been reprinted, and is no doubt now a marketable article for the bookseller; so that if some authors are not successful for themselves, it is a comfort to think how useful, in a variety of shapes, they are made so to others. Even Gilbert's "contracted scheme of publication" he was compelled to abandon! Yet the classic erudition of Wakefield was confessed, and is still remembered. No one will doubt that we have lost a valuable addition to our critical stores by this literary persecution, were it only in the present instance; but examples are too numerous!

tam a safer and a more honourable principle,—the true objects of LITERATURE, the cultivation of the intellectual faculties, stand entirely unconnected with POLITICS and RELIGION, let this be the imprescriptible right of an author. In our free country unhappily they have not been separated—they run together, and in the ocean of human opinions, the salt and bitterness of these mightier waves have infected the clear waters from the springs of the Muses. I once read of a certain river that ran through the sea without mixing with it, preserving its crystalline purity and all its sweetness during its course; so that it tasted the same at the Line as at the Poles. This stream indeed is only to be found in the geography of an old romance; literature should be this magical stream!

HOBBES, AND HIS QUARRELS;

INCLUDING

AN ILLUSTRATION OF HIS CHARACTER.

WHY Hobbes disguised his sentiments—why his philosophy degraded him—of the sect of the HOBBISTS—his LEVIATHAN; its principles adapted to existing circumstances—the author's difficulties on its first appearance—the system originated in his fears, and was a contrivance to secure the peace of the nation—its duplicity and studied ambiguity illustrated by many facts—the advocate of the national religion—accused of atheism—Hobbes's religion—his temper too often tried—attacked by opposite parties—Bishop Fell's ungenerous conduct—makes Hobbes regret that juries do not consider the quarrels of authors of any moment—the mysterious panic which accompanied him through life—its probable cause—he pretends to recant his opinions—he is speculatively bold, and practically timorous—an extravagant specimen of the anti-social philosophy—the SELFISM of

Hobbes—his high sense of his works, in regard to foreigners and
posterity—his monstrous egotism—his devotion to his literary pursuits—the despotic principle of the LEVIATHAN of an innocent tendency—the fate of systems of opinions.

THE history of the philosopher of Malmesbury exhibits
a large picture of literary controversy, where we
may observe how a persecuting spirit in the times drives
the greatest men to take refuge in the meanest arts of subterfuge. Compelled to disguise their sentiments, they
will not, however, suppress them; and hence all their
ambiguous proceedings, all that ridicule and irony, and
even recantation, with which ingenious minds, when
forced to their employ, have never failed to try the patience, or the sagacity, of intolerance.*

---

* Shaftesbury has thrown out, on this head, some important truths:
—" If men are forbid to speak their minds *seriously*, they will do it
iron ca ly. If they find it dangerous to do so, they will then redouble
their disguise. *inv lve t'em el es into mysteriousness*, and talk so as hardly
to be understood. The *p rsecuting* spirit has raised the *bantering* one.
The higher the slavery, the more exquisite the buffoonery."—Vol. i.
p. 71. The subject of our present inquiry is a very remarkable instance of "involving himself into mysteriousness." To this cause
we owe the strong raillery of Marvell; the cloudy " Oracles of Reason's
of Blount; and the formidable, though gross burlesque, of Hickeringill,
the rector of All-Saints, in Colchester. "Of him (says the editor of his
collected works, 1716), the greatest writers of our times trembled at his
pen; and as great a genius as Sir Roger L'Estrange's was, it submitted
to his *superior way of reaso ing*" that is, to a most extraordinary burlesque spirit in politics and religion. But even he who made others
tremble felt the terrors he inflicted: for he complains that " some who
have thought his pen too sharp and smart, those who have been galled,
sore men where the skin's off, have long lain to catch for somewhat
to accuse me—upon such touchy subjects, a man had need have the
d rterity t s lt a hair, to handle them pertinently, usefully, and yet *safely*
and *warily*."—Such men, however, cannot avoid their fate: they will
be persecuted, however they succeed in "splitting a hair;" and it is
then they have recourse to the most absurd *subt r u es*, to which our
Hobbes was compelled. Thus also it happened to Woolston, who wrote

The character of Hobbes will, however, serve a higher moral design. The force of his intellect, the originality of his views, and the keenest sagacity of observation, place him in the first order of minds; but he has mortified, and then degraded man into a mere selfish animal. From a cause we shall discover, he never looked on human nature but in terror or in contempt. The inevitable consequence of that mode of thinking, or that system of philosophy, is to make the philosopher the abject creature he has himself imagined ; and it is then he libels the species from his own individual experience.* More

in a ludicrous way "Blasphemies" against the miracles of Christ; calling them "tales and rodomontados." He rested his defence on this subterfuge, that "it was meant to place the Christian religion on a better footing," &c. But the Court answered, that "if the author of a treasonable libel should write at the conclusion, *God save the king!* it would not excuse him."

* The moral axiom of Solon " KNOW THYSELF " (*Nosce teipsum*), applied by the ancient sage as a corrective of our own pride and vanity, Hobbes contracts into a narrow principle, when, in his introduction to "The Leviathan," he would infer that, by this self-inspection, we are enabled to determine on the thoughts and passions of other men; and thus he would make the taste, the feelings, the experience of the individual decide for all mankind. This simple error has produced all the dogmas of cynicism; for the cynic is one whose insulated feelings, being all of the selfish kind, can imagine no other stirrer of even our best affections, and strains even our loftiest virtues into pitiful motives. Two noble authors, men of the most dignified feelings, have protested against this principle. Lord Shaftesbury keenly touches the characters of Hobbes and Rochester:—" Sudden courage, says our modern philosopher (Hobbes), is anger. If so, courage, considered as constant, and belonging to a character, must, in his account, be defined constant anger, or anger constantly recurring. All men, says a witty poet (Rochester), would be cowards, if they durst: that the poet and the philosopher both were cowards, may be yielded, perhaps, without dispute! they may have spoken the best of their knowledge."—Shaftesbury, vol. i. p. 119.

With an heroic spirit, that virtuous statesman, Lord Clarendon, rejects the degrading notion of Hobbes. When *he* looked into his own breast, he found that courage was a real virtue, which had induced him,

generous tempers, men endowed with warmer imaginations, awake to sympathies of a higher nature, will
indignantly reject the system, which has reduced the
unlucky system-maker himself to such a pitiable condition.

Hobbes was one of those original thinkers who creat
a new era in the philosophical history of their nation
and perpetuate their name by leaving it to a sect.*

had it been necessary. to have shed his blood as a patriot. But death,
in the judgment of Hobbes, was the most terrible event, and to be
avoided by any means. Lord Clarendon draws a parallel between a
"man of courage" and one of the disciples of Hobbes, "brought to die
together, by a judgment they cannot avoid." "How comes it to pass,
that one of these undergoes death, with no other concernment than as
if he were going any other journey: and the other with such confusion and trembling, that he is even without life before he dies; if it
were true that all men fear alike upon the like occasion?"—*Survey of
the Leviathan*, p. 14.

    * They were distinguished as *Hobbists*, and the opinions as *Hobbian-
ism*. Their chief happened to be born on a Good Friday; and in the
metrical history of his own life he seems to have considered it as a
remarkable event. An atom had its weight in the scales by which
his mighty egotism weighed itself. He thus marks the day of his birth,
innocently enough :—

         "Natus erat noster Servator Homo-Deus annos
         Mille et quingentos, octo quoque undecies."

But the *Hobbists* declared more openly (as Wood tells us), that "as our
Saviour Christ went out of the world on that day to save the men of
he world, so another saviour came into the world on that day to save
them !

    That the sect spread abroad. as well as at home. is told us by Lord
Clarendon. in the preface to his "Survey of the Leviathan." The
qualities of the author, as well as the book, were well adapted for pros-
elytism; for Clarendon, who was intimately acquainted with him,
notices his confidence in conversation—his never allowing himself to
be contradicted—his bold inferences—the novelty of his expressions—
and his probity, and a life free from scandal. "The humour and inclination of the time to all kind of paradoxes," was indulged by a pleasant clear style, an appearance of order and method, hardy paradoxes,
and accommodating principles to existing circumstances.

The eloquent and thinking Madame de Staël has asserted that "Hobbes was an *Atheist* and a *Slave*." Yet I still think that Hobbes believed, and proved, the necessary existence of a Deity, and that he loved freedom, as

Who were the sect composed of? The monstrous court of Charles II.—the grossest materialists! The secret history of that court could scarcely find a Suetonius among us. But our author was frequently in the hands of those who could never have comprehended what they pretended to admire; this appears by a publication of the times, intituled, "Twelve Ingenious Characters, &c" 1686, where, in that of a town-fop, who, "for genteel breeding, posts to town, by his mother's indulgence, three or four wild companions, half a dozen bottles of Burgundy, *two leaves of Leviathan*," and some few other obvious matters, shortly make this young philosopher nearly lose his moral and physical existence. "He will not confess himself an Atheist, yet he boasts aloud that he holds his *gospel* from *the Apostle of Malmesbury*, though it is more than probable he never read, at least understood, ten leaves of *that unlucky author*." If such were his wretched disciples, Hobbes was indeed "an unlucky author," for their morals and habits were quite opposite to those of their master. Eachard, in the preface to his Second Dialogue, 1673, exhibits a very Lucianic arrangement of his disciples—Hobbes's "Pit, Box, and Gallery Friends." The *Pit-friends* were sturdy practicants who, when they hear that "Ill-nature, Debauchery, and Irreligion were Mathematics and Demonstration, clap and shout, and swear by all that comes from Malmesbury." The *Gallery* are "a sort of small, soft, little, pretty, fine gentlemen, who having some little wit, some little modesty, some little remain of conscience and country religion, could not hector it as the former, but quickly learnt to chirp and giggle when t'other clapt and shouted." But "the Don-admirers, and *Box-friends* of Mr. Hobbes, are men of gravity and reputation, who will scarce simper in favour of the philosopher, but can make shift to nod and nod again." Even amid this wild satire we find a piece of truth in a dark corner: for the satirist confesses that "his Gallery-friends, who were such resolved practicants in *Hobbianism* (by which the satirist means all kinds of licentiousness) would most certainly have been so, had there never been any such man as Mr. Hobbes in the world." Why then place to the account of the philosopher those gross immoralities which he never sanctioned? The life of Hobbes is without a stain! He had other friends besides these "Box, Pit, and Gallery" gentry—the learned of Europe, and many of the great and good men of his own country.

every sage desires it. It is now time to offer an apology
for one of those great men who are the contemporaries
of all ages, and, by fervent inquiry, to dissipate that
traditional cloud which hangs over one of "those
monuments of the mind" which Genius has built with
imperishable materials.

The author of the far-famed "Leviathan" is considered
as a vehement advocate for absolute monarchy. This
singular production may, however, be equally adapted
for a republic; and the monstrous principle may be so
innocent in its nature, as even to enter into our own constitution, which presumes to be neither.*

As "The Leviathan" produced the numerous controversies of Hobbes, a history of this great moral curiosity
enters into our subject.

Hobbes, living in times of anarchy, perceived the
necessity of re-establishing authority with more than its
usual force. But how were the divided opinions of men
to melt together, and where in the State was to be placed
absolute power? for a remedy of less force he could not
discover for that disordered state of society which he
witnessed. Was the sovereign or the people to be in-
vested with that mighty power which was to keep every
other quiescent?—a topic which had been discussed for
ages, and still must be, as the humours of men incline—
was, I believe, a matter perfectly indifferent to our philosopher, provided that whatever might be the govern-

---

* Hobbes, in defending Thucydides, whom he has so admirably
translated, from the charge of some obscurity in his design, observes
that "Marcellinus ,saith he was obscure, on purpose that the common
people might not understand him; and not unlikely, for a wise man
should so write (though in words understood by all men), that wise
men only should be able to commend him." Thus early in life Hobbes
had determined on a principle which produced all his studied ambiguity,
involved him in so much controversy, and, in some respects, preserved
him in an inglorious security.

ment, absolute power could somewhere be lodged in it,
to force men to act in strict conformity. He discovers
his perplexity in the dedication of his work. "In a way
beset with those that contend on one side for too great
liberty, on the other side for too much authority, 'tis
hard to pass between the points of both unwounded."
It happened that our cynical Hobbes had no respect
for his species; terrified at anarchy, he seems to have
lost all fear when he flew to absolute power—a sovereign
remedy unworthy of a great spirit, though convenient
for a timid one like his own. Hobbes considered men
merely as animals of prey, living in a state of perpetual
hostility, and his solitary principle of action was self-
preservation at any price.

He conjured up a political phantom, a favourite and
fanciful notion, that haunted him through life. He imagined that the *many* might be more easily managed by
making them up into an artificial *One*, and calling this
wonderful political unity the *Commonwealth*, or the *Civil
Power*, or the *Sovereign*, or by whatever name was
found most pleasing; he personified it by the image of
" Leviathan." *

---

* Hobbes explains the image in his Introduction. He does not
disguise his opinion that *Men* may be converted into *Automatons;* and
if he were not very ingenious we might lose our patience. He was so
delighted with this whimsical fancy of his " artificial man," that he
carried it on to government itself, and employed the engraver to im-
press the monstrous personification on our minds, even clearer than
by his reasonings. The curious design forms the frontispiece of "The
Leviathan." He borrowed the name from that sea-monster, that
mightiest of powers, which Job has told is not to be compared with any
on earth. The sea-monster is here, however, changed into a colossal
man, entirely made up of little men from all the classes of society,
bearing in the right hand the sword, and in the left the crosier. The
compartments are full of political allegories. An expression of Lord
Clarendon's in the preface to his " Survey of the Leviathan," shows
our philosopher's infatuation to this " idol of the Den," as Lord Bacon

At first sight the ideal monster might pass for an innocent conceit; and there appears even consummate wisdom in erecting a colossal power for our common security; but Hobbes assumed that *Authority* was to be supported to its extreme pitch. *Force* with him appeared to constitute *right*, and *unconditional submission* then became a *duty:* these were consequences quite natural to one who at his first step degraded man by comparing him to a watch, and who would not have him go but with the same nicety of motion, wound up by a great key.

To be secure, by the system of Hobbes, we must at least lose the glory of our existence as intellectual beings. He would persuade us into the dead quietness of a commonwealth of puppets, while he was consigning into the grasp of his " Leviathan," or sovereign power, the wire that was to communicate a mockery of vital motion—a principle of action without freedom. The system was equally desirable to the Protector Cromwell as to the regal Charles. A conspiracy against mankind could not alarm their governors: it is not therefore surprising that the usurper offered Hobbes the office of Secretary of State; and that he was afterwards pensioned by the monarch.

might have called the intellectual illusion of the philosopher. Hobbes, when at Paris, showed a proof-sheet or two of his work to Clarendon, who, he soon discovered, could not approve of the hardy tenets. "He frequently came to me," says his lordship. "and told me his book (*which he would call* LEVIATHAN) was then printing in England. He said, that he knew when I read his book I would not like it, and mentioned some of his conclusions: upon which I asked him, why he would publish such doctrine ; to which, after a discourse, *between jest and earnest,* he said, *The truth is, I have a mind to go home!*" Some philosophical systems have, probably, been raised "between jest and earnest;" yet here was a text-book for the despot, as it is usually accepted, deliberately given to the world, for no other purpose than that the philosopher was desirous of changing his lodgings at Paris for his old apartments in London !

A philosophical system, moral or political, is often nothing more than a temporary expedient to turn aside the madness of the times by substituting what offers an appearance of relief; nor is it a little influenced by the immediate convenience of the philosopher himself; his personal character enters a good deal into the system. The object of Hobbes in his "Leviathan" was always ambiguous, because it was, in truth, one of these systems of expediency, conveniently adapted to what has been termed of late "existing circumstances." His sole aim was to keep all things in peace, by creating one mightiest power in the State, to suppress instantly all other powers that might rise in insurrection. In his times, the establishment of despotism was the only political restraint he could discover of sufficient force to chain man down, amid the turbulence of society; but this concealed end he is perpetually shifting and disguising; for the truth is, no man loved slavery less.*

* The duplicity of the system is strikingly revealed by Burnet, who tells of Hobbes, that "he put all the law in the will of the *prince* or the *people;* for he writ his book at *first* in favour of *absolute monarchy,* but turned it afterwards to gratify the *republican party.* These were his true principles, though he had disguised them for deceiving unwary readers." It is certain Hobbes became a suspected person among the royalists. They were startled at the open extravagance of some of his political paradoxes; such as his notion of the necessity of extirpating all the *Greek* and *Latin* authors, "by reading of which men from their childhood have gotten a habit of licentious controuling the actions of their sovereigns."—p. 111. But the doctrines of liberty were not found only among the Greeks and Romans : the *Hebrews* were stern republicans ; and liberty seems to have had a nobler birth in the North among our German ancestors, than perhaps in any other part of the globe. It is certain that the Puritans, who warmed over the Bible more than the classic historians, had their heads full of Pharaoh and his host in the Red Sea; the hanging of the five kings of Joshua; and the fat king of the Moabites, who in his summer-room received a present, and then a dagger, from the left-handed Jewish Jacobin. Hobbes curiously compares "The *tyrannophobia,* or fear of

The system of Hobbes could not be limited to politics:
he knew that the safety of the people's morals required
an *Established Religion.* The alliance between Church
and State had been so violently shaken, that it was ne-

being strongly governed," to the *hydrophobia.* " When a monarchy
is once bitten to the quick by those democratical writers, and, by their
poison, men seem to be converted into dogs," his remedy is, "a
strong monarch," or "the exercise of entire sovereignty," p. 171; and
that the authority he would establish should be immutable, he hardily
asserts that "the ruling power cannot be punished for mal-adminis-
tration." Yet in this elaborate system of despotism are interspersed
some strong republican axioms, as The safety of the people is the supreme law.—The public good to be preferred to that of the individual:
—and that God made the one for the many, and not the many for the one.
The effect the LEVIATHAN produced on the royal party was quite unexpected by the author. His hardy principles were considered as a
satire on arbitrary power, and Hobbes himself as a concealed favourer
of democracy. This has happened more than once with such vehement advocates. Our philosopher must have been thunderstruck at
the insinuation, for he had presented the royal exile, as Clarendon in
his "Survey" informs us, with a magnificent copy of "The Leviathan,"
written on vellum; this beautiful specimen of caligraphy may still be
seen, as we learn from the *Gentleman's Magazine* for January, 1813,
where the curiosity is fully described. The suspicion of Hobbes's
principles was so strong, that it produced his sudden dismissal from
the presence of Charles II. when at Paris. The king, indeed, said he
believed Hobbes intended him no hurt; and Hobbes said of the king,
"that his majesty understood his writings better than his accusers."
However, happy was Hobbes to escape from France, where the officers
were in pursuit of him, amid snowy roads and nipping blasts. The
lines in his metrical life open a dismal winter scene for an old man on
a stumbling horse :—

    " Frigus erat, nix alta, senex ego, ventus acerbus,
      Vexat equus sternax, et salebrosa via—"

A curious spectacle! to observe, under a despotic government, its vehement advocate in flight!
    The ambiguity of "The Leviathan" seemed still more striking, when
Hobbes came, at length, to place the right of government merely in
what he terms "the Seat of Power," a wonderful principle of expediency ; for this was equally commodious to the republicans and to the

cessary to cement them once more. As our philosopher had been terrified in his politics by the view of its contending factions, so, in religion, he experienced the same terror at the hereditary rancours of its multiplied sects.

royalists. By this principle, the republicans maintaine i the right of Cromwell, since his authority was established, while it absolv d the royalists from their burdensome allegiance ; for, accor ling to " The Leviathan," Charles was the English monarch only when in a condition to force obedience ; and, to calm tender consciences, the philosopher further fixed on that precise point of time, " when a subject may obey an unjust conqueror." After the Restoration, it was subtilely urged by the Hobbists, that this very principle had greatly served the royal cause ; for it afforded a plea for the emigrants to return, by compounding for their estates, and joining with those royalists who had remained at home in an open submission to the established government : and thus they were enabled to concert their measures in common, for reinstating the old monarchy. Had the Restoration never taken place, Hobbes would have equally insisted on the soundness of his doctrine ; he would have asserted the title of Richard Cromwell to the Protectorate, if Richard had had the means to support it, as zealously as he afterwards did that of Charles II. to the throne, when the king had firmly re-established it. The philosophy of Hobbes, therefore, is not dangerous in any government ; its sole aim is to preserve it from intestine divisions; but for this purpose, he was for reducing men to mere machines. With such little respect he treated the species, and with such tenderness the individual!

I will give Hobbes's own justification, after the Restoration of Charles II., when accused by the great mathematician, Dr. Wallis, a republican under Cromwell, of having written his work in defence of Oliver's government. Hobbes does not deny that "he placed the right of government wheresoever should be the strength." Most subtilely he argues, how this very principle "was designed in behalf of the faithful subjects of the king," after they had done their utmost to defend his rights and person. The government of Cromwell being established, these found themselves without the protection of a government of their own, and therefore might lawfully promise obedience to their victor for the saving of their lives and fortunes; and more, they ought even to protect that authority in war by which they were themselves protected in peace. But this plea, which he so ably urged in favour of the royalists, will not, however, justify those who, like Wallis, voluntarily submitted to Cromwell, because they were always

He could devise no other means than to attack the mysteries and dogmas of theologians, those after-inventions and corruptions of Christianity, by which the artifices of their chiefs had so long split them into perpetual factions:* he therefore asserted that the religion of the people ought to exist, in strict conformity to the will of the State.†

the enemies of the king; so that this submission to Oliver is allowed only to the royalists—a most admirable political paradox! The whole of the argument is managed with infinite dexterity, and is thus unexpectedly turned against his accusers themselves. The principle of "self-preservation" is carried on through the entire system of Hobbes. —*Considerations upon the Reputation, Loyalty, &c., of Mr. Hobbes.*

* The passage in Hobbes to which I allude is in "The Leviathan," c. 32. He there says, sarcastically, "It is with the *mysteries of religion* as with wholesome pills for the sick, which, swallowed whole, have the virtue to cure: but, chewed, are for the most part cast up again without effect." Hobbes is often a wit: he was much pleased with this thought, for he had it in his *De Cive;* which, in the English translation, bears the title of "Philosophical Rudiments Concerning Government and Society," 1651. There he calls "the wholesome pills," "bitter." He translated the *De Cive* himself; a circumstance which was not known till the recent appearance of Aubrey's papers.

† Warburton has most acutely distinguished between the intention of Hobbes and that of some of his successors. The bishop does not consider Hobbes as an enemy to religion, not even to the Christian; and even doubts whether he has attacked it in "The Leviathan." At all events, he has "taken direct contrary measures from those of Bayle, Collins, Tindal, Bolingbroke, and all that school. They maliciously endeavoured to show the Gospel was *unreasonable;* Hobbes, as reasonable as his admirable wit could represent it: they contended for the most unbounded *toleration,* Hobbes for the most rigorous *conformity.*" See the "Alliance between Church and State," book i. c. v. It is curious to observe the noble disciple of Hobbes, Lord Bolingbroke, a strenuous advocate for his political and moral opinions, enraged at what he calls his "High Church notions." Trenchard and Gordon, in their *Independent Whig,* No. 44, that libel on the clergy, accuse them of *Atheism* and *Hobbism;* while some divines as earnestly reject Hobbes as an Atheist! Our temperate sage, though angried at that spirit of contradiction which he had raised, must, however, have sometimes smiled both on his advocates and his adversaries!

When Hobbes wrote against mysteries, the mere po-
lemics sent forth a cry of his impiety; the philosopher
was branded with Atheism;—one of those artful calumnies, of which, after a man has washed himself clean, the
stain will be found to have dyed the skin.*

* The odious term of *Atheist* has been too often applied to many
great men of our nation by the hardy malignity of party. Were I to
present a catalogue, the very names would refute the charge. Let
us examine the religious sentiments of Hobbes. The materials for its
investigation are not common, but it will prove a dissertation of facts.
I warn some of my readers to escape from the tediousness, if they cannot value the curiosity.

Hobbes has himself thrown out an observation in his "Life of
Thucydides" respecting Anaxagoras, that "his opinions, being of a
strain above the apprehension of the vulgar, procured him the estimation of an *Atheist*, which name they bestowed upon all men that
thought not as they did of their ridiculous religion, and in the end
cost him his life." This was a parallel case with Hobbes himself, except its close, which, however, seems always to have been in the mind
of our philosopher.

Bayle, who is for throwing all things into doubt, acknowledging
that the life of Hobbes was blameless, adds, One might, however, have
been tempted to ask him this question:

Heus age responde; minimum est quod scire laboro;
De Jove quid sentis?—PERSIUS, Sat. ii. v. 17.

Hark, now! resolve this one short question, friend!
What are thy thoughts of Jove?

But Bayle, who compared himself to the Jupiter of Homer, powerful in gathering and then dispersing the clouds, dissipates the one he
had just raised, by showing how "Hobbes might have answered the
question with sincerity and belief, *according to the writers of his life.*"—
But had Bayle known that Hobbes was the author of all the lives of
himself, so partial an evidence might have raised another doubt with
the great sceptic. It appears, by Aubrey's papers, that Hobbes did
not wish his biography should appear when he was living, that he
might not seem the author of it.

Baxter, who knew Hobbes intimately, ranks him with Spinosa, by
a strong epithet for materialists—"The *Brutists*, Hobbes, and Spinosa."
He tells us that Selden would not have him in his chamber while

To me it appears that Hobbes, to put an end to these
religious wars, which his age and country had witnessed,

dying, calling out, "No Atheists!" But by Aubrey's papers it appears that Hobbes stood by the side of his dying friend. It's certain
his enemies raised stories against him, and told them as suited their
purpose. In the Lansdowne MSS. I find Dr. Grenville, in a letter,
relates how "Hobbes, when in France, and like to die, betrayed such
expressions of repentance to a great prelate, from whose mouth I had
this relation, that he admitted him to the sacrament. But Hobbes
afterwards made this a subject of ridicule in companies."—*Lansdowne
MSS.* 990—73.

Here is a strong accusation, and a fact too: yet when fully developed, the result will turn out greatly in favour of Hobbes.

Hobbes had a severe illness at Paris, which lasted six months, thus
noticed in his metrical life :

> Dein per sex menses morbo decumbo propinque
> Accinctus morti; nec fugio, illa fugit.

It happened that the famous Guy Patin was his physician; and in
one of those amusing letters, where he puts down the events of the
day, like a newspaper of the times, in No. 61, has given an account
of his intercourse with the philosopher, in which he says that Hobbes
endured such pain, that he would have destroyed himself—"*Qu'il
avoit voulu se tuer.*"—Patin is a vivacious writer: we are not to take
him *au pied de la lettre.* Hobbes was systematically tenacious of
life: and, so far from attempting suicide, that he wanted even the
courage to allow Patin to bleed him! It was during this illness that
the Catholic party, who like to attack a Protestant in a state of unresisting debility, got his learned and intimate friend, Father Mersenne, to
hold out all the benefits a philosopher might derive from their Church.
When Hobbes was acquainted with this proposed interview (says a
French contemporary, whose work exists in MS., but is quoted in Joly's
folio volume of Remarks on Bayle), the sick man answered, "Don't let
him come for this; I shall laugh at him; and perhaps I may convert
him myself." Father Mersenne did come: and when this missionary
was opening on the powers of Rome to grant a plenary pardon, he was
interrupted by Hobbes—"Father, I have examined, a long time ago, all
these points; I should be sorry to dispute now; you can entertain me
in a more agreeable manner. When did you see Mr. Gassendi?" The
monk, who was a philosopher, perfectly understood Hobbes, and this
interview never interrupted their friendship. A few days after, Dr.

perpetually kindled by crazy fanatics and intolerant dog-
matists, insisted that the *crosier* should be carried in

Cosin (afterwards Bishop of Durham), the great prelate whom Dr.
Grenville alludes to, prayed with Hobbes, who first *stipulated* that tho
prayers should be those authorised by the *Church of England;* and he
also received the sacrament with reverence. Hobbes says:—"Mag-
num hoc erga disciplinam Episcopalem signum erat reverentiæ."—It
is evident that the conversion of Father Mersenne, to which Hobbes
facetiously alluded, could never be to Atheism, but to Protestant-
ism: and had Hobbes been an Atheist, he would not have risked his
safety, when he arrived in England, by his strict attendance to the
Church of England, resolutely refusing to unite with any of the sects.
His views of the national religion were not only enlightened, but in
this respect he showed a boldness in his actions very unusual with
him.

But the religion of Hobbes was "of a strain beyond the apprehension of the vulgar," and not very agreeable to some of the Church. A
man may have peculiar notions respecting the Deity, and yet be far
removed from Atheism; and in his political system the Church may
hold that subordinate place which some Bishops will not like. When
Dr. Grenville tells us "Hobbes ridiculed in companies" certain matters which the Doctor held sacred, this is not sufficient to accuse a man
of Atheism, though it may prove him not to have held orthodox opinions. From the MS. collections of the French contemporary, who well
knew Hobbes at Paris, I transcribe a remarkable observation:—
"Hobbes said, that he was not surprised that the Independents, who
were enemies of monarchy, could not bear it in heaven, and that therefore they placed there three Gods instead of one; but he was astonished that the English bishops, and those Presbyterians who were
favourers of monarchy, should persist in the same opinion concerning
the Trinity. He added, that the Episcopalians ridiculed the Puritans,
and the Puritans the Episcopalians; but that the wise ridiculed both
alike."—*Lantiniana MS.* quoted by Joly, p. 434.

The *religion* of Hobbes was in *conformity* to *State and Church.* He
had, however, the most awful notions of the Divinity. He confesses
he is unacquainted with "the nature of God, but not with the *necessity* of the existence of the Power of all powers, and First Cause of all
causes; so that we know that God is, though not what he is." See
his "Human Nature," chap. xi. But was the God of Hobbes the in-
active deity of Epicurus, who takes no interest in the happiness or
misery of his created beings; or, as Madame de Staël has expressed
it, with the point and felicity of French antithesis, was this "an

the *left* hand of his Leviathan, and the *sword* in his right.* He testified, as strongly as man could, by his

Atheism with a God?" This consequence some of his adversaries would draw from his principles, which Hobbes indignantly denies. He has done more: for in his *De Corpore Politico*, he declares his belief of all the fundamental points of Christianity, part i. c. 4. p. 116, Ed. 1652. But he was an open enemy to those "who presume, out of Scripture, by their own interpretation, to raise any *doctrine to the understanding*, concerning those things which are incomprehensible;" and he refers to St. Paul, who gives a good rule "*to think soberly, according as God hath dea't to every man* the measure of faith."—Rom. xii. 3.

* This he pictures in a strange engraving prefixed to his book, and representing a crowned figure, whose description will be found in the note, p. 281. It is remarkable that when Hobbes adopted the principle that the *ecclesiastical* should be united with the *sovereign* power, he was then actually producing that portentous change which had terrified Luther and Calvin; who, even in their day, were alarmed by a new kind of political Antichrist; that "Cæsarean Popery" which Stubbe so much dreaded, and which I have here noticed, p. 174. Luther predicted that as the pope had at times seized on the political sword, so this "Cæsarean Popery," under the pretence of policy, would grasp the ecclesiastical crosier, to form a *political church*. The curious reader is referred to Wolfius *Lect'onum Memorabilium et reconditarum*, vol. ii. cent. x. p. 987. Calvin, in his commentary on Amos, has also a remarkable passage on this *political church*, animadverting on Amaziah, the priest, who would have proved the Bethel worship warrantable, because settled by the royal authority: "It is the king's chapel." Amos, vii. 13. Thus Amaziah, adds Calvin, assigns the king a double function, and maintains it is in his power to transform religion into what shape he pleases, while he charges Amos with disturbing the public repose, and encroaching on the royal prerogative. Calvin zealously reprobates the conduct of those inconsiderate persons, "who give the civil magistrate a sovereignty in religion, and dissolve the Church into the State." The supremacy in Church and State, conferred on Henry VIII., was the real cause of these alarms: but the passage of domination raged not less fiercely in Calvin than in Henry VIII.; in the enemy of kings than in kings themselves. Were the *forms* of religion more celestial from the sanguinary hands of that tyrannical reformer than from those of the reforming tyrant? The system of our philosopher was, to lay all the wild spirits which have haunted us in the chimerical shapes of *non-conformity*. I have often

public actions, that he was a Christian of the Church of England, "as by law established," and no enemy to the episcopal order; but he dreaded the encroachments of the Churchmen in his political system; jealous of that *supremacy* at which some of them aimed. Many enlightened bishops sided with the philosopher.* At a time when Milton sullenly withdrew from every public testimonial of divine worship, Hobbes, with more enlightened views, *attended Church service*, and strenuously supported *an established religion;* yet one is deemed a religious man, and the other an Atheist! Were the actions of men to be decisive of their characters, the reverse might be inferred.

The temper of our philosopher, so ill-adapted to contradiction, was too often tried; and if, as his adversary, Harrington, in the "Oceana," says, "Truth be a spark whereunto objections are like bellows," the mind of Hobbes, for half a century, was a very forge, where the hammer was always beating, and the flame was never allowed to be extinguished. Charles II. strikingly described his worrying assailants. "Hobbes," said the king, "was a bear against whom the Church played their

thought, after much observation on our Church history since the Reformation, that *the devotional feelings* have not been so much concerned in this bitter opposition to the National Church as the rage of dominion, the spirit of vanity, the sullen pride of sectarism, and the delusions of madness.

* Hobbes himself tells us that "some bishops are content to hold their authority from *the king's letters patents;* others will needs have somewhat more they know not what of *divine rights,* &c., *not acknowledging the power of the king.* It is a relic still remaining of the venom of popish ambition, lurking in that *seditious distinction and division* between the power *spiritual* and *civil.* The safety of the State does not depend on the safety of the clergy, but on the *entireness of the sovereign power."—Considerations upon the Reputation, &c., of Mr. Hobbes,* p. 44.

young dogs, in order to exercise them."* A strange
repartee has preserved the causticity of his wit. Dr.
Eachard, perhaps one of the prototypes of Swift, wrote
two admirable ludicrous dialogues, in ridicule of Hobbes's
"State of Nature."† These were much extolled, and
kept up the laugh against the philosophic misanthropist:
once when he was told that the clergy said that "Eachard
had crucified Hobbes," he bitterly retorted, "Why, then,
don't they fall down and *worship* me?"‡

"The Leviathan" was ridiculed by the wits, declaimed
against by the republicans, denounced by the monar-
chists, and menaced by the clergy. The commonwealth
man, the dreamer of equality, Harrington, raged at the
subtile advocate for despotic power; but the glittering
bubble of his fanciful "Oceana" only broke on the
mighty sides of the Leviathan, wasting its rainbow tints:
the mitred Bramhall, at "The Catching of Leviathan, or
the Great Whale," flung his harpoon, demonstrating
consequences from the principles of Hobbes, which he

* This royal observation is recorded in the "Sorberiana." Sorbiere
gleaned the anecdote during his residence in England. By the "Aubrey Papers," which have been published since I composed this
article, I find that Charles II was greatly delighted by the wit and
repartees of Hobbes, who was at once bold and happy in making his
stand amidst the court wits. The king, wherever he saw Hobbes,
who had the privilege of being admitted into the royal presence,
would exclaim, "Here comes the bear to be baited." This did not
allude to his native roughness, but the force of his resistance when
attacked.

† See "Mr. Hobbes's State of Nature considered in a Dialogue between Philautus and Timothy." The second of these is not contained
in the seventh edition of Eachard's Works, 1705, which, however,
was long after his death; so curious were the publishers of those days
of their authors' works. The literary bookseller, Tom Davies, who
ruined himself by giving good editions of our old authors, has preserved it in his own.

‡ "A Discourse Concerning Irony," 1729, p. 13.

as eagerly denied. But our ambiguous philosopher had
the hard fate to be attacked even by those who were
labouring to the same end.* The literary wars of Hobbes
were fierce and long; heroes he encountered, but heroes
too were fighting by his side. Our chief himself wore a
kind of magical armour; for, either he denied the consequences his adversaries deduced from his principles, or he
surprised by new conclusions, which many could not discover in them; but by such means he had not only the
art of infusing confidence among the *Hobbists*, but the
greater one of dividing his adversaries, who often retreated, rather fatigued than victorious. Hobbes owed
this partly to the happiness of a genius which excelled
in controversy, but more, perhaps, to the advantage of
the ground he occupied as a metaphysician: the usual
darkness of that spot is favourable to those shiftings and
turnings which the equivocal possessor may practise
with an unwary assailant. Far different was the fate of
Hobbes in the open daylight of mathematics: there his
hardy genius lost him, and his sophistry could spin no
web; as we shall see in the memorable war of twenty
years waged between Hobbes and Dr. Wallis. But the
gall of controversy was sometimes tasted, and the flames

* Men of very opposite principles, but aiming at the same purpose,
are reduced to a dilemma, by the spirit of party in controversy. Sir
Robert Filmer, who wrote against "The Anarchy of a Limited Monarchy," and "Patriarcha," to re-establish *absolute power*, derived it
from the scriptural accounts of the patriarchal state. But Sir Robert
and Hobbes, though alike the advocates for supremacy of power, were
as opposite as possible on theological points. Filmer had the same
work to perform, but he did not like the instruments of his fellow-
labourer. His manner of proceeding with Hobbes shows his dilemma:
he refutes the doctrine of the "Leviathan," while he confesses that
Hobbes is right in the main. The philosopher's reasonings stand on
quite another foundation than the scriptural authorities deduced by
Filmer. The result therefore is, that Sir Robert had the trouble to
confute the very thing he afterwards had to establish!

of persecution flashed at times in the closet of our philosopher. The ungenerous attack of Bishop Fell, who, in
the Latin translation of Wood's "History of the University of Oxford," had converted eulogium into the most
virulent abuse,* without the participation of Wood, who

* It may be curious to some of my readers to preserve that part of
Hobbes's Letter to Anthony Wood, in the rare tract of his "Latin
Life," in which, with great calmness, the philosopher has painfully
collated the odious interpolations. All that was written in favour of
the morals of Hobbes—of the esteem in which foreigners held him—
of the royal patronage, &c., were maliciously erased. Hobbes thus
notices the amendments of Bishop Fell:—

"Nimirum ubi mihi tu ingenium attribuis *Sobrium*, ille, deleto *Sobrio*,
substituit *Acri.*

"Ubi tu scripseras *Libellum scripsit de Cive*. interposuit ille inter *Libellum* et *de Cive, rebus permiscendis natum*, de *Cive*, quod ita manifestè
falsum est, &c.

"Quod, ubi tu de libro meo *Leviathan* scripsisti, primò, quod esset,
Vicinis gentibus notissimus interposuit ille, *publico damno*. Ubi tu scripseras, *scripsit librum*, interposuit ille *monstrosissimum.*"

A noble confidence in his own genius and celebrity breaks out in this
Epistle to Wood. "In leaving out all that you have said of my character and reputation, the dean has injured you, but cannot injure me; for
long since has my fame winged its way to a station from which it can
never descend." One is surprised to find such a Miltonic spirit in the
contracted soul of Hobbes, who in his own system might have cynically
ridiculed the passion for fame, which, however, no man felt more than
himself. In his controversy with Bishop Bramhall (whose book he
was cautious not to answer till ten years after it was published, and his
adversary was no more, pretending he had never heard of it till then!)
he breaks out with the same feeling:—"What my works are, he was
no fit judge; but now he has provoked me, I will say thus much of
them, that neither he, if he had lived, could—nor I, if I would, can—
extinguish the light which is set up in the world by the greatest part
of them."

It is curious to observe that an idea occurred to Hobbes, which some
authors have attempted lately to put into practice against their critics
—to prosecute them in a court of law: but the knowledge of mankind
was one of the liveliest faculties of Hobbes's mind: he knew well to
what account common minds place the injured feelings of authorship;
yet were *a jury of literary men* to sit in judgment, we might have a

resented it with his honest warmth, was only an arrow
snatched from a quiver which was every day emptying
itself on the devoted head of our ambiguous philosopher.
Fell only vindicated himself by a fresh invective on " the
most vain and waspish animal of Malmesbury," and
Hobbes was too frightened to reply. This was the Fell
whom it was so difficult to assign a reason for not
liking :

> I don't like thee, Dr. Fell,
> The reason why I cannot tell,
> But I don't like thee, Dr. Fell !

A curious incident in the history of the mind of this
philosopher, was the mysterious panic which accompanied
him to his latest day. It has not been denied that
Hobbes was subject to occasional terrors : he dreaded to
be left without company ; and a particular instance is
told, that on the Earl of Devonshire's removal from
Chatsworth, the philosopher, then in a dying state, insisted on being carried away, though on a feather-bed.
Various motives have been suggested to account for this
extraordinary terror. Some declared he was afraid of
spirits ; but he was too stout a materialist !*—another,

good deal of business in the court for a long time; the critics and the
authors would finally have a very useful body of reports and plead-
ings to appeal to; and the public would be highly entertained and
greatly instructed. On this attack of Bishop Fell, Hobbes says—" I
might perhaps have an action on the case against him, if it were worth
my while : but juries seldom consider the Quarrels of Authors as of much
moment."

* Bayle has conjured up an amusing theory of apparitions, to show
that Hobbes might fear that a certain combination of atoms agitating
his brain might so disorder his mind that it would expose him to spec-
tral visions ; and being very timorous, and distrusting his imagination,
he was averse to be left alone. Apparitions happen frequently in
dreams, and they may happen, even to an incredulous man, when
awake, for reading and hearing of them would revive their images—
these images, adds Bayle, might play him some unlucky trick ! Wo

that he dreaded assassination; an ideal poniard indeed
might scare even a materialist. But Bishop Atterbury,
in a sermon on *the Terrors of Conscience*, illustrates their
nature by the character of our philosopher. Hobbes is
there accused of attempting to destroy the principles of
religion against his own inward conviction: this would
only prove the insanity of Hobbes! The Bishop shows
that "the disorders of *conscience* are not a *continued*,
but an *intermitting* disease;" so that the patient may
appear at intervals in seeming health and real ease, till
the fits return: all this he applies to the case of our philosopher. In reasoning on human affairs, the shortest
way will be to discover human motives. The spirit, or
the assassin of Hobbes, arose from the bill brought into
Parliament, when the nation was panic-struck on the fire
of London, against Atheism and Profaneness; he had a
notion that a writ *de heretico comburendo* was intended
for him by Bishop Seth Ward, his *quondam* admirer.*

are here astonished at the ingenuity of a disciple of Pyrrho, who in
his inquiries, after having exhausted all human evidence, seems to
have demonstrated what he hesitates to believe! Perhaps the truth
was, that the sceptical Bayle had not entirely freed himself from the
traditions which were then still floating from the fireside to the philosopher's closet: he points his pen, as Æneas brandished his sword at
the Gorgons and Chimeras that darkened the entrance of Hell; wanting the admonitions of the sibyl, he would have rushed in—

Et frustra ferro diverberet umbras.

* The papers of Aubrey confirm my suggestion. I shall give the
words—"There was a report, and surely true, that in parliament, not
long after the king was settled, some of the bishops made a motion to
have the good old gentleman burne? for a heretique; which he hearing, feared that his papers might be searched by their order, and he
told me he had burned part of them."—p. 612. When Aubrey requested Waller to write verses on Hobbes, the poet said that he was
afraid of the Churchmen. Aubrey tells us—"I have often heard him say
that he was not afraid of *Sprights*, but afraid of being knocked on the
head for five or ten pounds which rogues might think he had in his

His spirits would sink at those moments; for in the philosophy of Hobbes, the whole universe was concentrated in the small space of SELF. There was no length he refused to go for what he calls "the natural right of preservation, which we all receive from the uncontrollable dictates of NECESSITY." He exhausts his imagination in the forcible descriptions of his extinction: "the terrible enemy of nature, Death," is always before him. The "inward horror" he felt of his extinction, Lord Clarendon thus alludes to: "If Mr. Hobbes and some other man were both condemned to death (which is the most formidable thing Mr. Hobbes can conceive)"—and Dr. Eachard rallies him on the infinite anxiety he bestowed on his *body*, and thinks that "he had better compound to be kicked and beaten twice a day, than to be so dismally tortured about an old rotten carcase." Death was perhaps the only subject about which Hobbes would not dispute.

Such a materialist was then liable to terrors; and though, when his works were burnt, the author had not a hair singed, the convulsion of the panic often produced, as Bishop Atterbury expresses it, "an intermitting disease."

Persecution terrified Hobbes, and magnanimity and courage were no virtues in his philosophy. He went about hinting that he was not obstinate (that is, before the Bench of Bishops); that his opinions were mere conjectures, proposed as exercises for the powers of reason-

chamber." This reason given by Hobbes for his frequent alarms was an evasive reply for too curious and talkative an inquirer. Hobbes has not concealed the cause of his terror in his metrical life—

> "Tunc venit in mentem mihi Dorislaus et Ascham,
> Tanquam proscripto terror ubique aderat."

Dr. Dorislaus and Ascham had fallen under the daggers of proscription. [The former was assassinated in Holland, whither he had fled for safety.]

ing. He attempted (without meaning to be ludicrous) to make his *opinions* a distinct object from his *person*; and, for the good order of the latter, he appealed to the family chaplain for his attendance at divine service, from whence, however, he always departed at the sermon, insisting that the chaplain could not teach him anything. It was in one of these panics that he produced his "Historical Narrative of Heresy, and the Punishment thereof," where, losing the dignity of the philosophic character, he creeps into a subterfuge with the subtilty of the lawyer; insisting that "The Leviathan," being published at a time when there was no distinction of creeds in England (the Court of High Commission having been abolished in the troubles), that therefore none could be heretical.*

* It is said that Hobbes completely recanted all his opinions; and proceeded so far as to declare that the opinions he had published in his "Leviathan," were not his real sentiments, and that he neither maintained them in public nor in private. Wood gives this title to a work of his—"An Apology for Himself and his Writings," but without date. Some have suspected that this Apology, if it ever existed, was not his own composition. Yet why not? Hobbes, no doubt, thought that "The Leviathan" would outlast any recantation; and, after all, that a recantation is by no means a refutation!—recantations usually prove the force of authority, rather than the force of conviction. I am much pleased with a Dr. Pocklington, who hit the etymology of the word *recantation* with the spirit. Accused and censured, for a penance he was to make a recantation, which he began thus:—"If *canto* be to *sing*, *recanto* is to sing again:" so that he *re-chanted* his offensive principles by his *recantation!*

I suspect that the apology Wood alludes to was only a republication of Hobbes's Address to the King, prefixed to the "Seven Philosophical Problems," 1662, where he openly disavows his opinions, and makes an apology for the "Leviathan." It is curious enough to observe how he acts in this dilemma. It was necessary to give up his opinions to the clergy, but still to prove they were of an innocent nature. He therefore acknowledges that "his theological notions are not his opinions, but propounded with submission to the power ecclesiastical, never afterwards having maintained them in writing or discourse."

No man was more speculatively bold, and more practically timorous;* and two very contrary principles enabled him, through an extraordinary length of life, to deliver his opinions and still to save himself: these were his excessive vanity and his excessive timidity. The one inspired his hardy originality, and the other prompted him to protect himself by any means. His love of glory roused his vigorous intellect, while his fears shrunk him into his little self. Hobbes, engaged in the cause of truth, betrayed her dignity by his ambiguous and abject conduct : this was a consequence of his selfish philosophy; and this conduct has yielded no dubious triumph to the noble school which opposed his cynical principles.

A genius more luminous, sagacity more profound, and morals less tainted, were never more eminently combined than in this very man, who was so often reduced to the most abject state. But the antisocial philosophy of Hobbes terminated in preserving a pitiful state of exist-

Yet, to show the king that the regal power incurred no great risk in them, he laid down one principle, which could not have been unpleasing to Charles II. He asserts, truly, that he never wrote against episco-pacy; "yet he is called an Atheist, or man of no religion, because he has made the authority of the Church depend wholly upon the re-gal power, which, I hope, your majesty will think is neither Atheism nor Heresy." Hobbes considered the *religion* of his country as a sub-ject of *law*, and not *philosophy*. He was not for *separating* the Church from the State; but, on the contrary, for *joining them* more closely. The bishops ought not to have been his enemies; and many were not.

* In the MS. collection of the French contemporary, who personally knew him, we find a remarkable confession of Hobbes. He said of himself that "he sometimes made openings to let in light, but that he could not discover his thoughts but by half-views: like those who threw open the window for a short time, but soon closing it, from the dread of the storm." "*Il d soit qu'il faisoit quelquefois des ouvertures, mais qu'il ne pouvoit découvrir ses pensées qu' i-demi ; qu'il imitoit ceux qui ouvrent la fenêtre pendant quelques momens, mais qui la referment promptement de peur de l'orage.*"—Lantiniana MSS., quoted by Joly in his volume of "Remarques sur Bayle."

ence. He who considered nothing more valuable than life, degraded himself by the meanest artifices of self-love,* and exulted in the most cynical truths.† The

* Could one imagine that the very head and foot of the stupendous "Leviathan" bear the marks of the little artifices practised for self by its author? This grave work is dedicated to Francis Godolphin, a person whom its author had never seen, merely to remind him of a certain legacy which that person's brother had left to our philosopher. If read with this fact before us, we may detect the concealed claim to the legacy, which it seems was necessary to conceal from the Parliament, as Francis Godolphin resided in England. It must be confessed this was a miserable motive for dedicating a system of philosophy which was addressed to all mankind. It discovers little dignity. This secret history we owe to Lord Clarendon, in his "Survey of the Leviathan," who adds another. The postscript to the "Leviathan," which is only in the English edition, was designed as an easy summary of the principles; and his lordship adds, as a sly address to Cromwell, that he might be induced to be master of them at once, and "as a pawn of his new subject's allegiance." It is possible that Hobbes might have anticipated the sovereign power which the *general* was on the point of assuming in the *protectorship*. It was natural enough that Hobbes should deny this suggestion.

† The story his antagonist (Dr. Wallis) relates is perfectly in character. Hobbes, to show the Countess of Devonshire his attachment to life, declared that "were he master of all the world to dispose of, he would give it to live one day." "But you have so many friends to oblige, had you the world to dispose of!" "Shall I be the better for that when I am dead?" "No." repeated the sublime cynic, "I would give the whole world to live one day." He asserted that "it was lawful to make use of ill instruments to do ourselves good," and illustrated it thus:—"Were I cast into a deep pit, and the devil should put down his cloven foot, I would take hold of it to be drawn out by it." It must be allowed this is a philosophy which has a chance of being long popular; but it is not that of another order of human beings! Hobbes would not, like Curtius, have leaped into a "deep pit" for his country; or, to drop the fable, have died for it in the field or on the scaffold, like the Falklands, the Sidneys, the Montroses—all the heroic brotherhood of genius! One of his last expressions, when informed of the approaches of death, was—"I shall be glad to find a hole to creep out of the world at." Everything was seen in a little way by this great man, who, having reasoned himself into an abject being, "licked the dust" through life.

philosophy of Hobbes, founded on fear and suspicion, and which, in human nature, could see nothing beyond himself, might make him a wary politician, but always an imperfect social being. We find, therefore, that the philosopher of Malmesbury adroitly retained a friend at court, to protect him at an extremity; but considering all men alike, as bargaining for themselves, his friends occasioned him as much uneasiness as his enemies. He lived in dread that the Earl of Devonshire, whose roof had ever been his protection, should at length give him up to the Parliament! There are no friendships among cynics!

To such a state of degradation had the selfish philosophy reduced one of the greatest geniuses; a philosophy true only for the wretched and the criminal.* But those

---

* In our country, Mandeville, Swift, and Chesterfield have trod in the track of Hobbes; and in France, Helvetius, Rochefoucauld in his "Maxims," and L'Esprit more openly in his "Fausette des Vertus Humaines." They only degrade us—they are polished cynics! But what are we to think of the tremendous cynicism of Machiavel? That great genius eyed human nature with the ferocity of an enraged savage. Machiavel is a vindictive assassin, who delights even to turn his dagger within the mortal wound he has struck; but our Hobbes, said his friend Sorbiere, "is a gentle and skilful surgeon, who, with regret, cuts into the living flesh, to get rid of the corrupted." It is equally to be regretted that the same system of degrading man has been adopted by some, under the mask of religion.

Yet Hobbes, perhaps, never suspected the arms he was placing in the hands of wretched men, when he furnished them with such fundamental positions as, that "Man is naturally an evil being; that he does not love his equal; and only seeks the aid of society for his own particular purposes." He would at least have disowned some of his diabolical disciples. One of them, so late as in 1774, vented his furious philosophy in "An Essay on the Depravity and Corruption of Human Nature, wherein the Opinions of Hobbes, Mandeville, Helvetius, &c. are supported against Shaftesbury, Hume, Sterne, &c. by Thomas O'Brien M'Mahon." This gentleman, once informed that he was *born wicked*, appears to have considered that wickedness was his paternal

who feel moving within themselves the benevolent principle, and who delight in acts of social sympathy, are
conscious of passions and motives, which the others have
omitted in their system. And the truth is, these " unnatural philosophers," as Lord Shaftesbury expressively
terms them, are by no means the monsters they tell us
they are : their practice is therefore usually in opposition
to their principles. While Hobbes was for chaining
down mankind as so many beasts of prey, he surely
betrayed his social passion, in the benevolent warnings

estate, to be turned to as profitable an account as he could.   The titles
of his chapters, serving as a string of the most extraordinary propositions, have been preserved in the "Monthly Review," vol. lii. 77.   The
demonstrations in the work itself must be still more curious.   In
these axioms we find that " Man has an *enmity* to all beings ; that had
he *power*, the first victims of his revenge would be his wife, children,
&c.—a sovereign, if he could reign with the *unbounded authority* every
man *longs for*, free from apprehension of punishment for misrule, would
slaughter all his subjects ; perhaps he would not leave one of them
alive at the end of his reign."   It was perfectly in character with this
wretched being, after having quarrelled with human nature, that he
should be still more inveterate against a small part of her family, with
whom he was suffered to live on too intimate terms ; for he afterwards
published another extraordinary piece—" The Conduct and Good-
Nature of Englishmen Exemplified in their charitable way of Characterising the Customs, Manners, &c. of Neighbouring Nations; their
Equitable and Humane Mode of Governing States, &c.; their Elevated
and Courteous Deportment, &c. of which their own Authors are everywhere produced as Vouchers," 1777.   One is tempted to think that
this O'Brien M'Mahon, after all, is only a wag, and has copied the
horrid pictures of his masters, as Hogarth did the School of Rembrandt
by his " Paul before Felix, designed and *scratched* in the true Dutch
taste."   These works seem, however, to have their use.   To have
carried the conclusions of the Anti-social Philosophy to as great lengths
as this writer has, is to display their absurdity.   But, as every
rational Englishman will appeal to his own heart, in declaring the one
work to be nothing but a libel on the nation ; so every man, not destitute of virtuous emotions, will feel the other to be a libel on human
nature itself.

he was perpetually giving them; and while he affected to hold his brothers in contempt, he was sacrificing laborious days, and his peace of mind, to acquire celebrity. Who loved glory more than this sublime cynic? " *Glory*," says our philosopher, " by those whom it displeaseth, is called *Pride;* by those whom it pleaseth, it is termed *a just valuation of himself.*"* Had Hobbes defined, as critically, the passion of *self-love*, without resolving all our sympathies into a single monstrous one, we might have been disciplined without being degraded.

Hobbes, indeed, had a full feeling of the magnitude of his labours, both for foreigners and posterity, as he has expressed it in his life. He disperses, in all his works, some Montaigne-like notices of himself, and they are eulogistic. He has not omitted any one of his virtues, nor even an apology for his deficiency in others. He notices with complacency how Charles II. had his portrait placed in the royal cabinet; how it was frequently asked for by his friends, in England and in France.† He has written his life several times, in verse and

---

* "Human Nature," c. ix.

† Hobbes did not exaggerate the truth. Aubrey says of Cooper's portrait of Hobbes, that "he intends to borrow the picture of his majesty, for Mr. Loggan to engrave an accurate piece by, which will sell well at home and abroad." We have only the rare print of Hobbes by Faithorne, prefixed to a quarto edition of his Latin Life, 1682, remarkable for its expression and character. Sorbiere, returning from England, brought home a portrait of the sage, which he placed in his collection; and strangers, far and near, came to look on the physiognomy of a great and original thinker. One of the honours which men of genius receive is the homage the public pay to their images: either, like the fat monk, one of the heroes of the *Epistol e obscurorum Virorum*, who, standing before a portrait of Erasmus, spit on it in utter malice; or when they are looked on in silent reverence. It is alike a tribute paid to the masters of intellect. They have had their shrines and pilgrimages.

in prose; and never fails to throw into the eyes of his adversaries the reputation he gained abroad and at home.* He delighted to show he was living, by annual publications; and exultingly exclaims, "That when he had silenced his adversaries, he published, in the eighty-seventh year of his life, the Odyssey of Homer, and the next year the Iliad, in English verse."

His greatest imperfection was a monstrous egotism—the fate of those who concentrate all their observations in their own individual feelings. There are minds which may think too much, by conversing too little with books and men. Hobbes exulted he had read little; he had not more than half-a-dozen books about him; hence he always saw things in his own way, and doubtless this was the cause of his mania for disputation.

He wrote against dogmas with a spirit perfectly dog-matic. He liked conversation on the terms of his own political system, provided absolute authority was established, peevishly referring to his own works whenever contradicted; and his friends stipulated with strangers, that "they should not dispute with the old man." But

None of our authors have been better known, nor more highly considered, than our Hobbes, abroad. I find many curious particulars of him and his conversations recorded in French works, which are not known to the English biographers or critics. His residence at Paris occasioned this. See Ancillon's Mélange Critique, Basle, 1698: Patin's Letters, 61; Sorberiana; Niceron, tome iv.; Joly's Additions to Bayle.—All these contain original notices on Hobbes.

* To his Life are additions, which nothing but the self-love of the author could have imagined.

"Amicorum Elenchus."—He might be proud of the list of foreigners and natives.

"Tractuum contra Hobbium editorum Syllabus."

"Eorum qui in Scriptis suis Hobbio contradixerunt Indiculus."

"Qui Hobbii meminerunt seu in bonam seu in sequiorem partem."

"In Hobbii Defensionem."—Hobbes died 1679, aged 91. These two editions are, 1681, 1682.

what are we to think of that pertinacity of opinion which he held even with one as great as himself? Selden has often quitted the room, or Hobbes been driven from it, in the fierceness of their battle.* Even to his latest day, the " war of words" delighted the man of confined reading. The literary duels between Hobbes and another hero celebrated in logomachy, the Catholic priest, Thomas White, have been recorded by Wood. They had both passed their eightieth year, and were fond of paying visits to one another: but the two literary Nestors never met to part in cool blood, "wrangling, squabbling, and scolding on philosophical matters," as our blunt and lively historian has described.†

His little qualities were the errors of his own selfish philosophy; his great ones were those of nature. He was a votary to his studies:‡ he avoided marriage, to

---

* This fact has been recorded in one of the pamphlets of Richard Baxter, who, however, was no well-wisher to our philosopher. "Additional Notes on the Life and Death of Sir Matthew Hale," 1682, p. 40.

† "Athen. Oxon.," vol. ii. p. 665, ed. 1721. No one, however, knew better than Hobbes the vanity and uselessness of *words:* in one place he compares them to "a spider's web; for, by contexture of words, tender and delicate wits are insnared and stopped, but strong wits break easily through them." The pointed sentence with which Warburton closes his preface to Shakspeare, is Hobbes's—that "words are the counters of the wise, and the money of fools."

‡ Aubrey has minutely preserved for us the manner in which Hobbes composed his "Leviathan:" it is very curious for literary students. "He walked much, and contemplated; and he had in the head of his cane a pen and inkhorn, and carried always a note-book in his pocket; and as soon as a thought darted, he presently entered it into his book, or otherwise might have lost it. He had drawn the design of the book into chapters, &c., and he knew whereabouts it would come in. Thus that book was made."—Vol. ii. p. 607. Aubrey, the little Boswell of his day, has recorded another literary peculiarity, which some authors do not assuredly sufficiently use. Hobbes said that he sometimes would set his thoughts upon researching and contemplating, always with this proviso: "that he very much and deeply considered one thing at a time—for a week, or sometimes a fortnight."

which he was inclined; and refused place and wealth, which he might have enjoyed, for literary leisure. He treated with philosophic pleasantry his real contempt of money.* His health and his studies were the sole objects of his thoughts; and notwithstanding that panic which so often disturbed them, he wrote and published beyond his ninetieth year. He closes the metrical history of

* A small annuity from the Devonshire family, and a small pension from Charles II., exceeded the wants of his philosophic life. If he chose to compute his income, Hobbes says facetiously of himself, in French sols or Spanish maravedis, he could persuade himself that Crœsus or Crassus were by no means richer than himself; and when he alludes to his property, he considers wisdom to be his real wealth:—

> "An quàm dives, id est, quàm sapiens fuerim?"

He gave up his patrimonial estate to his brother, not wanting it himself; but he tells the tale himself, and adds, that though small in extent, it was rich in its crops. Anthony Wood, with unusual delight, opens the character of Hobbes: "Though he hath an ill name from some, and good from others, yet he was a person endowed with an excellent philosophical soul, was a contemner of riches, money, envy, the world, &c.; a severe lover of justice, and endowed with great morals; cheerful, open, and free of his discourse, yet without offence to any, which he endeavoured always to avoid." What an enchanting picture of the old man in the green vigour of his age has Cowley sent down to us!

> "Nor can the snow which now cold age does shed
>   Upon thy reverend head,
> Quench or allay the noble fires within;
>   But all which thou hast been,
> And all that youth can be, thou'rt yet:
>   So fully still dost thou
> Enjoy the manhood and the bloom of wit,
>   And all the natural heat, but not the fever too.
> So contraries on Ætna's top conspire:
>   Th' embolden'd snow next to the flame does sleep.—
> To things immortal time can do no wrong:
> And that which never is to die, for ever must be young."

his life with more dignity than he did his life itself; for his mind seems always to have been greater than his actions. He appeals to his friends for the congruity of his life with his writings; for his devotion to justice; and for a generous work, which no miser could have planned; and closes thus:—

> And now complete my four-and-eighty years,
> Life's lengthen'd plot is o'er, and the last scene appears.*

Of the works of Hobbes we must not conclude, as Hume tells us, that "they have fallen into neglect;" nor, in the style with which they were condemned at Oxford, that "they are pernicious and damnable." The sanguine opinion of the author himself was, that the mighty "Leviathan" will stand for all ages, defended by its own strength; for the rule of justice, the reproof of the ambitious, the citadel of the Sovereign, and the peace of the people.† But the smaller treatises of Hobbes

---

* "Ipse meos nôsti, Verdusi candide, mores,
    Et tecum cuncti qui mea scripta legunt:
Nam mea vita meis non est incongrua scriptis;
    Justitiam doceo, Justitiamque colo.
Improbus esse potest nemo qui non sit avarus,
    Nec pulchrum quisquam fecit avarus opus.
Octoginta ego jam complevi et quatuor annos;
    Pene acta est vitæ fabula longa meæ."

† Hobbes, in his metrical (by no means his poetical) life, says, the more the "Leviathan" was written against, the more it was read; and adds,

> "Firmiùs inde stetit, spero stabitque per omne
>   Ævum, defensus viribus ipse suis.
> Justitiæ mensura, atque ambitionis elenchus,
>   Regum arx, pax populo, si doceatur, erit."

The term *arx* is here peculiarly fortunate, according to the system of the author—it means a citadel or fortified place on an eminence, to which the people might fly for their common safety.

His works were much read; as appears by "The Court Burlesqued," a satire attributed to Butler.

are not less precious. Locke is the pupil of Hobbes, and it may often be doubtful whether the scholar has rivalled the nervous simplicity and the energetic originality of his master.

The genius of Hobbes was of the first order; his works abound with the most impressive truths, in all the simplicity of thought and language, yet he never elevates nor delights. Too faithful an observer of the miserable human nature before him, he submits to expedients; he acts on the defensive; and because he is in terror, he would consider security to be the happiness of man. In *Religion* he would stand by an established one; yet thus he deprives man of that moral freedom which God himself has surely allowed us. Locke has the glory of having first given distinct notions of the nature of toleration. In *Politics* his great principle is the establishment of *Authority*, or, as he terms it, an "entireness of sovereign power:" here he seems to have built his arguments with such eternal truths and with such a contriving wisdom as to adapt his system to all the changes of government. Hobbes found it necessary in his day to

> "So those who wear the holy robes
> That rail so much at *Father Hobbs*,
> Because he has exposed of late
> *The nakedness of Church and State;*
> Yet tho' they do his books condemn,
> They love to buy and read the same."

Our author, so late as in 1750, was still so commanding a genius, that his works were collected in a handsome folio: but that collection is not complete. When he could not get his works printed at home, he published them in Latin, including his mathematical works, at Amsterdam, by Blaew, 1668, 4to. His treatises, "De Cive," and "On Human Nature," are of perpetual value. Gassendi recommends these admirable works, and Puffendorff acknowledges the depth of his obligations. The Life of Hobbes in the "Biographia Britannica," by Dr. Campbell, is a work of curious research.

place this despotism in the hands of his colossal monarch; and were Hobbes now living, he would not relin-
quish the principle, though perhaps he might vary the
application; for if Authority, strong as man can create
it, is not suffered to exist in our free constitution, what
will become of our freedom? Hobbes would now maintain his system by depositing his " entireness of sovereign
power" in the Laws of his Country. So easily shifted
is the vast political machine of the much abused " Leviathan!" The *Citizen* of Hobbes, like the *Prince* of
Machiavel, is alike innocent, when the end of their
authors is once detected, amid those ambiguous means
by which the hard necessity of their times constrained
their mighty genius to disguise itself.

It is, however, remarkable of *Systems of Opinions*,
that the founder's celebrity has usually outlived his
sect's. Why are systems, when once brought into practice, so often discovered to be fallacies? It seems to me
the natural progress of system-making. A genius of
this order of invention long busied with profound observations and perpetual truths, would appropriate to
himself this assemblage of his ideas, by stamping his
individual mark on them; for this purpose he strikes out
some mighty paradox, which gives an apparent connexion to them all: and to this paradox he forces all
parts into subserviency. It is a minion of the fancy,
which his secret pride supports, not always by the most
scrupulous means. Hence the system itself, with all its
novelty and singularity, turns out to be nothing more
than an ingenious deception carried on for the glory of
the inventor; and when his followers perceive they were
the dupes of his ingenuity, they are apt, in quitting the
system, to give up all; not aware that the parts are as
true as the whole together is false; the sagacity of Genius collected the one, but its vanity formed the other!

HOBBES'S QUARRELS

WITH

DR. WALLIS THE MATHEMATICIAN.

HOBBES'S passion for the study of Mathematics began late in life—
attempts to be an original discoverer—attacked by Wallis—various
replies and rejoinders—nearly maddened by the opposition he encountered—after four years of truce. the war again renewed—
character of Hobbes by Dr. Wallis, a specimen of invective and
irony; serving as a remarkable instance how the greatest genius
may come down to us disguised by the arts of an adversary—
Hobbes's noble defence of himself; of his own great reputation; of
his politics; and of his religion—a literary stratagem of his—reluctantly gives up the contest, which lasted twenty years.

THE Mathematical War between Hobbes and the
celebrated Dr. Wallis is now to be opened. A series
of battles, the renewed campaigns of more than twenty
years, can be described by no term less eventful. Hobbes
himself considered it as a war, and it was a war of idle
ambition, in which he took too much delight. His
"Amata Mathemata" became his pride, his pleasure,
and at length his shame. He attempted to maintain his
irruption into a province he ought never to have entered
in defiance, by "a new method;" but having invaded
the powerful natives, he seems to have almost repented
the folly, and retires, leaving "the unmanageable brutes"
to themselves:

> Ergo meam statuo non ultra perdere opellam
> Indocile expectans discere posse pecus.

His language breathes war, while he sounds his retreat, and confesses his repulse. The Algebraists had all
declared against the Invader.

Wallisius contra pugnat; victusquo videbar
Algebristarum Theiologumque scholis,
Et simul eductus Castris exercitus omnis
Pugnæ securus Wallisianus ovat.

And,

Pugna placet vertor—
Bella mea audisti—&c.

So that we have sufficient authority to consider this Literary Quarrel as a war, and a "Bellum Peloponnesiacum" too, for it lasted as long. Political, literary, and even personal feelings were called in to heat the temperate blood of two Mathematicians.

What means this tumult in a Vestal's veins?

Hobbes was one of the many victims who lost themselves in squaring the circle, and doubling the cube. He applied, late in life, to mathematical studies, not so much, he says, to learn the subtile demonstrations of its figures, as to acquire those habits of close reasoning, so useful in the discovery of new truths, to prove or to refute. So justly he reasoned on mathematics; but so ill he practised the science, that it made him the most unreasonable being imaginable, for he resisted mathematical demonstration itself!*

His great and original character could not but prevail in everything he undertook; and his egotism tempted him to raise a name in the world of Science, as he had in that of Politics and Morals. With the ardour of a young mathematician, he exclaimed, "*Eureka!*" "I have found

* The origin of his taste for mathematics was purely accidental; begun in love, it continued to dotage. According to Aubrey, he was forty years old when, "being in a gentleman's library, Euclid's Elements lay open at the 47th Propos. lib. i., which, having read, he swore 'This is impossible!' He read the demonstration, which referred him back to another—at length he was convinced of that truth. This made him in love with geometry. I have heard Mr. Hobbes say that he was wont to draw lines on his thighs and on the sheets a-bed."

it." The quadrature of the circle was indeed the common Dulcinea of the Quixotes of the time; but they had all been disenchanted. Hobbes alone clung to his ridiculous mistress. Repeatedly confuted, he was perpetually resisting old reasonings and producing new ones. Were only genius requisite for an able mathematician, Hobbes had been among the first; but patience and docility, not fire and fancy, are necessary. His reasonings were all paralogisms, and he had always much to say, from not understanding the subject of his inquiries.

When Hobbes published his "De Corpore Philosophico," 1655, he there exulted that he had solved the great mystery. Dr. Wallis, the Savilian professor of mathematics at Oxford,* with a deep aversion to Hobbes's political and religious sentiments, as he understood them, rejoiced to see this famous combatant descending into his own arena. He certainly was eager to meet him single-handed; for he instantly confuted Hobbes, by his " Elenchus Geometriæ Hobbianæ." Hobbes, who saw the newly-acquired province of his mathematics in dan-

---

* The author of the excellent Latin grammar of the English language, so useful to every student in Europe, of which work that singular patriot, Thomas Hollis, printed an edition, to present to all the learned Institutions of Europe. Henry Stubbe, the celebrated physician of Warwick, to whom the reader has been introduced, joined, for he loved a quarrel, in the present controversy, when it involved philosophical matters, siding with Hobbes, because he hated Wallis. In his "Oneirocritica, or an Exact Account of the Grammatical Parts of this Controversy," he draws a strong character of Wallis, who was indeed a great mathematician, and one of the most extraordinary decypherers of letters ; for perhaps no new system of character could bo invented for which he could not make a key; by which means he had rendered the most important services to the Parliament. Stubbe quaintly describes him as "the sub-scribe to the tribe of Adoniram " (i. e. Adoniram Byfield, who, with this cant name, was scribe to tho fanatical Assembly of Divines), and "as the glory and pride of the Presbyterian faction."

ger, and which, like every new possession, seemed to
involve his honour more than was necessary, called on
all the world to be witnesses of this mighty conflict.
He now published his work in English, with a sarcastic
addition, in a magisterial tone, of "*Six Lessons to the
Professors of Mathematics in Oxford.*" These were
Seth Ward* and Wallis, both no friends to Hobbes, and
who hungered after him as a relishing morsel. Wallis now
replied in English, by "Due Correction for Mr. Hobbes,
or School-discipline for not saying his Lessons Right,"
1656. That part of controversy which is usually the last
had already taken place in their choice of phrases."†

* Dr. Seth Ward, after the Restoration made Bishop of Salisbury,
said, some years before this event was expected, that "he had rather
be the author of one of Hobbes's books than be king of England." But
afterwards he seemed not a little inclined to cry out *Crucifige!* He
who, to one of these books, the admirable treatise on "Human Nature," had prefixed one of the highest panegyrics Hobbes could receive!—*Athen. Oxon.* vol. ii. p. 617.

† It is mortifying to read *such language* between two mathematicians,
in the calm inquiries of square roots, and the finding of mean propor-
tionals between two straight lines. I wish the example may prove a
warning. Wallis thus opens on Hobbes:—"It seems, Mr. Hobbes,
that you have a mind to *say your lesson*, and that the mathematic professors of Oxford should *hear* you. You are too old to learn, though
you have as much need as those that be younger, and yet will think
much to be whipped.

"What moved you to say your lessons in English, when the books
against which you do chiefly intend them were written in Latin? Was
it chiefly for the perfecting your natural rhetoric whenever you thought
it convenient to repair to Billingsgate?—You found that the oyster-
women could not teach you to rail in Latin. Now you can, upon all
occasion, or without occasion, give the titles of *fool, beast, ass, dog,*
&c., which I take to be but barking; and they are no better than a
man might have at Billingsgate for a box o' the ear.

"You tell us, 'though the beasts that think our railing to be roar-
ing have for a time admired us; yet now you have showed them our
ears, they will be less affrighted.' Sir, those persons (the professors
themselves) needed not the sight of *your ears,* but could tell by the

In the following year the campaign was opened by
Hobbes with "ΣΤΙΓΜΑΙ; or, *marks* of the absurd
Geometry, *rural Language*, Scottish Church-politics,
and Barbarisms, of John Wallis." Quick was the rout-
ing of these fresh forces; not one was to escape alive !
for Wallis now took the field with "Hobbiani Puncti
dispunctio! or, the undoing of Mr. Hobbes's Points;
in answer to Mr. Hobbes's ΣΤΙΓΜΑΙ, *id est*, Stigmata
Hobbii." Hobbes seems now to have been reduced to
great straits; perhaps he wondered at the obstinacy of
his adversary. It seems that Hobbes, who had been
used to other studies, and who confesses all the algebraists were against him, could not conceive a point to
exist without quantity; or a line could be drawn without latitude; or a superficies be without depth or thickness; but mathematicians conceive them without these
qualities, when they exist abstractedly in the mind;
though, when for the purposes of science they are produced to the senses, they necessarily have all the qualities. It was understanding these figures, in the vulgar
way, which led Hobbes into a labyrinth of confusions
and absurdities.* They appear to have nearly maddened
the clear and vigorous intellect of our philosopher; for
he exclaims, in one of these writings :—

" I alone am mad, or they are all out of their senses :
so that no third opinion can be taken, unless any will
say that we are all mad."

Four years of truce were allowed to intervene between
the next battle; when the irrefutable Hobbes, once more
collecting his weak and his incoherent forces, arranged

voice what kind of creature *brayed* in your books: you dared not have
said this to their faces."—He bitterly says of Hobbes, that "he is a
man who is always writing what was answered before he had written."

* Dr. Campbell's art. on Hobbes, in " Biog. Brit." p. 2619.

them, as well as he was able, into "Six Dialogues,"
1661. The utter annihilation he intended for his antag-
onist fell on himself. Wallis borrowing the character of
"The Self-tormentor" from Terence, produced "Hobbius
Heauton-timorumenos (Hobbes the Self-tormentor); or, a
Consideration of Mr. Hobbes's Dialogues; addressed to
Robert Boyle," 1662.

This attack of Wallis is of a very opposite character
to the arid discussion of abstract blunders in geometry.
He who began with points, and doubling the cube, and
squaring the circle, now assumes a loftier tone, and
carrying his personal and moral feelings into a mere
controversy between two idle mathematicians, he has
formed a solemn invective, and edged it with irony. I
hope the reader has experienced sufficient interest in the
character of Hobbes to read the long, but curious extract
I shall now transcribe, with that awe and reverence
which the old man claims. It will show how even the
greatest genius may be disguised, when viewed through
the coloured medium of an adversary. One is, however,
surprised to find such a passage in a mathematical work.

"He doth much improve; I mean he doth, *proficere
in pejus;* more, indeed, than I could reasonably have
expected he would have done;—insomuch, that I cannot
but profess some relenting thoughts (though I had
formerly occasion to use him somewhat coarsely), to see
an old man thus fret and torment himself to no purpose.
You, too, should pity your antagonist; not as if he did
deserve it, but because he needs it; and as Chremes, in
Terence, of his Senex, his self-tormenting Menedemus—

> Cum videam miserum hunc tam excruciarier
> Miseret me ejus.   Quod potero adjutabo senem.

"Consider the temper of the man, to move your pity;
a person *extremely passionate and peevish, and wholly*

impatient of contradiction. A temper which, whether it be a greater fault or torment (to one who must so often meet with what he is so ill able to bear), is hard to say.

"And to this fretful humour you must add another as bad, which feeds it. You are therefore next to consider him as *one highly opinionative and magisterial. Fanciful* in his conceptions, and deeply enamoured with those *phantasmes,* without a rival. He doth not spare to profess, upon all occasions, how incomparably he thinks himself to have *surpassed all,* ancient, modern, schools, academies, persons, societies, philosophers, divines, heathens, Christians; how despicable he thinks all their writings in comparison of his; and what hopes he hath, that, by *the sovereign command of some absolute prince, all other doctrines being exploded, his new dictates should be peremptorily imposed, to be alone taught in all schools and pulpits, and universally submitted to.* To recount all which he speaks of himself *magnificently,* and *contemptuously* of others, would fill a volume. Should some idle person read over all his books, and collecting together his arrogant and supercilious speeches, applauding himself, and despising all other men, set them forth in one *synopsis,* with this title, *Hobbius de se*—what a pretty piece of pageantry this would make!

"The admirable sweetness of your own nature has not given you the experience of such a temper; yet your contemplation must have needs discerned it, in those symptoms which you have seen it work in others, like the strange effervescence, ebullition, fumes, and fetors, which you have sometimes given yourself the content to observe, in some active *acrimonious* chymical *spirits* upon the injection of some contrariant *salts* strangely vexing, fretting, and tormenting itself, while it doth but administer *sport* to the unconcerned spectator. Which

temper, being so eminent in the person we have to deal
with, your generous nature, which cannot but pity afflic-
tion, how much soever deserved, must needs have some
compassion for him: who, besides those exquisite *torments* wherewith he doth afflict himself, like that

> ——- quo Siculi non invenere Tyranni
> Tormentum majus—

is unavoidably exposed to those two great *mischiefs ;* an
incapacity to be *taught what he doth not know*, or to be
advised when he thinks amiss ; and moreover, to this
inconvenience, that he must never *hear his faults but
from his adversaries;* for those who are willing to be
reputed *friends* must either not advertise what they see
amiss, or incommode themselves.

"But, you will ask, what need he thus torment himself? What need of pity? If *he have hopes* to be admitted the *sole dictator in philosophy,* civil and natural,
in schools and pulpits, and to be owned as the only *ma-
gister sententiarum,* what would he have more?

"True, *if he have ;* but what *if he have not ?* That
he *had* some hopes of such an honour, he hath not been
sparing to let us know, and was providing against the
envy that might attend it (*nec deprecabor invidiam, sed
augendo, ulciscar,* was his resolution); but I doubt these
hopes are at an end. He did not find (as he expected)
that the *fairies and hobgoblins* (for such he reputes all
that went before him) did vanish presently, upon the
first appearance of his *sunshine :* and, which is worse,
while he was on the one side guarding himself against
envy, he is, on the other side, unhappily *surprised* by a
worse enemy, called *contempt,* and with which he is less
able to grapple.

"I forbear to mention (lest I might seem to reproach
that age which I reverence) the *disadvantages* which he

may sustain by his old age. 'Tis possible that time and age, in a person somewhat *morose*, may have riveted faster that preconceived opinion of his own worth and excellency beyond others. 'Tis possible, also, that he may have *forgotten* much of what once he knew. He may, perhaps, be sometimes more *secure* than *safe;* while trusting to what he thinks a firm foundation, his footing fails him; nor always so vigilant or quicksighted as to discern the *incoherence* or *inconsequence* of his own discourses; unwilling, notwithstanding, to make use of the eyes of other men, lest he should seem thereby to disparage his own; but certainly (though his *will* may be as good as ever) his *parts* are less vegete and nimble, as to *invention* at least, than in his younger days.

"While he had endeavoured only to *raise an expectation*, or put the world in hopes of what great things he had in hand (*to render all philosophy as clear and certain as Euclid's Elements*), if he had then *died*, it might, perhaps, have been thought by some that the world had been deprived of *a great philosopher*, and learning sustained an invaluable loss, by the abortion of *so desired a piece*. But since that *Partus Montis* is come to light, and found to be no more than what little animals have brought forth, and that *deformed* enough and *unamiable*, he might have sooner gone off the stage with more advantage than now he is like to do; such is the misfortune for a man to *outlive his reputation!*

" By this time, perhaps, you may see cause to *pity* him while you see him *falling*. But if you consider him *tumbling headlong* from so great a height, 'twill make some addition to that *compassion* which doth already begin to work. You are therefore next to consider that when, upon the account of *geometry*, he was unsafely mounted to that height of vanity, he did unhappily fall into the hands of two mathematicians, who have used

him so unmercifully as would have put a person of
greater patience into *passion*, and meeting with such a
temper, have so discomposed him that he hath ever since
talked idly: and to augment the grief, these mathematicians were both divines—he had rather have fallen by
any other hand. These *mathematical divines* (a term
which he had thought incomponible) began to unravel
the wrong end; and while he thought they should have
first *untiled the roof*, and by degrees gone downward,
they strike at the *foundation*, and make the building
tumble all at once; and that in such confusion, that by
dashing one part against another, they make each help
to destroy the whole. They first fall upon his *last reserve*, and rout his *mathematics* beyond a possibility of
rallying; and by *firing his magazine* upon the first as-
sault, make his own weapons *fight against him*. Not
contented herewith, they enter the *breach*, and pursue
the *rout* through his Logics, Physics, Metaphysics, Theology, where they find all in confusion."

This invective and irony from this celebrated mathematician, so much out of the path of his habitual studies,
might have proved a tremendous blow; but the genius
of Hobbes was invulnerable to mere human opposition,
unless accompanied by the supernatural terrors of penal
fires or perpetual dungeons. Our hero received the
whole discharge of this battering train, and stood invulnerable, while he returned the fire in "Considerations
upon the Reputation, Loyalty, Manners, and Religion of
Thomas Hobbes, of Malmesbury, written by way of
Letter to a learned person, Dr. Wallis," 1662.

It is an extraordinary production. His lofty indignation retorts on the feeble irony of his antagonist with
keen and caustic accusations; and the green strength of
youth was still seen in the old man whose head was
covered with snows.

From this spirited apology for himself I shall give
some passages. Hobbes thus replied to Dr. Wallis, who
affected to consider the old man as a fit object for com-
miseration.

" You would make him contemptible, and move Mr.
Boyle to pity him. This is a way of railing too much
beaten to be thought witty: besides, 'tis no argument of
your contempt to spend upon him so many angry lines,
as would have furnished you with a dozen of sermons.
If you had in good earnest despised him, you would
have let him alone, as he does Dr. Ward, Mr. Baxter,
Pike, and others, that have reviled him as you do. As
for his reputation beyond the seas, it fades not yet ; and
because, perhaps, you have no means to know it, I will cite
you a passage of an epistle written by a learned French-
man to an eminent person in France, in a volume of
epistles." Hobbes quotes the passage at length, in which
his name appears joined with Galileo, Descartes, Bacon,
and Gassendi.

In reply to Wallis' sarcastic suggestion that an idle
person should collect together Hobbes's arrogant and
supercilious speeches applauding himself, under one title,
Hobbius de se, he says—

" Let your idle person do it ; Mr. Hobbes shall acknowledge them under his hand, and be commended for
it, and you scorned. A certain Roman senator having
propounded something in the assembly of the people,
which they, misliking, made a noise at, boldly bade
them hold their peace, and told them he knew better
what was good for the commonwealth than all they ;
and his words are transmitted to us as an argument of
his virtue ; *so much do truth and vanity alter the complexion of self-praise.* You can have very little skill in
morality, that cannot see the justice of commending a
man's self, as well as of anything else, in his own defence ;

and it was want of prudence in you to constrain him to a thing that would so much displease you.

"When you make his *age* a reproach to him, and show no cause that might impair the faculties of his mind, but only age, I admire how you saw not that you reproached all old men in the world as much as him, and warranted all young men, at a certain time which they themselves shall define, to call you *fool!* Your dislike of old age you have also otherwise sufficiently signified, in venturing so fairly as you have done to escape it. But that is no great matter to one that hath so many marks upon him of much greater reproaches. By Mr. Hobbes's calculation, that derives prudence from experience, and experience from age, you are a very young man; but, by your own reckoning, you are older already than Methuselah."

"During the late trouble, who made both Oliver and the people mad but the preachers of your principles? But besides the wickedness, see the folly of it. You thought to make them mad, but just to such a degree as should serve your own turn; that is to say, mad, and yet just as wise as yourselves. Were you not very imprudent to think to govern madness!"—p. 15.

"The king was hunted as a partridge in the mountains, and though the hounds have been hanged, yet the hunters were as guilty as they, and deserved no less punishment. And the decypherers (Wallis had decyphered the royal letters),* and all that blew the horn, are to be reckoned among the hunters. Perhaps you would not have had the prey killed, but rather have kept it tame. And yet who can tell? I have read of few kings deprived

* Found in the king's tent at Naseby, and which were written to the queen on important political subjects, in a cypher of which they only had the key. They were afterwards published in a quarto pamphlet, and did much mischief to the royal cause.—ED.

of their power by their own subjects that have lived any
long time after it, for reasons that every man is able to
conjecture."

He closes with a very odd image of the most cynical
contempt :—

" Mr. Hobbes has been always far from provoking any
man, though, when he is provoked, you find his pen as
sharp as yours. All you have said is error and railing;
that is, *stinking wind*, such as a jade lets fly when he is
too hard girt upon a full belly. I have done. I have
considered you now, but will not again, whatsoever preferment any of your friends shall procure you."

These were the pitched battles; but many skirmishes
occasionally took place. Hobbes was even driven to a
ruse de guerre. When he found his mathematical character in the utmost peril, there appeared a pamphlet,
entitled "Lux Mathematica, &c., or, Mathematical Light
struck out from the clashings between Dr. John Wallis,
Professor of Geometry in the celebrated University of
Oxford (celeberrima Academia), and Thomas Hobbes, of
Malmesbury; augmented with many and shining rays
of the Author, R. R." 1672.

Here the victories of Hobbes are trumpeted forth, but
the fact is, that R. R. should have been T. H. It was
Hobbes's own composition! R. R. stood for *Roseti
Repertor*, that is, the Finder of the Rosary, one of the
titles of Hobbes's mathematical discoveries. Wallis
asserts that this R. R. may still serve, for it may answer
his own book, " Roseti Refutator, or the Refuter of
the Rosary."

Poor Hobbes gave up the contest reluctantly; if,
indeed, the controversy may not be said to have lasted
all his life. He acknowledges he was writing to no purpose; and that the medicine was obliged to yield to the
disease.

Sed nil profeci, magnis authoribus Error
Fultus erat, cessit sic Medicina malo.

He seems to have gone down to the grave, in spite of all the reasonings of the geometricians on this side of it, with a firm conviction that its superficies had both depth and thickness.* Such were the fruits of a great genius, entering into a province out of his own territories; and, though a most energetic reasoner, so little skilful in these new studies, that he could never know when he was confuted and refuted.†

---

* The strange conclusions some mathematicians have deduced from their principles concerning the *real quantity of matter*, and the *reality of space*, have been noticed by Pope, in the *Dunciad*:—

"Mad *Mathésis* alone was unconfined,
Too mad for mere material chains to bind:
Now to *pure space* lifts her ecstatic stare;
Now running round *the circle*, finds its *square.*"

Dunciad, Book iv. ver. 31.

† When all animosities had ceased, after the death of Hobbes, I find Dr. Wallis, in a very temperate letter to Tenison, exposing the errors of Hobbes in mathematical studies; Wallis acknowledges that philology had never entered into his pursuits,—in this he had never designed to oppose his superior genius; but it was Hobbes who had too often turned his mathematical into a philological controversy. Wallis has made a just observation on the nature of mathematical truths:—"Hobbes's argumentations are destructive in one part of what is said in another. This is more convincingly evident, and more unpardonable, in mathematics than in other discourses, which are things capable of cogent demonstration, and so evident, that though a good mathematician may be subject to commit an error, yet one who understands but little of it cannot but see a fault when it is showed him."

Wallis was an eminent genius in scientific pursuits. His art of decyphering letters was carried to amazing perfection; and among other phenomena he discovered was that of teaching a young man, born deaf and dumb, to speak plainly. He humorously observes, in one of his letters:—"I am now employed upon another work, as hard almost as to make Mr. Hobbes understand mathematics. It is to teach a person dumb and deaf to speak, and to understand a language."

JONSON AND DECKER.

BEN JONSON appears to have carried his military spirit into the literary republic—his gross convivialities, with anecdotes of the prevalent taste in that age for drinking-bouts—his " Poetaster" a sort of *Dunciad*, besides a personal attack on the frequenters of the theatres, with anecdotes—his Apological Dialogue, which was not allowed to be repeated—characters of Decker and of Marston—Decker's Satiromastix, a parody on Jonson's " Poetaster"—Ben exhibited under the character of " Horace Junior"—specimens of that literary satire ; its dignified remonstrance, and the honourable applause bestowed on the great bard—some foibles in the literary habits of Ben, alluded to by Decker—Jonson's noble reply to his detractors and rivals.

THIS quarrel is a splendid instance how genius of the first order, lavishing its satirical powers on a number of contemporaries, may discover, among the crowd, some individual who may return with a right aim the weapon he has himself used, and who will not want for encouragement to attack the common assailant : the greater genius is thus mortified by a victory conceded to the inferior, which he himself had taught the meaner one to obtain over him.

Jonson, in his earliest productions, " Every Man in his Humour," and " Every Man out of his Humour," usurped that dictatorship, in the Literary Republic, which he so sturdily and invariably maintained, though long and hardily disputed. No bard has more courageously foretold that posterity would be interested in his labours ; and often with very dignified feelings he casts this declaration into the teeth of his adversaries : but a bitter contempt for his brothers and his contemporaries was not less vehement than his affections for those who crowded under his wing. To his " sons" and his ad-

mirers he was warmly attached, and no poet has left
behind him, in MS., so many testimonies of personal
fondness, in the inscriptions and addresses, in the copies
of his works which he presented to friends: of these I
have seen more than one fervent and impressive.

Drummond of Hawthornden, who perhaps carelessly
and imperfectly minuted down the heads of their literary
conference on the chief authors of the age, exposes the
severity of criticism which Ben exercised on some spirits
as noble as his own. The genius of Jonson was rough,
hardy, and invincible, of which the frequent excess
degenerated into ferocity; and by some traditional
tales, this ferocity was still inflamed by large potations:
for Drummond informs us, "Drink was the element in
which he lived."* Old Ben had given on two occasions
some remarkable proofs of his personal intrepidity. When

---

* The gross convivialities of the times, from the age of Elizabeth,
were remarkable for several circumstances. Hard-drinking was a
foreign vice, imported by our military men on their return from the
Netherlands: and the practice, of whose prevalence Camden complains,
was even brought to a kind of science. They had a dialect peculiar
to their orgies. See "Curiosities of Literature," vol ii. p. 294 (last
edition).

Jonson's inclinations were too well suited to the prevalent taste, and
he gave as largely into it as any of his contemporaries. Tavern-habits
were then those of our poets and actors. Ben's *Humours*, at "the
Mermaid," and at a later period, his *Leges Convivales* at "the Apollo,"
the club-room of "the Devil," were doubtless one great cause of a
small personal unhappiness, of which he complains and which had a
very unlucky effect in rendering a mistress so obdurate, who,
"through her eyes had stopt her ears." This was, as his own verse
tells us,

		" His mountain-belly and his rocky face."

He weighed near twenty stone, according to his own avowal—an
Elephant-Cupid! One of his "Sons," at the "Devil," seems to think
that his *Catiline* could not fail to be a miracle, by a certain sort of inspiration which Ben used on the occasion.

a soldier, in the face of both armies, he had fought single-handed with his antagonist, had slain him, and carried off his arms as trophies. Another time he killed his man in a duel. Jonson appears to have carried the same military spirit into the Literary Republic.

> " With strenuous sinewy words that *Catiline* swells,
> I reckon it not among men-miracles.
> How could that poem heat and vigour lack,
> *When each line oft cost* Ben *a cup of sack!*"
>
> R. Baron's *Pocula Castalia*, p. 113, 1650.

Jonson, in the Bacchic phraseology of the day, was "a Canary-bird." "He would (says Aubrey) many times exceed in drink; canary was his beloved liquor; then he would tumble home to bed; and when he had thoroughly perspired, then to study."

Tradition, too, has sent down to us several tavern-tales of " Rare Ben." A good-humoured one has been preserved of the first interview between Bishop Corbet, when a young man, and our great bard. It occurred at a tavern, where Corbet was sitting alone. Ben, who had probably just drank up to the pitch of good fellowship, desired the waiter to take to the gentleman "a quart of *raw* wine; and tell him," he added, "I *sacrifice* my service to him."—"Friend," replied Corbet, "I thank him for his love; but tell him, from me, that he is mistaken; for *sacrifices are always burned.*" This pleasant allusion to the mulled wine of the time by the young wit could not fail to win the affection of the master-wit himself. Harl. MSS. 6395.

Ben is not viewed so advantageously, in an unlucky fit of ebriety recorded by Oldys, in his MS. notes on Langbaine; but his authority is not to me of a suspicious nature: he had drawn it from a MS. collection of Oldisworth's, who appears to have been a curious collector of the history of his times. He was secretary to that strange character, Philip, Earl of Pembroke. It was the custom of those times to form collections of little traditional stories and other good things; we have had lately given to us by the Camden Society an amusing one, from the L'Estrange family, and the MS. already quoted is one of them. There could be no bad motive in recording a tale, quite innocent in itself, and which is further confirmed by Isaac Walton, who, without alluding to the tale, notices that Jonson parted from Sir Walter Raleigh and his son "not in cold blood." Mr. Gifford, in a MS. note on this work, does not credit this story, it not being accordant with dates. Such stories may not accord with dates or persons, and yet may be

Such a genius would become more tyrannical by success, and naturally provoked opposition, from the prone-
ness of mankind to mortify usurped greatness, when
they can securely do it. The man who hissed the poet's
play had no idea that he might himself become one of
the dramatic personages. Ben then produced his "Poetaster," which has been called the *Dunciad* of those times;
but it is a *Dunciad* without notes. The personages
themselves are now only known by their general resemblance to nature, with the exception of two characters,
those of *Crispinus and Demetrius.**

founded on some substantial fact. I know of no injury to Ben's
poetical character, in showing that he was, like other men, quite incapable of taking care of himself, when he was sunk in the heavy
sleep of drunkenness. It was an age when kings, as our James I.
and his majesty of Denmark, were as often laid under the table as
their subjects. My motive for preserving the story is the incident
respecting *carrying men in baskets:* it was evidently a custom, which
perhaps may have suggested the memorable adventure of Falstaff.
It was a convenient mode of conveyance for those who were incapable
of taking care of themselves before the invention of hackney coaches,
which was of later date, in Charles the First's reign.

Camden recommended Jonson to Sir Walter Raleigh as a tutor to
his son, whose gay humours not brooking the severe studies of Jonson, took advantage of his foible, to degrade him in the eyes of his
father, who, it seems, was remarkable for his abstinence from wine:
though, if another tale be true, he was no common sinner in "the
true Virginia." Young Raleigh contrived to give Ben a surfeit, which
threw the poet into a deep slumber; and then the pupil maliciously
procured a buck-basket, and a couple of men, who carried our Ben to
Sir Walter, with a message that "their young master had sent home
his tutor." There is nothing improbable in the story; for the circumstance of *carrying drunken men in baskets* was a usual practice. In the
Harleian MS. quoted above, I find more than one instance; I will
give one. An alderman, carried in *a porter's basket*, at his own door,
is thrown out of it in a *qualmish* state. The man, to frighten away the
passengers, and enable the grave citizen to creep in unobserved, exclaims, that the man had the *falling sickness!*

* These were Marston and Decker, but as is usual with these sort
of caricatures, the originals sometimes mistook their likenesses. They

In "The Poetaster," Ben, with flames too long smoth-
ered, burst over the heads of all rivals and detractors.
His enemies seem to have been among all classes; per-

were both town-wits, and cronies, of much the same stamp; by a
careful perusal of their works, the editor of Jonson has decided that
Marston was Crispinus. With him Jonson had once lived on the
most friendly terms: afterwards the great poet quarrelled with both,
or they with him.

Dryden, in the preface to his "Notes and Observations on the Empress of Morocco," in his quarrel with Settle, which has been sufficiently narrated by Dr. Johnson, felt, when poised against this miserable
rival, who had been merely set up by a party to mortify the superior
genius, as Jonson had felt when pitched against *Crispinus*. It is thus
that literary history is so interesting to authors. How often, in recording the fates of others, it reflects their own! "I know indeed
(says Dryden) that to write against him was to do him too great an
honour: but I considered Ben Jonson had done it before to Decker,
our author's predecessor, whom he chastised in his Poetaster, under
the character of *Crispinus*." Langbaine tells us the subject of the
"Satiromastix" of Decker, which I am to notice, was "the witty Ben
Jonson;" and with this agree all the notices I have hitherto met with
respecting "the Horace Junior" of Decker's *Satiromastix*. Mr. Gilchrist has published two curious pamphlets on Jonson; and in the
last, p. 56, he has shown that Decker was "the poet ape of Jonson,"
and that he avenged himself under the character of *Crispinus* in his
"Satiromastix:" to which may be added, that the *Fannius*, in the same
satirical comedy, is probably his friend Marston.

Jonson allowed himself great liberty in *personal satire*, by which,
doubtless, he rung an alarum to a waspish host; he lampooned *Inigo
Jones*, the great machinist and architect. The lampoons are printed
in Jonson's works [but not in their entirety. The great architect had
sufficient court influence to procure them to be cancelled; and the
character of *In-and-in Medley*, in "The Tale of a Tub," has come down
to us with no other satirical personal traits than a few fantastical ex-
pressions]; and I have in MS. an answer by Inigo Jones, in verse, so
pitiful that I have not printed it. That he condescended to bring obscure individuals on the stage, appears by his character of *Carlo
Buffoon*, in *Every Man out of his Humour*. He calls this "a second un-
truss," and was censured for having drawn it from personal revenge.
The Aubrey Papers, recently published, have given us the character
of this *Carlo Buffoon*, "one Charles Chester, a bold impertinent fellow;

sonages recognised on the scene as soon as viewed; poetical, military, legal, and histrionic. It raised a host in arms. Jonson wrote an apologetical epilogue, breathing a firm spirit, worthy of himself; but its dignity was too haughty to be endured by contemporaries, whom genius must soothe by equality. This apologetical dialogue was never allowed to be repeated; now we may do it with pleasure. Writings, like pictures, require a particular light and distance to be correctly judged and inspected, without any personal inconvenience.

One of the dramatic personages in this epilogue inquires:

> I never saw the play breed all this tumult,
> What was there in it could so deeply offend,
> And stir so many hornets?

The author replies:

> ———— I never writ that piece
> More innocent, or empty of offence:
> Some salt it had, but neither tooth nor gall.
> ———— Why, they say you tax'd
> The law and lawyers, captains, and the players,
> By their particular names.
> ———— It is not so:
> I used no names. My books have still been taught
> To spare the persons, and to speak the vices.

---

and they could never be at quiet for him; a perpetual talker, and made a noise like a drum in a room. So one time at a tavern Sir Walter Raleigh beats him, and seals up his mouth; i. e., his upper and nether beard, with hard wax."—p. 514. Such a character was no unfitting object for dramatic satire. Mr. Gilchrist's pamphlets defended Jonson from the frequent accusations raised against him for the freedom of his muse, in such portraits after the life. Yet even our poet himself does not deny their truth, while he excuses himself. In the dedication of "The Fox," to the two Universities, he boldly asks, "Where have I been particular? Where personal?—Except to a mimic, cheater, bawd, buffoon, creatures (for their insolencies) worthy to be taxed." The mere list he here furnishes us with would serve to crowd one of the "twopenny audiences" in the small theatres of that day.

And he proceeds to tell us, that to obviate this accusation, he had placed his scenes in the age of Augustus.

> To show that Virgil, Horace, and the rest
> Of those great master-spirits, did not want
> Detractors then, or practisers against them:
> And by this line, although no parallel,
> I hoped at last they would sit down and blush.

But instead of their "sitting down and blushing," we find—

> That they fly buzzing round about my nostrils;
> And, like so many, screaming grasshoppers
> Held by the wings, fill every ear with noise.

Names were certainly not necessary to portraits, where every day the originals were standing by their side. This is the studied pleading of a poet, who knows he is concealing the truth.

There is a passage in the play itself where Jonson gives the true cause of "the tumult" raised against him. Picturing himself under the character of his favourite Horace, he makes the enemies of Horace thus describe him, still, however, preserving the high tone of poetical superiority.

"Alas, sir, Horace is a mere sponge. Nothing but humours and observations he goes up and down sucking from every society, and when he comes home squeezes himself dry again. He will pen all he knows. He will sooner lose his best friend than his least jest. What he once drops upon paper against a man, lives eternally to upbraid him."

Such is the true picture of a town-wit's life! The age of Augustus was much less present to Jonson than his own; and Ovid, Tibullus, and Horace were not the personages he cared so much about, as "that society in which," it was said, "he went up and down sucking in and squeezing himself dry:" the formal lawyers, who were cold to his genius; the sharking captains, who would not draw to save their own swords, and would cheat "their friend, or their friend's friend," while they would bully down Ben's genius; and the little sycophant histrionic, "the twopenny* tear-mouth, copper-laced scoundrel, stiff-toe, who used to travel with pumps full of gravel after a blind jade and a hamper, and stalk upon boards and barrel-heads to an old crackt trumpet;" and who all now made a party with some rival of Jonson.

All these personages will account for "the tumult" which excites the innocent astonishment of our author. These only resisted him by "filling every ear with noise." But one of the "screaming grasshoppers held by the wings," boldly turned on the holder with a scorpion's bite; and Decker, who had been lashed in "The Poetaster," produced his "Satiromastix, or the untrussing of the humorous Poet." Decker was a subordinate author, indeed; but, what must have been very galling to Jonson, who was the aggressor, indignation proved such an inspirer, that Decker seemed to have caught some portion of Jonson's own genius, who had the art of making even Decker popular; while he discovered that his own laurel-wreath had been dexterously changed by the "Satiromastix" into a garland of "stinging nettles."

In "The Poetaster," *Crispinus* is the picture of one of those impertinent fellows who resolve to become poets, having an equal aptitude to become anything that is in fashionable request. When Hermogenes, the finest singer in Rome, refused to sing, *Crispinus* gladly seizes the occasion, and whispers the lady near him—"Entreat the ladies to entreat me to sing, I beseech you." This character is marked by a ludicrous peculiarity which, turning on an individual characteristic, must have assisted the

* Alluding, no doubt, to the price of seats at some of the minor theatres.

audience in the true application. Probably Decker had
some remarkable head of hair,* and that his locks hung
not like "the curls of Hyperion;" for the jeweller's wife
admiring among the company the persons of Ovid, Tibullus, &c., *Crispinus* acquaints her that they were poets,
and, since she admires them, promises to become a poet
himself. The simple lady further inquires, "if, when he
is a poet, his looks will change? and particularly if his
hair will change, and be like those gentlemen's?" "A
man," observes *Crispinus.* "may be a poet, and yet not
change his hair." "Well," exclaims the simple jeweller's
wife, "we shall see your cunning; yet if you can change
your hair, I pray do it."

In two elaborate scenes, poor Decker stands for a full-
length. Resolved to be a poet, he haunts the company
of Horace: he meets him in the street, and discovers all
the variety of his nothingness: he is a student, a stoic,
an architect: everything by turns, "and nothing long."
Horace impatiently attempts to escape from him, but
Crispinus foils him at all points. This affectionate admirer is even willing to go over the world with him. He
proposes an ingenious project, if Horace will introduce
him to Mæcenas. *Crispinus* offers to become "his as-
sistant," assuring him that "he would be content with
the next place, not envying thy reputation with thy
patron;" and he thinks that Horace and himself "would
soon lift out of favour Virgil, Varius, and the best of
them, and enjoy them wholly to ourselves." The rest-
lessness of Horace to extricate himself from this "Hydra
of Discourse," the passing friends whom he calls on to assist him, and the glue-like pertinacity of *Crispinus*, are
richly coloured.

* It was the fashion with the poets connected with the theatre to
wear long hair. Nashe censures Greene "for his fond (foolish) disguising of a Master of Arts (which was Greene's degree) with ruffianly
hair."—ED.

A ludicrous and exquisitely satirical scene occurs at the trial of *Crispinus* and his colleagues. Jonson has here introduced an invention, which a more recent satirist so happily applied to our modern Lexiphanes, Dr. Johnson, for his immeasurable polysyllables. Horace is allowed by Augustus to make *Crispinus* swallow a certain pill; the light vomit discharges a great quantity of hard matter, to clear

> His brain and stomach of their tumorous heats.

These consist of certain affectations in style, and adulteration of words, which offended the Horatian taste: "the basin" is called quickly for and *Crispinus* gets rid easily of some, but others were of more difficult passage :—

> 'Magnificate!' that came up somewhat hard!
> *Crispinus.* 'O barmy froth——'
> *Augustus.* What's that?
> *Crispinus.* 'Inflate!—Turgidous!—and Ventositous'—
> *Horace.* 'Barmy froth, inflate, turgidous, and ventosity' are come up.
> *Tibullus.* O terrible windy words!
> *Gallus.* A sign of a windy brain.

But all was not yet over: "Prorumpt" made a terrible rumbling, as if his spirit was to have gone with it; and there were others which required all the kind assistance of the Horatian "light vomit." This satirical scene closes with some literary admonitions from the grave Virgil, who details to *Crispinus* the wholesome diet to be observed after his surfeits, which have filled

> His blood and brain thus full of crudities.

Virgil's counsels to the vicious neologist, who debases the purity of English diction by affecting new words or phrases, may too frequently be applied.

> You must not hunt for wild outlandish terms
> To stuff out a peculiar dialect;
> But let your matter run before your words.

> And if at any time you chance to meet
> Some Gallo-Belgick phrase, you shall not straight
> Rack your poor verse to give it entertainment,
> But let it pass; and do not think yourself
> Much damnified, if you do leave it out,
> When not the sense could well receive it.

Virgil adds something which breathes all the haughty spirit of Ben: he commands *Crispinus :*

> ———— Henceforth, learn
> To bear yourself more humbly. nor to swell
> Or breathe your insolent and idle spite
> On him whose laughter can your worst affright:

and dismisses him

> To some dark place, removed from company;
> He will talk idly else after his physic.

"The Satiromastix" may be considered as a parody on "The Poetaster." Jonson, with classical taste, had raised his scene in the court of Augustus: Decker, with great unhappiness, places it in that of William Rufus. The interest of the piece arises from the dexterity with which Decker has accommodated those very characters which Jonson has satirised in his "Poetaster." This gratified those who came every day to the theatre, delighted to take this mimetic revenge on the arch bard.

In Decker's prefatory address "To the World," he observes, "Horace haled his Poetasters to the bar;* the Poetasters untrussed Horace: Horace made himself believe that his Burgonian wit† might desperately chal-

---

* Alluding to the trial of the Poetasters, which takes place before Augustus and his poetical jury of Virgil, Ovid, Tibullus, &c., in Ben's play.

† Decker alludes here to the bastard of Burgundy, who considered himself unmatchable, till he was overthrown in Smithfield by Woodville, Earl Rivers.

lenge all comers, and that none durst take up the foils against him." But Decker is the Earl Rivers! He had been blamed for the personal attacks on Jonson; for "whipping his fortunes and condition of life; where the more noble reprehension had been of his mind's deformity;" but for this he retorts on Ben. Some censured Decker for barrenness of invention, in bringing on those characters in his own play whom Jonson had stigmatised; but "it was not improper," he says, "to set the same dog upon Horace, whom Horace had set to worry others." Decker warmly concludes with defying the Jonsonians.

"Let that mad dog Detraction bite till his teeth be worn to the stumps; Envy, feed thy snakes so fat with poison till they burst; World, let all thy adders shoot out their Hydra-headed forked stings! I thank thee, thou true Venusian Horace, for these good words thou givest me. *Populus me sibilat, at mihi plaudo.*"

The whole address is spirited. Decker was a very popular writer, whose numerous tracts exhibit to posterity a more detailed narrative of the manners of the town in the Elizabethan age than is elsewhere to be found.

In Decker's Satiromastix, Horace junior is first exhibited in his study, rehearsing to himself an ode: suddenly the Pindaric rapture is interrupted by the want of a rhyme; this is satirically applied to an unlucky line of Ben's own. One of his "sons," Asinius Bubo, who is blindly worshipping his great idol, or "his Ningle," as he calls him, amid his admiration of Horace, perpetually breaks out into digressive accounts of what sort of a man his friends take him to be. For one, Horace in wrath prepares an epigram: and for *Crispinus* and *Fannius*, brother bards, who threaten "they'll bring your life and death on the stage, as a bricklayer in a play," he says, "I can bring a prepared troop of gallants, who, for

my sake, shall distaste every unsalted line in their fly-
blown comedies." "Ay," replies Asinius, "and all men
of my rank!" *Crispinus*, Horace calls "a light volup-
tuous reveller," and *Fannius* "the slightest cobweb-lawn
piece of a poet." Both enter, and Horace receives them
with all friendship.

The scene is here conducted not without skill. Horace
complains that

> —————————— When I dip my pen
> In distill'd roses, and do strive to drain
> Out of mine ink all gall—
> Mine enemies, with sharp and searching eyes,
> Look through and through me.
> And when my lines are measured out as straight
> As even parallels, 'tis strange, that still,
> Still some imagine that they're drawn awry.
> The error is not mine, but in their eye,
> That cannot take proportions.

To the querulous satirist, *Crispinus* replies with dignified gravity—

> Horace! to stand within the shot of galling tongues
> Proves not your guilt; for, could we write on paper
> Made of these turning leaves of heaven, the clouds,
> Or speak with angels' tongues, yet wise men know
> That some would shake the head, though saints should sing;
> Some snakes must hiss, because they're born with stings.
> ——— ——— ——— Be not you grieved
> If that which you mould fair, upright, and smooth,
> Be screw'd awry, made crooked, lame, and vile,
> By racking comments.—
> So to be bit it rankles not, for Innocence
> May with a feather brush off the foul wrong.
> But when your *dastard wit will strike at men*
> *In corners, and in riddles fold the vices*
> *Of your best friends, you must not take to heart*
> If they take off all gilding from their pills,
> And only offer you the bitter core.—

At this the galled Horace winces. *Crispinus* continues, that it is in vain Horace swears, that

> ————————— He puts on
> The office of an executioner,
> Only to strike off the swoln head of sin
> Where'er you find it standing. Say you swear,
> And make damnation, parcel of your oath,
> That when your lashing jests make all men bleed,
> Yet you whip none—court, city, country, friends,
> Foes, all must smart alike.—

Fannius, too, joins, and shows Ben the absurd oaths he takes, when he swears to all parties, that he does not mean them. How, then, of five hundred and four, five hundred

> Should all point with their fingers in one instant,
> At one and the same man?

Horace is awkwardly placed between these two friendly remonstrants, to whom he promises perpetual love.

Captain Tucca, a dramatic personage in Jonson's Poetaster, and a copy of his own Bobadil, whose original the poet had found at " Powles," the fashionable lounge of that day, is here continued with the same spirit; and as that character permitted from the extravagance of its ribaldry, it is now made the vehicle for those more personal retorts, exhibiting the secret history of Ben, which perhaps twitted the great bard more than the keenest wit, or the most solemn admonition which Decker could ever attain. Jonson had cruelly touched on Decker being out at elbows, and made himself too merry with the histrionic tribe: he, who was himself a poet, and had been a Thespian! The blustering captain thus attacks the great wit:—" Do'st stare, my Saracen's head at Newgate? I'll march through thy Dunkirk guts, for shooting jests at me." He insists that as Horace, " that sly knave, whose shoulders were once seen lapp'd in a player's old cast cloak," and who had reflected on *Cris-pinus's* satin doublet being ravelled out; that he should wear one of *Crispinus's* "old cast sattin suits," and that *Fannius* should write a couple of scenes for his own "strong garlic comedies," and Horace should swear that they were his own—he would easily bear the "guilt of conscience." "Thy Muse is but a hagler, and wears clothes upon best be trust (a humorous Deckerian phrase) —thou'rt *great* in somebody's books for this!" Did it become Jonson to gibe at the histrionic tribe, who is himself accused of "treading the stage, as if he were treading mortar."* He once put up—"a supplication to be a poor journeyman player, and hadst been still so, but that thou couldst not set *a good face* upon't. Thou hast forget how thou ambled'st in leather-pilch, by a play-waggon in the highway; and took'st mad Jeronimo's part, to get service among the mimics," &c.

Ben's person was, indeed, not gracious in the playfulness of love or fancy. A female, here, thus delineates Ben :—

"That same Horace has the most ungodly face, by my fan; it looks for all the world like a rotten russet-apple, when 'tis bruised. It's better than a spoonful of cinnamon-water next my heart, for me to hear him speak; he sounds it so i' th' nose, and talks and rants like the poor fellows under Ludgate—to see his face make faces, when he reads his songs and sonnets."

Again, we have Ben's face compared with that of his favourite, Horace's—"You staring Leviathan! look on the sweet visage of Horace; look, parboil'd face, look—

---

* Horace acknowledges he played Zulziman at Paris-garden. "Sir Vaughan: Then, master Horace, you played the part of an honest man—"

Tucca exclaims: "Death of Hercules! he could never play that part well in 's life!"

he has not his face punchtfull of eyelet-holes, like the cover of a warming-pan."

Joseph Warton has oddly remarked that most of our poets were handsome men. Jonson, however, was not poetical on that score; though his bust is said to resemble Menander's.

Such are some of the personalities with which Decker recriminated.

Horace is thrown into many ludicrous situations. He is told that "admonition is good meat." Various persons bring forward their accusations; and Horace replies that they envy him,

> Because I hold more worthy company.

The greatness of Ben's genius is by no means denied by his rivals; and Decker makes *Fannius* reply, with noble feelings, and in an elevated strain of poetry :—

> Good Horace, no! my cheeks do blush for thine,
> As often as thou speakst so; where one true
> And nobly virtuous spirit, for thy best part
> Loves thee, I wish one, ten; even from my heart!
> I make account, I put up as deep share
> In any good man's love, which thy worth earns,
> As thou thyself; we envy not to see
> Thy friends with bays to crown thy poesy.
> No, here the gall lies:—We, that know what stuff
> Thy very heart is made of, know the stalk
> On which thy learning grows, and can give life
> To thy, once dying, baseness; yet must we
> Dance anticke on your paper —.
> But were thy warp'd soul put in a new mould,
> I'd wear thee as a jewel set in gold.

To which one adds, that "jewels, master Horace, must be hanged, you know." This "Whip of Men," with Asinius his admirer, are brought to court, transformed into satyrs, and bound together; "not lawrefied, but nettle-fied;" crowned with a wreath of nettles.

With stinging-nettles crown his stinging wit.

Horace is called on to swear, after Asinius had sworn to give up his "Ningle."

"Now, master Horace, you must be a more horrible swearer; for your oath must be, like your wits, of many colours; and like a broker's book, of many parcels."

Horace offers to swear till his hairs stand up on end, to be rid of this sting. "Oh, this sting!" alluding to the nettles. "'Tis not your sting of conscience, is it?" asks one. In the inventory of his oaths, there is poignant satire, with strong humour; and it probably exhibits some foibles in the literary habits of our bard.

He swears "Not to hang himself, even if he thought any man could write plays as well as himself; not to bombast out a new play with the old linings of jests stolen from the *Temple's Revels;* not to sit in a gallery, when your comedies have entered their actions, and there make vile and bad faces at every line, to make men have an eye to you, and to make players afraid; not to venture on the stage, when your play is ended, and exchange courtesies and compliments with gallants, to make all the house rise and cry—'That's Horace; that's he that pens and purges humours.' When you bid all your friends to the marriage of a poor couple, that is to say, your Wits and Necessities—*alias*, a poet's Witsunale—you shall swear that, within three days after, you shall not abroad, in bookbinders' shops, brag that your viceroys, or tributary-kings, have done homage to you, or paid quarterage. Moreover, when a knight gives you his passport to travel in and out to his company, and gives you money for God's sake—you will swear not to make scald and wry-mouthed jests upon his knighthood. When your plays are misliked at court, you shall not cry Mew! like a puss-cat, and say, you are glad you write out of the courtier's element; and in brief, when

you sup in taverns, amongst your betters, you shall
swear not to dip your manners in too much sauce; nor,
at table, to fling epigrams or play-speeches about you."
The king observes, that

> ———————— He whose pen
> Draws both corrupt and clear blood from all men
> Careless what vein he pricks; let him not rave
> When his own sides are struck; blows, blows do crave.

Such were the bitter apples which Jonson, still in his
youth, plucked from the tree of his broad satire, that
branched over all ranks in society. That even his intrepidity and hardiness felt the incessant attacks he had
raised about him, appears from the close of the Apologetical Epilogue to "The Poetaster;" where, though he
replies with all the consciousness of genius, and all its
haughtiness, he closes with a determination to give over
the composition of comedies! This, however, like all
the vows of a poet, was soon broken; and his master-
pieces were subsequently produced.

Friend. Will you not answer then the libels?
Author. No.
Friend. Nor the Untrussers?
Author. Neither. ▲
Friend. You are undone, then.
Author. With whom?
Friend. The world.
Author. The bawd!
Friend. It will be taken to be stupidity or tameness in you.
Author. But they that have incensed me, can in soul
Acquit me of that guilt. They know I dare
To spurn or baffle them : or squirt their eyes
With ink or urine: or I could do worse,
Arm'd with Archilochus' fury, write iambicks,
Would make the desperate lashers hang themselves.—

His Friend tells him that he is accused that "all his
writing is mere railing;" which Jonson nobly compares

to " the salt in the old comedy ;" that they say, that he
is slow, and " scarce brings forth a play a year."

> *Author.* ————————— 'Tis true,
> I would they could not say that I did that.

He is angry that their

> ———————— Base and beggarly conceits
> Should carry it, by the multitude of voices,
> Against the most abstracted work, opposed
> To the stufft nostrils of the drunken rout.—

And then exclaims with admirable enthusiasm—

> O this would make a learn'd and liberal soul
> To rive his stained quill up to the back,
> And damn his long-watch'd labours to the fire;
> Things, that were born, when none but the still night,
> And the dumb candle, saw his pinching throes.

And again, alluding to these mimics—

> This 'tis that strikes me silent. seals my lips,
> And apts me rather to sleep out my time,
> Than I would waste it in contemned strifes
> With these vile Ibides, these unclean birds,
> That make their mouths their clysters, and still purge
> From their hot entrails.*   But I leave the monsters
> To their own fate.   And since the Comic Muse

* Among those arts of imitation which man has derived from the
practice of animals, naturalists assure us that he owes *the use of clysters*
to the Egyptian Ibis.   There are some who pretend this medicinal invention comes from the stork.   The French are more like *Ibises* than
we are : *ils se donnent des lavements eux-mêmes.*   But as it is rather uncertain what the Egyptian *Ibis* is ; whether, as translated in Leviticus
xi. 17, the cormorant, or a species of stork, or only " a great owl," as we
find in Calmet ; it would be safest to attribute the invention to the unknown bird.   I recollect, in Wickliffe's version of the Pentateuch,
which I once saw in MS. in the possession of my valued friend Mr.
Douce, that that venerable translator interpolates a little, to tell us
that the Ibis " giveth to herself a purge."

Hath proved so ominous to me, I will try
If Tragedy have a more kind aspect.
Leave me! There's something come into my thought
That must and shall be sung, high and aloof,
Safe from the wolf's black jaw, and the dull ass's hoof.
Friend. I reverence these raptures, and obey them.

Such was the noble strain in which Jonson replied to his detractors in the town and to his rivals about him. Yet this poem, composed with all the dignity and force of the bard, was not suffered to be repeated. It was stopped by authority. But Jonson, in preserving it in his works, sends it "TO POSTERITY, that it may make a difference between their manners that provoked me then, and mine that neglected them ever."

CAMDEN AND BROOKE.

LITERARY, like political history, is interested in the cause of an obscure individual, when deprived of his just rights—character of Camden—Brooke's "Discovery of Errors" in the "Britannia"—his work disturbed in the printing—afterwards enlarged, but never suffered to be published—whether Brooke's motive was personal rancour!—the persecuted author becomes vindictive—his keen reply to Camden—Camden's beautiful picture of calumny—Brooke furnishes a humorous companion-piece—Camden's want of magnanimity and justice—when great authors are allowed to suppress the works of their adversary, the public receives the injury and the insult.

IN the literary as well as the political commonwealth, the cause of an obscure individual violently deprived of his just rights is a common one. We protest against the power of genius itself, when it strangles rather than wrestles with its adversary, or combats in mail against a naked man. The general interests of literature are involved by the illegitimate suppression of a work, of which the purpose is to correct another, whatever may be the invective which accompanies the correction : nor are we always to assign to malignant motives even this spirit of invective, which, though it betrays a contracted genius, may also show the earnestness of an honest one.

The quarrel between Camden, the great author of the " Britannia," and Brooke, the " York Herald," may illustrate these principles. It has hitherto been told to the shame of the inferior genius ; but the history of Brooke was imperfectly known to his contemporaries. Crushed by oppression, his tale was marred in the telling. A century sometimes passes away before the world can discover the truth even of a private history.

Brooke is aspersed as a man of the meanest talents, insensible to the genius of Camden, rankling with envy at his fame, and correcting the "Britannia" out of mere spite.

When the history of Brooke is known, and his labours fairly estimated, we shall blame him much less than he has been blamed ; and censure Camden, who has escaped all censure, and whose conduct, in the present instance, was destitute of magnanimity and justice.

The character of the author of " Britannia " is great, and this error of his feelings, now first laid to his charge, may be attributed as much to the weakness of the age as to his own extreme timidity, and perhaps to a little pride. Conscious as was Camden of enlarged views, we can easily pardon him for the contempt he felt, when he compared them with the subordinate ones of his cynical adversary.

Camden possessed one of those strongly directed minds which early in life plan some vast labour, while their imagination and their industry feed on it for many successive years ; and they shed the flower and sweetness of their lives in the preparation of a work which at its maturity excites the gratitude of their nation. His passion for our national antiquities discovered itself even in his school-days, grew up with him at the University; and, when afterwards engaged in his public duties as master at Westminster school, he there composed his "Britannia," "at spare hours, and on festival days." To the perpetual care of his work, he voluntarily sacrificed all other views in life, and even drew himself away from domestic pleasures; for he refused marriage and preferments, which might interrupt his beloved studies! The work at length produced, received all the admiration due to so great an enterprise; and even foreigners, as the work was composed in the universal language of learning, could sympathise with Britons, when they contemplated the stupendous labour. Camden was honoured by the titles (for the very names of illustrious genius become such), of the Varro, the Strabo, and the Pausanias of Britain.

While all Europe admired the "Britannia," a cynical genius, whose mind seemed bounded by his confined studies, detected one error amidst the noble views the mighty volume embraced; the single one perhaps he could perceive, and for which he stood indebted to his office as "York Herald." Camden, in an appendage to the end of each county, had committed numerous genealogical errors, which he afterwards affected, in his defence, to consider as trivial matters in so great a history, and treats his adversary with all the contempt and bitterness he could inflict on him; but Ralph Brooke entertained very high notions of the importance of heraldical studies, and conceived that the "Schoolmaster" Camden, as he considered him, had encroached on the rights and honours of his College of Heralds. When particular objects engage our studies, we are apt to raise them in the scale of excellence to a degree disproportioned to their real value; and are thus liable to incur ridicule. But it should be considered that many useful students

are not philosophers, and the pursuits of their lives are
never ridiculous to them. It is not the interest of the
public to degrade this class too low. Every species of
study contributes to the perfection of human knowledge,
by that universal bond which connects them all in a
philosophical mind.

Brooke prepared "A Discovery of Certain Errors in
the Much-commended Britannia." When we consider
Brooke's character, as headstrong with heraldry as Don
Quixote's with romances of chivalry, we need not attribute his motives (as Camden himself, with the partial
feelings of an author, does, and subsequent writers echo)
to his envy at Camden's promotion to be Clarencieux
King of Arms; for it appears that Brooke began his
work before this promotion. The indecent excesses of
his pen, with the malicious charges of plagiarism he
brings against Camden for the use he made of Leland's
collections, only show the insensibility of the mere
heraldist to the nobler genius of the historian. Yet
Brooke had no ordinary talents; his work is still valuable for his own peculiar researches; but his *naïve*
shrewdness, his pointed precision, the bitter invective,
and the caustic humour of his cynical pen, give an air
of originality, if not of genius, which no one has dared
to notice. Brooke's first work against Camden was
violently disturbed in its progress, and hurried, in a
mutilated state, into the world, without licence or a
publisher's name. Thus impeded, and finally crushed,
the howl of persecution followed his name; and subsequent writers servilely traced his character from their
partial predecessors.

But Brooke, though denied the fair freedom of the
press, and a victim to the powerful connexions of Camden, calmly pursued his silent labour with great magnanimity. He wrote his "Second Discovery of Errors,"

an enlargement of the first. This he carefully finished for the press, but could never get published. The secret history of the controversy may be found there.*

Brooke had been loudly accused of indulging a personal rancour against Camden, and the motive of his work was attributed to envy of his great reputation; a charge constantly repeated.

Yet this does not appear, for when Brooke first began his "Discovery of Errors," he did not design its publication; for he liberally offered Camden his Observations and Collections. They were fastidiously, perhaps haughtily, rejected; on this pernicious and false principle, that to correct his errors in genealogy might discredit the whole work. On which absurdity Brooke shrewdly remarks—" As if healing the sores would have maimed the body." He speaks with more humility on this occasion than an insulted, yet a skilful writer, was likely to do, who had his labours considered, as he says, "worthy neither of thanks nor acceptance."

"The rat is not so contemptible but he may help the lion, at a pinch, out of those nets wherein his strength is hampered; and the words of an inferior may often carry matter in them to admonish his superior of some important consideration; and surely, of what account soever I might have seemed to this learned man, yet, in respect to my profession and courteous offer, (I being an officer-of-arms, and he then but a schoolmaster), might well have vouchsafed the perusal of my notes."

When he published, our herald stated the reasons of

* This work was not given to the public till 1724, a small quarto, with a fine portrait of Brooke. More than a century had elapsed since its forcible suppression. Anstis printed it from the fair MS. which Brooke had left behind him. The author's paternal affection seemed fondly to imagine its child might be worthy of posterity, though calumniated by its contemporaries.

writing against Camden with good-humour, and rallies
him on his "incongruity in his principles of heraldry—
for which I challenge him!—for depriving some nobles
of issue to succeed them, who had issue, of whom are
descended many worthy families : denying barons and
earls that were, and making barons and earls of others
that were not; mistaking the son for the father, and the
father for the son ; affirming legitimate children to be
illegitimate, and illegitimate to be legitimate; and framing incestuous and unnatural marriages, making the
father to marry the son's wife, and the son his own
mother."

He treats Camden with the respect due to his genius,
while he judiciously distinguishes where the greatest
ought to know when to yield.

"The most abstruse arts I profess not, but yield the
palm and victory to mine adversary, that great learned
Mr. Camden, with whom, yet, a long experimented navi-
gator may contend about his chart and compass, about
havens, creeks, and sounds; so I, an ancient herald, a
little dispute, without imputation of audacity, concerning the honour of arms, and the truth of honourable
descents."

Brooke had seen, as he observes, in four editions of
the "Britannia," a continued race of errors, in false descents, &c., and he continues, with a witty allusion :—

"Perceiving that even the brains of many learned men
beyond the seas had misconceived and miscarried in the
travail and birth of their relations, being gotten, as it
were, with child (as Diomedes's mares) by the blasts of
his erroneous puffs; I could not but a little question the
original father of their absurdities, being so far blown,
with the trumpet of his learning and fame, into foreign
lands."

He proceeds with instances of several great authors on

8

the Continent having been misled by the statements of Camden.

Thus largely have I quoted from Brooke, to show, that at first he never appears to have been influenced by the mean envy, or the personal rancour, of which he is constantly accused. As he proceeded in his work, which occupied him several years, his reproaches are whetted with a keener edge, and his accusations are less generous. But to what are we to attribute this? To the contempt and persecution Brooke so long endured from Camden: these acted on his vexed and degraded spirit, till it burst into the excesses of a man heated with injured feelings.

When Camden took his station in the Herald's College with Brooke, whose offers of his notes he had refused to accept, they soon found what it was for two authors to live under the same roof, who were impatient to write against each other. The cynical York, at first, would twit the new king-of-arms, perpetually affirming that "his predecessor was a more able herald than any who lived in this age:" a truth, indeed, acknowledged by Dugdale. On this occasion, once the king-of-arms gave malicious York "the lie!" reminding the crabbed herald of "his own learning; who, as a scholar, was famous through all the provinces of Christendom." "So that (adds Brooke) now I learnt, that before him, when we speak in commendation of any other, to say, I must always except Plato." Camden would allow of no private communication between them; and in *Sermonibus Convivalibus*, in his table-talk, "the heat and height of his spirit" often scorched the contemned Yorkist, whose rejected "Discovery of Errors" had no doubt been too frequently enlarged, after such rough convivialities. Brooke now resolved to print; but, in printing the work, the press was disturbed, and his house was entered by

"this learned man, his friends, and the stationers." The
latter were alarmed for the sale of the "Britannia," which
might have been injured by this rude attack. The work
was therefore printed in an unfinished state: part was
intercepted; and the author stopped, by authority, from
proceeding any further. Some imperfect copies got
abroad.

The treatment the exasperated Brooke now incurred
was more provoking than Camden's refusal of his notes,
and the haughtiness of his "Sermonibus Convivalibus."
The imperfect work was, however, laid before the public,
so that Camden could not refuse to notice its grievous
charges. He composed an angry reply in Latin, addressed *ad Lectorem!* and never mentioning Brooke by
name, contemptuously alludes to him only by a *Quidam*
and *Iste* (a certain person, and He!)—"He considers me
(cries the mortified Brooke, in his second suppressed
work) as an *Individuum vagum*, and makes me but a
Quidam in his pamphlet, standing before him as a
school-boy, while he whips me. Why does he reply in
Latin to an English accusation? He would disguise
himself in his school-rhetoric; wherein, like the cuttle-
fish, being stricken, he thinks to hide and shift himself
away in the ink of his rhetoric. I will clear the waters
again."

He fastens on Camden's former occupation, virulently
accusing him of the manners of a pedagogue:—"A man
may perceive an immoderate and eager desire of vainglory growing in hand, ever since he used to teach and
correct children for these things, according to the opinion
of some, *in mores et naturam abeunt.*" He complains of
"the school-hyperboles" which Camden exhausts on
him, among which Brooke is compared to "the strumpet
Leontion," who wrote against "the divine Theophrastus." To this Brooke keenly replies:

"Surely, had Theophrastus dealt with women's matters, a woman, though mean, might in reason have contended with him. A king must be content to be laughed at if he come into Apelles's shop, and dispute about colours and portraiture. I am not ambitious nor envious to carp at matters of higher learning than matters of heraldry, which I profess: that is the slipper, wherein I know a slip when I find it. But see your cunning; you can, with the blur of your pen, dipped in copperas and gall, make me learned and unlearned; nay, you can almost change my sex, and make me a whore, like Leontion; and, taking your silver pen again, make yourself the divine Theophrastus."

At the close of Camden's answer, he introduced the allegorical picture of Calumny, that elegant invention of the Grecian fancy of Apelles, painted by him when suffering under the false accusations of a rival. The picture is described by Lucian; but it has received many happy touches from the classical hand of the master of Westminster School. As a literary satire, he applies it with great dignity. I give here a translation, but I preserve the original Latin in the note, as Camden's reply to Brooke is not easily to be procured.

"But though I am not disposed to waste more words on these, and this sort of men, yet I cannot resist the temptation of adding a slight sketch, for I cannot give that vivacity of colouring of the picture of the great artist Apelles that our Antiphilus and the like, whose ears are ever open to calumny, may, in contemplating it, find a reflection of themselves.

"On the right hand sits a man, who, to show his credulity, is remarkable for his prodigious ears, similar to those of Midas. He extends his hand to greet Calumny, who is approaching him. The two diminutive females around him are Ignorance and Suspicion. Opposite to

them, Calumny advances, betraying in her countenance
and gesture the savage rage and anger working in her
tempestuous breast : her left hand holds a flaming torch;
while with her right she drags by the hair a youth, who,
stretching his uplifted hands to Heaven, is calling on the
immortal powers to bear testimony to his innocence
She is preceded by a man of a pallid and impure appear
ance, seemingly wasting away under some severe disease, except that his eye sparkles, and has not the
dulness usual to such. That Envy is here meant, you
readily conjecture. Some diminutive females, frauds and
deceits, attend her as companions, whose office is to encourage and instruct, and studiously to adorn their mistress. In the background, Repentance, sadly arrayed in
a mournful, worn-out, and ragged garment, who, with
averted head, with tears and shame, acknowledges and
prepares to receive Truth, approaching from a distance." *

* " Verum enimverò de his et hoc genere hominum ne verbum am-
plius addam, tabellam tamen summi illius artificis Apell s, cùm colorum
vivacitate depingere non possim, verbis leviter adumbrabo et proponam,
ut Antiphilus noster, suique similes, et qui calumniis credunt, hanc, et
in hac seipsos semel simulque intueantur.

" Ad dextram sedet quidam, quia credulus, auribus prælongis insig-
nis, quales ferè illæ Midæ feruntur. Manum porrigit procul accedenti
Calumniæ. Circumstant eum mulierculæ duæ, Ignorantia ac Suspicio.
Adit aliunde propiùs Calumnia eximiè compta, vultu ipso et gestu
corporis efferens rabiem, et iram æstuanti conceptam pectore præ se
ferens : sinistra facem tenens flammantem, dextra secum adolescen-
tem, capillis arreptum. manus ad superos tendentem. obtestantemque
immortalium deorum fidem, trahit. Anteit vir pallidus, in speciem
impurus, acie oculorum minimè hebeti, cæterùm planè iis similis, qui
gravi aliquo morbo contabuerunt. Hic livor est, ut facilè conjicias.
Quin. et mulierculæ aliquot Insidiæ et Fallaciæ ut comites Calumniam
comitantur. Harum est munus, dominam hortari, instruere, comere,
et subornare. A tergo, habitu lugubri, pullato, laceroque Pœnitentia
subsequitur, quæ capite in tergum deflexo, cum lachrymis, ac pudore
procul venientem Veritatem agnoscit, et excipit."

This elegant picture, so happily introduced into a piece of literary controversy, appears to have only slightly affected the mind of Brooke, which was probably of too stout a grain to take the folds of Grecian drapery. Instead of sympathising with its elegance, he breaks out into a horse-laugh; and, what is quite unexpected among such grave inquiries into a ludicrous tale in verse, which, though it has not Grecian fancy, has broad English humour, where he maliciously insinuates that Camden had appropriated to his own use, or "new-coated his 'Britannia'" with Leland's MSS., and disguised what he had stolen.

"Now, to show himself as good a painter as he is a herald, he propounded, at the end of his book, a table (*i. e.* a picture) of his own invention, being nothing comparable to 'Apelles,' as he himself confesseth, and we believe him; for, like the rude painter that was fain to write, 'This is a Horse,' upon his painted horse, he writes upon his picture the names of all that furious rabble therein expressed—which, for to requite him, I will return a tale of John Fletcher (some time of Oxford) and his horse. Neither can this fable be any disparagement to his table, being more ancient and authenticall, and far more conceipted than his envious picture. And thus it was:—

A TALE (NOT OF A ROASTED) BUT OF A PAINTED HORSE.
John Fletcher, famous, and a man well known,
But using not his sirname's trade alone,*
Did hackney out poor jades for common hire,
Not fit for any pastime but to tire.

His conscience, once, surveying his jade's stable,
Prick'd him, for keeping horses so unable.
'Oh why should I,' saith John, 'by scholars thrive,
For jades that will not carry, lead, nor drive?'

---

* A *Fletcher* is a maker of bows and arrows.—ASH.

To mend the matter, out he starts. one night,
And having spied a palfrey somewhat white,
He takes him up, and up he mounts his back,
Rides to his house, and there he turns him black;

Marks him in forehead, feet, in rump, and crest,
As coursers mark those horses which are best.
So neatly John had coloured every spot,
That the right owner sees him, knows him not.

Had he but feather'd his new-painted breast,
He would have seemèd Pegasus at least.
Who but John Fletcher's horse. in all the town,
Amongst all hackneys, purchased this renown?

But see the luck : John Fletcher's horse. one night,
By rain was wash'd again almost to white.
His first right owner, seeing such a change,
Thought he should know him, but his hue was strange !

But eyeing him, and spying out his steed,
By flea-bit spots of his now washèd weed,
Seizes the horse ; so Fletcher was attainted,
And did confess the horse—he stole and painted."

To close with honour to Brooke ; in his graver moments he warmly repels the accusation Camden raised against him, as an enemy to learning, and appeals to many learned scholars, who had tasted of his liberality at the Universities, towards their maintenance ; but, in an elevated tone, he asserts his right to deliver his animadversions as York Herald.

"I know (says Brooke) the great advantage my adversary has over me, in the received opinion of the world. If some will blame me for that my writings carry some characters of spleen against him, men of pure affections, and not partial, will think reason that he should, by ill hearing, lose the pleasure he conceived by ill speaking. But since I presume not to understand above that which is meet for me to know, I must not be discouraged, nor fret myself, because of the malicious; for I find myself

seated upon a rock, that is sure from tempest and waves,
from whence I have a prospect into his errors and waver-
ings. I do confess his great worth and merit, and that
we Britons are in some sort beholding to him; and
might have been much more, if God had lent him the
grace to have played the faithful steward, in the talent
committed to his trust and charge."

Such was the dignified and the intrepid reply of Ralph
Brooke, a man whose name is never mentioned without
an epithet of reproach; and who, in his own day, was
hunted down, and not suffered, vindictive as he was no
doubt, to relieve his bitter and angry spirit, by pouring
it forth to the public eye.*

But the story is not yet closed. Camden, who wanted
the magnanimity to endure with patient dignity the corrections of an inferior genius, had the wisdom, with the
meanness, silently to adopt his useful corrections, but
would never confess the hand which had brought them.†

* Brooke died at the old mansion opposite the Roman town of
Reculver in Kent. The house is still known as Brooke-farm; and the
original gateway of decorative brickwork still exists. He was buried
in Reculver Church, now destroyed, where a mural monument was
erected to his memory, having a rhyming inscription, which told the
reader:—

> "Fifteenth October he was last alive,
> One thousand six hundred and twenty-five,
> Seaventy-three years bore he fortune's harms,
> And forty-five an officer of armes."

Brooke was originally a painter-stainer. His enmity to Camden
appears to have originated in the appointment of the latter to the
office of Clarencieux on the death of Richard Lee; he believing himself to be qualified for the place by greater knowledge, and by his long
connexion with the College of Arms. His mode of righting himself
lacked judgment, and he was twice suspended from his office, and was
even attempted to be expelled therefrom.—ED.

† In Anstis's edition of "A Second Discoverie of Errors in the
Much-commended 'Britannia,' &c.," 1724, the reader will find all the

Thus hath Ralph Brooke told his own tale undisturbed,
and, after the lapse of more than a century, the press has
been opened to him. Whenever a great author is suffered to gag the mouth of his adversary, Truth receives
the insult. But there is another point more essential to
inculcate in literary controversy. Ought we to look too
scrupulously into the motives which may induce an inferior author to detect the errors of a greater? A man
from no amiable motive may perform a proper action:
Ritson was useful after Warton; nor have we a right to
ascribe it to any concealed motives, which, after all, may
be doubtful. In the present instance, our much-abused
Ralph Brooke first appears to have composed his elaborate work from the most honourable motives: the offer
he made of his Notes to Camden seems a sufficient evi
dence. The pride of a great man first led Camden into
an error, and that error plunged him into all the bar-
barity of persecution; thus, by force, covering his folly.
Brooke over-valued his studies: it is the nature of those
peculiar minds adapted to excel in such contracted pursuits. He undertook an ungracious office, and he has
suffered by being placed by the side of the illustrious
genius with whom he has so skilfully combated in his
own province; and thus he has endured contempt, without being contemptible. The public are not less the
debtors to such unfortunate, yet intrepid authors.*

passages in the "Britannia" of the edition of 1594 to which Brooke
made exceptions, placed column-wise with the following edition of it
in 1600. It is, as Anstis observes, a debt to truth, without making
any reflections.

* There is a sensible observation in the old "Biographia Britannica"
on Brooke. "From the splenetic attack originally made by Fafe
Brooke upon the 'Britannia' arose very *great advantages to the publc,*
by the shift ng and bringing to light as good, perhaps a better and
more authentic account of our nobility, than had been given at that
time of those in any other country of Europe."—p. 1135.

MARTIN MAR-PRELATE.

Of the two prevalent factions in the reign of Elizabeth, the Catholics and the Puritans—Elizabeth's philosophical indifference offends both —Maunsell's Catalogue omits the books of both parties—of the Puritans, "the mild and moderate, with the fierce and fiery," a great religious body covering a political one—Thomas Cartwright, the chief of the Puritans and his rival Whitgift—attempts to make the Ecclesiastical paramount to the Civil Power—his plan in dividing the country into comitial. provincial. and national assemblies, to be concentrated under the secret head at Warwick, where Cartwright was elected "perpetual Moderator!"—after the most bitter controversies, Cartwright became very compliant to his old rival Whitgift, when Archbishop of Canterbury—of Martin Mar-Prelate—his sons —specimens of their popular ridicule and invective—Cartwright approves of this mode of controversy—better counteracted by the wits than by the grave admonishers—specimens of the Anti-Martin Mar-Prelates—of the authors of these surreptitious publications.

THE Reformation, or the new Religion, as it was then called, under Elizabeth, was the most philosophical she could form, and therefore the most hateful to the zealots of all parties. It was worthy of her genius, and of a better age! Her sole object was, a deliverance from the Papal usurpation. Her own supremacy maintained, she designed to be the great sovereign of a great people; and the Catholic, for some time, was called to her council-board, and entered with the Reformer into the same church. But wisdom itself is too weak to regulate human affairs, when the passions of men rise up in obstinate insurrection. Elizabeth neither won over the Reformers nor the Catholics. An excommunicating bull, precipitated by Papal Machiavelism, driving on the brutalised obedience of its slaves, separated the friends. This was a political error arising from a misconception

of the weakness of our government; and when discovered
as such, a tolerating dispensation was granted "till better times;" an unhealing expedient, to join again a dis-
membered nation! It would surprise many, were they
aware how numerous were our ancient families and our
eminent characters who still remained Catholics.* The
country was then divided, and Englishmen who were
heroic Romanists fell the terrible victims.

On the other side, the national evil took a new form.
It is probable that the Queen, regarding the mere cere-
monies of religion, now venerable with age, as matters
of indifference, and her fine taste perhaps still lingering
amid the solemn gorgeousness of the Roman service, and
her senses and her emotions excited by the religious
scenery, did not share in that abhorrence of the paintings and the images, the chant and the music, the censer
and the altar, and the pomp of the prelatical habits,
which was prompting many well-intentioned Reformers
to reduce the ecclesiastical state into apostolical naked-
ness and primitive rudeness. She was slow to meet this
austerity of feeling, which in this country at length ex-
tirpated those arts which exalt our nature, and for this
these pious Vandals nicknamed the Queen "the untamed
heifer;" and the fierce Knox expressly wrote his "First
Blast Against the Monstrous Government of Women."
Of these Reformers, many had imbibed the republican
notions of Calvin. In their hatred of Popery, they

---

* The Church History by Dodd, a Catholic, fills three vols. folio: it
is very rare and curious. Much of our own domestic history is interwoven in that of the fugitive papists, and the materials of this work
are frequently drawn from their own archives, preserved in their
seminaries at Douay, Valladolid, &c., which have not been accessible
to Protestant writers. Here I discovered a copious nomenclature of
eminent persons, and many literary men, with many unknown facts,
both of a private and public nature. It is useful, at times, to know
whether an English author was a Catholic.

imagined that they had not gone far enough in their
wild notions of reform, for they viewed it, still shadowed
out in the new hierarchy of the bishops. The fierce
Calvin, in his little church at Geneva, presumed to rule
a great nation on the scale of a parish institution; copying the apostolical equality at a time when the Church
(say the Episcopalians) had all the weakness of infancy,
and could live together in a community of all things,
from a sense of their common poverty. Be this as it
may, the dignified ecclesiastical order was a vulnerable
institution, which could do no greater injury, and might
effect as much public good as any other order in the
state.* My business is not with this discussion. I mean
to show how the republican system of these Reformers
ended in a political struggle which, crushed in the reign
of Elizabeth, and beaten down in that of James, so furiously triumphed under Charles. Their history exhibits
the curious spectacle of a great religious body covering
a political one—such as was discovered among the Jesuits, and such as may again distract the empire, in some
new and unexpected shape.

Elizabeth was harassed by the two factions of the in-
triguing Catholic and the disguised Republican. The
age abounded with libels.† Many a *Benedicite* was

---

* I refer the reader to Selden's "Table Talk" for many admirable
ideas on "Bishops." That enlightened genius, who was no friend to
the ecclesiastical temporal power, acknowledges the absolute necessity
of this order in a great government. The preservers of our literature
and our morals they ought to be, and many have been. When the
political reformers ejected the bishops out of the house, what did they
gain? a more vulgar prating race, but even more lordly! Selden
says—" The bishops being put out of the house, whom will they lay
the fault upon now? When the dog is beat out of the room, where
will they lay the stink?"

† The freedom of the press hardly subsisted in Elizabeth's reign;
and yet libels abounded! A clear demonstration that nothing is really
gained by those violent suppressions and expurgatory indexes which

handed to her from the Catholics; but a portentous personage, masked, stepped forth from a club of PURITANS,
and terrified the nation by continued visitations, yet
was never visible till the instant of his adieus—"starting
like a guilty thing upon a fearful summons!"

power in its usurpation may enforce. At a time when they did not
dare even to publish the titles of such libels, yet were they spread
about, and even hoarded. The most ancient catalogue of our vernacular literature is that by Andrew Maunsell, published in 1595. It consists of Divinity, Mathematics, Medicine, &c.: but the third part which
he promised, and which to us would have been the most interesting,
of "Rhetoric, History, Poetry, and Policy," never appeared. In the
Preface, such was the temper of the times, and of Elizabeth, we discover that he has deprived us of a catalogue of the works alluded to
in our text, for he thus distinctly points at them:—"The books written
by the *fugitive papistes*, as also those that are *written against the present
government* (meaning those of the Puritans), I doe not thinke meete for
me to meddle withall." In one part of his catalogue, however, he contrived to insert the following passage; the burden of the song seems
to have been chorused by the ear of our cautious Maunsell. He is
noticing a Pierce Plowman in prose. "I did not see the beginning of
this booke, but it ended thus:—

> " God save the king, and speed the plough,
>   And send the *prelats* care inough,
>   Inough, inough, inough."—p. 80.

Few of our native productions are so rare as the *Martin Mar-Prelate*
publications. I have not found them in the public repositories of our
national literature. There they have been probably rejected with in-
dignity, though their answerers have been preserved: yet even these
are almost of equal rarity and price. They were rejected in times less
enlightened than the present. In a national library every book deserves preservation. By the rejection of these satires, however absurd or infamous, we have lost a link in the great chain of our National
Literature and History. [Since the above was written, many have
been added to our library; and the Rev. William Maskell, M.A., has
published his "History of the Martin Mar-Prelate Controversy." It
is a most careful summary of the writings and proceedings of all connected with this important event, and is worthy the attentive perusal
of such as desire accurate information in this chapter of our Church
history.]

Men echo the tone of their age, yet still the same unvarying human nature is at work; and the Puritans,*

* We know them by the name of Puritans, a nickname obtained by
their affecting superior sanctity; but I find them often distinguished
by the more humble appellative of Precisians. As men do not leap
up, but climb on rocks, it is probable they were only *precise* before
they were *pure*. A satirist of their day, in "Rythmes against Martin
Marre-Prelate," melts their attributes into one verse:—

"The sacred sect, and perfect *pure precise*."

A more laughing satirist. "Pasquill of England to Martin Junior,"
persists in calling them Puritans, *a pruritu!* for their perpetual itching,
or a desire to do something. Elizabeth herself only considered them
as "a troublesome sort of people:" even that great politician could
not detect the political monster in a mere chrysalis of reform. I find,
however, in a poet of the Elizabethan age, an evident change in the
public feeling respecting the *Puritans*, who being always most active
when the government was most in trouble, their political views were
discovered. Warner, in his "Albion's England," describes them:—

"If ever England will in aught prevent her own mishap,
	Against these Skonmes (no terme too grosse) let England shut the
		gap;
	With giddie heads—
		Their country's foes they helpt, and most their country harm'd.
	If *Hypocrites* why *Puritaines* we term, be asked, in breefe,
	'Tis but an *ironised terme:* good-fellow so spells theefe!"

The gentle-humoured Fuller, in his "Church History," felt a tenderness for the name of *Puritan*, which, after the mad follies they had
played during the Commonwealth, was then held in abhorrence. He
could not venture to laud the good men of that party, without employing a new term to conceal the odium. In noticing, under the date of
1563, that the bishops urged the clergy of their dioceses to press uniformity, &c., he adds—"Such as refused were branded with the name
of Puritans—a name which in this nation began in this year, subject
to several senses, and various in the acceptions. *Puritan* was taken
for the opposers of hierarchy and church service, as resenting of
superstition. But the nickname was quickly improved by profane
mouths to abuse pious persons. We will decline the word to prevent exceptions, which, if casually slipping from our pen, the reader
knoweth that only *nonconformists* are intended," lib. ix. p. 76. Fuller,

who in the reign of Elizabeth imagined it was impossible
to go too far in the business of reform, were the spirits

however, divided them into classes—"the mild and moderate, and the
fierce and fiery." Heylin, in his "History of the Presbyterians,"
blackens them as so many political devils; and Neale, in his "History of the Puritans," blanches them into a sweet and almond white-
ness.

Let us be thankful to these PURITANS for a political lesson. They
began their quarrels on the most indifferent matters. They raised
disturbances about the "Romish Rags," by which they described the
decent surplice as well as the splendid scarlet chimere[1] thrown over
the white linen rochet, with the square cap worn by the bishops. The
scarlet robe. to please their sullen fancy, was changed into black satin;
but these men soon resolved to deprive the bishops of more than a
scarlet robe. The affected niceties of these PRECISIANS. dismembering
our images, and scratching at our paintings, disturbed the uniformity
of the religious service. A clergyman in a surplice was turned out
of the church. Some wore square caps, some round, some abhorred
all caps. The communion-table placed in the East was considered as
an idolatrous altar. and was now dragged into the middle of the
church. where, to show their contempt. it was always made the filth-
iest seat in the church. They used to kneel at the sacrament: now
they would sit. because that was a proper attitude for a supper;
then they would not sit. but stand: at length they tossed the elements about, because the bread was wafers, and not from a loaf.
Among their *preciseness* was a qualm at baptism : the water was to be
taken from a basin. and not from a fount; then they would not name
their children, or if they did. they would neither have Grecian, nor
Roman, nor Saxon names. but Hebrew ones, which they ludicrously
translated into English, and which, as Heylin observes, "many of
them when they came of age were ashamed to own"—such as
"Accepted, Ashes, Fight-the-good-Fight-of-Faith, Joy-again, Kill-
sin, &c."

Who could have foreseen that some pious men quarrelling about
the square caps and the rochets of bishops should at length attack
bishops themselves; and, by an easy transition, passing from bishops
to kings, finally close in levellers !

---

[1] So Heylin writes the word; but in the "Rythmes against Martin," a contemporary production, the term is *Chiver*. It is not in
Cotgrave.

called *Roundheads* under Charles, and who have got
another nickname in our days. These wanted a Reformation of a Reformation—they aimed at reform, but
they designed Revolution; and they would not accept
of toleration, because they had determined on predom-
inance.*

Of this faction, the chief was Thomas Cartwright, a
person of great learning, and doubtless of great ambition. Early in life a disappointed man, the progress was
easy to a disaffected subject. At a Philosophy Act, in
the University of Cambridge, in the royal presence, the
queen preferred and rewarded his opponent for the
slighter and more attractive elegances in which the
learned Cartwright was deficient. He felt the wound
rankle in his ambitious spirit. He began, as Sir George
Paul, in his "Life of Archbishop Whitgift," expresses it,
"to kick against her Ecclesiastical Government." He
expatriated himself several years, and returned fierce
with the republican spirit he had caught among the
Calvinists at Geneva, which aimed at the extirpation of
the bishops. It was once more his fate to be poised
against another rival, Whitgift, the Queen's Professor
of Divinity. Cartwright, in some lectures, advanced
his new doctrines; and these innovations soon raised a
formidable party, " buzzing their conceits into the green

* The origin of the controversy may be fixed about 1588. " A far
less easy task," says the Rev. Mr. Maskell, "is it to guess at the
authors. The tracts on the Mar-Prelate side have been usually attributed to Penry, Throgmorton, Udal, and Fenner. Very considerable
information may be obtained about these writers in Wood's ' Athenæ,'
art. *Penry;* in Collier, Strype, and Herbert's edition of 'Arnes.' to
whom I would refer. After a careful examination of these and other
authorities on the subject, the question remains, in my judgment,
as obscure as before; and I think that it is very far from clear that
either one of the three last-named was actually concerned in the
authorship of any of the pamphlets."--ED.

heads of the University."* Whitgift regularly preached
at Cartwright, but to little purpose; for when Cartwright preached at St. Mary's they were forced to take
down the windows. Once our sly polemic, taking advantage of the absence of Whitgift, so powerfully operated,
in three sermons on one Sunday, that in the evening his
victory declared itself, by the students of Trinity College
rejecting their surplices, as Papistical badges. Cartwright was now to be confuted by other means. The
University refused him his degree of D.D.; condemned
the lecturer to silence; and at length performed that last
feeble act of power, expulsion. In a heart already alienated from the established authorities, this could only
envenom a bitter spirit. Already he had felt a personal
dislike to royalty, and now he had received an insult
from the University: these were motives which, though
concealed, could not fail to work in a courageous mind,
whose new forms of religion accorded with his political
feelings. The "Degrees" of the University, which he
now declared to be "unlawful," were to be considered
"as limbs of Antichrist." The whole hierarchy was to
be exterminated for a republic of Presbyters; till, through
the church, the republican, as we shall see, discovered a
secret passage to the Cabinet of his Sovereign, where he
had many protectors.

Such is my conception of the character of Cartwright.
The reader is enabled to judge for himself by the note.†

* In the "Just Censure and Reproof of Martin Junior" (circæ 1589),
we are told: "There is Cartwright, too, at Warwick; he hath got him
such a company of disciples, both of the worshipfull and other of the
poorer sort, as wee have no cause to thank him. Never tell me that
he is too grave to trouble himself with Martin's conceits. Cartwright
seeks the peace of the Church no otherwise than his platform may
stand." He was accused before the commissioners in '1590 of knowing
who wrote and printed these squibs, which he did not deny.—ED.

† I give a remaikble extract from the writings of Cartwright. It

But Cartwright, chilled by an imprisonment, and witnessing some of his party condemned, and some executed, after having long sustained the most elevated and rigid

will prove two points. First, that the *religion* of those men became a cover for a *political* design: which was *to raise the ecclesiastical above the civil power.* Just the reverse of Hobbes's alter scheme; but while theorists thus differ and seem to refute one another, they in reality work for an identical purpose. Secondly, it will show the not uncommon absurdity of man; while these nonconformists were affecting to annihilate the hierarchy of England as a remains of the Romish supremacy, they themselves were designing one according to their own fresher scheme. It was to be a state or republic of Presbyters, in which all *Sovereigns* were to hold themselves, to use their style, as " Nou isses, or servants under the Church: the Sovereigns were to bo as subjects; they were to vail their sceptres and to offer their crowns as the prophet speaketh, *to lick the dust of the feet of the Church.*" These are Cartwright's words, in his "Defence of the Admonition." But ho is still bolder, in a joint production with *Travers.* He insists that " the *Monarchs of the World* should give up their *sceptres and crowns* unto him (Jesus Christ) who is *represent d by the Officers of the Church.*" See "A Full and Plain Declaration of Ecclesiastical Discipline," p. 185. One would imagine he was a disguised Jesuit, and an advocate for tho Pope's supremacy. But observe how these saintly Republicans would govern the State. Cartwright is explicit, and very ingenious. "Tho world is now deceived that thinketh that the *Church* must be framed according to the *Commonwealth,* and the *Church Covernment* according to the *Civil Government,* which is as much as to say, as if a man should fashion his house according to his hangings; whereas, indeed, it is clean contrary. That as the hangings are made fit for the house, so the Commonwealth must be made to agree with the Church, and tho government thereof with her government; for, as the house is before the hangings, therefore the hangings, which come after, must be framed to the house, which was before; so the Church being before there was a commonwealth, and the commonwealth coming after, must bo fashioned and made suitable to the Church; otherwise, God is made to give place to men, heaven to earth."—Cartwright's *Defence of the Admonition,* p. 181.

Warburton's "Alliance between Church and State," which was in his time considered as a hardy paradox, is mawkish in its pretensions, compared with this sacerdotal republic. It is not wonderful that tho wisest of our Sovereigns, that great politician Elizabeth, should have

tone, suddenly let his alp of ice dissolve away in the gentlest thaw that ever occurred in political life. Ambitious he was, but not of martyrdom! His party appeared once formidable,* and his protection at Court

punished with death these democrats: but it is wonderful to discover that these inveterate enemies to the Church of Rome were only trying to transfer its absolute power into their own hands! They wanted to turn the Church into a democracy. They fascinated the people by telling them that there would be no beggars were there no bishops; that every man would be a governor by setting up a Presbytery. From the Church. I repeat, it is scarcely a single step to the Cabinet. Yet the early Puritans come down to us as persecuted saints. Doubtless, there were a few honest saints among them; but they were as mad politicians as their race afterwards proved to be, to whom they left so many fatal legacies. Cartwright uses the very language a certain cast of political reformers have recently done. He declares " An establishment may be made without the magistrate;" and told the people that " if every hair of their head was a life, it ought to be offered for such a cause." Another of this faction is for " registering the names of the fittest and hottest brethren without lingering for Parliament;" and another exults that " there are a hundred thousand hands ready." Another, that " we may overthrow the bishops and all the government in one day." Such was the style, and such the confidence in the plans which the lowest orders of revolutionists promulgated during their transient exhibition in this country. More in this strain may be found in " Maddox's Vindication Against Neale," the advocate for the Puritans, p. 255; and in an admirable letter of that great politician, Sir Francis Walsingham, who, with many others of the ministers of Elizabeth, was a favourer of the Puritans, till he detected their secret object to subvert the government. This letter is preserved in "Collier's Eccl. Hist." vol. ii. 607. They had begun to divide the whole country into *classes*, provincial synods, &c. They kept registers, which recorded all the heads of their debates, to be finally transmitted to the secret head of the *Classis* of Warwick, where Cartwright governed as *the perpetual moderator! Heylin's Hist. of Presbyt.* p. 277. These violent advocates for the freedom of the press had. however, an evident intention to monopolise it; for they decreed that " no book should be put in print but by consent of the *Classes*."—Sir G. Paul's *Life of Whitgift*, p. 65. The very Star-Chamber they justly protested against, they were for raising among themselves!

* Under the denomination of *Barrowists* and *Brownists*. I find Sir

sure. I have read several letters of the Earl of Leicester, in MS., that show he always shielded Cartwright, whenever in danger. Many of the ministers of Elizabeth were Puritans; but doubtless this was before their state policy had detected the politicians in mask. When some of his followers had dared to do what he had only thought, he appears to have forsaken them. They reproached him for this left-handed policy, some of the boldest of them declaring that they had neither acted nor written anything but what was warranted by his principles. I do not know many political ejaculations more affecting than that of Henry Barrow, said to have been a dissipated youth, when Cartwright refused, before Barrow's execution to allow of a conference. The deluded man, after a deep sigh, said: "Shall I be thus forsaken by him? Was it not he that brought me first into these briars? and will he now leave me in the same? Was it not from him alone that I took my grounds? Or did I not, out of such premises as he pleased to give me, infer those propositions, and deduce those conclusions, for which I am now kept in these bonds?" He was soon after executed, with others.

Then occurred one of those political spectacles at which the simple-minded stare, and the politic smile; when, after the most cruel civil war of words,* Cart-

Walter Raleigh declaring, in the House of Commons, on a motion for reducing disloyal subjects, that "they are worthy to be rooted out of a Commonwealth." He is alarmed at the danger, "for it is to be feared that men not guilty will be included in the law about to be passed. I am sorry for it. I am afraid there is near twenty thousand of them in England; and when they be gone (that is, expelled) who shall maintain their wives and children?"—Sir Simonds D'Ewes' *Journal*, p. 517.

* The controversies of Whitgift and Cartwright were of a nature which could never close, for toleration was a notion which never occurred to either. These rivals from early days wrote with such bitterness against each other, that at length it produced mutual reproaches.

wright wrote very compliant letters to his old rival,
Whitgift, now Archbishop of Canterbury; while the
Archbishop was pleading with the Queen in favour of
the inveterate Republican, declaring that had Cartwright not so far engaged himself in the beginning, he
thought he would have been, latterly, drawn into conformity.   To clear up this mysterious conduct, we must
observe that Cartwright seems to have graduated his
political ambition to the degree the government touched
of weakness or of strength; and besides, he was now
growing prudent as he was growing rich.   For it seems
that he who was for scrambling for the Church revenues
while telling the people of the Apostles, *silver and gold
they had none,* was himself " feeding too fair and fat"
for the meagre groaning state of a pretended reformation.   He had early in life studied that part of the law
by which he had learned the marketable price of landed
property; and as the cask still retains its old flavour,
his despiser of bishops was still making the best interest,
for his money by land-jobbing.*

Whitgift complains to Cartwright; "If you were writing against the
veriest Papist, or the ignorantest dolt, you could not be more spiteful
and malicious."   And Cartwright replies: " If peace had been so
precious unto you as you pretend, you would not have brought so
many hard words and bitter reproaches, as it were sticks and coals, to
double and treble the heat of contention."

After this it is curious, even to those accustomed to such speculations, to observe some men changing with the times, and furious
rivals converted into brothers.   Whitgift, whom Elizabeth, as a mark
of her favour, called " her black husband," soliciting Cartwright's
pardon from the Queen; and the proud Presbyter Cartwright styling
Whitgift his Lord the Archbishop's Grace of Canterbury, and visiting
him !

* Sir George Paul, a contemporary, attributes his wealth " to the
benevolence and bounty of his followers."   Dr. Sutcliffe, one of his
adversaries, sharply upbraids him, that " in the persecution he perpetually complained of, he was grown rich."   A Puritan advocate
reproves Dr. Sutcliffe for always carping at Cartwright's purchases:—

One of the memorable effects of this attempted inno-
vation was that continued stream of libels which ran
throughout the nation, under the portentous name of
Martin Mar-Prelate.* This extraordinary personage, in
his collective form, for he is to be splitted into more than
one, long terrified Church and State. He walked about
the kingdom invisibly, dropping here a libel, and there a
proclamation for sedition; but wherever *Martinism* was
found, *Martin* was not. He prided himself in what he
calls " Pistling the Bishops." Sometimes he hints to his
pursuers how they may catch him, for he prints, " within
two furlongs of a bouncing priest," or " in Europe;"
while he acquaints his friends, who were so often uneasy
for his safety, that " he has neither wife nor child," and
prays " they may not be anxious for him, for he wishes
that his head might not go to the grave in peace."—

" Why may not Cartwright sell the lands he had from his father, and
buy others with the money, as well as some of the bishops, who by
bribery, simony, extortion, racking of rents, wasting of woods, and such
like stratagems, wax rich, and purchase great lordships for their
posterity?"

To this Sutcliffe replied :

" I do not carpe alway, no, nor once, at Master Cartwright's purchase.
I hinder him not: I envy him not. Only thus much I must tell him,
that Thomas Cartwright, a man that hath more laudes of his own in possession than any bishop that I know, and that fareth daintily every
day, and feedeth fayre and fatte, and lyeth as soft as any tenderling of
that brood, and hath wonne much wealth in short time, and will leave
more to his posterity than any bishop, should not cry out either of persecution or of excess of bishop's livinges."—Sutcliffe's *Answer to Certain Calumnious Petitions.*

* " The author of these libels," says Bishop Cooper, in his " Admonition to the people of England," 1589, " calleth himself by a
feigned name, *Martin Mar-Prelate*, a very fit name undoubtedly. But
if this outrageous spirit of boldness be not stopped speedily, I fear he
will prove himself to be, not only *Mar-Prelate*, but Mar-Prince, Mar-
State, Mar-Law, Mar-Magistrate, and altogether, until he bring it to an
Anabaptistical equality and community."—ED.

" I come, with the rope about my neck, to save you, how-
soever it goeth with me." His press is interrupted, he
is silent, and Lambeth seems to breathe in peace. But
he has "a son; nay, five hundred sons!" and *Martin
Junior* starts up! He inquires

" Where his father is ; he who had studied the art of
pistle-making ? Why has he been tongue-tied these
four or five months ? Good Nuncles (the bishops), have
you closely murthered the gentleman in some of your
prisons? Have you choaked him with a fat prebend or
two ? I trow my father will swallow down no such pills,
for he would thus soon purge away all the conscience
he hath. Do you mean to have the keeping of him?
What need that ? he hath five hundred sons in the land.
My father would be sorry to put you to any such cost
as you intend to be at with him. A meaner house, and
less strength than the Tower, the Fleet, or Newgate,
would serve him well enough. He is not of that ambitious
vein that many of his brethren the bishops are, in seeking
for more costly houses than even his father built for him."

This same " Martin Junior," who, though he is but
young, as he says, " has a pretty smattering gift in this
pistle-making ; and I fear, in a while, I shall take a pride
in it." He had picked up beside a bush, where it had
dropped from somebody, an imperfect paper of his
father's :—

" Theses Martinianæ—set forth as an after-birth of the
noble gentleman himselfe, by a pretty stripling of his,
Martin Junior, and dedicated by him to his good nuncka,
Maister John Cankerbury (i.e. Canterbury). Printed
without a sly privilege of the Cater Caps "—(i. e. the
square caps the bishops wore).

But another of these five hundred sons, who declares
himself to be his " reverend and elder brother, heir to the
renowned *Martin Mar-Prelate* the Great," publishes

"The just Censure and Reproof of Martin Junior; where, lest the Springall should be utterly discouraged in his good meaning, you shall finde that he is not bereaved of his due commendation."

Martin Senior, after finding fault with *Martin Junior* for " his rash and indiscreet headiness," notwithstanding agrees with everything he had said. He confirms all, and cheers him ; but charges him,

" Should he meet their father in the street, never to ask his blessing, but walke smoothly and circumspectly ; and if anie offer to talk with thee of Martin, talke thou straite of the voyage into Portugal, or of the happie death of the Duke of Guise, or some such accident ; but meddle not with thy father. Only, if thou have gathered anie thing in visitation for thy father, intreate him to signify, in some secret printed pistle, where a will have it lefte. I feare least some of us should fall into John Canterburie's hand."

Such were the mysterious personages who, for a long time, haunted the palaces of the bishops and the vicarages of the clergy, disappearing at the moment they were suddenly perceived to be near. Their slanders were not only coarse buffooneries, but the hottest effusions of hatred, with an unparalleled invective of nicknames.* Levelled at the bishops, even the natural de-

---

* Cartwright approved of them, and well knew the concealed writers, who frequently consulted him : this appears by Sir G. Paul's "Life of Whitgift," p. 65. Being asked his opinion of such books, he said, that " since the bishops, and others there touched, would not amend by grave books, it was therefore meet they should be dealt withal to their farther reproach ; and that some books must be *earnest*, some *more mild and temperate*, whereby they may be both of the spirit of Elias and Eliseus ;" the one the great mocker, the other the more solemn reprover. It must be confessed Cartwright here discovers a deep knowledge of human nature. He knew the power of ridicule and of invective. At a later day, a writer of the same stamp, in " The

fects, the personal infirmities, the domestic privacies, much more the tyranny, of these now " petty popes," now " bouncing priests," now " terrible priests," were the inexhaustible subjects of these popular invectives.†

Second Wash, or the *Moore Scoured o ce more*," (written against Dr. Henry More, the Platonist), in defence of that vocabulary of *names* which he has poured on More, asserts it is a practice allowed by the high authority of Christ himself. I transcribe the curious passage:— " It is the practice of Christ himself to character *men* by those *things* to which they assimilate. Thus hath he called *Herod* a *fox; Judas* a *devil; false pastors* he calls *wolves;* the *buyers and sellers. theeves;* and those Hebrew Puritans the *Pharisees, hypocrites.* This rule and justice of his Master St. Paul hath well observed, and he acts freely thereby ; for when he reproves the Cretians, he makes use of that ignominious proverb, *Evil beasts and slow bellies.* When the high priest commanded the Jews to *smite* him on the face, he replied to him, not without some bitterness, *God shall smite thee, thou white wall.* I cite not these places to justify an injurious spleen, but to argue the liberty of the truth."— *The Second Wash, or the More Scoured once more.* 1651. P. 8.

† One of their works is " A Dialogue, wherein is laid open the tyrannical dealing of L. Bishopps against God's children." It is full of scurrilous stories, probably brought together by two active cobblers who were so useful to their junto. Yet the bishops of that day were not of dissolute manners; and the accusations are such, that it only proves their willingness to raise charges against them. Of one bishop they tell us, that after declaring he was poor, and what expenses he had been at, as Paul's church could bear witness, shortly after hanged four of his servants for having robbed him of a considerable sum. Of another, who cut down all the woods at Hampstead, till the towns-women " fell a swaddling of his men," and so saved Hampstead by their resolution. But when *Mart n* would give a proof that the Bishop of London was one of the bishops of the devil, in his " Pistle to the terrible priests," he tells this story:—" When tho bishop throws his bowl (as he useth it commonly upon the Sabbath-day), he runnes after it; and if it be too hard, he cr es *Rub! rub! rub! the diuel goe with thee!* and he goeth himself with it: so that by these words he names himself the Bishop of the Divel, and by his tirannical practice prooveth himselfe to be." He tells, too, of a parson well known, who, being in the pulpit, and " hearing his dog cry, he out with this text: ' Why, how now, host can you not let my dog alone there? Come, Springe! come, Springe!' and whistled the dog

Those " pillars of the State " were now called "its cater-
pillars ;" and the inferior clergy, who perhaps were not
always friendly to their superiors, yet dreaded this new

to the pulpit." One of their chief objects of attack was Cooper,
Bishop of Lincoln, a laborious student, but married to a dissolute
woman, whom the University of Oxford offered to separate from him ؛
but he said he knew his infirmity, and could not live without his wife,
and was tender on the point of divorce. He had a greater misfortune
than even this loose woman about him—his *name* could be punned on ;
and this bishop may be placed among that unlucky class of authors
who have fallen victims to their *names*. Shenstone meant more than
Le expressed, when he thanked God that he could not be punned on.
Mar-Prelate, besides many cruel hits at Bishop Cooper's wife, was
now always " making the *Cooper's hoops to flye off*, and the bishop's
tubs to leake out." In " The Protestatyon of Martin Marprelat,"
where he tells of two bishops, " who so contended in throwing
down elmes, as if the wager had bene whether of them should most
have impoverished their bishopricks. Yet I blame not *Mar-Elme* so
much as Cooper for this fact, because it is no less given him by his
name to spoil elmes, than it is allowed him by the secret judgment of
God to mar the Church. A man of *Cooper's* age and occupation, so
wel scene in that trade, might easily knowe that tubs made of green
timber must needs leak out ; and yet I do not so greatly marvel ; for
he that makes no conscience to be a deceiver in the building of the
churche, will not stick for his game to be a *deceitfull workeman in
making of tubbs.*"—p. 19. The author of the books against Bishop
Cooper is said to have been Job Throckmorton, a learned man, affecting raillery and humour to court the mob.

Such was the strain of ribaldry and malice which Martin Mar-Prelate indulged, and by which he obtained full possession of the minds
of the people for a considerable time. His libels were translated, and
have been often quoted by the Roman Catholics abroad and at home
for their particular purposes, just as the revolutionary publications in
this country have been concluded abroad to be the general sentiments
of the people of England; and thus our factions always will serve the
interests of our enemies. Martin seems to have written little verse ;
but there is one epigram worth preserving for its bitterness.

Martin Senior, in his " Reproofe of Martin Junior," complains that
his younger brother has not taken a little paines in ryming with
Mar-Martin (one of their poetical antagonists), that the Cater-Caps may
know how the meanest of my father's sonnes is able to answeare them

race of innovators, were distinguished as "halting neu-
trals." These invectives were well farced for the gross
taste of the multitude; and even the jargon of the lowest of the populace affected, and perhaps the coarse malignity of two *cobblers* who were connected with the
party, often enlivened the satirical page. The *Martin
Mar-Prelate* productions are not, however, effusions of
genius; they were addressed to the coarser passions of
mankind, their hatred and contempt. The authors were
grave men, but who affected to gain over the populace
with a popular familiarity.*   In vain the startled bishops

both at blunt and sharpe." He then gives his younger brother a
specimen of what he is hereafter to do. He attributes the satire of
Mar-Martin to Dr. Bridges, Dean of Sarum, and John Whitgift, Archbishop of Canterbury.

"The first Rising, Generation, and Original of *Mar-Martin.*

"From Sarum came a goos's egg,
    With specks and spots bepatched;
A priest of Lambeth coucht thereon,
    Thus was *Mar-Martin* hatched.

Whence hath *Mar-Martin* all his wit,
    But from that egge of Sarum?
The rest comes all from great Sir **John,**
    Who rings us all this 'larum.

What can the cockatrice hatch up
    But serpents like himselfe?
What sees the ape within the glasse
    But a deformed elfe?

Then must *Mar-Martin* have some smell
    Of forge, or else of fire:
A sotte in wit, a beaste in minde,
    For so was damme and sire."

* It would, however, appear that these revolutionary publications
reached the universities, and probably fermented "the green heads"
of our students, as the following grave admonition directed to them
evidently proves:—

remonstrated : they were supposed to be criminals, and
were little attended to as their own advocates. Besides,
they were solemn admonishers, and the mob are composed of laughers and scorners.

"Anti-Martinus sive monitio cujusdam Londinensis ad adolescentes
vtrimque academiæ contra personatum quendam rabulam qui se
Anglice Martin Marprelat, &c. Londini, 1589, 4°."
A popular favourite as he was, yet even Martin, *in proprid persona*,
acknowledges that his manner was not approved of by *either party*.
His "Theses Martinianæ" opens thus: "I see my doings and my
course misliked of many, both the good and the bad; though also I
have favourers of both sortes. The bishops and their traine, though
they stumble at the cause, yet especially mislike my maner of writing.
Those whom foolishly men call *Puritanes*, like of the matter I have
handled, but the forme they cannot brooke. So that herein I have
them both for mine adversaries. But now what if I should take the
course in certain theses or conclusions, without *inveighing* against
either *person* or *cause*." This was probably written after Martin had
swallowed some of his own sauce, or taken his "Pap (offered to him)
with a Hatchet," as one of the most celebrated government pamphlets
is entitled. But these "Theses Martinianæ," without either scurrility
or invective are the dullest things imaginable; abstract propositions
were not palatable to the multitude; and then it was, after the trial
had been made, that *Martin Junior and Senior* attempted to revive the
spirit of the old gentleman : but if sedition has its progress, it has also
its decline; and if it could not strike its blow when strongest, it only
puled and made grimaces, prognostics of weakness and dissolution.
This is admirably touched in "Pappe with an Hatchet." "Now Old
Martin appeared, with a wit worn into the socket, twinkling and pink-
ing like the snuffe of a candle; *quantum mutatus ab illo*, how unlike
the knave he was before, not for malice, but for sharpnesse! The
hogshead was even come to the haunceing, and nothing could be drawne
from him but dregs; yet the emptie caske sounds lowder than when
it was full, and protests more in his waining than he could perform in
his waxing. I drew neere the sillie soul, whom I found quivering in
two sheets of protestation paper (alluding to the work mentioned here
in the following note). O how meager and leane he looked, so crest
falne that his combe hung downe to his bill ; and had I not been sure
it was the picture of Envie, I should have sworn it had been the image
of Death : so like the verie anatomie of Mischief, that one might see
through all the ribbes of his conscience."

The Court-party did not succeed more happily when
they persecuted Martin, broke up his presses, and im-
prisoned his assistants. Never did sedition travel so
fast, nor conceal itself so closely; for they employed a
moveable press; and, as soon as it was surmised that
Martin was in Surrey, it was found he was removed to
Northamptonshire, while the next account came that he
was showing his head in Warwickshire. And long they
invisibly conveyed themselves, till in Lancashire the
snake was scotched by the Earl of Derby, with all its
little brood.*

In another rare pamphlet from the same school, "Pasquill of England to Martin Junior, in a countercuffe given to Martin Junior," he
humorously threatens to write "The Owle's Almanack, wherein your
night labours be set down;" and "some fruitful volumes of 'The Lives
of the Saints,' which, maugre your father's five hundred sons, shall be
printed," with "hays, jiggs, and roundelays, and madrigals, serving
for epitaphs for his father's hearse."

* Some of these works still bear evident marks that the "pur-
suivants" were hunting the printers. "The Protestatyon of Martin
Mar-Prelate, wherein, notwithstanding the surprising of the printer,
he maketh it knowne vnto the world that he feareth neither proud
priest, tirannous prelate, nor godlesse cater-cap; but defieth all the
race of them," including "a challenge" to meet them personally;
was probably one of their latest efforts. The printing and the orthography show all the imperfections of that haste in which they were
forced to print this work. As they lost their strength, they were getting more venomous. Among the little Martins disturbed in the hour
of parturition, but already christened, there were: "Episto Mastix;"
"The Lives and Doings of English Popes;" "Itinerarium, or Visitations; "'Lambethisms." The "Itinerary" was a survey of every
clergyman of England! and served as a model to a similar work,
which appeared during the time of the Commonwealth. The "Lambethisms" were secrets divulged by Martin, who, it seems, had got
into the palace itself! Their productions were, probably, often got
up in haste, in utter scorn of the Horatian precept. [These pamphlets
were printed with difficulty and danger, in secrecy and fear, for they
were rigidly denounced by the government of Elizabeth. Sir George
Paul, in his "Life of Archbishop Whitgift," informs us that they were
printed with a kind of wandering press, which was first set up at

These pamphlets were "speedily dispersed and greedily read," not only by the people; they had readers and even patrons among persons of condition. They were found in the corners of chambers at Court; and when a prohibition issued that no person should carry about them any of the Mar-Prelate pamphlets on pain of punishment, the Earl of Essex observed to the Queen, "What then is to become of me?" drawing one of these pamphlets out of his bosom, and presenting it to her.

The Martinists were better counteracted by the Wits, in some extraordinary effusions, prodigal of humour and

Moulsey, near Kingston-on-Thames, and from thence conveyed to Fauseley in Northamptonshire, and from thence to Norton, afterwards to Coventry, from thence to Welstone in Warwickshire, from which place the letters were sent to another press in or near Manchester; where by the means of Henry, Earl of Derby, the press was discovered in printing "More Work for a Cooper;" an answer to Bishop Cooper's attack on the party, and a work so rare Mr. Maskell says, "I believe no copy of it, in any state, remains."]

As a great curiosity, I preserve a fragment in the *Scottish* dialect, which well describes them and their views. The title is wanting in the only copy I have seen; but its extreme rarity is not its only value: there is something venerable in the criticism, and poignant in the political sarcasm.

"Weil lettred clarkis endite their warkes, quoth Horace, slow and
    geasoun,
Bot thou can wise forth buike by buike, at every spurt and seasoun;
For men of litrature t'endite so fast, them doth not fitte,
Enanter in them, as in thee, their pen outrun thair witte.
The shaftis of foolis are soone shot out, but fro the merke they stray,
So art thou glibbe to guibe and taunte, but rouest all the way.
Quhen thou hast parbrackt out thy gorge, and shot out all thy arrowes,
See that thou hold thy clacke, and hang thy quiver on the gallows,
Els Clarkis will soon all be Sir Johns, the priestis craft will empaire,
And Dickin, Jackin, Tom, and Hob, mon sit in Rabbies chaire.
Let Georg and Nichlas, cheek by jol, bothe still on cock-horse yode,
That dignitie of Pristis with thee may hau a long abode.
Els Litrature mon spredle her wings, and piercing welkin bright,
To Heaven, from whence she did first wend, retire and take her flight."

invective. Wit and raillery were happily exercised
against these masked divines: for the gaiety of the Wits
was not foreign to their feelings. The Mar-Prelates
showed merry faces, but it was with a sardonic grin
they had swallowed the convulsing herb; they horridly
laughed against their will—at bottom all was gloom and
despair. The extraordinary style of their pamphlets,
concocted in the basest language of the populace, might
have originated less from design than from the impo-
tence of the writers. Grave and learned persons have
often found to their cost that wit and humour must
spring from the soil; no art of man can plant them
there. With such, this play and grace of the intellect
can never be the movements of their nature, but its
convulsions.

Father Martin and his two sons received " A sound
boxe of the eare," in "a pistle" to "the father and the
two sonnes, Huffe, Ruffe, and Snuffe, the three tame ruf-
fians of the Church, who take pepper in the nose because
they cannot marre prelates grating," when they once met
with an adversary who openly declared—

" I profess rayling, and think it is as good a cudgel for
a Martin as a stone for a dogge, or a whip for an ape, or
poison for a rat. Who would curry an ass with an ivory
comb? Give this beast thistles for provender. I doe
but yet angle with a silken flie, to see whether Martins
will nibble; and if I see that, why then I have wormes
for the nonce, and will give them line enough, like a
trowte, till they swallow both hooke and line, and then,
Martin, beware your gills, for I'll make you daunce at the
pole's end."

" Fill thy answer as full of lies as of lines, swell like a
toade, hiss like an adder, bite like a dog, and chatter like
a monkey, my pen is prepared, and my mind; and if
you chaunce to find anie worse words than you broughte,

let them be put in your dad's dictionarie. Farewell, and
be hanged; and I pray God you fare no worse.—Yours
at an hour's warning."

This was the proper way to reply to such writers, by
driving them out of the field with their own implements
of warfare. "Pasquill of England"* admirably observed
of the papers of this faction—"Doubt not but that the
same reckoning in the ende will be made of you which
your favourers commonly make of their old shooes—
when they are past wearing, they barter them awaie for
newe broomes, or carrie them forth to the dunghill and
leave them there." The writers of these Martin Mar-
Prelate books have been tolerably ascertained,† considering the secrecy with which they were printed—sometimes at night, sometimes hid in cellars, and never long
in one place: besides the artifices used in their disper-
sion, by motley personages, held together by an invisible
chain of confederacy. Conspiracy, like other misery,
"acquaints a man with strange bedfellows;" and the
present confederacy combined persons of the most vari-

---

* "Pasquill of England to Martin Junior, in a countercuffe given to
Martin Junior."

† "Most of the books under Martin's name were composed by John
Penry, John Udall, John Field, and Job Throckmorton, who all concurred in making Martin. See 'Answer to Throgmorton's Letter by
Sutcliffe,' p. 70; 'More Work for a Cooper;' and 'Hay any Work for
a Cooper;' and 'Some layd open in his Colours;' were composed by
Job Throckmorton."—MS. Note by Thomas Baker. Udall, indeed,
denied having any concern in these invectives, and professed to disap-
prove of them. We see Cartwright, however, of quite a different
opinion. In Udall's library some MS. notes had been seen by a person who considered them as materials for a Martin Mar-Prelate work
in embryo, which Udall confessed were written "by a friend." All
the writers were silenced ministers; though it is not improbable that
their scandalous tales, and much of the ribaldry, might have been contributed by their lowest retainers, those purveyors for the mob, of
what they lately chose to call their "Pig's-meat."

ous descriptions, and perhaps of very opposite views. I
find men of learning, and of rigid lives, intimately associated with dissipated, or with too ardently-tempered
youths; connected, too, with maniacs, whose lunacy had
taken a revolutionary turn; and men of rank combining
with old women and cobblers.*   Such are the party-

---

* The execution of Hacket, and condemnation of his party, who
had declared him "King of Europe," so that England was only a
province to him, is noted in our "General History of England." This
was the first serious blow which alarmed the Puritanic party. Doubtless, this man was a mere maniac, and his ferocious passions broke
out early in life; but, in that day, they permitted no lunacy as a plea
for any politician. Cartwright held an intercourse with that party, as
he had with Barrow, said to have been a debauched youth; yet we
had a sect of Barrowists; and Robert Brown, the founder of another
sect, named after him *Brownists*; which became very formidable. This
Brown, for his relationship, was patronised by Cecil, Earl of Burleigh.
He was a man of violent passions. He had a wife, with whom he
never lived; and a church, wherein he never preached, observes the
characterising Fuller, who knew him when Fuller was young. In one
of the pamphlets of the time I have seen, it is mentioned that being
reproached with beating his wife, he replied, "I do not beat Mrs.
Brown as my wife, but as a curst cross old woman." He closed his
life in prison; not for his opinions, but for his brutality to a constable.
The old women and the cobblers connected with these Martin Mar-
Prelates are noticed in the burlesque epitaphs on Martin's death, supposed to be made by his favourites; a humorous appendix to "Martin's Monthminde." Few political conspiracies, whenever religion
forms a pretext, is without a woman. One Dame Lawson is distinguished, changing her "silke for sacke;" and other names might be
added of ladies. Two cobblers are particularly noticed as some of the
industrious purveyors of sedition through the kingdom—Cliffe, the
cobbler, and one Newman. Cliffe's epitaph on his friend Martin is not
without humour:—

> "Adieu, both naule and bristles now for euer;
> The shoe and soale—ah, woe is me!—must sever.
> Bewaile, mine awle, thy sharpest point is gone;
> My bristle's broke, and I am left alone.
> Farewell old shoes, thumb-stall, and clouting-leather;
> Martin is gone, and wo undone together."

coloured apostles of insurrection! and thus their honourable and dishonourable motives lie so blended together, that the historian cannot separate them. At the moment the haughty spirit of a conspirator is striking at the head of established authority, he is himself crouching to the basest intimates; and to escape often from an ideal degradation, he can bear with a real one.

Of the heads of this party, I shall notice Penry and Udall, two self-devoted victims to Nonconformity. The

Nor is Newman, the other cobbler, less mortified and pathetic. "The London Corresponding Society" had a more ancient origin than that sodality was aware.

"My hope once was, my old shoes should be sticht;
My thumbs ygilt, that were before bepicht:
Now Martin's gone, and laid full deep in ground,
My gentry's lost, before it could be found."

Among the Martin Mar-Prelate books was one entitled "The Cobbler's Book." This I have not seen; but these cobblers probably picked up intelligence for these scandalous chronicles. The writers, too, condescended to intersperse the cant dialect of the populace, with which the cobblers doubtless assisted these learned men, when busied in their buffoonery. Hence all their vulgar gibberish; the Shibboleth of the numerous class of their admirers—such as, "O, whose *tat*?" John *Kanker*bury, for Canterbury: *Paltri*-politans, for Metropolitans; *See Villains*, for Civilians; and Doctor of *Devilty*, for Divinity! and more of this stamp. Who could imagine that the writers of these scurrilities were learned men, and that their patrons were men of rank! We find two knights heavily fined for secreting these books in their cellars. But it is the nature of rebellion to unite the two extremes; for *want* stirs the populace to rise, and *excess* the higher orders. This idea is admirably expressed in one of our elder poets:—

"Want made them murmur; for the people, who
To get their bread, do wrestle with their fate,
Or those, who in superfluous riot flow,
Soonest rebel. Convulsions in a State,
Like those which natural bodies do oppress,
Rise from repletion, or from emptiness."

Alcyne's *Henry VII.*

most active was John Penry, or *Ap Henry*. He exulted
that " he was born and bred in the mountains of Wales ;"
he had, however, studied at both our Universities. He
had all the heat of his soil and of his party. He " wished
that his head might not go down to the grave in peace,"
and was just the man to obtain his purpose. When he
and his papers were at length seized, Penry pleaded that
he could not be tried for sedition, professing unbounded
loyalty to the Queen : such is the usual plea of even violent Reformers. Yet how could Elizabeth be the sovereign, unless she adopted the mode of government planned
by these Reformers? In defence of his papers, he declared that they were only the private memorandums of
a scholar, in which, during his wanderings about the
kingdom, he had collected all the objections he had heard
against the government. Yet these, though written
down, might not be his own. He observed that they
were not even English, nor intelligible to his accusers ;
but a few Welshisms could not save Ap Henry ; and the
judge, assuming the hardy position, that *scribere est agere*,
the author found more honour conferred on his MSS. than
his genius cared to receive. It was this very principle
which proved so fatal, at a later period, to a more elevated politician than Penry ; yet Algernon Sidney, perhaps, possessed not a spirit more Roman.*   State neces-

---

* The writer of Algernon Sidney's Memoirs could not have known
this fact, or he would not have said that "this was the first indict-
ment of high treason upon which any man lost his life for *writing anything without publishing it.*"—Edit. 1751, p. 21.   It is curious to have
Sidney's own opinion on this point. We discover this on his trial.
He gives it, assuming one of his own noble principles, not likely to
have been allowed by the wretched Tories of that day.   Addressing
the villanous Jeffries, the Lord Chief Justice :—" My Lord, I think it is
a right of mankind, and 'tis exercised by all studious men, to write, in
their own closets, what they please, for their own memory ; and no
man can be answerable for it, unless they publish it."   Jeffries ro-

sity claimed another victim; and this ardent young man, whose execution had been at first unexpectedly postponed, was suddenly hurried from his dinner to a temporary gallows; a circumstance marked by its cruelty, but designed to prevent an expected tumult.*

plied :—" Pray don't go away with *that right of mankind*, that it is lawful for me to write what I will in my own closet, so I do not publish it. We must not endure men to talk thus, that by the *right of nature* every man may contrive mischief in his own chamber, and is not to be punished till he thinks fit to be called to it." Jeffries was a profligate sophist, but his talents were as great as his vices.

* Penry's unfinished petition, which he designed to have presented to the Queen before the trial, is a bold and energetic composition; his protestation, after the trial, a pathetic prayer! Neale has preserved both in his " History of the Puritans." With what simplicity of eloquence he remonstrates on the temporising government of Elizabeth. He thus addresses the Queen, under the title of Madam!—" Your standing is, and has been, by the Gospel: it is little beholden to you for anything that appears. The practice of your government shows that if you could have ruled without the Gospel, it would have been doubtful whether the Gospel should be established or not; for now that you are established in your throne by the Gospel, you suffer it to reach no farther than the end of your sceptre limiteth unto it." Of a milder, and more melancholy cast, is the touching language, when the hope of life, but not the firmness of his cause had deserted him. " I look not to live this week to an end. I never took myself for a rebuker, much less for a reformer of states and kingdoms. I never did anything in this cause for contention, vainglory, or to draw disciples after me. Great things, in this life, I never sought for; sufficiency I had, with great outward trouble; but most content I was with my lot, and content with my untimely death, though I leave behind me a friendless widow and four infants."—Such is often the pathetic cry of the simple-hearted, who fall the victims to the political views of more designing heads.

We could hardly have imagined that this eloquent and serious young man was that Martin Mar-Prelate who so long played the political ape before the populace, with all the mummery of their low buffoonery, and even mimicking their own idioms. The populace, however, seems to have been divided in their opinions respecting the sanity of his politics, as appears by some ludicrous lines, made on Penry's death, by a northern rhymer.

Contrasted with this fiery Mar-Prelate was another,
the learned subtile John Udall. His was the spirit
which dared to do all that Penry had dared, yet conducting himself in the heat of action with the tempered
wariness of age: "If they silence me as a minister,"
said he, "it will allow me leisure to write; and then I
will give the bishops such a blow as shall make their
hearts ache." It was agreed among the party neither to
deny, or to confess, writing any of their books, lest
among the suspected the real author might thus be discovered, or forced solemnly to deny his own work; and
when the Bishop of Rochester, to catch Udall by surprise,
suddenly said, "Let me ask you a question concerning
your book," the wary Udall replied, "It is not yet
proved to be mine!" He adroitly explained away the
offending passages the lawyers picked out of his book,
and in a contest between him and the judge, not only
repelled him with his own arms, but when his lordship
would have wrestled on points of divinity, Udall ex-
pertly perplexed the lawyer by showing he had committed an anachronism of four hundred years! He was
equally acute with the witnesses; for when one deposed
that he had seen a catalogue of Udall's library, in which
was inserted "The Demonstration of Discipline," the
anonymous book for which Udall was prosecuted; with
great ingenuity he observed that this was rather an

"The Welshman is honged,
    Who at our kirke fl.uged,
    And at the state banged,
        And brened are his buks.
    And though he be hanged,
    Yet he is not wranged;
    The deil has him fanged
        In his kruked kluks."
Weever's *Funerall Monuments*, p. 56.   Edit. 1631.

argument that he was not the author, for " scholars use
not to put their own books in the catalogue of those
they have in their study." We observe with astonishment the tyrannical decrees of our courts of justice,
which lasted till the happy Revolution. The bench was
as depraved in their notions of the rights of the subject
in the reign of Elizabeth as in those of Charles II. and
James II. The Court refused to hear Udall's witnesses,
on this strange principle, that " witnesses in favour of
the prisoner were against the queen!" To which Udall
replied, " It is for the queen to hear all things when the
life of any of her subjects is in question." The criminal
felt what was just more than his judges; and yet the
judge, though to be reprobated for his mode, calling so
learned a man "Sirrah!" was right in the thing, when he
declared that " you would bring the queen and the
crown under your girdles." It is remarkable that Udall
repeatedly employed that expression which Algernon
Sidney left as his last legacy to the people, when he told
them he was about to die for " that *Old Cause* in which
I was from my youth engaged." Udall perpetually
insisted on " *The Cause.*" This was a term which served
at least for a watchword : it rallied the scattered members of the republican party. The precision of the
expression might have been difficult to ascertain; and,
perhaps, like every popular expedient, varied with
"existing circumstances." I did not, however, know it
had so remote an origin as in the reign of Elizabeth;
and suspect it may still be freshened up, and varnished
over, for any present occasion.

The last stroke for Udall's character is the history of
his condemnation. He suffered the cruel mockery of a
pardon granted conditionally, by the intercession of the
Scottish monarch but never signed by the Queen—and
Udall mouldered away the remnant of his days in a

rigid imprisonment.* Cartwright and Travers, the chief
movers of this faction, retreated with haste and caution
from the victims they had conducted to the place of
execution, while they themselves sunk into a quiet for-
getfulness and selfish repose.

SUPPLEMENT TO MARTIN MAR-PRELATE.

AS a literary curiosity, I shall preserve a very rare
poetical tract, which describes with considerable
force the Revolutionists of the reign of Elizabeth.
They are indeed those of wild democracy; and the subject of this satire will, I fear, be never out of time. It
is an admirable political satire against a mob-govern-
ment. In our poetical history, this specimen too is
curious, for it will show that the stanza in alternate
rhymes, usually denominated elegiac, is adapted to very
opposite themes. The solemnity of the versification is
impressive, and the satire equally dignified and keen.

The taste of the mere modern reader had been more
gratified by omitting some unequal passages; but, after

* Observe what different conclusions are drawn from the same fact
by opposite writers. Heylin, arguing that Udall had been justly condemned, adds, "the man remained a *living monument* of the archbishop's
extraordinary goodness to him in the preserving of that life which by
the law he had forfeited." But Neale, on the same point, considers
him as one who "died for his conscience, and stands upon record *as a
monument* of the oppression and cruelty of the government." All this
opposition of feeling is of the nature of party-spirit; but what is more
curious in the history of human nature, is the change of opinion in the
same family in the course of the same generation. The son of this
Udall was as great a zealot for Conformity, and as great a sufferer for
it from his father's party, when they possessed political power. This
son would not submit to their oaths and covenants, but, with his bed-
ridden wife, was left unmercifully to perish in the open streets.—
Walker's *Sufferings of the Clergy*, part ii. p. 178.

deliberation, I found that so short a composition would be injured by dismembering extracts. I have distinguished by italics the lines to which I desire the reader's attention, and have added a few notes to clear up some passages which might appear obscure.

RYTHMES AGAINST MARTIN MARRE-PRELATE.*

Ordo Sacerdotum fatuo turbatur ab omni,
Labitur et passim Religionis honos.

SINCE Reason, *Martin*, cannot stay thy pen,
We 'll see what rime will do; have at thee then!

A Dizard late skipt out upon our stage,
　But in a sacke, that no man might him see;
And though we know not yet the paltrie page,
　Himselfe hath *Martin* made his name to bee.
A proper name, and for his feates most fit;
The only thing wherein he hath shew'd wit.

Who knoweth not, that Apes, men *Martins* call,†
　Which beast, this baggage seems as 't were himselfe:
So as both nature, nurture, name, and all,
　Of that's expressed in this apish elfe.
Which Ile make good to Martin Marre-als face,
In three plaine poynts, and will not bate an ace.

For, first, *the Ape delights with moppes and mowes,*
　And mocketh Prince and Peasants all alike;

---

* In Herbert's "Typographical Antiquities," p. 1689, this tract is ntituled, "A Whip for an Ape, or Martin Displaied." I have also seen the poem with this title. Readers were then often invited to an old book by a change of title: in some cases, I think the same work has been published with several titles.

† *Martin* was a name for a *bird*, and a cant term for an *Ass;* and, as it appears here, an *Ape.* Our *Martins*, considered as birds, were often reminded that their proper food was "hempen seed," which at length choked them. That it meant an *Ass*, appears from "Pappe with a Hatchet." "Be thou Martin the bird or Martin the beast, a bird with the longest bill, or a *beast with the longest ears*, there's a net spread for your neck."—Sign. B. 5. There is an old French proverb, quoted by Cotgrave, voce Martin:—"*Plus d'un* ASNE *à la foire, a nom* Martin."

This jesting Jacke, that no good manners knows,
With his Asse-heeles presumes all states to strike.
Whose scoffes so stinking in each nose doth smell,
As all mouthes saie of Dolts he beares the bell

Sometimes his chappes do walke in poynts too high,
    Wherein the Ape himself a Woodcock tries
Sometimes with floutes he drawes his mouth awrie,
    And sweares by his ten bones, and falselie lies.
Wherefore be he what he will I do not passe;
He is the paltriest Ape that euer was.

Such fleering, leering, jeering fooles bopeepe,
    Such hahas! techees! weehees! wild colts play;
Such Sohoes! whoopes and hallowes; hold and keepe;
    Such rangings, ragings, reuelings, roysters ray;
With so foule mouth, and knius at euery catch,
'Tis some knaue's nest did surely *Martin* hatch.

Now out he runnes with Cuckowe king of May,
    Then in he leapes with a wild Morrice daunce;
Then strikes he up *Dune Lawson's** lustie lay;
    Then comes Sir *Jeffrie's* ale-tub, tapped by chaunce,
Which makes me gesse, and I can shrewd'y smell,
He loues both t' one and t'other passing well.

Then straight, as though he were distracted quite,
    He chaft't like a cut-purse layde in warde;
And rud-ly railes with all his maine and might,
    Ag inst both knights and lords w thout regard:
So as *Bridewell* must tame his dronken fits,
And *Bedlem* help to bring him to his wits.

---

* Martin was a *protégé* of this *Dame Lawson.* There appear to
have been few political conspiracies without a woman, whenever
religion forms a part. This dame is thus noticed in the mock epitaphs
on Martin's funeral—

    " Away with silk, for I will mourn in sacke;
    Martin is dead, our new sect goes to wrack.
    Come, gossips mine, put finger in the eie,
    He made us laugh, but now must make us crie."
                                    DAME LAWSON.

" Sir Jeffrie's Ale-tub" alludes to two knights who were ruinously
fined, and hardly escaped with life, for their patronage of Martin.

But, *Martin*, why, in matters of such weight,
  Dost thou thus *play the dawe, and dauncing foole?*
O sir (quoth he) *this is a play ant baite*
  For men of sorts, to traine them to my schoole.
Ye noble states, how can you like hereof,
A shamelesse Ape at your sage head should so ffe?

Good *Noddie*, now leaue scribbling in such matters;
  They are no too'es for fooles to tend vnto:
Wise men regard not what mad monkies patters!
  'Twere trim a beast should teach men what to do.
Now *Tarletou's* dead, the consort lackes a Vice,
For knaue and foole thou maist bear prick and price.

The sacred sect, and perfect pure precise,
  Whose cause must be by *Scoggiu's* jests mainteinde,
Ye shewe, although that Purple, Apes disguise,
  Yet Apes are still, and so must be, disdainde.
For though your Lyons lookes weake eyes escapes,
Your babling lookes bewraies you all for Apes.

The next point is, *Apes use to tosse and leare*
  What once their fidling fingers fasten on;
And clime aloft, and caste downe every where,
  And neuer staie till all that stands be gon!
Now whether this in *Mart'n* be not true,
You wiser heads marke here what doth ensue.

What is it not that *Mart'n* doth not rent?
  Cappes, tippets, gownes, black chimers, rotchets white;
Communion bookes, and homelies: yea, so bent
  To teare, as women's wimples feele his spite.
Thus tearing all, as all apes use to do,
He teares withall the Church of Christ in two.

Marke now what thinges he meanes to tumble downe,
  For to this poynt to look is worth the while,
In one that makes no choice 'twixt cap and crowne,
  Cathedral churches he would faine vntile,
And snatch up bishops' lands, and catch away
All gaine of learning for his prouling pray.

And thinke you not he will pull downe at length
  As well the top from tower as cocks from steeple;

And when his heade hath gotten some more strength,
To play with Prince as now he doth with People:
Yes, he that now saith, Why should Bishops bee?
Will next crie out, *Why Kings?* *The Sainets are free!*

The Germaine boores with Clergiemen began,
But neuer left till Prince and Peeres were dead.
Jacke Leyden was a holy zealous man,
But cea~t not till the Crowne was on his head.
And *Martin's* mate, *Jacke Strawe,* would alwaies ring,
The Clergie's faults, but sought to kill the King.

"Oh that," quoth *Martin,* "*chwere* a Nobleman!" *
Avaunt, vile villain! 'tis not for such swads.
And of the Counsell, too: marke Princes then:
These roomes are raught at by these lustie lads.
For Apes must climbe. and neuer stay their wil,
Untill on top of highest hilles they sit.

What meane they els, in euery towne to craue
Their Priest and King like Christ himself to be:
And for one Pope ten thousand Popes to have,
And to controll the highest he or she?
Aske Scotland that, whose King so long they crost,
As he was like his kingdome to haue lost.

Beware ye States and Nobles of this lande,
The Clergie is but one of these men's buttes.
The Ape at last on master's necke will stande:
Then gegge betimes these gaping greedie gutts.
Least that too soone. and then too late ye jeele,
He strikes at head that first began with heele.

The third tricke is, *what Apes by flattering waies*
Cannot come by with biting, they will snatch;
Our *Martin* makes no bones, but plainely saies,
Their fists shall walke, they will both bite and scratch.
He'll make their hearts to ake, and will not faile,
Where pen cannot, their penknife shall prevail.†

---

* *Chwere, i. e.,* "that I were," alluding to their frequently adopting the corrupt phraseology of the populace, to catch the ears of the mob.
† It is a singular coincidence that Aruauld, in his caustic retort on

But this is false, he saith he did but mock:
   A foole he was, that so his words did scanne.
He only meant with pen their pates to knocke;
   A knaue ho is, that so turns cat in pan.
But, *Martin*, sweare and stare as deepe as hell,
Thy sprite, thy spite and mischeuous minde doth tell.

The thing that neither Pope with booke nor bull,
   Nor Spanish King with ships could doe without,
Our MARTINS *heere at home will worke at full:*
   If Prince curbe not betimes that rabble rout.
That is, destroy both Church and State and all;
For if t' one faile, the other needes must fall.

Thou England, then, whom God doth make so glad
   Through Gospel's grace and Prince's prudent reigne,
Take heede lest thou at last be made as sad,
   Through *Martin's* makebates marring, to thy paine.
For he marrs all and maketh nought, nor will,
Saue lies and strife, and works for *England's* ill.

And ye graue men that answere MARTIN'S *mowes,*
   He mocks the more, and you in vain loose times.
Leaue Apes to Doggs to baite, their skins to Crowes,
   And let old *Lanom** lashe him with his rimes.
The beast is proud when men read his enditings;
Let his workes goe the waie of all wast writings.

Now, *Martin*, you that say you will spawne out
   Your brawling brattes, in euery towne to dwell,
We will prouide in each place for your route,
   A bell and whippe that Apes do loue so well.
And if yo skippe, and will not wey the checke,
We 'il haue a springe, and catche you by the necke.

---

the Jesuits, said—"I do not fear your *pen*, but your *penknife*." The
play on the word, tells even better in our language than in the original—*plume* and *canife.*

   * I know of only one *Laneham*, who wrote "A Narrative of the
Queen's Visit to Kenilworth Castle," 1575. He was probably a re-
doubtable satirist. I do not find his name in Ritson's "Bibliographia
Poetica."

And so adieu, mad *Martin*-mar-the-land
   Leaue off thy worke, and "more work"* hearest thou me;
Thy work's nought worth, take better worke in hand.
   Thou ma r'st thy worke, and thy work will marre thee.
Worke not anewe, least it doth worke thy wracke,
And then make worke for him that worke doth lacke.

And this I warn thee, Martin Monckies-face,
   Take heed of me; my rime doth charm thee bad.
I am a rimer of the Irish race,
   And haue alreadie rimde thee staring mad.
But if thou cease not thy bald jests to spread,
I'le never leaue till I have rimde thee dead.

---

* Alluding to the title of one of their most virulent libels against Bishop Cooper ["Hay any worke for Cooper," which was a pun on the Bishop's name, conveyed in the street cry of an itinerant trader, and was followed by another entitled] "More work for a Cooper." Cooper, in his "Admonition to the People of England," had justly observed that this *Mar-Prelate* ought to have many other names. See note. p. 360.

I will close this note with an extract from "Pappe with a Hatchet,' which illustrates the ill effects of all sudden reforms, by an apposite and original image.

"There was an aged man that lived in a well-ordered Commonwealth by the space of threescore years, and finding at the length, that by the heate of some men's braines, and the warmness of other men's blood, that newe alteratiens were in hammering, and that it grewe to such an height, that all the desperate and discontented persons were readie to runne their heads against their head; coming into the midst of these mutiners, cried, as loude as his yeeres would allow:—'Spring-alls, and vnripened youthes, whose wisedomes are yet in the blade, when this snowe shall be melted (laying his hand on his siluer haires) then shall you find store of dust, *and rather wish for the continuance of a long frost, than the incomming of an vntimely thaw.'*"—*Sig. D. 3. verso.*

LITERARY QUARRELS

FROM

PERSONAL MOTIVES.

ANECDOTE of a Bishop and a Doctor—Dr. Middleton and Dr. Bentley—
—Warburton and Dr. Taylor—Warburton and Edwards—Swift and
Dryden—Pope and Bentley—why fiction is necessary for satire,
according to Lord Rochester's confession—Rowe and Addison—
Pope and Atterbury—Sir John Hawkins and George Steevens—a
fierce controversial author a dangerous neighbour—a ludicrous instance of a literary quarrel from personal motives between Bohun
and the Wykehamists.

LITERARY QUARRELS have abundantly sprung
from mere personal motives; and controversies
purely literary, sometimes of magnitude, have broken
out, and been voluminously carried on, till the public are
themselves involved in the contest, while the true origin
lies concealed in some sudden squabble; some neglect of
petty civility; some unlucky epithet; or some casual
observation dropped without much consideration, which
mortified or enraged the author. How greatly has passion prevailed in literary history! How often the most
glorious pages in the chronicles of literature are tainted
with the secret history which must be placed by their
side, so that the origin of many considerable works,
which do so much honour to the heads of their authors,
sadly accuse their hearts. But the heaven of Virgil was
disturbed with quarrels—

> Tantæne animis cœlestibus iræ ?
>
> *Æneid.*
>
> Can heavenly minds such high resentment show ?
>
> *Dryden.*

And has not a profound observer of human affairs declared, *Ex privatis odiis respublica crescit?* individual hatreds aggrandize the republic. This miserable philosophy will satisfy those who are content, from private vices, to derive public benefits. One wishes for a purer morality, and a more noble inspiration.

To a literary quarrel from personal motives we owe the origin of a very remarkable volume. When Dr. Parr delivered his memorable sermon, which, besides the "*sesquipedalia verba*," was perhaps the longest that ever was heard—if not listened to—Bishop Hurd, who had always played the part of one of the most wary of politicians in private life, and who had occasion once adroitly to explain the French word *Retenue*, which no man better understood, in a singularly unguarded moment, sarcastically observed that he did not like "the doctor's long vernacular sermon." The happy epithet was soon conveyed to the classical ear of the modern Grecian: it was a wasp in it! The bishop had, in the days of literary adventure, published some pieces of irony, which were thought more creditable to his wit than his feelings— and his great patron, Warburton, certain juvenile prose and verse—all of which they had rejected from their works. But this it is to be an author!—his errors remain when he has outlived and corrected them. The mighty and vindictive Grecian in rage collected them all; exhausted his own genius in perpetuating follies; completed the works of the two bishops in utter spite; and in "Tracts by Warburton and a Warburtonian," has furnished posterity with a specimen of the force of his own "vernacular" style, giving a lesson to the wary bishop, who had scarcely wanted one all his life—of the dangers of an unlucky epithet!

Dr. Conyers Middleton, the author of the "Life of Cicero," seldom wrote but out of pique; and he prob-

ably owed his origin as an author to a circumstance of
this nature. Middleton when young was a *Dilettante* in
music; and Dr. Bentley, in contempt, applied the epithet
"fiddling Conyers." Had the irascible Middleton broken
his violin about the head of the learned Grecian, and thus
terminated the quarrel, the epithet had then cost Bentley's honour much less than it afterwards did. It seems
to have excited Middleton to deeper studies, which the
great Bentley not long after felt when he published proposals for an edition of the New Testament in Greek.
Middleton published his "Remarks, paragraph by paragraph, upon the proposals," to show that Bentley had
neither talents nor materials proper for the work. This
opened a great paper-war, and again our rabid wolf
fastened on the majestic lion, "paragraph by paragraph."
And though the lion did affect to bear in contempt the
fangs of his little active enemy, the flesh was torn. " The
proposals" sunk before the "paragraph by paragraph,"
and no edition of the Greek Testament by Bentley ever
appeared. Bentley's proposals at first had met with the
greatest success; the subscription-money amounted to
two thousand pounds, and it was known that his nephew
had been employed by him to travel abroad to collect
these MSS. He declared he would make use of no MS.
that was not a thousand years old, or above; of which
sort he had collected twenty, so that they made up a
total of twenty thousand years. He was four years
studying them before he issued his proposals. The
Doctor rested most on eight Greek MSS., the most recent of which was one thousand years old. All this
wore a very imposing appearance. At a touch the whole
magnificent edifice fell to pieces! Middleton says, " His
twenty old MSS. shrink at once to eight, and he is forced
again to own that even of these eight there are only four
which had not been used by Dr. Mill;" and these Mid-

dleton, by his sarcastic reasoning, at last reduces to
"some pieces only of the New Testament in MS." So
that twenty MSS. and their twenty thousand years were
battered by the "fiddling Conyers" into a solitary fragment of little value! Bentley returned the subscription-
money, and would not publish; the work still lies in its
prepared state, and some good judges of its value have
expressed a hope to see it yet published. But Bentley
himself was not untainted in this dishonourable quarrel:
he well knew that Middleton was the author of this severe
attack; but to show his contempt of the real author, and
desirous, in his turn, of venting his disappointment on a
Dr. Colbatch, he chose to attribute it to him, and fell on
Colbatch with a virulence that made the reply perfectly
libellous, if it was Bentley's, as was believed.

The irascibility of Middleton, disguising itself in a
literary form, was still more manifested by a fact recorded of him by Bishop Newton. He had applied to
Sir Robert Walpole for the mastership of the Charter-
house, who honestly informed him that Bishop Sherlock,
with the other Bishops, were against his being chosen.
Middleton attributed the origin of this opposition to
Bishop Sherlock, and wreaked his vengeance by publishing his "Animadversions upon Sherlock's Discourses on
Prophecy." The book had been long published, and had
passed through successive editions; but Middleton pretended he had never seen them before, and from this
time Lambeth-house was a strong provocative for his
vindictive temper.

Nor was the other great adversary of Middleton, he
who so long affected to be the lord paramount, the
Suzerain in the feudal empire, rather than the republic
of letters—Warburton himself—less easily led on to
these murderous acts of personal rancour. A pamphlet
of the day has preserved an anecdote of this kind. Dr.

Taylor, the Chancellor of Lincoln, once threw out in company an opinion derogatory to the scholarship of Warburton, who seems to have had always some choice spirits of his legion as spies in the camp of an enemy, and who sought their tyrant's grace by their violation of the social compact. The tyrant himself had an openness, quite in contrast with the dark underworks of his satellites. He boldly interrogated our critic, and Taylor replied, undauntedly and more poignantly than Warburton might have suspected, that " he did not recollect ever *saying* that Dr. Warburton was no scholar, but that indeed he had always *thought* so." To this intrepid spirit the world owes one of the remarkable prefaces to the "Divine Legation "—in which the Chancellor of Lincoln, intrepid as he was, stands like a man of straw, to be buffeted and tossed about with all those arts of distortion which the wit and virulence of Warburton almost every day was practising at his "established places of execution," as his prefaces and notes have been wittily termed.

Even Warburton himself, who committed so many personal injuries, has, in his turn, most eminently suffered from the same motive. The personal animosity of a most ingenious man was the real cause of the utter destruction of Warburton's critical reputation. Edwards, the author of the " Canons of Criticism," when young and in the army, was a visitor at Allen's of Prior-park, the patron of Warburton ; and in those literary conversations which usually occupied their evenings, Warburton affected to show his superiority in his acquaintance with the Greek writers, never suspecting that a red coat covered more Greek than his own—which happened unluckily to be the case. Once, Edwards in the library, taking down a Greek author, explained a passage in a manner which did not suit probably with some new theory of the great inventor of so many; a contest arose, in which Edwards discovered how Warburton came by his illegitimate knowledge of Greek authors: Edwards attempted to convince him that he really did not understand Greek, and that his knowledge, such as it was, was derived from French translations—a provoking act of literary kindness, which took place in the presence of Ralph Allen and his niece, who, though they could not stand as umpires, did as witnesses. An incurable breach took place between the parties, and from this trifling altercation, Edwards produced the bitter "Canons of Criticism," and Warburton those foaming notes in the *Dunciad.*

Such is the implacable nature of literary irascibility! Men so tenderly alive to intellectual sensibility, find even the lightest touch profoundly enter into the morbid constitution of the literary temper; and even minds of a more robust nature have given proof of a sickly delicacy hanging about them quite unsuspected. Swift is a remarkable instance of this kind: the foundation of the character of this great wit was his excellent sense. Yet having, when young, composed one of the wild Pindarics of the time, addressed to the Athenian Society, and Dryden judiciously observing that "cousin Jonathan would never be a poet," the enraged wit, after he had reached the maturity of his own admirable judgment, and must have been well aware of the truth of the friendly prediction, could never forgive it. He has indulged the utmost licentiousness of personal rancour; he even puns miserably on his name to degrade him as the *emptiest* of writers. His spirited translation of Virgil, which was admired even by Pope, he levels by the most grotesque sarcastic images to mark the poet's diminutive genius—he says this version-maker is so lost in Virgil, that he is like " the lady in a lobster; a mouse

under a canopy of state; a shrivelled beau within the
penthouse of a full-bottomed perriwig." He never was
generous enough to contradict his opinion, and persisted
in it to the last. Some critic, about Swift's own time,
astonished at his treatment of Dryden, declares he must
have been biassed by some prejudice—the anecdote here
recorded, not then probably known, discovers it.

What happened to Pope on the publication of his
Homer shows all the anxious temper of the author.
Being in company with Bentley, the poet was very desirous of obtaining the doctor's opinion of it, which
Bentley contrived to parry as well as he could; but in
these matters an author who calculates on a compliment,
will risk everything to obtain it. The question was more
plainly put, and the answer was as plainly given. Bentley declared that "the verses were good verses, but the
work is not Homer—it is Spondanus!" From this
interview posterity derives from the mortified poet the
full-length figure of "*the slashing* Bentley," in the fourth
book of the Dunciad:

> The mighty Scholiast, whose unwearied pains
> Made Horace dull, and humbled Milton's strains.

When Bentley was told by some officious friend that
Pope had abused him, he only replied, "Ay, like enough!
I spoke against his Homer, and the *portentous cub* never
forgives!" Part of Pope's severe criticism only is true;
but to give full effect to their severity, poets always
infuse a certain quantity of fiction, This is an artifice
absolutely necessary to practise; so I collect from a great
master in the arts of satire, and who once honestly
avowed that no satire could be composed unless it was
personal; and no personalities would sufficiently adorn
a poem without *lies.* This great satirist was Rochester.
Burnet details a curious conversation between himself

and his lordship on this subject. The bishop tells us that
"he would often go into the country, and be for some
months wholly employed in study, or the sallies of his
wit chiefly directed to satire. And this he often defended to me by saying, there were some people that
could not be kept in order, or admonished, but in this
way." Burnet remonstrated, and Rochester replied—
" A man could not write with life unless he were *heated
by revenge;* for to make a satire without resentments,
upon the cold notions of philosophy, was as if a man
would, in cold blood, cut men's throats who had never
offended him. And he said, the *lies* in these libels came
often in as *ornaments,* that could not be spared without
spoiling the beauty of the poem." It is as useful to know
how the materials of satire are put together; as thus the
secret of pulling it to pieces more readily may sometimes
be obtained.

These facts will sufficiently establish this disgraceful
principle of the personal motives which have influenced
the quarrels of authors, and which they have only disguised by giving them a literary form. Those who are
conversant in literary history can tell how many works,
and some considerable ones, have entirely sprung out of
the vengeance of authors. Johnson, to whom the feelings of the race were so well known, has made a curious observation, which none but an author could have
made :—" The best advice to authors would be, that they
should keep out of the way of one another." He says
this in the " Life of Rowe," on the occasion of Addison's
Observations on Rowe's Character. Rowe had expressed
his happiness to Pope at Addison's promotion; and Pope,
who wished to conciliate Addison towards Rowe, mentioned it, adding, that he believed Rowe was sincere.
Addison replied, "That he did not suspect Rowe
feigned; but *the levity of his heart is such, that he is*

struck with any new adventure: and it would affect him
just in the same manner as if he heard I was going to
be hanged." Warburton adds that Pope said he could
not deny but Addison understood Rowe well. Such is
the fact on which Johnson throws out an admirable
observation:—"This censure time has not left us the
power of confirming or refuting; but observation daily
shows that much stress is not to be laid on hyperbolical
accusations and pointed sentences, which even he that
utters them desires to be applauded, rather than credited.
Addison can hardly be supposed to have meant all that
he said. *Few characters can bear the microscopic scrutiny
of* WIT *quickened by* ANGER." I could heap up facts to
demonstrate this severe truth. Even of Pope's best
friends, some of their severities, if they ever reached him,
must have given the pain he often inflicted. His friend
Atterbury, to whom he was so partial, dropped an expression, in the heat of conversation, which Pope could
never have forgiven; that our poet had "a crooked
mind in a crooked body." There was a rumour, after
Pope's death, that he had left behind him a satirical
"Life of Dean Swift." Let genius, whose faculty detects
the foibles of a brother, remember he is a rival, and be a
generous one. In that extraordinary morsel of literary
history, the "Conversations of Ben Jonson with his
friend Drummond of Hawthornden," preserving his
opinions of his contemporaries, if I err not in my recol-
lection, I believe that he has not spoken favourably of
a single individual !

The personal motives of an author, influencing his literary conduct, have induced him to practise meannesses
and subterfuges. One remarkable instance of this nature
is that of Sir John Hawkins, who indeed had been hardly
used by the caustic pleasantries of George Steevens.
Sir John, in his edition of Johnson, with ingenious malice

contrived to suppress the acknowledgment made by
Johnson to Steevens of his diligence and sagacity, at the
close of his preface to Shakspeare. To preserve the
panegyric of Steevens mortified Hawkins beyond en-
durance; yet, to suppress it openly, his character as an
editor did not permit. In this dilemma he pretended he
reprinted the preface from the edition of 1765; which, as
it appeared before Johnson's acquaintance with Steevens,
could not contain the tender passage. However, this
was unluckily discovered to be only a subterfuge, to get
rid of the offensive panegyric. On examination, it
proved not true; Hawkins did not reprint from this early
edition, but from the latest, for all the corrections are inserted in his own. "If Sir John were to be tried at
Hicks's Hall (long the seat of that justice's glory), he
would be found guilty of *clipping*," archly remarks the
periodical critic.

A fierce controversial author may become a dangerous
neighbour to another author: a petulant fellow, who does
not write, may be a pestilent one; but he who prints a
book against us may disturb our life in endless anxieties.
There was once a dean who actually teased to death his
bishop, wore him out in journeys to London, and at
length drained all his faculties—by a literary quarrel
from personal motives.

Dr. Thomas Pierce, Dean of Sarum—a perpetual controversialist, and to whom it was dangerous to refuse a
request, lest it might raise a controversy—wanted a prebend of Dr. Ward, Bishop of Salisbury, for his son
Robert. He was refused; and now, studying revenge,
he opened a controversy with the bishop, maintaining
that the king had the right of bestowing all dignities in
all cathedrals in the kingdom, and not the bishops.
This required a reply from the bishop, who had been
formerly an active controversialist himself. Dean Pierce

renewed his attack with a folio volume, entitled " A Vindication of the King's Sovereign Right, &c.," 1683.—
Thus it proceeded, and the web thickened around the
bishop in replies and rejoinders. It cost him many
tedious journeys to London, through bad roads, fretting
at "the King's Sovereign Right" all the way; and, in
the words of a witness, "in unseasonable times and
weather, that by degrees his spirits were exhausted, his
memory quite gone, and he was totally unfitted for
business." * Such was the fatal disturbance occasioned
by Dean Pierce's folio of " The King's Sovereign Right,"
and his son Bob being left without a prebend!

I shall close this article with a very ludicrous instance
of a literary quarrel from personal motives. This piece
of secret history had been certainly lost, had not Bishop
Lowth condescended to preserve it, considering it as
necessary to assign a sufficient reason for the extraordinary libel it produced.

Bohun, an antiquarian lawyer, in a work entitled "The
English Lawyer," in 1732, in illustrating the origin of
the Act of *Scandalum Magnatum*, which arose in the
time of William of Wykeham, the chancellor and
bishop of Edward III. and the founder of New College,
in Oxford; took that opportunity of committing the
very crime on the venerable manes of Wykeham himself.
He has painted this great man in the darkest colours.
Wykeham is charged with having introduced " Alice
Piers, his niece or," &c., for the truth is he was uncertain who she was, to use his peculiar language, "into the
king's bosom;" to have joined her in excluding the
Black Prince from all power in the state ; and he hints
at this hero having been poisoned by them ; of Wykeham's embezzling a million of the public money, and,

---

* Lansdowne MSS. 1042—1316.

when chancellor, of forging an Act of Parliament to indemnify himself, and thus passing his own pardon. It is
a singularity in this libellous romance, that the contrary
of all this only is true. But Bohun has so artfully interwoven his historical patches of misrepresentations, sur
mises, and fictions, that he succeeded in framing an
historical libel.

Not satisfied with this vile tissue, in his own obscure
volume, seven years afterwards, being the editor of a
work of high reputation, Nathaniel Bacon's " Historical
and Political Discourse of the Laws and Government of
England," he further satiated his frenzy by contriving
to preserve his libel in a work which he was aware would
outlive his own.

Whence all this persevering malignity? Why this
quarrel of Mr. Bohun, of the Middle Temple, with the
long-departed William of Wykeham?

> What's Hecuba to him, or he to Hecuba?

He took all these obscure pains, and was moved with
this perpetual rancour against William of Wykeham,
merely to mortify the Wykehamists; and slandered
their founder, with the idea that the odium might be
reflected on New College. Bohun, it seems, had a quarrel with them concerning a lease on which he had
advanced money; but the holder had contrived to assign
it to the well-known Eustace Budgell: the college confirmed the assignment. At an interview before the
warden, high words had arisen between the parties: the
warden withdrew, and the wit gradually shoved the
antiquary off the end of the bench on which they were
sitting: a blow was struck, and a cane broken. Bohun
brought an action, and the Wykehamites travelled down
to give bail at Westminster Hall, where the legal quarrel was dropped, and the literary one then began. Who

could have imagined that the venerable bishop and chancellor of Edward III. was to be involved in a wretched squabble about a lease with an antiquary and a wit? "Fancying," says Bishop Lowth, "he could inflict on the Society of New College a blow which would affect them more sensibly by wounding the reputation of their founder, he set himself to collect everything he could meet with that was capable of being represented to his discredit, and to improve it with new and horrible calumnies of his own invention." Thus originated this defamatory attack on the character of William of Wykeham! And by arts which active writers may practise, and innocent readers cannot easily suspect, a work of the highest reputation, like that of Nathaniel Bacon's, may be converted into a vehicle of personal malignity, while the author himself disguises his real purpose under the specious appearance of literature! The present case, it must be acknowledged, is peculiar, where a dead person was attacked with a spirit of rancour to which the living only appear subject; but the author was an antiquary, who lived as much with the dead as the living: his personal motive was the same as those already recorded, and here he was acting with a double force on the dead and the living!

But here I stop my hand, my list would else be too complete. Great names are omitted—Whitaker and Gibbon;* Pope and Lord Hervey;† Wood and South;‡ Rowe, Mores, and Ames;§ and George Steevens and Gough.‖

This chapter is not honourable to authors; but his-

* Gibbon's *Miscellaneous Works*, vol. i. 243.
† Walpole's *Memoirs*, vol. iii. 40.
‡ The Life of Wood, by Gutch, vol. 1.
§ Nichol's *Literary Anecdotes*.
‖ "Curiosities of Literature," vol. iii. p. 303–4.

torians are only Lord Chief Justices, who must execute
the laws, even on their intimate friends, when standing
at the bar. The chapter is not honourable—but it may
be useful; and that is a quality not less valuable to the
public. It lets in their readers to a kind of knowledge,
which opens a necessary comment on certain works, and
enlarges our comprehension of their spirit.

If in the heat of controversy authors imprudently
attack each other with personalities, they are only scat-
tering mud and hurling stones, and will incur the ridicule or the contempt of those who, unfriendly to the
literary character, feel a secret pleasure in its degradation; but let them learn, that to open a literary controversy from mere personal motives; thus to conceal the
dagger of private hatred under the mantle of literature,
is an expedient of short duration, for the secret history
is handed down with the book; and when once the dignity of the author's character sinks in the meanness of
his motives, powerful as the work may be, even Genius
finds its lustre diminished, and Truth itself becomes suspicious.

INDEX.

Disraeli's Complete Works

THE AUTHORIZED AND COMPLETE EDITION,

Edited, with Notes, by his Son, the Right Hon. B. DISRAELI
Ex-Premier of England. In 9 vols. crown 8vo. Large clear
type, on fine toned paper, bound in handsome library style in
extra cloth, comprising : —

THE CURIOSITIES OF LITERATURE. 4 vols. . $7.00

THE AMENITIES OF LITERATURE. 2 vols. . 3 50

THE CALAMITIES AND QUARRELS OF AUTHORS.
  2 vols. 3 50

THE LITERARY CHARACTER. 1 vol. . . . 2.25

Any of the works sold separately as above, or the entire
set of nine volumes in a case for $15.00; half calf, $30.00.

This set of books contains what may be called the cream
of reading and research, from the time of Dr. Johnson to
our own, and of the superiority of this edition there is no
room for question; a comparison with the English, —
crowded into six volumes of small type, — decides at a
glance.

For sale at the principal Bookstores throughout the
country, and sent by mail or express, on receipt of price by

W. J. WIDDLETON, PUBLISHER, .

27 Howard Street, New York

DISRAELI'S WORKS.

THE CURIOSITIES OF LITERATURE. By
Isaac Disraeli. With a view of the Life of the
Author, by his Son. Handsomely printed on choice tinted
paper, from the *fourteenth* corrected London edition. With
a Memoir and fine steel portrait. 4 vols. crown 8vo, cloth,
cut or uncut edges, $7; half calf or half Turkey morocco, $14.
Each set of books in a box.

"These 'Curiosities of Literature' have passed through a remarkable ordeal
of time; they have survived a generation of rivals; they are found wherever books
are bought, and they have been repeatedly reprinted at foreign presses, as well as
translated. These volumes have imbued our youth with their first tastes for modern literature, have diffused a delight in critical and philosophical speculation
among circles of readers who were not accustomed to literary topics; and, finally,
they have been honored by eminent contemporaries, who have long consulted
them, and set their stamp on the metal." — *Extract from Editor's Preface.*

DISRAELI'S AMENITIES OF LITERA-
TURE. Consisting of Sketches and Characters of
English Literature. By Isaac Disraeli. Edited by his son,
the Right Hon. B. Disraeli. A new edition, on choice
tinted paper, uniform with Curiosities of Literature.
2 vols. crown 8vo, cloth, cut or uncut edges, $3.50; half calf
or half Turkey morocco, $7.

"One of the most remarkable works ever written. The varied learning and
research of the author are proverbial; and the unique title conveys a good idea of
the value and interest of the book."

THE CURIOSITIES AND AMENITIES
TOGETHER. In uniform sets of 6 vols. Cloth, $10.50
half calf, $21.00.

For sale at principal Bookstores throughout the country,
and mailed by Publisher on receipt of price.

W. J. WIDDLETON, Publisher

New York.

DISRAELI'S WORKS.

The Calamities and Quarrels of Authors,

With some inquiries respecting their moral and literary characters, and memoirs for our literary history. By ISAAC DISRAELI. Edited by his son, the Right Hon. B. DISRAELI. 2 vo s. crown 8vo. Cloth, $3.50; half calf, $7.00.

The " Calamities and Quarrels of Authors " are, like the " Curiosities of Literature," and the "Amenities," rich in entertaining and instructive information, such as can be found nowhere else. To the younger class of readers, who treasure up every scrap of biography or personal gossip, relating to the distinguished authors of the past, these volumes must prove a storehouse of inestimable value

The Literary Character;

Of the History of MEN OF GENIUS, drawn from their own feelings and confessions. LITERARY MISCELLANIES, and an inquiry into THE CHARACTER OF JAMES THE FIRST. By ISAAC DISRAELI. Edited by his son, the Right Hon. B. DISRAELI. A handsome crown 8vo volume, with Steel Portraits of Disraeli, and uniform with our editions of the " Curiosities " and " Amenities of Literature," by the same author. Cloth, $2.25; half calf, $4.00.

THE LITERARY CHARACTER is contained in a single volume, but to our notion it is one of the best and most interesting of the whole. It not merely treats of authors and books, but through the variety of character portrayed, gives a comprehensive view of human nature.

For sale at principal Bookstores, and mailed, postpaid, on receipt of price, by

W. J. WIDDLETON, PUBLISHER,

No. 27 Howard Street, New York.

Milman's History of the Jews.

THE HISTORY OF THE JEWS. From the Earliest Period down to Modern Times. By HENRY HART
MILMAN, Dean of St. Paul's. A New Edition, thoroughly
revised and extended. In 3 Volumes, crown 8vo. Cloth,
$5.25; half calf, $10.50.

" . . . . Though the Jewish people are especially called the people of God,
though their polity is grounded on their religion, though God be held the author of
their theocracy, as well as its conservator and administrator. yet the Jewish nation is
one of the families of mankind ; their history is part of the world's history. The func-
tions which they have performed in the progress of human development and civilization
are so important, so enduring ; the veracity of their history has been made so entirely
to depend on the rank which they are entitled to hold in the social scale of mankind;
their barbarism has been so fiercely and contemptuously exaggerated, their premature
wisdom and humanity so contemptuously depreciated or denied ; above all, the bar-
riers which kept them in their holy seclusion have long been so utterly prostrate ;
friends as well as foes, the most pious Christians as well as the most avowed enemies
of Christian faith, have so long expatiated on this open field, that it is as impossible, in
my judgment. as it would be unwise to limit the full freedom of inquiry.
" Such investigations, then, being inevitable, and, as I believe, not only inevitable. but the only safe way of attaining to the highest religious truth, what is the right,
what is the duty of a Christian historian of the Jews (and the Jewish history has, I
think, been shown to be a legitimate province for the historian) in such investigations?
The views adopted by the author in early days he still conscientiously maintains.
These views, more free, it was then thought, and bolder than common. he dares to say
not irreverent, have been his safeguard during a long and not unreflective life against
the difficulties arising out of the philosophical and historical researches of our times ;
and from such views many, very many, of the best and wisest men whom it has been
his blessing to know with greater or less intimacy, have felt relief from pressing doubts,
and found that peace which is attainable only through perfect freedom of mind."—
Extract from Author's Preface.

Uniform with "History of the Jews,"

MILMAN'S HISTORY OF CHRISTIANITY.
New and Revised Edition. 3 Volumes, crown 8vo. Cloth,
$5.25; half calf, $10.50.

And

MILMAN'S LATIN CHRISTIANITY. 8 Volumes,
crown 8vo. Cloth, $14.00; half calf, $28.00.

. or sale at principal Bookstores throughout the country, and
mailed by Publisher on receipt of Price.

W. J. WIDDLETON, PUBLISHER,
27 Howard Street, New York.

www.ingramcontent.com/pod-product-compliance
Lightning Source LLC
Chambersburg PA
CBHW032314280326
41932CB00009B/810